CAMBRIDGE TEXTBOOKS IN LINGUISTICS

General Editors: B. COMRIE, C. J. FILLMORE, R. LASS, R. B. LEPAGE, J. LYONS,
P. H. MATTHEWS, F. R. PALMER, R. POSNER, S. ROMAINE, N. V. SMITH,
J. L. M. TRIM, A. ZWICKY

SYNTAX

SYNTAX

P. H. MATTHEWS

PROFESSOR OF LINGUISTICS,
UNIVERSITY OF CAMBRIDGE

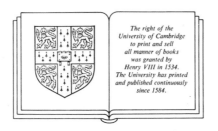

The right of the
University of Cambridge
to print and sell
all manner of books
was granted by
Henry VIII in 1534.
The University has printed
and published continuously
since 1584.

CAMBRIDGE UNIVERSITY PRESS

CAMBRIDGE

LONDON   NEW YORK   NEW ROCHELLE

MELBOURNE   SYDNEY

Published by the Press Syndicate of the University of Cambridge
The Pitt Building, Trumpington Street, Cambridge CB2 1RP
32 East 57th Street, New York, NY 10022, USA
10 Stamford Road, Oakleigh, Melbourne 3166, Australia

First published 1981
Reprinted 1982, 1984, 1987

Printed in Great Britain at the University Press, Cambridge

British Library Cataloguing in Publication Data
Matthews, Peter Hugoe
Syntax. – (Cambridge textbooks in linguistics).
1. English language – Syntax
I. Title II. Series

425 PE1361 80–41664

ISBN 0 521 22894 8 hard covers
ISBN 0 521 29709 5 paperback

To my friends in Reading

CONTENTS

PREFACE

This is the last thing that I will send to the press from the University of Reading, where I have worked for fifteen years. I would like to believe that it is a fitting tribute to the ideal conditions which the University has provided, and to the inspiration which the Head of the Linguistics Department, Frank Palmer, has given me all the time that I have been with him.

I am grateful to David Allerton, Ron Brasington, David Crystal, Giulio Lepschy, John Lyons, Jeremy Mynott and Irene Warburton, for reading a penultimate draft and making clear where it had to be improved. I doubt if I could ever have put my material in order if I had not spent a year in 1977–8 as a fellow of the Netherlands Institute for Advanced Studies in Wassenaar, and I owe a great debt to the Board of the Institute, and the Dutch Ministry of Education, for making this possible.

June 1980   P.H.M.

PRINCIPAL REFERENCES

The following abbreviations cover all books and articles which I have
referred to for two or more separate points. Other references are given in full
at the point of citation.

ALLERTON = D. J. Allerton, *Essentials of Grammatical Theory: a Consensus View
of Syntax and Morphology* (London: Routledge & Kegan Paul, 1979).
ANDERSON = J. M. Anderson, *The Grammar of Case: towards a Localistic Theory*
(Cambridge: Cambridge University Press, 1971).
ArchL = *Archivum Linguisticum* (Glasgow, 1949–65; n.s. Menston, 1970–   ).
BACH = E. Bach, *Syntactic Theory* (New York: Holt, Rinehart & Winston,
1974).
BLOOMFIELD = L. Bloomfield, *Language*, British edn (London: Allen &
Unwin, 1935). (American edn, New York: Holt, 1933.)
BOLINGER (ed.) = D. L. Bolinger (ed.), *Intonation: Selected Readings*
(Harmondsworth: Penguin Books, 1972).
BRESNAN = Joan Bresnan, 'A realistic transformational grammar', in M.
Halle, Joan Bresnan & G. A. Miller (eds.), *Linguistic Theory and
Psychological Reality* (Cambridge, Mass.: MIT Press, 1978), pp. 1–59.
BRINKER = K. Brinker, *Modelle und Methoden der strukturalistischen Syntax*
(Stuttgart: Kohlhammer, 1977).
BSL = *Bulletin de la Société de Linguistique de Paris* (Paris, 1869–   ).
CHEVALIER = J.-C. Chevalier, *Histoire de la syntaxe: naissance de la notion de
complément dans la grammaire française (1530–1750)* (Geneva: Droz, 1968).
CHOMSKY, *Structures* = N. Chomsky, *Syntactic Structures* (The Hague:
Mouton, 1957).
CHOMSKY, *Aspects* = N. Chomsky, *Aspects of the Theory of Syntax* (Cambridge,
Mass.: MIT Press, 1965).
CHOMSKY, *Topics* = N. Chomsky, *Topics in the Theory of Generative Grammar*
(The Hague: Mouton, 1966). Also in T. A. Sebeok (ed.), *Current Trends in
Linguistics*, Vol. 3: *Theoretical Foundations* (The Hague: Mouton, 1966), pp.
1–60.
CHOMSKY, 'Nominalization' = N. Chomsky, 'Remarks on nominalization',
in JACOBS & ROSENBAUM (ed.), pp. 184–221. Reprinted in CHOMSKY,
Studies, pp. 11–61.
CHOMSKY, *Studies* = N. Chomsky, *Studies on Semantics in Generative Grammar*
(The Hague: Mouton, 1972).

CHOMSKY, *Essays* = N. Chomsky, *Essays on Form and Interpretation* (New York: Elsevier/North-Holland, 1977).

COLE & SADOCK (ed.) = P. Cole & J. M. Sadock (eds.), *Grammatical Relations* (New York: Academic Press, 1977).

CULICOVER = P. W. Culicover, *Syntax* (New York: Academic Press, 1976).

CULICOVER *et al.* (ed.) = P. Culicover, T. Wasow & A. Akmajian (eds.), *Formal Syntax* (New York: Academic Press, 1977).

DE GROOT, *Syntaxis* = A. W. de Groot, *Structurele Syntaxis* (The Hague: Servire, 1949).

DE GROOT, 'Classification' = A. W. de Groot, 'Classification of word-groups', *Lingua*, 6 (1957), pp. 113–57.

DE SAUSSURE = F. de Saussure, *Cours de linguistique générale*, with notes from the Italian edition by T. de Mauro (Paris: Payot, 1972). (First published 1916.)

DIK = S. C. Dik, *Coordination: its Implications for the Theory of General Linguistics* (Amsterdam: North-Holland, 1968).

DUBOIS *et al.* = J. Dubois *et al.*, *Dictionnaire de linguistique* (Paris: Larousse, 1973).

ENGEL = U. Engel, *Syntax der deutschen Gegenwartssprache* (Berlin: Erich Schmidt, 1977).

ERNOUT & THOMAS = A. Ernout & F. Thomas, *Syntaxe latine*, 2nd edn (Paris: Klincksieck, 1953).

FILLMORE = C. J. Fillmore, 'The case for case', in E. Bach & R. T. Harms (eds.), *Universals in Linguistic Theory* (New York: Holt, Rinehart & Winston, 1968), pp. 1–88.

FL = *Foundations of Language* (Dordrecht, 1965–76).

FODOR & KATZ (ed.) = J. A. Fodor & J. J. Katz (eds.), *The Structure of Language: Readings in the Philosophy of Language* (Englewood Cliffs: Prentice-Hall, 1964).

GARVIN = P. L. Garvin, *On Linguistic Method: Selected Papers* (The Hague: Mouton, 1964).

HALLIDAY, 'Categories' = M. A. K. Halliday, 'Categories of the theory of grammar', *Word*, 17 (1961), pp. 241–92.

HALLIDAY, 'Transitivity and theme' = M. A. K. Halliday, 'Notes on transitivity and theme in English', Parts 1 & 2, *JL*, 3 (1967), pp. 37–81, 199–244; Part 3, *JL*, 4 (1968), pp. 179–215.

HARRIS, *Methods* = Z. S. Harris, *Methods in Structural Linguistics* (Chicago: University of Chicago Press, 1951). Reissued in paperback as *Structural Linguistics*.

HARRIS, 'Co-occurrence and transformation' = Z. S. Harris, 'Co-occurrence and transformation in linguistic structure', *Lg*, 33 (1957), pp. 283–340. Reprinted in FODOR & KATZ (ed.), pp. 155–210; HARRIS, *Papers*, pp. 390–457; HOUSEHOLDER (ed.), pp. 151–85.

HARRIS, *Papers* = Z. S. Harris, *Papers in Structural and Transformational Linguistics* (Dordrecht: Reidel, 1970).

HELBIG (ed.) = G. Helbig (ed.), *Beiträge zur Valenztheorie* (The Hague: Mouton, 1971).

HERINGER = H. J. Heringer, *Theorie der deutschen Syntax*, 2nd edn (Munich: Hueber, 1973). (1st edn, 1970.)

HILL = A. A. Hill, *Introduction to Linguistic Structures: from Sound to Sentence in English* (New York: Harcourt, Brace, 1958).

HILL (ed.) = A. A. Hill (ed.), *Third Texas Conference on Problems of Linguistic Analysis in English, May 9–12, 1958* (Austin: University of Texas, 1962).

HOCKETT = C. F. Hockett, *A Course in Modern Linguistics* (New York: Macmillan, 1958).

HOUSEHOLDER (ed.) = F. W. Householder (ed.), *Syntactic Theory 1: Structuralist: Selected Readings* (Harmondsworth: Penguin Books, 1972).

HUDDLESTON = R. D. Huddleston, *An Introduction to English Transformational Syntax* (London: Longman, 1976).

HUDSON = R. A. Hudson, *Arguments for a Non-transformational Grammar* (Chicago: University of Chicago Press, 1976).

IJAL = *International Journal of American Linguistics* (Baltimore, 1917–).

JACKENDOFF, *Semantic Interpretation* = R. S. Jackendoff, *Semantic Interpretation in Generative Grammar* (Cambridge, Mass.: MIT Press, 1972).

JACKENDOFF, $\bar{X}$ *Syntax* = R. Jackendoff, $\bar{X}$ *Syntax: a Study of Phrase Structure* (Cambridge, Mass.: MIT Press, 1977).

JACOBS & ROSENBAUM (ed.) = R. A. Jacobs & P. S. Rosenbaum (eds.), *Readings in English Transformational Grammar* (Waltham, Mass.: Ginn & Co., 1970).

JESPERSEN, *MEG* = O. Jespersen, *A Modern English Grammar on Historical Principles*, Parts 1–7 (Heidelberg: Winter, 1909–31; Copenhagen: Munksgaard, 1940–9).

JESPERSEN, *Philosophy* = O. Jespersen, *The Philosophy of Grammar* (London: Allen & Unwin, 1924).

JESPERSEN, *Syntax* = O. Jespersen, *Analytic Syntax* (London: Allen & Unwin, 1937).

JL = *Journal of Linguistics* (Cambridge, 1965–).

JOOS (ed.) = M. Joos (ed.), *Readings in Linguistics* (New York: American Council of Learned Societies, 1958).

KORHONEN = J. Korhonen, *Studien zu Dependenz, Valenz und Satzmodell*, Vol. 1: *Theorie und Praxis der Beschreibung der deutschen Gegenwartssprache: Dokumentation, kritische Besprechung, Vorschläge* (Bern: Lang, 1977).

LAFITTE = P. Lafitte, *Grammaire basque (navarro-labourdin littéraire)*, 2nd edn (Bayonne: 'Amis du musée basque' et 'Ikas', 1962).

LAn = *Linguistic Analysis* (New York, 1974–).

LEES = R. B. Lees, *The Grammar of English Nominalizations* (Bloomington: Indiana University Research Center in Anthropology, Folklore & Linguistics, 1960).

Lg = *Language: Journal of the Linguistic Society of America* (Baltimore, 1925–).

LIGHTFOOT = D. W. Lightfoot, *Principles of Diachronic Syntax* (Cambridge: Cambridge University Press, 1979).

LIn = *Linguistic Inquiry* (Cambridge, Mass., 1970–).

Lingua = *Lingua: International Review of General Linguistics/Revue internationale de linguistique générale* (Amsterdam, 1947–).

LONGACRE = R. E. Longacre, *Grammar Discovery Procedures* (The Hague: Mouton, 1964).

LYONS, *Introduction* = J. Lyons, *Introduction to Theoretical Linguistics* (Cambridge: Cambridge University Press, 1968).

LYONS, *Semantics* = J. Lyons, *Semantics*, 2 vols. (Cambridge: Cambridge University Press, 1977).

MCCAWLEY = J. D. McCawley, *Grammar and Meaning: Papers on Syntactic and Semantic Topics* (Tokyo: Taishukan, 1973).

MARTINET, *Elements* = A. Martinet, *Éléments de linguistique générale* (Paris: Colin, 1960). English translation, *Elements of General Linguistics*, by Elizabeth Palmer (London: Faber & Faber, 1964).

MARTINET, *Studies* = A. Martinet, *Studies in Functional Syntax/Études de syntaxe fonctionelle* (Munich: Fink, 1975).

MATTHEWS, *Morphology* = P. H. Matthews, *Morphology: an Introduction to the Theory of Word-structure* (Cambridge: Cambridge University Press, 1974).

MATTHEWS, *Generative Grammar* = P. H. Matthews, *Generative Grammar and Linguistic Competence* (London: Allen & Unwin, 1979).

OED = *The Oxford English Dictionary*, ed. Sir James Murray *et al.*, with Supplement (Oxford: Clarendon Press, 1933). New Supplement, ed. R. W. Burchfield, 1972– .

PALMER = F. R. Palmer, *The English Verb* (London: Longman, 1974).

PAUL = H. Paul, *Prinzipien der Sprachgeschichte*, 5th edn (Halle: Niemeyer, 1920). (1st edn, 1880.) English adaptation, *Introduction to the Study of the History of Language*, by H. A. Strong *et al.* (London, 1891).

PIKE = K. L. Pike, *Language in Relation to a Unified Theory of the Structure of Human Behavior*, 2nd edn (The Hague: Mouton, 1967). (1st edn, 1954–60.)

PIKE & PIKE = K. L. Pike & Evelyn G. Pike, *Grammatical Analysis* (Dallas: Summer Institute of Linguistics, 1977).

POSTAL = P. M. Postal, *Constituent Structure: a Study of Contemporary Models of Syntactic Description* (Bloomington: Indiana University; The Hague: Mouton, 1964).

QUIRK *et al.* = R. Quirk, S. Greenbaum, G. Leech & J. Svartvik, *A Grammar of Contemporary English* (London: Longman, 1972).

RADFORD = A. Radford, *Italian Syntax: Transformational and Relational Grammar* (Cambridge: Cambridge University Press, 1977).

REIBEL & SCHANE (ed.) = D. A. Reibel & S. A. Schane (eds.), *Modern Studies in English: Readings in Transformational Grammar* (Englewood Cliffs: Prentice-Hall, 1969).

ROBINS = R. H. Robins, *General Linguistics: an Introductory Survey* (London: Longmans, 1964).

SAPIR = E. Sapir, *Language: an Introduction to the Study of Speech* (New York: Harcourt, Brace, 1921).

SMITH & WILSON = N. Smith & Deirdre Wilson, *Modern Linguistics: the Results of Chomsky's Revolution* (Harmondsworth: Penguin, 1979).

STUART (ed.) = C. I. J. M. Stuart (ed.), *Report of the Fifteenth Annual (First International) Round Table Meeting on Linguistics and Language Studies* (Washington: Georgetown University Press, 1964).

SWEET = H. Sweet, *A New English Grammar: Logical and Historical*, 2 vols. (Oxford: Clarendon Press, 1891–8).

Terminology = *On the Terminology of Grammar, being the Report of the Joint Committee on Grammatical Terminology* (London: John Murray, 1911).

TESNIÈRE = L. Tesnière, *Éléments de syntaxe structurale* (Paris: Klincksieck, 1959).

TLP = *Travaux linguistiques de Prague* (Prague, 1964–).

TPhS = *Transactions of the Philological Society* (London, 1842–).

WALL = R. Wall, *Introduction to Mathematical Linguistics* (Englewood Cliffs: Prentice-Hall, 1972).

Word = *Word: Journal of the Linguistic Circle of New York* (New York, 1945–).

NOTICE TO THE READER

When I wrote *Morphology*, which was published in 1974 as the first volume of this series, it was clear enough what such a book should contain but none too easy to convince people that it was needed. I therefore began with a chapter explaining why I thought the subject was important. This time I have quite the opposite problem. My colleagues will agree that syntax must be studied. But many of them may be puzzled by the form which this introduction takes. I must therefore begin by making clear how it is to be read, and what it is and is not trying to do.

Firstly, it is not an introduction to a particular syntactic theory, such as transformational grammar, systemic grammar, and so on. In the past twenty years I have learned most from the transformational grammarians and would urge any student of linguistics to familiarise himself with their work, from the originals as well as from the excellent textbooks that are now available. But there are many topics that they have covered poorly or not at all, and some that cannot be dealt with properly, or cannot be dealt with in a way that I find illuminating, unless their basic assumptions are rejected. A further problem concerns the sort of transformational grammar that one might expound. Five years ago it was possible to see the latest work of Chomsky and his associates as no more than a series of extensions, in different directions, of a basic method that had been firmly established in the 60s. But this is no longer so. On issues central to grammatical theory, such as the distinction between syntax and semantics or transformations and the lexicon, the views reflected in leading generativist work are now much closer to those urged by their critics ten or fifteen years ago than to the practices those critics objected to. Nor is it clear exactly what their present principles are.

An alternative is to discuss the history of successive theories, from the 50s or from the 30s and earlier. This is a book that would be well worth writing, and would make a fascinating essay in the development of ideas. It might also appeal to students, who often ask to be taught in that way and who read much of the relevant literature in tutorials. But a course on what linguists have said is no substitute for one on language itself, and many of the facts that have been taken as crucial for one theory or another (including those discussed in very recent articles) are either well known or in other respects not very revealing. They also cover a rather small range. That is neither surprising nor discreditable. But since many of the theories are now dead, and many of the arguments are seen to be invalid, the examples which have been prominent in the literature are often only of historical interest.

A further problem is that although we have learned a great deal from the theorists of specific schools, a scholar does not have to call himself a thingummybob grammarian, or publish work on such and such a component of the whatsit model, to say important things either about syntax in general or about specific constructions. A student can also gain much from the descriptive traditions of individual languages. But for those studying English this is at present rather difficult, since the books recommended for the structure of the language often differ strikingly, in terminology, in references and in a large part of their substance, from those recommended for transformational and other syntactic theories, even though the latter have English illustrations. This is a bad state of affairs and any responsible introduction ought to try and improve it. It will be made worse unless theoretical and more traditional work are both taken into account.

For these reasons I have organised my text thematically, in a way that reflects the dominant models only as they are relevant to given issues. The central chapters deal with the nature of syntactic relations and the fundamental types of construction (predication, attribution, coordination and so on) as I understand them. This account begins with Chapter 4 ('Constituency and dependency') and ends or culminates in Chapter 10, with the discussion of apposition and correlative constructions. Those who know the subject will see at once that I have not limited myself to the problems that happen to have attracted the most attention in recent decades. I have also been forced at times to adopt original positions. The first three chapters address preliminary questions, with which a student is already likely to have some familiarity. But the general textbooks do not always cope with them satisfactorily, and some of the primary treatments are now quite old. I have also given prominence to topics that are crucial to later stages of my argument, such as the roots of indeterminacy (at the end of Chapter 1) and the notion of ellipsis (in the middle part of Chapter 2), though it may not be till later that the reader will fully appreciate why they are important.

After the survey of constructions, the last two chapters deal with the means by which syntactic relations are realised and the forms of statement in which they can be described. It is here, I believe, that transformational grammar has made, or can make, its best contribution. I have therefore ended with a critical sketch of its history, which may be taken as a plea, both to the generativists and to their out and out opponents, to look at its possibilities in a fresh light. By this point it will be clear why a common or garden course in established formalisms cannot, in my view, be an adequate introduction.

A thematic exposition inevitably leaves much that can only be covered, or alluded to, in the small print. The sections of 'Notes and references' are mainly designed to give an account of my sources and to direct the reader to further studies, both secondary and primary. In many cases there is no recent survey, and I have had to include a thumbnail history of what has been said on the topic. But I have also felt that other forms of note might be of value. Some deal with problems of terminology: a book of this kind must choose among alternative uses, and although one may make the choice as rationally as one can, a student will and must read work in varying traditions. I have tried to sort out some of the discrepancies which seem to me to be most confusing. Other notes summarise the contribution of a school, or the main points of a model that has been referred to. I have also explained why I think that certain proposals are mistaken. Some of these have in the past been influential (thus the note on endocentricity at the end of Chapter 7). Others are recent, but too much at variance with my own view for convenient inclusion in the text. So far as possible, I have tried to shape the notes for each chapter into a continuous bibliographical survey.

These notes are indexed as carefully as the text, so that an inquiring reader will not overlook them.

Finally, I must apologise (if apologies are needed) for two deliberate restrictions of my subject matter. Firstly, I have given relatively few examples from languages other than English. The languages of Europe are basically similar, and to illustrate from German or Italian instead of English would in most cases be decorative rather than truly helpful. I have therefore stuck to English throughout the body of the work, except where good examples are lacking. On other languages the information available to Western scholars is less complete, and I do not sufficiently trust my own grasp of it. Some may wish that I had been more confident, and had included more discussion of typological theories. But the most careful studies in this field tend to have limited conclusions, and those which are more spectacular are often known to contain bad errors. So far as an introduction is concerned, I think this subject is better left for the moment.

Secondly, I have said very little, and that only in passing, about the analysis of discourse or the structure of a sentence in relation to its setting. This is partly because I agree with the old-fashioned definition of syntax, as a subject distinct from stylistics and in terms of which expressions such as 'syntax beyond the sentence' are meaningless. But it is also because I am convinced that these fields are too important, and their methods too much of their own, for them to be handled as an appendage to a book which is basically on relations within phrases and clauses. They need separate introductions, and I look forward to seeing them in this series.

I
Constructions

Traditional concept of syntax. Constructions; characterised as wholes and by internal elements. Constructions and meaning; which differences are relevant? *Identification of constructions:* Semantic connections; lexical co-variance; collocational restrictions. Rules: for realisation; of valency. Tests for units: transference of function; replacement by single words; as confirming semantic distinctions. Transformational relations: as oppositions of construction; as separating constructions. Can transformations be the only evidence? Regularity of transformations: exceptions vs. semantic unpredictability. Collocational evidence not sufficient.
Indeterminacy: Distinctions sometimes uncertain. Reasons for indeterminacy: rules and tendencies; marginal codification.

The term '**syntax**' is from the Ancient Greek *sýntaxis*, a verbal noun which literally means 'arrangement' or 'setting out together'. Traditionally, it refers to the branch of grammar dealing with the ways in which words, with or without appropriate inflections, are arranged to show connections of meaning within the sentence. For example, in *It tastes nice* there are connections of meaning among *it, tastes* and *nice* which are shown by the order of words (*it + tastes + nice*, not *nice + tastes + it*, or other permutations) and also, in part, by inflectional agreement between the verb and pronoun (*it tastes*, not *it taste*). Similar connections are found in other combinations: for example, in *They smell fresh* and *It felt softer* or, as parts of larger sentences, among *he, looked* and *thinner* in *I thought he looked thinner*, or among *which, tastes* and *peppery* in *He likes food which tastes peppery*. The individual connections can also form part of a different whole, distinguished by another pattern of arrangement: for example, in the exclamation *How nice it tastes!* or, as part of a larger sentence, in *However nice it tastes, you are not to eat any more*. The field of syntax covers both what is shown (that *How nice it tastes!* is an exclamation, that *tastes* stands in a certain meaning relationship to *nice*) and the means by which it is done (agreement, order of words, and other devices).

For the syntactic characterisation of a sentence, or of any smaller unit that we can distinguish within it, grammarians use the equivalent Latin term '**construction**'. In *I thought he looked thinner* the last three words have a construction of their own; by that token they form a syntactic unit, or (we will later say) a **syntagm**. We can then talk of a larger construction in which this unit as a whole (*he looked thinner*) is related to *thought*, which in turn is related to *I*. Such relations may be called **constructional relations**. For example, in *He likes food which tastes peppery* there is a syntactic unit, *which tastes peppery*, in which *peppery* and *which* stand in constructional relations to, or are **construed with**, *tastes*. This forms part of a larger unit, *food which tastes peppery*, in which the whole of *which tastes peppery* is construed with *food*; that in turn construes with *likes* within the sentence as a whole. The constructional relation which obtains between, for example, *tastes* and *peppery* is the same as that obtaining between *looked* and *thinner* in *I thought he looked thinner*, or between *looks* and *how thin* in *How thin he looks!*, though other aspects of the construction are different.

Any syntactic unit (*which tastes peppery*, *food which tastes peppery*, *however nice it tastes*, *It tastes nice*, and so on) can now be looked at from two angles. First we can consider it as a whole, for its function either in isolation or as part of a larger unit. In *food which tastes peppery* the last three words form what grammarians call a Relative Clause – a clause (this term we will return to later) whose function is 'in relation to' an antecedent noun. The four words together are seen as a Noun Phrase – a phrase (this too we will return to) whose functions are the same as those of a single noun. In *It tastes nice* we have a Main Clause – a clause functioning as a sentence – which in addition is Declarative (having the form appropriate to a statement) as opposed to Interrogative (having the form appropriate to a question), and so on. We will say that these exhibit a 'relative clause construction' (shown by a pattern of arrangement appropriate to clauses with that function), a noun phrase construction (with a pattern appropriate to such phrases) and a declarative construction, or the construction of a declarative main clause, respectively. It will be seen that any unit can be characterised on more than one dimension. Thus *It tastes nice* is at once a clause and not a phrase, declarative and not interrogative, main and not (for example) relative, and so on.

The second characterisation is in terms of a unit's internal connections. In *It tastes nice*, the relationship of *it* to *tastes* is that of a Subject to (as we will call it) a Predicator. The pronoun is the 'subject of' the verb; a grammarian will also describe it as 'the subject' within the clause or sentence as a whole. In the same unit, the relationship of *tastes* to *nice* is that of a predicator to its Complement: specifically, what most grammarians call a Subject Complement. So, the adjective is at once the 'complement of' the verb (relation of part to part) and also 'the complement' within the clause (relation of part to whole), in which the verb is in turn the predicator. The unit can then be said to have a 'subject–predicator–complement' construction, whose terms or **elements** (subject, predicator, complement) are successive functions established by the individual constructional relations. Likewise, in the construction of the noun phrase *food which tastes peppery*, there are two elements to which we assign, or which are represented by, the noun *food* on the one hand and the relative clause on the other. This is one type of Head–Modifier construction, with the clause as a modifier of a head *food*. These too are categories to which we will return in a later chapter.

The roots of all this lie in the grammatical tradition, though terms such as 'element' and 'predicator' are fairly recent. In two essential points we will take it as correct. Firstly, constructions are to be described in terms of functions and relations, and not simply in terms of parts of speech and their sequential distribution. In *It tastes nice*, the first word is a subject related to a predicator *tastes*; it is not simply a pronoun (one of the eight parts of speech inherited from the ancient grammarians) which is immediately followed by a verb. Secondly, constructional relations are at bottom relationships of meaning. On both points, the main tradition differs from at least one major school of structural linguists, for whom the distribution of units has been the primary object of study. Patterns of arrangement are important. But that is because they are the means by which constructions are shown, not because constructions ARE arrangements.

A difference of construction can now be seen as a difference of meaning, either of the whole or in at least one relationship between elements. But not every difference of meaning is relevant. *He sounded a fool* means that, from what one heard, it seems that he is foolish; *He sounded a trumpet* that he held the instrument and blew it. For almost all grammarians that is a difference of construction as well as simply a difference of words, *a fool* having the function of subject complement (like *nice* in *It tastes nice*) and *a trumpet* that of a Direct Object. *It was cold, if not freezing* could mean either that, although it was not freezing, it was nevertheless cold or that it was cold and may indeed have been freezing too. But it is doubtful if any grammarian has ever seen this as a difference of syntax, even though the words are the same. We must therefore ask on what grounds a construction is identified. Why do we say that *a fool* and *a trumpet* have different constructional relationships to *sounded*, when we do not say that *if not freezing* can have different relationships to *cold* or *it was cold*?

IDENTIFICATION OF CONSTRUCTIONS

Let us begin with the basic notion of a relation. In the opening line of a poem by Ted Hughes:[1]

Terrifying are the attent sleek thrushes on the lawn

we can see a connection of meaning between, for example, *on the lawn* and *thrushes*. This too is described as a relation between a modifier and a head, with the modifier locating the birds referred to. We can also see connections between *terrifying* and *thrushes* (the birds are in themselves frightening), or between *terrifying* and *on the lawn* (the birds might not be terrifying if they were at their respective song posts), or between *terrifying* and *attent* (they are terrifying because they are watching for prey). We might even see a connection between *terrifying* and *the lawn* (the lawn has become terrifying because there are thrushes on it). A grammarian will subsume these under a constructional relation between *terrifying* and the entire unit *the attent sleek thrushes on the lawn*. But it is hard to see any direct connection of meaning between, for example, *sleek* and *the lawn* or *terrifying* and *on*. In short, some pairs of units are potential relata while others are not.

For a relation in general a natural criterion is that of **lexical co-variance**. In *Terrifying are the thrushes* ... we could replace *thrushes* with *crocodiles* (*Terrifying are the crocodiles on the lawn*), *toadstools*, *shadows*, and so on. This establishes a variable – let us call it n – ranging over a class of plural nouns. We could also replace *terrifying* with *agile* (*Agile are the thrushes on the lawn*), *frightened*, *scrumptious*, and so on. This establishes another variable – call it a – ranging over a class of adjectives. But n and a are not independent. Although it would be easy to understand *frightened* with *crocodiles* (*Frightened are the crocodiles on the lawn*), it takes more imagination to connect it with *shadows*

[1] 'Thrushes', in *Selected Poems, 1957–1967* (London: Faber & Faber, 1972), p. 53.

(*Frightened are the shadows on the lawn*), or *shadows* with *scrumptious* (*Scrumptious are the shadows on the lawn*), or *agile* with *toadstools*. The values co-vary, adjective a_1 going more readily with noun n_1 than noun n_2, or n_1 more readily with a_1 than a_2. For 'goes with' we will say '**collocates** with'. Similarly, in the construction with a direct object, a noun such as *brandy* collocates with verbs like 'to drink' or 'to sip' (*He drank the brandy, They were sipping brandy*) and a noun such as *cake* with verbs like 'to eat' or 'to munch'. But it is harder to make sense of *He was munching brandy* (was it perhaps frozen?), *He often drinks cake* (does he perhaps break it up and stir it into his tea?), and so on.

In these examples the co-variance is explained by the nature of shadows or thrushes or brandy or cake, by the states of fright or scrumptiousness, and by the actions involved in drinking or munching. But in other cases it is less predictable. For instance, one would normally talk of 'toasting bread' and 'grilling meat', not 'grilling bread' or 'toasting meat', although the actual operations (of cooking a flat piece of food on a rack beneath a fierce heat) may not otherwise be distinguishable. Likewise one would say *They sautéd the potatoes* but not, or not usually, *They sautéd the rice*. In such cases we must speak of specific **collocational restrictions**: in terms of a dictionary, the meaning of 'to sauté' is 'of potatoes' not 'of rice', and that of 'to grill' is 'of meat' not 'of toast'. In my speech there is a further restriction by which 'to bake' collocates readily with *potatoes* or *apple pie*, but not with *chestnuts* (though one can naturally cook chestnuts in the same way) or *steak and kidney pie*.

On such grounds we can talk of a relation, though not yet a constructional relation, between *sipped* and *brandy* in *They sipped brandy*, or *sounded* and *(a) trumpet* in *He sounded a trumpet*. In *It tastes nice* or *It looks good* we can establish a similar relation between the subject complement and the subject. For example, one would usually say *The milk looks sour* or *The meat looks bad*, rather than *The milk looks bad* or *The meat looks sour*; likewise *The beer tastes flat* (rather than *The beer tastes stale*), *The bread tastes stale* (but not *The meat tastes stale*), and so on. It is to the link attested by such restrictions that the term 'subject complement' in part refers. But in sentences like *He tasted the brandy* there is no direct co-variance between the subject and object. Provided that each goes naturally with the verb (*your daughter was nibbling, the thrushes were eating; was nibbling cheese, were eating the cake*), and the sense of the verb remains the same in both collocations, the combination of all three

5

together (*Your daughter was nibbling cheese, The thrushes were eating the cake*) is subject to no other specific restrictions. On collocational evidence, the difference between sentences like *It tastes nice* and *He tasted the cake* is not simply in the parts of speech which follow the verb, but also in the relations which they enter into.

For a constructional or syntactic relation we will now require not just that there should be co-variance but also that it should be subject to a **rule**, or that a rule should be associated with it. An obvious instance is the agreement in, for example, *It sounds good* and *They sound good*. Although there are cases where the inflectional co-variance is not obligatory (*The family were delighted*, as well as *The family was . . .*; *The number of visitors have increased*, as well as *The number . . . has . . .*), combinations like *They sounds good* or *It sound good* are errors which could in principle be corrected, or put into more acceptable English, by any speaker who said or encountered them. To learn English is, in part, to learn to conform to the rule by which this is so. It will be noted that the same pattern of co-variance is found in sentences like *Terrifying are the thrushes . . .* (compare *Terrifying is the thrushes . . .* or *Terrifying are the thrush*), although the variables are in the opposite order. That suggests that the construction of the line from 'Thrushes' is, in one respect at least, the same as that of *The thrushes are terrifying*.

But lexical co-variance is not, as such, subject to rule. Suppose that someone did say, for example, *He is toasting the chops*. One's natural reaction is not to try and correct it, but to try and find some way in which it can, in fact, make sense. (Thus perhaps he has put them into a toasting machine, or perhaps he 'merely toasts' them – just browning them on the outside – instead of cooking them properly.) Nor would it be wrong English to say, for instance, *The milk looks rancid*; it is merely that *rancid* is less usual, and less automatically understood, with *milk* rather than *butter*. Statements relating to individual collocations (that *rancid* is used 'of butter', *sour* 'of milk', and so on) rightly belong to a dictionary, and not to a grammar as it is traditionally conceived. It does not follow that a grammar should say nothing about the relationship. But if it does it must be for other reasons.

Two sorts of reason are immediately relevant. Firstly, although there are no rules for the pairs that particular words can form, there ARE rules for the order in which they can be arranged. One can say *I will taste the brandy* or *The BRANdy I WILL taste* (with intonational stress on *brandy* and *will*). But one could not say *I the brandy will taste*, or *I will the brandy taste*, and so on. In ordinary speech such forms are as wrong, and as corrigible, as those which gratuitously break the rule of agreement. Similarly, one can say *It tastes nice* but not, for example, *It nice tastes*. The different relations allow a slightly different range of patterns. Thus the line from 'Thrushes' has a literary order which reverses that of the more usual *The thrushes are terrifying*. But *Brandy like they* is not a similar alternative to *They like brandy*. Although one can say BRAN*dy I de*TEST (intonational stress again shown by small capitals), I do not think I would say *At*TRAC*tive it* LOOKS, or RAN*cid the butter* DOES *taste* (compare WHIS*ky the Scots* DO *love*). If relation *a* cannot be shown in quite the same ways as relation *b* there is more than just a difference of meaning between them.

The second reason concerns the range of verbs with which the relations are compatible. One can say both *They smelled fresh* and *They smelled the roses*, both *He sounded a fool* and *He sounded a trumpet*, with the same verbs, 'to smell' and 'to sound', in senses not otherwise dissimilar. But consider such collocations as *He took fresh* or *He looked a trumpet*. The former will make sense only if *fresh* can be understood in the direct object relation (he took something called 'fresh', or something 'which was' fresh), but not with freshness attributed to 'he'. (Compare A. *Do they like sour milk?* – B. *No, they only take fresh.*) The latter could be interpreted only if *a trumpet* is related to the subject: he 'looked like' a trumpet, not he did something called 'looking' to it. Likewise *He boiled an idiot* must mean that the idiot was boiled; conversely, *He seemed the roses* could only mean that 'his being the roses' seemed the case, and so on. There is a co-variance between the predicator and the remaining elements, in which different categories of verb ('to drink' and 'to boil', 'to look' and 'to seem') allow different collocational relationships. These too are absolute restrictions; it is not just that the verbs are naturally or commonly used in these ways. The choice of words is again subject to rules.

The first of these arguments appeals to the patterns of **realisation**. Likewise, the evidence of agreement concerned the permissible realisation of the relation between subject and predicator. The second argument appeals to the **valency** (as we will later call it) of the verbs. The conclusion from both is that the two sets of collocational relationships – of subject, predicator and subject complement in *It tastes nice* or *He sounded a fool*, and of subject, predicator and direct object in *I will taste the brandy* or *He sounded a trumpet* – are associated with rules that are

7

partly different. Hence the differences between the relations are constructional. But although this illustrates a characteristic form of demonstration, there are other forms of argument which, on occasion, we may also use. These have had a large place in earlier discussion of this issue, and it is therefore important to consider how they fit with what we have already said.

One type of argument is concerned with the identification of subsidiary units. In the line from 'Thrushes':

Terrifying are the attent sleek thrushes on the lawn

we assumed that *on the lawn* was directly connected to *thrushes*: on a natural interpretation, the poem refers to birds 'which are' on a lawn, and it is these 'attent sleek thrushes on the lawn' which are said to be terrifying. Accordingly, the whole of *the attent sleek thrushes on the lawn* was taken as a unit and treated, as a whole, as subject of *(are) terrifying*. Likewise, one interpretation of a more prosaic sentence such as

Leave the meat in the kitchen

is that *leave* has as its object a subsidiary unit formed by the whole of *the meat in the kitchen*. There is some meat 'which is' in the kitchen, and it is this 'meat in the kitchen' that is to be left.

The collocational links are not the only evidence which supports these groupings. One important finding is that both units can be transferred en bloc to other relations. In *The meat in the kitchen is finished* the same words *the ... kitchen* would be grouped together, in this case as the subject of *is finished*; in *I watched the attent sleek thrushes on the lawn* or *I threw bread to the attent sleek thrushes on the lawn* the same words *the ... lawn* would be the direct object of *watched* or the Indirect Object of *threw*. We have also implied that there is a unit *on the lawn*, paralleled in the second example by *in the kitchen*. These too can be transferred en bloc to other functions: for example, in *I sleep on the lawn* or *They eat in the kitchen*. In each case the unit remains the same: the internal connections are constant, even though its external relation alters.

Another finding is that each of these units, in each of its putative functions, can be replaced by a single word. Thus one can say *Leave it* or *Leave them*, replacing *the meat in the kitchen* with the single pronouns *it* or *them*; similarly *Thrushes are terrifying* or *I watched thrushes*, with *thrushes* alone in the role of subject or object. Now a word such as *it* is indivisible, and cannot but function as a whole. Therefore any group of words which it can replace, still with the remaining connections of meaning held constant, must itself form a unit. In *The meat in the kitchen is finished* or *The thrushes on the lawn are terrifying* we could make similar replacements for *in the kitchen* and *on the lawn*: for example, *The thrushes above are terrifying* or *They sleep above*, *The meat here is finished* or *They eat here*. Let *x* stand for any of *above, here, in the kitchen* or *on the lawn*. Then in *They sleep x* and so on, the semantic roles of *x* are constant for both single words and larger groupings.

These findings confirm that there are units such as *in the kitchen* which can form part of a larger unit in which they are preceded by a noun. But in other sentences the evidence is different. For example, in a line from another of Ted Hughes's poems:

Takes his changed body into the holes of lakes

(line 13 of 'An Otter', *ibid.*, p. 50) a single word cannot fill the roles of both *his changed body* and *into the holes of lakes*. One can say, for example, *takes bodies* or *takes it*. But these refer only to something that is taken, whereas the line refers both to what is taken ('his changed body') and to the places ('the holes of lakes') that it is taken to. Nor can they stand together in another function: compare *His changed body into the holes of lakes is terrifying*. But a word like *it* could replace just *his changed body* (⟨*The otter*⟩ *takes it into the holes of lakes*) and a word like *here* or *there* could independently replace *into the holes of lakes* (⟨*The otter*⟩ *takes his changed body there*, or *takes it there*). This evidence divides the line into three separate elements (*takes, his ... body* and *into ... lakes*), not just two.

There is also another interpretation of *Leave the meat in the kitchen*, by which it refers not to some 'meat which is in the kitchen', but to a kitchen as the place where some meat – identified independently – is to be left. In that case the connections of meaning are like those of *Leave it there* or *Leave it in the kitchen*, and unlike those of the simple *Leave it* or *Leave meat*. Nor can *the meat in the kitchen* stand in other relations, as in *The meat in the kitchen is finished*, unless another connection is made. This argues that the sentence has two different constructions, or is **constructionally ambiguous**. In one case *in the kitchen* is a modifier of *meat*, just as *on the lawn* modified *thrushes*. In the other *leave* has an object *the meat* and is accompanied by *in the kitchen* as an Adverbial. Similarly, *into the holes of lakes* was an adverbial alongside *takes* and *his changed body*.

9

Such arguments attracted much attention in the decade after the Second World War, when they were formulated as part of an analysis of distributions. But they too may be seen as confirming the evidence of collocational relationships. In the construction with an object and an adverbial, another finding is that the preposition – *in*, *on*, and so on – can vary with the verb. Thus *leave* makes sense with *in* but not with, for example, *via* or *from*. If one said *Leave the meat from the kitchen* the natural reference is to meat 'which is from' there, with a construction in which *from the kitchen* is a modifier. *Fetch* collocates with *from* but not with *in*; it would also be less usual, at the least, with *through* or *into* (*Fetch the meat through the kitchen*, *Fetch him into the house*). *Bring* goes with *into*, *onto*, *through* or *from*, but less easily with, for example, *under*: compare *Bring the books under the table* with *Leave the books under the table* or *Bring the books onto the table*. This attests a link between the verb and the final unit, and it is this that the term 'adverbial' (Latin *ad* 'to' or 'adjoined to') traditionally acknowledges. Our earlier findings merely confirm that this final unit is not linked to the object.

In the other construction the verb and the preposition vary independently, but certain prepositions do not readily make sense with every noun that might precede them. Thus one can say *the meat in the kitchen* or *the meat on the table*; but what could be meant by, for example, *the meat into* ... or *the meat onto* ... ? In *Take the meat onto the table* the natural meaning is that the table is where some meat is to be taken, with *onto the table* an adverbial. *Leave the meat onto the table* does not readily make sense in either way – is there perhaps a trail or strip of meat which is somehow seen as leading onto it? This attests the link by which in, for example, *the attent sleek thrushes on the lawn* the unit *on the lawn* is specifically the modifier of *thrushes*. Our earlier findings merely confirm that there is a larger unit of which *the*, *attent*, *sleek*, *thrushes* and *on the lawn* are all part. Such confirmation is important. But it is only when we add the evidence of collocations that we can see in full what the relations are that we are investigating.

Our remaining arguments are concerned not with the evidence of links within each sentence, but with collocational similarities that can obtain between them. For example, the collocation of *nice*, *it* and 'to taste' is found in both the exclamation *How nice it tastes!* and the declarative *It tastes nice*; likewise that of *cool*, *water* and 'to look' in both *How cool the water looks!* and *The water looks cool*, that of *depressing*, *man* and 'to sound' in both *How depressing the man sounds* and *The man sounds depressing*, and so on. In general, any collocation which appears in the declarative can also appear in a corresponding exclamation, and vice versa. The change of meaning is also regular for each pair. *How nice it tastes!* differs in meaning from *It tastes nice* just as *How horrible it tastes!* differs from *It tastes horrible, How cool the water looks!* from *The water looks cool* just as *How cool the stream looks!* differs from *The stream looks cool*, and so on, so that a general opposition of Exclamative and declarative can be described without reference to the particular adjectives or nouns or verbs. On this evidence we will say that each declarative can be **transformed** into a corresponding exclamative and, conversely, each exclamative can be transformed into the corresponding declarative. We will then speak of a **transformational relation** between each pair, and between exclamative and declarative constructions generally.

Such relations are important in distinguishing the categories that enter into them. Thus it is because a regular change of form correlates with regular changes of meaning that the exclamation *How nice it tastes!* can be assigned to a syntactic category different, in at least one respect, from the statement *It tastes nice*, and is not simply an alternative realisation of the same construction. Further transformational relations hold between the declarative and the interrogative (*It tastes nice* and *Does it taste nice?*) or between the exclamative and the interrogative (*How nice it tastes!* and *Does it taste nice?*). This establishes syntactic oppositions among all three constructions.

But a transformation can also distinguish constructions that do and do not allow it. In pairs like *My sister also drinks brandy* and *Brandy is also drunk by my sister, The twelfth man keeps the score* and *The score is kept by the twelfth man* there is tentative evidence that an Active construction (with an active verb such as *drinks* or *keeps*) is transformationally related to a Passive (... *is drunk* ... or ... *is kept* ...). The same lexical collocations, of *sister*, 'to drink' and *brandy* or of *twelfth man*, 'to keep' and *score*, appear in both, with any change of meaning again attributable to the general opposition. But sentences like *His sister looks a fool* or *Reading seems a nice place* cannot be transformed into *A fool is looked by his sister* or *A nice place is seemed by Reading*. Similarly, *A fool is sounded by him* could only mean that he 'sounds out' a fool or that a fool is somehow made to make a sound, with a connection like that of a direct object. It could not mean that he 'sounds like' one, as with a subject complement. We already have sufficient grounds for dis-

11

tinguishing these elements. But this evidence may be seen as further confirmation.

A famous example, which attracted much attention in the early days of transformational grammar, is the constructional ambiguity of phrases such as *flying planes*, in sentences like *Flying planes can be dangerous*. On one interpretation, this means that flying them can be a dangerous thing to do: in traditional terms, *planes* is construed as the direct object of a Gerund *flying* just as, in earlier examples, *brandy* was the direct object of Finite verb forms such as *drank* or *likes*. Part of the justification is that a phrase with a gerund is transformationally related to a main clause. Just as *Bringing brandy* ⟨*is useless*⟩ stands to *They bring brandy* or *Eating chocolate* ⟨*is fattening*⟩ to *They eat chocolate*, so *Flying planes* ⟨*is dangerous*⟩ stands to *They fly planes*, and so on for all other collocations.

On another interpretation, *Flying planes can be dangerous* means that planes 'which fly' can be dangerous, or can be dangerous when they are doing so: in that case, a grammarian would describe *flying* as a Participle which modifies *planes* just as, in *the attent sleek thrushes*, the adjectives *attent* and *sleek* modify *thrushes*. Similarly, in *Screaming children are a nuisance*, the first two words refer to children 'who are' screaming or in the habit of doing so. One reason for distinguishing the construction of the participle from that of the gerund is that *screaming children* cannot be transformed into a main clause such as *They scream children*; nor *flying planes*, with this second interpretation, into *They fly planes*. If any transformation is possible, it is into a clause with the noun as subject. Thus *Screaming children* ⟨*are a nuisance*⟩ stands to *Children scream* as *The setting sun* ⟨*is beautiful*⟩ stands to *The sun sets*, or *Flying planes* ⟨*are dangerous*⟩ to *Planes fly*.

A criterion based on transformational relations can be adopted without commitment to the theory of transformational grammar as it has historically developed (see Chapter 12). But there are certain problems. Firstly, it must be noted that in examples like *flying planes* the distinction can be drawn on other grounds. In *Hanging gardens delight him*, the verb *delight* agrees with *gardens*, with which it stands in a collocational relationship. Replace it with *delights*, and one is forced to take *hanging* as a gerund. (So, what would delight him would be the act or practice of hanging them.) In *Eating chocolates delights him* it has singular agreement, despite plural *chocolates*. *Eating chocolates delight . . .* would be an error, or else one is forced to take *eating* as a modifier:

perhaps they are an 'eating sort' of chocolate (compare *eating apples* or *cooking sherry*). The different meanings are distinguished by a rule which, in *Flying planes can be dangerous*, merely happens to be inoperative. Nor is it just the identity of collocations that allows us to equate the relation of object to gerund with that of object to finite verb. Another identity is in the relative order of the direct object and other elements that can follow a predicator. In *Flying planes badly is dangerous*, the order of *planes* and *badly* is the same as in *They fly planes badly*; a gerundial phrase *flying badly planes* and a clause *They fly badly planes* would break the same rule. Likewise, *feeding buns to elephants* follows the same rule as *They feed buns to elephants*, *feeding them buns* (without *to*) the same rule as *They feed them buns*, and so on.

Sentences like *My sister drinks brandy* and *His sister looks a fool* can also be distinguished on other grounds, as we have shown. We may add that it is because their realisations are different that the relation of subject to passive verb (*Brandy is drunk ...*, *The score is kept ...*) is not identified with that of the direct object to the active (*... drinks brandy*, *... keeps the score*), even though the collocations correspond. We must therefore ask if constructions can ever be distinguished solely by this form of evidence.

A related question concerns the degree of regularity which transformational relations have to show. Our first examples met an absolute criterion. For instance, I know of no declarative of the form *It tastes nice* or *He drinks brandy* whose meaning is not matched by a corresponding interrogative of the form *Does it taste nice?* or *Does he drink brandy?* This is also true of main clauses and the corresponding gerunds. But the relation of participles is more problematic. *Screaming children* corresponds, as we said, to *The children scream*. But the meaning of *hanging gardens* is much clearer than that of *The gardens hang* or *The gardens are hanging*, and that of *a drinking man* ('a man who habitually drinks alcohol') corresponds to only one sense of *A man drinks*. (For the non-habitual sense one would usually say *a man drinking*.) It would also be hard to understand, for example, *the arriving people* (alongside *The people arrive* or *The people are arriving*). Is there still a transformation when we find exceptions of that kind?

These questions are rarely posed explicitly, and the varying practice of linguists indicates that there are no agreed answers. But so far as the first is concerned, a reasonable requirement is that, if a transformation is the only evidence for a distinction, the constructions to be

13

established should be based on a clear difference of meaning. A sentence like *I contributed £10* can be transformed into the passive *£10 were contributed by me* (or *£10 were contributed by* ME). But *It costs £10* cannot be transformed into *£10 were cost by it*; nor *His brother weighs twelve stone* (meaning that that is his weight) into *Twelve stone are weighed by his brother*, or *It measures three feet* (meaning that that is its measurement) into *Three feet are measured by it*. This might suggest that *£10* represents two different elements, and that a sentence like *He weighed the whole of it* (meaning either that that was his weight or that that was what he measured the weight of) is constructionally ambiguous. But consider a sentence like *He married my sister* or *This hat fits me*. One does not say *My sister was married by him* (meaning that they got married) or *I am fitted by this hat*; so, on transformational evidence, these belong with *It costs £10* or *It measures three feet*. Yet the connection of meaning between, for example, *married* and *my sister* is more like that of *He courted my sister* (with the passive correlate *My sister was courted by him*), or indeed that of *He weighed the rice* or *He measured the stick*, than those between *costs* and *£10* or *weighs* and *twelve stone*. Hence there is no constructional difference unless, perhaps, other evidence could be adduced.

The other issue is more controversial. But for a transformation to be a regularity, the most we can allow is that it should have specified exceptions. If we assume that *This hat fits me* has the direct object construction, the verb 'to fit' is one exception to the transformation of actives into passives. But this is an absolute restriction: 'to fit' is incompatible with the passive construction just as, for example, 'to seem' was incompatible with a direct object, or 'to drink' with a subject complement. Nor are there other types of lexical irregularity. If a noun, a verb and a noun collocate readily in the active, and the verb or sense of the verb is not itself an exception, then in principle they collocate as readily in the corresponding passive, without changes of meaning that must be attributed to the particular words from which the collocation is formed. The passive will often seem more awkward: thus *Brandy is drunk by me* (or even *Brandy is drunk by* ME) is a less likely sentence than *I drink brandy*. But that is because the uses of the passive construction are in general more restricted, and is not due to the specific words *brandy*, 'to drink' and *I*.

There are different exceptions if, for example, we try to relate *He was exhausted* and *The journey exhausted him*, or *He was delighted* and *The book delighted him*. Thus the most likely meaning of *She is engaged* does not match that of *He engaged her*, and that of *He was worried* corresponds to only one sense of *It worried him*. In these and many other cases the change of form produces semantic changes that are partly unpredictable. A grammarian's explanation is that *engaged, exhausted* and so on are adjectives as well as forms of verbs, so that the exceptions have the same construction as, for example, *The thrushes are sleek*. The transformation is then restricted to true passives, like *The brandy is drunk (by my sister)*, *The burglar has been caught (by the police)* or *He is often worried (by the neighbours' dogs)*. But its regularity would be destroyed if, for example, *She is engaged to Bill* and *She was engaged by the National Theatre* were both seen as passive constructions.

If our general view is accepted it is easy to find putative transformations that will not hold. Another famous example concerns phrases such as *the shooting of the hunters*, in a sentence like *The shooting of the hunters was disgraceful*. In *the marking of the papers is very thorough*, the collocation of 'to mark' and *(the) papers* is identical to that of *They mark the papers thoroughly*. In traditional terms, *of the papers* is an Objective Genitive (the genitive being the Latin case most nearly translating *of*), with *the papers* connected to *marking* in a manner like that of an object to a finite predicator. But in *The singing of the children is very beautiful* the genitive is Subjective: the collocation of 'to sing' and *(the) children* shows a semantic connection like that of the same words in *The children sing beautifully*. In Chomsky's first account of such phrases, *the shooting of the hunters* was seen as constructionally ambiguous. On one interpretation, *of the hunters* is objective (the disgrace was in the act of shooting them), and the phrase was related by transformation to sentences like *They shot the hunters*. On another interpretation it is subjective (the disgrace was in the way the hunters shot), and the phrase was related by transformation to sentences like *The hunters were shooting*.

But when we look at other collocations the transformational relations are immediately suspect. There is nothing awkward about, for example, *They read the papers thoroughly* or *The children walk beautifully*; but *The reading of the papers is very thorough* or *The walking of the children is very beautiful*, though not wrong, are decidedly less likely than *The marking of the papers ...* or *The singing of the children ...* The causes must lie in the individual words *marking, reading, singing* and *walking*. In many cases it is hard to say if one or other interpretation is possible:

for example, would one say *The charging of the cavalry was decisive* (in the subjective sense of *the charge of the cavalry* or *the cavalry charge*)? As an ordinary speaker I was at first very doubtful about the ambiguity of *the shooting of the hunters*, though as a scholar I have now been brainwashed into accepting it. We find similar problems with ordinary nouns: thus could one say, objectively, *the charge of the stockade*? It does not follow that the forms in *-ing* are also ordinary nouns, any more than the participles in *-ing* (as in *screaming children*) are ordinary adjectives. But by our criterion the transformations are invalid and, in default of other evidence, subjective and objective genitives are not distinct constructions.

Some linguists might still be unhappy with this conclusion, since in our first examples the subjective and objective connections are quite plain. But if syntax is concerned with regularities syntactic functions must be distinguished by something more than a sporadic difference in collocational meaning. In *My aunt is cooking* the natural sense is that cooking is something she is doing; on that interpretation *my aunt* denotes an actor. But there is another sense in which cooking is something that is happening to her – the ultimate dream of a child in one of Saki's stories. On that interpretation *my aunt* does not denote an actor; nor does *dinner* in *Dinner is cooking*, or *the sausages* in *The sausages are frying*, and so on. For these examples there is a collocational parallel with sentences in which the noun is a direct object (*They are cooking my aunt, My aunt is cooking dinner, She is frying the sausages*). But others do not show it. *My aunt fell down* also describes something that happened to her (compare *My aunt lay down*); but one cannot say *They fell my aunt down*. *The fat is smoking* has a meaning like that of *The fat is burning* (compare *The fat must smoke but not burn*); but one would not say *She always smokes the fat*, with a meaning parallel to that of *She always burns the fat*. There is again no regular transformation.

Despite this, there have been attempts to describe the 'non-actor' function (of *the fat* in both *The fat is smoking* and *The fat is burning*, of *my aunt* in both *My aunt fell down* and the Sakiesque sense of *My aunt is cooking*) as grammatically distinct. But there are other semantic functions which are no less clear. If one says *She fried the sausages* one means that the sausages existed and were then fried; according to a terminology that is sometimes borrowed from German, *the sausages* is an 'affected' object ('affiziertes Objekt'), denoting an entity to which something is done. But in the case of *She made a cake* the cake exists only as a result of the making; *a cake* is semantically an 'effected' object ('effiziertes Objekt') or, in the more usual English term, an Object of Result. There are as good grounds for distinguishing these.

But if we do there is no way of knowing when to stop. *My aunt fell down* could be distinguished from both *My aunt lay down* and *My aunt is cooking nicely*; perhaps its subject has a third function (denoting an 'involuntary actor'). *She brought him up herself* might be said to mean that 'he', as he now is, is the result of her actions, or simply that the existing 'he' was so dealt with. Is it then constructionally ambiguous, with either object construction? We discussed the ambiguity of *Leave the meat in the kitchen*, but did our analysis go deep enough? It could mean that there are several lots of meat around the place; the hearer is being told which to leave and which to bring. Or perhaps there is just one lot; but the hearer does not know about it and is therefore being warned that it is there. Further distinctions could be made with *in the kitchen* taken as adverbial. Perhaps the hearer is in there and about to follow the speaker upstairs; but he is carrying some meat and is told not to bring it with him. Or perhaps they are passing the house and the hearer is going to drop the meat in; but he is stupid enough to ask which room the speaker wants it put in. When we start to draw distinctions of that sort, our analysis loses itself in episodic details.

In the view adopted here, neither *the shooting of the hunters* nor *My aunt is cooking* has a constructional ambiguity, and the object of result is a semantic function predictably associated with the meanings of certain verbs, such as 'to make' or 'to build'. If we thought otherwise we would have no rational delimitation of our field.

INDETERMINACY

In the preceding section we have found criteria by which certain distinctions are clearly syntactic and others are clearly not. But we will also find borderline cases, where the status of functions is not clear, or where it is uncertain which of two constructions, or types of construction, a specific form has. In ordinary grammars these do not cause a great deal of trouble, since most constructions, as such, are decisively identified. But a theoretical study must pay careful attention to them.

An elementary illustration is the type of *with*-phrase in, for example, *He walked with a stick*. The most natural interpretation is that the stick was used as an aid to walking; in traditional terms, *with a stick* has the semantic function of an Instrumental. But *He walked with his mother* means merely that his mother accompanied him; *with his mother* has the function of a Comitative. These functions are not distinguished by any rule of realisation. Thus the relative order is the same in, for example, *She hits boys with a stick* and *She hunts foxes with his mother*, *He flipped it to her with a spoon* and *He lowered it to the floor with his brother*, *With a spoon you can do it easily* and *With the vicar you can sing anything*. Although the collocational meanings are supported by other constructions (*He cut the cheese with a knife* and *The knife cut the cheese*; *He went for a walk with his mother* and *He and his mother went for a walk*), there is no precise transformational distinction. So far, then, the syntactic element appears to be identical.

The problem, however, is whether there is a class of verbs with whose valency either function must be described as incompatible. 'To walk' allows an instrumental, as we have seen; so also 'to climb' (*They were climbing with a rope*), and many others. But what of, for example, 'to come' or 'to go'? In present-day English *He went with a stick* means simply that he took one with him (compare *He walked with a haversack*). One would give a similar interpretation to, let us say, *They came with snow shoes*. It might be argued that these verbs exclude the instrumental, just as 'to take' or 'to boil' exclude a subject complement (as in *He took fresh*). The verbs which take it would then form their own class, and would distinguish the constructions of *He walked with a stick* and *He went with a stick* by the same reasoning that distinguished *He looked a fool* and *He saw a fool*.

But would any special rules be necessary? 'To go' and 'to come' are general verbs of motion, indicating no specific means of locomotion. But sticks and snow shoes are aids not to movement generally, but to movement on foot in particular; for *with a stick* or *with snow shoes* to be understood instrumentally, it is natural that the verb should have to indicate the same means (*He walked, He hobbled*, and so on). On such reasoning, the non-instrumental interpretation of *He went with a stick* would follow from the meaning of that verb, just as, for example, the 'effected' interpretation of *She made a cake* follows from the meaning of 'to make'. No further statement of incompatibility would be needed. It is significant that the collocation of 'to go' and *with* has lost the instrumental meaning often borne in earlier literature, precisely as the verb itself has lost a more specific 'walking' sense (*OED*, §1.1).[2] It is also relevant that 'to go' or 'to come' can readily collocate with phrases such as *by car* or *on horseback* in which the means, and not merely the instrument, is specified.

In the case of objects versus subject complements, it seems clear that syntactic incompatibility is involved. There is nothing else in the meanings of, for example, 'to look' and 'to listen' which explains why one can say *It looks good* but not *It listens good*, or in those of 'to bounce' and 'to rebound' (in *The ball bounced* and *The ball rebounded*) to explain why only the former can also take a direct object (*He bounced the ball*). For the different types of object a syntactic explanation seems quite unnecessary; an object of result is simply the object of a verb denoting a resultative process. But for the instrumental neither line of reasoning is quite decisive. The meanings of 'to come' and 'to go' are clearly relevant. Yet the instrumental interpretation is awkward even when it is reinforced by the context (compare *His artificial leg broke, so he had to come with a stick instead*). Does this or does this not warrant a separate rule of valency?

Such hesitation is intellectually dissatisfying, and in describing a language we will do our best to resolve it, by looking for more evidence or proposing fresh criteria. In this and similar cases, it is natural to suspect that there is something which we have missed, which would emerge from deeper investigation. But it is often hard to see what such a something might be. We must therefore ask at the outset why indeterminacies should be found, and whether they are more than artefacts of our method.

According to one view of language, the problems arise because, in treating syntax as a separate field, we are trying to draw a distinction which does not exist. There is no real notion of a construction apart from that of semantic connectivity in general; hence there cannot be a consistent basis for what grammarians have traditionally done. According to another view, the distinction is genuine; but syntax has its basis in something other than semantic relations. Therefore we are bound to have difficulty if we do not free it of criteria based on semantic differences. But in the theory which I have assumed the

---

[2] *OED* = *Oxford English Dictionary*. See the 'Principal references' for this and other abbreviations.

indeterminacy is inherent in the system we are describing. A central thesis is that to speak a language is, in part, to conform to rules of that language. Thus *They smell fresh* is in conformity with the rules of English, while *They smells fresh* and *They fresh smell* are (in my judgment) not. Such statements can be challenged: the best-trained mind is sometimes confused by school grammar, or by an irrelevant analogy, or by knowledge of some other language or dialect. But they reflect one sort of judgment that speakers can learn to make, in which a sentence is seen as comprehensible but corrigible, as contrary to grammar and not simply contrary to sense. In that respect the system is **codified**; there is a code ('code' in the sense of 'code of morals' and not in that of 'the Morse code') which they are said to break.

But languages are not wholly subject to rules. We remarked on the tendency for 'to grill' to be used of meat but not of bread, for beer to be called 'flat' rather than 'stale', and so on. These too are linguistic matters; the restrictions belong to the dictionary, or to some other form of lexical description, and do not simply reflect the things that the individual words denote. But a sentence like *He grilled the toast* is not wrong, and might on occasion be entirely appropriate. It merely departs from what we have just described as a **tendency**. Thus the system is only **partly codified**, with rules for some but not all aspects.

In such a system it is not surprising that the boundary between rules and tendencies, between what is codified and what is not codified, should itself be underdetermined. For the rules are rarely explicit, and are implicitly learned and followed, by each speaker, only to the point at which his speech is natural and received within the community. That point can clearly vary, without any difference which other speakers will remark. Thus A might have a tendency not, for example, to use *x* in a certain semantic relationship; but occasionally he says something which forces him to go against it. Likewise B might follow a rule, by which *x* is wrong in that relationship; but on occasion he is compelled to break it. From A's viewpoint B would depart from a tendency, like A himself. From B's viewpoint A too would be breaking a rule, but again because it is forced. Their utterances would be equally intelligible, since it is only when their meaning is grasped that the question of oddity or error arises. If that were the only difference between A's and B's speech, or one of only a handful of differences, it is hard to see how either should seem unusual to the other, or at all foreign to their shared community. The distinctions we have drawn would indeed be academic.

That does not mean that they are ALWAYS academic. If A follows a rule of frequent application, and B appears gratuitously to break it, their different usage, or B's imperfect command of A's language, will be plain enough. But we can anticipate borderline cases, in which a relation of meaning is only **marginally codified**. That is precisely the case with the instrumental. It is because there is marginal codification that our criteria, however rational, will sometimes fail to give definite results.

NOTES AND REFERENCES

For traditional views of syntax compare *Webster's Third International*, s.v., §a (cited at the beginning of Chapter 2); *OED*, s.v., §2.a; also, for example, SWEET, 1, p. 32 (§87) and generally, for 'logical relations' vs. 'means of grammatical expression'. For the distinction of construction and arrangement compare DE GROOT, *Syntaxis*, Ch. 4 ('syntactische structuur' vs. 'woordvolgorde'); TESNIÈRE, pp. 16–22 ('ordre structural' vs. 'ordre linéaire'); also F. R. Palmer's very useful '"Sequence" and "order"', in STUART (ed.), pp. 123–30 (reprinted in HOUSEHOLDER (ed.), pp. 140–7). On the general issue of linearity in structural linguistics see G. C. Lepschy, 'Sintagmatica e linearità', reprinted in his *Intorno a Saussure* (Turin: Stampatori, 1979), pp. 39–55; relevant textbook discussion in LYONS, *Introduction*, pp. 76–9. For the typology of means of realisation see Chapter 11 (and notes) below.

For distributional analysis see Z. S. Harris, 'Distributional structure', *Word*, 10 (1954), pp. 146–62 (reprinted in FODOR & KATZ (ed.), pp. 33–49; HARRIS, *Papers*, pp. 775–94); HARRIS, *Methods*, especially Ch. 2; textbook account in LYONS, *Introduction*, pp. 70ff., 143ff. But its origins go back to BLOOMFIELD. Thus for Bloomfield the basic lexical unit was the morpheme (see Chapter 3 below), defined as a combination of phonemes. Likewise the basic unit of grammar was the 'tagmeme', defined as a combination of sequential and other realisational features (p. 166). Both had meanings (*loc. cit.*), and constructions are referred to by notional labels (such as 'actor–action construction', p. 190). But in his view meaning was and would remain 'the weak point in language-study' (p. 140); hence a standing temptation to identify units independently of it. For criticism of distributional methods see W. Haas, 'On defining linguistic units', *TPhS* (1954), pp. 54–84, 'Linguistic structures' (review of HILL), *Word*, 16 (1960), pp. 251–76; brief assessment in his general essay, 'Linguistics 1930–1980', *JL*, 14 (1978), pp. 293–308 (see pp. 294–5). Compare, for example, de Groot: 'The aim of a structural classification has been defined as the establishment of similarities and dissimilarities, i.e. *oppositions, of meaning*, as far as features of meaning have *correlates*' (DE GROOT, 'Classification', p. 144; also critical remark on Bloomfield, p. 132).

For Chomsky's earliest views on the relation of syntax to meaning see CHOMSKY, *Structures*, especially Ch. 9; compare this with his recent 'Questions of form and interpretation', *LAn*, 1 (1975), pp. 75–109 (reprinted in CHOMSKY, *Essays*, pp. 25–59). The views of his followers have varied. For some syntax is still distributional: see, for example, CULICOVER, pp. 2, 9 (definitions of 'syntax' and 'syntactic category'), 45 (nature of 'syntactic arguments'). For others the 'base component' gives a full 'semantic interpretation' of sentences; hence 'generative semantics' (Chapter 12 below and notes). Now that both extremes have been tried we can return to traditional views with enhanced understanding.

Syntactic function is central to various theories developed in the 50s and 60s. In 'tagmemics' a role such as subject is a slot or point within a larger pattern (subject plus intransitive predicator, with the further slot 'intransitive predicator'; subject plus transitive predicator plus direct object, and so on). This slot may be 'filled' by various classes of unit (for example, noun phrases), which then have patterns of their own (for example, modifier plus head), and so on until all units are analysed. The theory was originally explored by PIKE (preliminary edition 1954–60), a work which unfortunately requires determination from its readers. But it was eventually systematised by Longacre: see R. E. Longacre, 'Some fundamental insights of tagmemics', *Lg*, 41 (1965), pp. 65–76, and his practical manual of 1964 (LONGACRE), especially the introductory chapter. It is also exemplified in numerous studies by their missionary organisation, the Summer Institute of Linguistics. For an early version see, for example, Viola Waterhouse, *The Grammatical Structure of Oaxaca Chontal* (Bloomington: Indiana University Research Center in Anthropology, Folklore, and Linguistics, 1962); Longacre's formulation is illustrated in detail by, among others, K. Jacobs & R. E. Longacre, 'Patterns and rules in Tzotzil grammar', *FL*, 3 (1967), pp. 325–89. For Pike's latest version see PIKE & PIKE, Ch. 3.

In systemic or 'scale and category' grammar a function is originally an element or place in a 'structure'. Thus *The milk tastes sour* has a structure 'subject predicator complement'; the subject element is then the 'place of operation' of a noun phrase, which in turn has a 'determiner head' structure, and so on. For the leading account see HALLIDAY, 'Categories', pp. 254ff.: more readably in M. A. K. Halliday, A. McIntosh & P. Strevens, *The Linguistic Sciences and Language Teaching* (London: Longman, 1964), Ch. 2; also in Margaret Berry's textbook, *An Introduction to Systemic Linguistics*, Vol. 1: *Structures and Systems* (London: Batsford, 1975), pp. 62ff. The origins of the theory lie in Halliday's dissertation, *The Language of the Chinese 'Secret History of the Mongols'* (published Oxford: Blackwell, 1959) and are, of course, quite independent of Pike's. But their similarities have often been noted: see, in particular, DIK's account of 'functional grammar' (Chs. 8–9), which draws heavily on both. They also share a central failing, in that they do not distinguish specific relations between elements. In *He eats cake, he* would simply be 'the subject'; likewise *eats* 'the predicator'. But we can also establish a direct relation between them, by which one is specifically the 'subject of' the other. In *It tastes nice* we have established a relation between the subject and the subject complement; but there is no direct relation between a subject and an object. This too cannot be shown merely by labelling object and subject complement as different 'slots'. Compare my review of DIK, *Lingua*, 23 (1969), pp. 360f., and later discussion of 'fused' constructions (Chapter 8).

A functional theory has also been sketched, several times, by Martinet: see, for example, A. Martinet, 'The foundations of a functional syntax', in STUART (ed.), pp. 25–36 (reprinted in MARTINET, *Studies*, pp. 111–22). But this has never got beyond its protreptic stage. See too Dik's later characterisation of a functional approach: S. C. Dik, *Functional Grammar* (Amsterdam: North-Holland, 1978).

'Collocation' is a term introduced by Firth, particularly for the habitual accompaniment of one word by another: see J. R. Firth, 'Modes of meaning', *Essays and Studies*, n.s. 4 (1951), pp. 118–49 (reprinted in his *Papers in Linguistics 1934–1951* (London: Oxford University Press, 1957), pp. 190–214), and textbook discussion in ROBINS, pp. 67ff.; very brief but penetrating comment in F. R. Palmer (ed.), *Selected Papers of J. R. Firth 1952–59* (London: Longman, 1968), 'Introduction', p. 6. My use may be compared with Harris's 'co-occurrence' (HARRIS, 'Co-occurrence and transformation') and Chomsky's 'selection' (CHOMSKY, *Aspects*, Ch. 2). For valency see notes to Chapter 5. For the substitution test for syntagms see HARRIS, *Methods*, Ch. 16, and other primary references in notes to Chapter 4 below, for immediate constituents; textbook account of this and other criteria in H. A. Gleason, *Introduction to Descriptive Linguistics*, 2nd edn (New York: Holt, Rinehart & Winston, 1961), Ch. 10. A special variant is the test of 'dropping' (substitution of *A* for *AB* or *BA*): see P. L. Garvin, 'A study of inductive method in syntax', *Word*, 18 (1962), pp. 107–20 (reprinted in GARVIN, pp. 62–77; HOUSEHOLDER (ed.), pp. 287–300); also discussion of obligatoriness in Chapters 6 and 7 below. For the ambiguity of *Leave the meat in the kitchen* compare the famous example *old men and women*, as discussed in particular by C. F. Hockett, 'Two models of grammatical description', *Word*, 10 (1954), pp. 210–34 (reprinted in JOOS (ed.), pp. 386–99), §3.1.

For transformational relations compare HARRIS, 'Co-occurrence and transformation'; discussion, and references for transformational grammar generally, in notes to Chapter 12 below. *The shooting of the hunters* is one of Chomsky's earliest examples: see N. Chomsky, 'Three models for the description of language', in R. D. Luce, R. R. Bush & E. Galanter (eds.), *Readings in Mathematical Psychology*, Vol. 2 (New York: Wiley, 1965), pp. 105–24 (originally in *IRE Transactions on Information Theory*, IT-2 (1956), pp. 113–24); CHOMSKY, *Structures*, pp. 88f. Compare discussion of both this and *flying planes* in LYONS, *Introduction*, pp. 249–53. On the subjective/objective genitive in Latin compare E. Benveniste, 'Pour l'analyse des fonctions casuelles: le génitif latin', *Lingua*, 11 (1962), pp. 10–18 (reprinted in his *Problèmes de linguistique générale* (Paris: Gallimard, 1966), pp. 140–48). For the general problem of ambiguity see LYONS, *Semantics*, 2, pp. 396–409; the fullest study is by J. G. Kooij, *Ambiguity in Natural Language: an Investigation of Certain Problems in its Linguistic Description* (Amsterdam: North-Holland, 1971). See also A. M. Zwicky & J. M. Sadock, 'Ambiguity tests and how to fail them', *Syntax and Semantics*, 4 (1975), pp. 1–36 (with brief discussion of *the shooting of the hunters*, p. 13). Constructional ambiguity – or 'homonymity' as CHOMSKY inelegantly called it (*Structures*, p. 86) – is naturally only one aspect.

For the active–passive transformation see CHOMSKY, *Structures*, p. 43, where it is said to apply without exceptions. For *marry, fit* and so on compare CHOMSKY, *Aspects*, pp. 103f.; but it is wrong to equate these with a class that cannot take adverbs of manner (examples in last section of Chapter 6 below). Early criticism is against the abstraction from stylistic and other restrictions on use: thus, for example, the brief remarks in R. Quirk, 'Towards a description of English usage', *TPhS* (1960), pp. 40–61 (later version, 'The survey of English usage', in his *Essays on the English Language, Mediaeval and Modern* (London: Longman, 1968), pp. 70–87). But later criticism is partly based on a conflation of syntactic passives with participial adjectives: see Gabriele Stein, *Studies in the Function of the Passive* (Tübingen: Gunter Narr, 1979); paralleled, ironically, by one of the present wave of Chomsky's followers (BRESNAN, pp. 14–36). For the distinction between syntax and lexicon see T. Wasow, 'Transformations and the lexicon', in CULICOVER *et al.* (ed.), pp. 327–60 (with comments by S. R. Anderson, pp. 361–77); corresponding account in LIGHTFOOT, pp. 252ff. For irregularity as a general feature of lexical derivations see, for example, my *Morphology*, Chs. 3 and 10.

Sentences like *Dinner is cooking* and *My aunt is cooking dinner* were related in 'case grammar': see FILLMORE and contemporary discussion in LYONS, *Introduction*, §8.2; later textbook account in HUDDLESTON, pp. 231ff. See too ANDERSON; also Fillmore's (final?) retrospection, 'The case for case re-opened', in COLE & SADOCK (ed.), pp. 59–81. On voluntary and involuntary actors see the sensitive paper by D. A. Cruse, 'Some thoughts on agentivity', *JL*, 9 (1973), pp. 11–23; also G. L. Dillon, 'Some postulates characterising volitive NPs', *JL*, 10 (1974), pp. 221–33. On the category 'object of result' see JESPERSEN, *Philosophy*, pp. 159f.; *MEG*, 3, pp. 232–4.

For partial codification see my *Generative Grammar*, especially §§141ff. For rules and tendencies compare C. E. Bazell, 'Three misconceptions of grammaticalness', in STUART (ed.), pp. 3–9 (on 'constraint' and 'restraint'); W. Haas, 'Meanings and rules', *Proceedings of the Aristotelian Society* (1972–3), pp. 135–55; also Haas's review article, 'John Lyons "Introduction to theoretical linguistics"', *JL*, 9 (1973), pp. 71–113 (important for various points in this chapter). It is worth recalling Coseriu's distinction of system and norm:

E. Coseriu, 'Sistema, norma y habla', in *Teoría del lenguaje y lingüística general* (Madrid: Gredos, 1962), pp. 11–113 (originally published separately, Montevideo, 1952). But this has only brief examples from syntax (pp. 83f.). For further recent discussion see LYONS, *Semantics*, 2, pp. 373–86 (on the criterion of corrigibility and syntax vs. semantics generally); also pp. 418–20 (on the related problem of acceptability).

The meanings of *with* have been much discussed. For the continuity of instrumental and comitative see I. M. Schlesinger, 'Cognitive structures and semantic deep structures: the case of the instrumental', *JL*, 15 (1979), pp. 307–24; for an attempt at a unified description, H.-J. Seiler, 'The principle of concomitance', *FL*, 12 (1974–5), pp. 215–47 (with references to a series of papers within a transformational framework). For other references see W. Koch, *Kasus – Kognition – Kausalität: zur semantischen Analyse der instrumentalen 'mit'-Phrase* (Lund: Gleerup, 1978); Koch distinguishes the instrumental and the comitative very sharply (pp. 125ff.).

2
Sentences

Popular definition; sentence not definable by thoughts; problem of completeness.
One sentence or two? Sentence as maximal linguistic form (Bloomfield's definition); as maximal unit subject to rule. Parataxis; intonation a continuous feature; therefore not subject to rule. Indeterminacy (roles of *please* and tag questions).
Incomplete sentences: Latency and ellipsis. Syntactic incompleteness: vs. semantic variables; vs. incomplete utterances; vs. contracted sentences; vs. sentences without ellipsis.
Generative syntax: Grammatical vs. ungrammatical; grammar as generative system. Advantage of generative grammar; and qualifications.

In defining syntax, a dictionary will usually refer to the **sentence**: thus 'the arrangement of word forms to show their mutual relations in the sentence' (*Webster's Third International*, s.v. §a).[1] But of all linguistic units this is the most problematic, and the one whose nature has been most debated. In a monograph published in the early 30s, Ries listed seventeen pages of varying definitions,[2] to which later schools have added several more, still with no consensus. We must try to appreciate the reasons for this difficulty, which lie partly in the form of definition adopted by earlier theorists, and partly in the relative indeterminacy of our field, as we have just explained it in Chapter 1.

In the popular view, a sentence is 'a series of words in connected speech or writing, forming the grammatically complete expression of a single thought' (*OED*, §6). The example

> Go away! I'm busy

would thus involve two thoughts, one that the hearer should go away and the other that the speaker is busy; each of these has a grammatically complete expression in one of which the verb *go* is connected with the adverb *away*, while in the other the pronoun *I* is connected

---

[1] *Webster's Third New International Dictionary of the English Language*, (Springfield, Mass.: Merriam, 1961).
[2] J. Ries, *Was ist ein Satz?* (Prague, 1931), pp. 208–24.

with the verb *am* and the adjective *busy*. Such definitions are similar to those proposed in antiquity. Priscian, for example, defines an 'oratio' ('sentence' or more literally 'utterance') as 'a concordant ordering of words' ('ordinatio dictionum congrua') which 'expounds a complete idea' ('sententiam perfectam demonstrans').[3] In both accounts the sentence is linked to something that the modern tradition calls a thought. In both there is a notion of grammatical or semantic completeness, and in both a notion of concordance or connectedness. For example, in *I'm busy* the verb is concordant with the pronoun in that its form is the 1st singular *am*, not the 3rd singular *is* or the general present tense form *are*.

The basic defect of this view lies in the notion of a thought (originally the Greek *diánoia*) which is said to be expressed. For there is no way in which this thought can be conceived independently of the utterance. It is only when we have heard what he says that we can attribute to a speaker the expression of this thought and not that thought, or first one thought and then another thought. Nor is the speaker himself in any better position. In uttering these sentences I might be speaking to someone who I found very tiresome; I had the thought, perhaps, that if I spoke to him like that he might not trouble me again. Perhaps I might not in fact have been busy; but I had the thought that, if I sent him packing, it would be nice to lock the door and take a nap. But yet *I'm busy* expresses the thought (it would be said) that I am busy. It is obvious that such thoughts are simply a projection of the sentences themselves. The same holds for the notion of a 'single thought' (*OED*). In our example there are two thoughts precisely in that there are two sentences. There are not two sentences because, on independent evidence, we can establish that there are two thoughts.

Let us abandon a semantic theory based on thoughts or ideas. But we must not imagine that there is some other entity, or set of entities, that can be put in their place. To the popular definition already cited, the *OED* adds a second, more technical formulation:

> *In grammar*, the verbal expression of a proposition, question, command, or request, containing normally a subject and a predicate ...

[3] H. Keil (ed.), *Grammatici Latini*, 2 (Leipzig, 1855), p. 53. Here as elsewhere Priscian transmits a Greek (Alexandrian) formulation.

which incorporates a semantic classification of sentences, into questions, statements, and so on, first proposed by the Greek sophist Protagoras (fifth century B.C.).[4] According to *Webster's Third International*, a sentence is a 'group of words that expresses an assertion, a question, a command, a wish, or an exclamation, . . .' (s.v., §3). But these too must be seen as characterisations, not as independent objects. *I'm busy* does not EXPRESS a statement, but IS a statement. If our example contains two sentences it is not because its parts express two different kinds of thing. It is because they must be characterised separately, the first AS a command and the second AS a statement, and not together. The semantic units are the sentences themselves, not something else that lies outside them.

The division of sentence types need not occupy us further at this point. But we cannot avoid the broader problems which such definitions try to solve. If we turn to another example:

> They were drunk. Certainly I was

a grammarian will again establish two sentences, both of the same type. For comparison he might cite forms with *and* as a linker (*They were drunk and certainly I was*), or with the first statement made a condition for the second (*If they were drunk then certainly I was*), where the tradition sees one sentence only. On what grounds is this justified? Plainly we must seek some principle of continuity, by which *drunk* is connected to *were*, or *certainly* to *I* or *I was*, in a manner different from the connection between the sentences as wholes, or between *drunk* and *certainly* in particular. Hence the grammarian's division, and the written full stop corresponding to it. The continuity must then change when, for example, *and* is inserted. What principle should it be?

In the same example, *They were drunk* would be described as a **complete** sentence: in traditional terms it expresses an idea in its entirety (compare the formula from Priscian), or is a 'grammatically complete expression' of it (*OED*). The second sentence is **incomplete**, the idea in question (that the speaker was drunk) being expressed only partially, with the adjective *drunk* not made explicit. Here too we must abandon the appeal to ideas. If a sentence is grammatically incomplete, it is so precisely by virtue of its grammar,

---

[4] *eukhōlḗ* 'prayer, wish', *erōtḗsis* 'question', *apókrisis* 'answer', *entolḗ* 'order'; see Diogenes Laertius, IX. 53–4.

not because there is an object on some other plane (the thought 'Certainly I was drunk') one of whose parts does not find expression in it. So on what grounds might *Certainly I was* be seen as incomplete compared to, for example, *Certainly I was drunk*, whereas *They were drunk* is not incomplete compared to, for example, *They were drunk last night*?

Let us begin with the problem of continuity, which has attracted the most attention in the last half-century. The problem of completeness we may treat as secondary.

ONE SENTENCE OR TWO?

The traditional strategy is to define the sentence, and then define syntax as the study of relationships within it. But we can clearly turn the problem round. In Chapter 1 we tried to distinguish constructional from other relations. Thus in our first example we would establish a construction linking *go* and *away*, with another linking *I* and *(a)m* and *busy*. 'Syntax' we define as the study of constructions; the sentence in turn can be defined as the maximal unit of syntax, or the largest unit over which constructional relations hold. In the same example we would establish no constructional relation between *Go away!* and *I'm busy*, or between *away* and *I*, and so on. By that token there are two sentences and not one.

This strategy is essentially that of BLOOMFIELD (pp. 170ff.). In Bloomfield's formulation, *go* and *away* are both 'linguistic forms'; each can recur in many different contexts (*I must GO out, Take me AWAY from here*, and so on), both as the same 'phonetic form' and with features of meaning that remain constant. So too is the whole form *go away*, which recurs, again with a regularity of meaning, in such larger phonetic forms as *Go away till Monday!* or *I told you to go away from here*. So too are these larger forms themselves. But naturally there is an upper limit. In our first example it is reached with *Go away!* and *I'm busy*: although each is itself a linguistic form, Bloomfield's criterion is designed to recognise no larger unit of this sort – no further regularity of phonetic form and meaning – which includes both. In any utterance the set of sentences is the set of maximal linguistic forms. *Go away!* is accordingly a sentence when followed by *I'm busy*, though in *Go away till Monday* it is no sentence, since the whole is also a linguistic form. In our other example (*They were drunk. Certainly I was*) both *They were drunk* and *Certainly I was* would likewise be conceived as maximal; by definition they too are sentences.

This strategy has obvious attractions. For instead of taking the sentence as given, and determining our field by reference to its boundaries, we begin by asking if a relation is of interest to us, and establish a boundary, or no boundary, purely by that decision. But Bloomfield's notion of a linguistic form is not satisfactory. He defines it as 'a phonetic form which has meaning' (BLOOMFIELD, p. 138); so, the term should apply to any form which has this property. But what of our two sentences together (*Go away! I'm busy*)? Surely this too has meaning – as a whole, not simply as two parts. So does the whole of Bloomfield's *Language*, or that chapter of it, or the opening lecture in my next course on phonology. If my lecture has meaning it is apparently a linguistic form; by definition it must then be a sentence, provided that my course of lectures is not seen as an even larger linguistic form.

It is tempting to answer that such meaning lies outside linguistics. It concerns the way in which an utterance is composed on a particular occasion (in Saussurean terms it is a feature of 'parole'), and has nothing to do with the language ('langue') as such. But just as a language has its grammar or its syntax so, traditionally, it also has a stylistics. Within it there are statements to be made about connections between sentences, or even among larger units, which belong as clearly to the characterisation of style in particular languages (in one language or in a group of languages generally), as a statement about the meaning of words belongs to their lexicon, or a rule of agreement to their syntax, or a description of rhythm to their phonology or prosody, and so on. Such larger forms have meaning in a way which interests the linguist; therefore they too can appropriately be called linguistic forms. Yet they are not sentences, since they do not interest our field specifically.

What do interest us, according to the view developed in Chapter 1, are linguistic forms which are subject to rule. In Bloomfield's own illustration (BLOOMFIELD, p. 170), the speaker begins with the greeting *How are you?* The verb is subject to agreement; in his terms, there is a grammatical feature of selection (pp. 164f.) by which it is *are* and not *am* or *is*. There is also a grammatical feature of order (p. 163), exemplified in the sequence of words. In Priscian's terms, *Are how you?* or *You are how?* would not be a 'concordant ordering' ('ordinatio dictionum congrua'). The speaker then continues with two further sentences (*It's a fine day. Are you playing tennis this afternoon?*), each of which conforms to the same or similar restrictions. Thus we may add a feature of order by which *fine* precedes *day* (not *It's a day fine*), or a feature of selection by which one says *Are you playing . . . ?* and not, for example, *Have you playing . . . ?* But no such features link the sentences themselves. Although the last two might be connected in meaning (the tennis perhaps depending on the weather), and we could also see the first two as stylistically connected (remarks on the weather being an ordinary accompaniment of greetings), no rightness or wrongness can be demonstrated. One of the three could easily be dropped, or another form put in its place. (*How are you? My bike's got a flat tyre. Are you playing tennis this afternoon?*) Nor do we need a linguistic rule to explain why the forms are said in that order and not, say, with the greeting last. (*It's a fine day. Are you playing tennis this afternoon? How are you?*) Bloomfield does not use the term 'rule'; it was only after Chomsky's work in the 50s that it began to lose an earlier stigma. But it is the evidence of rules that allows his 'grammatical features' to be distinguished.

Let us now take an example which is more problematic. In Orwell's *Animal Farm* the sheep chant a slogan which is in two parts:

Four legs good, two legs bad

– punctuated, as shown, with a comma.[5] This is undoubtedly a linguistic form; indeed the whole chant would be such a form, the mass repetition of slogans being at least of stylistic interest. The comma also marks an intonational connection. If uttered once the first part might, for example, have a low rise:

Four legs ‚GOOD

and the second a complementary fall:

Two legs ‚BAD

If chanted the whole would form a striking rhythmical unit, even with a pause in the middle. In either form of utterance, the first part has a non-final intonation, showing clearly that the second is to follow. (So, if a speaker paused at that point, his hearers might expect him to go

[5] George Orwell, *Animal Farm: a Fairy Story* (London, 1945), Ch. 3 *et passim*.

on, or might wonder why he had stopped.) All this should be the subject of linguistic description, whether the form is one sentence or two. Then shall we acknowledge Orwell's comma, and treat it as one?

According to Bloomfield, two or more forms stand in a relation of **parataxis** (Greek *táxis* 'arrangement', *pará* 'beside') if they are joined only by their intonation. So, if there is nothing else, there is at least parataxis between *four legs good* and *two legs bad*; according to Bloomfield's treatment of intonation, they would be 'united by the use of only one sentence-pitch' (BLOOMFIELD, p. 171). In our earlier example, *Go away!* could likewise be related paratactically to *I'm busy*:

> Go away I'm BUsy!

– with a rhythm just like *Go away till Monday*. Now if an item such as *as* were inserted:

> Go away as I'm BUsy!

a grammarian would at once treat the second part (*as I'm busy*) as syntactically subordinate to the first. Could the intonation also realise a similar construction?

For Bloomfield himself the answer was already given. For if there is parataxis the whole utterance must be a linguistic form, the intonation being clearly a subject for linguistic description. Hence only the whole can be a maximal linguistic form. Accordingly the pitches were themselves seen as a feature of grammatical arrangement, belonging to a category of 'modulation' (BLOOMFIELD, p. 163). But if we take this line the features proposed will soon prove hopelessly elusive. In the example from Orwell it is easy to show the linkage, as this form of slogan has limited and rigid patterns. But could there also be parataxis between, for example, *It's a fine day* and *Are you playing tennis* ...? Presumably there could; compare Bloomfield's further example:

> It's ten o'clock, I have to go home

where the comma marks no more than a 'pause-pitch' (p. 171). But exactly which tunes have a pause-pitch – or a first part which is intonationally non-final – and which have a sentence-pitch? The more tunes we consider the more uncertain any answer will become. Or we might start from the paratactic form of our original example (*Go away I'm BUsy!*) and shift it gradually towards a form with separate nuclei (*Go aWAY! I'm BUsy*). There would be no certain point at which we could say that the relationship changed.

The root problem is that intonation is a **continuous** feature. A word, for example, is either there or not there: in *Four legs good* there is a plural *legs*, in *Four leg good* the singular *leg*, and in *Four good* no noun at all. There is nothing between these that is neither quite plural nor quite singular, nor quite present nor quite absent. In brief, words are **discrete** items. The same holds for the order of words: in *four legs* the noun is second and in *legs four* it is first, again with no intermediate range. Such discreteness is essential to the formulation of rules. In *Four leg good* a rule of selection has been broken, which in *Four legs good* has been obeyed; there are just these possibilities, either to get it wrong or to get it right. Likewise the order is correct in *four legs*, but incorrect in *legs four*. In general we could not properly talk of rules (for plural not singular, for numeral + noun not noun + numeral) unless, in principle, we could determine when the forms included in these oppositions (*legs* not *leg*, *fishes* not *fish*, *three fishes* not *fishes three*, and so on) were being used.

To Bloomfield and his successors it appeared that intonation could be treated in the same way. For English he himself proposed a discrete set of 'pitch phonemes' (BLOOMFIELD, pp. 91f., 130), in which pause-pitch can be opposed to sentence-pitch just as, among consonant phonemes, *p* in *paint* is opposed to *f* in *faint* or *t* in *taint*. But it is hard to see why such analogies should have been thought valid. Among vowels and consonants we will naturally find phonetic continua, such that in practice speakers can mishear. That in itself confirms the principle of discreteness, by which an intermediate sound is necessarily taken one way or the other. But with intonation the continuity is fundamental. Although as phoneticians we can hear two tunes as different, or transcribe form *a* as having a different pitch from form *b*, in the end there is no way of saying whether they enter into a simple opposition (like the English front *e* and back *o*, or the fortis *p* and lenis *b*), or an opposition with more terms in between (like the close *i* and the open *a*, or the labial *p* and velar *k*), or no opposition at all. The phonemic principle cannot apply, there being no evidence for clear-cut sameness or distinctness, but only for greater or lesser similarity.

This does not mean that the intonation should be ignored. For it can have a crucial role both in realising a given construction (thus the intonation of interrogatives tends to differ from that of declaratives) and in marking boundaries between syntactic units. One such unit is the sentence itself, though in normal speech the cues are often lacking. But all this is a matter of more or less; there are no rules by which a set of right tunes is distinguished from a set of wrong tunes. Hence there are no rules covering parataxis, as Bloomfield defines it. In his own example, *I have to go home* may indeed be linked by intonation to *It's ten o'clock*. But there is no other linkage; one could as readily say *I have to go home, it's ten o'clock* (with the forms in the opposite order), or *It's ten o'clock, time to go* (with an alternative to *I have to go home*), or any other combination that obeys the rules internal to each part, and makes sense. Accordingly there are two sentences, following our general principle. Likewise *Go away!* is a separate sentence from *I'm busy*, however unified their tune may be.

In Orwell's slogan there is at least parataxis, as we said. If that were the only link, both *four legs good* and *two legs bad* would be maximal syntactic forms. But perhaps it is not. The two forms have identical constructions, each consisting of a numeral, noun and adjective, in the same order and with the same roles. In Bloomfield's terms, this too could be a matter of grammatical arrangement, with features of order and selection (for example, the non-selection of a copula) as well as modulation. Then this too might be seen as subject to rule. If so, the parallel would be described as a constructional relationship; so again one sentence, not two. The problem here is typical of many that arise in practical applications, or that would arise if the tradition did not offer ready-made solutions. There is certainly a pattern to be described. But to what branch or mode of description does it belong?

In this case a rule would be limited to a certain style of utterance. It is only in such chanting that a form which broke the parallel (*Four legs good, but two bad*; *Four legs O.K., two legs are not O.K.*) could properly be classed as wrong, or even awkward. We might therefore see this as a pattern in stylistics – a special case of parallel patterning in general. But there are parallel forms that do belong to syntax: *The harder we work the less we earn*, *The fewer the better*. Is the sheep's slogan more like these, or more like a purely stylistic antithesis:

> One has to belong to the intelligentsia to believe things like that:
> no ordinary man could be such a fool

– from the same author?[6] Perhaps there is no definitive answer. In one case the pattern is codified (Chapter 1 above); in another we find no

[6] George Orwell, *The Decline of the English Murder and Other Essays* (Harmondsworth: Penguin Books, 1965), p. 178.

more than a stylistic tendency. But marginal codification must also be expected.

It is not surprising that different scholars can at times arrive at different conclusions. *Please*, for example, can appear as the only word in an utterance; hence the only word in a sentence. Thus:

(*a*) Please!

– meaning 'Please be quiet!', 'Yes, I'd love a cup of coffee', or whatever the situation suggests. Like *Go away!* this sentence can appear in parataxis:

(*b*) Please! I'm busy

again with a non-final intonation. But one could also make the request explicit:

(*c*) Please could you be quiet?

where the same role might be played by *please* in final position:

(*d*) Could you be quiet please?

or, of course, in the middle:

(*e*) Could you please be quiet?

where *quiet* alone might carry a nuclear stress. For many grammarians, the last three establish *please* as an adverb (so, for instance, QUIRK *et al.*, pp. 470ff.). But dictionaries still tend to class it as a verb, with the *please* of the historical *(if you) please* a form of the same word as the infinitive *please* of *I like to please her* or the past tense *pleased* of *It pleased me* (so, for example, at the end of the entry in *Webster's Third International*). For Bloomfield its role is paratactic; even in case *e*, it is grammatically no more than an interruption (compare BLOOMFIELD, p. 186) of the larger form *Could you … be quiet?*, with which it is intonationally linked.

In this last case it seems clear that Bloomfield is in error. For there is a rule of adverbial position – in his terms, a grammatical feature of order – by which *please* comes after *you* and before *be*, not before *you* (*Could please you be quiet?*) or directly before *quiet* (*Could you be please quiet?*). But the others are less straightforward. In case *b* the second part is declarative (*I'm busy*); since adverbial *please* is normally used to qualify requests, we might continue to take *Please!* as a separate unit, syntactically as in case *a*. In case *c* we do have a request; therefore it seems natural to take this as case *e*. But suppose that *c* is uttered with two separate contours:

,PLEASE! Could you be ˬQUIet?

Is this still just one request, or rather two requests (or a request and an attention-getting prelude), with *Please!* once more paratactic? If the latter, then why not when the intonation is continuous? For there could also be a single contour in case *b* (*Please I'm* BUsy!). We will also find genuine instances of interruption:

(*f*) I'm busy – please! – till Tuesday

(where the main form is again declarative). If requests are found with a similar pattern (*Could you put them, please, on the table?*, *Will you stop, please, doing that?*), do we still treat *please* as an adverb (as in case *e*) or should they go instead with case *f*? There is no single correct way of deciding which forms should come under the rule.

A similar problem arises in the analysis of Tag Questions. In an example such as the following:

They will be coming, won't they?

the final question is a tag whose verb and subject (*won't they?*) pick up the preceding subject and first verb (*They will*) of the statement. The pattern would be broken if one said *They will be coming, won't he?* (with subjects *they . . . he*), or *They will be coming, aren't they?* (with verbs *will . . . are*); so too in *He comes tomorrow, won't he?* (instead of *doesn't he?*), *We are seeing him on Tuesday, don't I?* (instead of *aren't we?*), and so on. Most grammarians would state this as a rule (so, for example, QUIRK *et al.*, pp. 390f.). But not every example fits so neatly. The tag is not invariably at the end: *It was Mary – wasn't it? – who came yesterday.* Nor does it always pick up the main verb: *He said it was Mary who was coming, wasn't it?* (compare *He said it was Mary, didn't he?*). Nor in that case need the verbs so strictly correspond: *He said it would take us three hours, won't it?* In other cases only a noun is picked up: *He's playing a glockenspiel, isn't it?* or *I spoke to your brother – wasn't it? – on Saturday.* In the last example *wasn't it?* can reasonably be treated as an interruption (like *please!* in *I'm busy – please! – till Tuesday*). But what of the others? Are they too outside the rule, and so no more than paratactic? Or should some, at least, be brought within it?

We could construct two opposite lines of argument. On the one hand, it is clear that each form could be altered for the worse: for example, *He said it would take us three hours, doesn't it?* (with *doesn't it* substituted for our earlier *won't*) or *He's playing a glockenspiel, isn't she?* This last form can be corrected (as any grammarian will tell us) by the change of *she* to *he*: thus *He's playing a glockenspiel, isn't he?* But it can also be corrected (so we would argue) by the change of *she* to *it*; just as there is a rule for correspondence with the verb and subject, so we could postulate a second rule, for correspondence with other noun phrases. The form with *doesn't it?* might be corrected either by replacing the whole tag with *didn't he?* (*He said it would take us three hours, didn't he?*) or by matching *would* in *would take* with at least a form of the same verb (*wouldn't* or *won't*). Both changes would be offered as evidence for a rule: in both cases by our usual test of corrigibility.

On the other hand, it is not clear that the worsening illustrated is any more than a worsening of sense. In ... *a glockenspiel, isn't she?* there is nothing that *she* can be taken to refer to, neither 'he' nor the glockenspiel being eligible. If we restore *it* we are not, perhaps, correcting a form which is wrong, but merely substituting paratactic forms which make sense for others that make nonsense. (Similarly *It's ten o'clock, I must go* makes more obvious sense than *It's ten o'clock, two and two makes four*.) Nor need we postulate a rule (so, again, we would argue) to explain why it is hard to understand *He said it would take us three hours, doesn't it?*, or why *won't* or *wouldn't* – note either – is more intelligible. But we do need a rule by which *It would take us three hours, won't it?*, with the tag linked to the main verb, is corrected to *It would take us three hours, wouldn't it?*, with *would* and *wouldn't* matching exactly.

In short, when are forms that correspond in sense more than merely forms corresponding in sense, and specifically forms corresponding by rule? Our only expedient is to ask how systematic the correspondence is. In our first cases a grammarian finds a neat and general pattern, covering forms of up to a dozen verbs (*will*/*would*, *can*/*could*, and so on) and frequently exemplified in speech. Therefore he states a rule, which (with additional features we have not mentioned) takes perhaps half a page. But if we try to extend this to the whole range of examples (including ... *your brother – wasn't it?* –) all neatness and generality will be lost. Therefore no grammarian does, at least to the writer's knowledge. However, the precise line might be drawn at various points. The pattern is not substantially changed when tags come in the middle (*It was Mary – wasn't it? – who* ...); so perhaps we should still talk of a single sentence, with the rule varied accordingly. There are also final tags whose correspondence is less firmly established. For example, I am not myself so happy with a tag in *oughtn't* (*He ought to go, oughtn't he?*), and could easily say *shouldn't*, especially if the verbs are well separated (*It ought to work better at that sort of price, shouldn't it?*). Is this last example within the rule, as a variant, or is there again parataxis, with *ought* and *shouldn't* merely going together in meaning? The facts themselves do not dictate an answer.

INCOMPLETE SENTENCES

Our other problem concerned the notion of completeness. In the example given earlier:

They were drunk. Certainly I was

the meaning of the second sentence has to be gathered from its context. All else being equal it means that the speaker was drunk; in traditional terms, the adjective *drunk* must be **understood**. Thus:

Certainly I was ⟨*sc.* drunk⟩

In other contexts the hearer might understand, or be meant to understand, something else – thus a verb and an adverb:

A. Don't you think we were driving too fast?
B. Certainly I was ⟨*sc.* driving too fast⟩

or a clause:

Certainly I was ⟨*sc.* where I should have been⟩

and so on. But some element or elements are always missing from – or, we will say, are **latent** in – the construction. Thus one construction of this sentence has a latent predicative element:

Adverb	*Subject*	*Copula*	*Predicative*
Certainly	I	was	⟨ ⟩

In such cases the sentence itself is described as **elliptical**. So, in our first interpretation, there is an **ellipsis** of the predicative element *drunk*.

In this example the evidence is quite clear. For the sentence cannot be uttered out of the blue; there must be some context – verbal or non-verbal, immediate or non-immediate – which shows what words are intended. The speaker can also be made to complete it, if necessary. Suppose, for example, that we are looking at some facetious notice: 'Were you drunk last night?' I laugh and say 'Certainly I was.' But perhaps you do not follow; 'Were what?', you ask. I might then point to the notice and say 'Drunk, of course', supplying the element which was missing. The problem, however, is that any utterance is in some sense incomplete, in that there is always something which the speaker might in principle have said, or might in principle have said more precisely, had it been necessary. Nor is this the only type of ellipsis that grammarians have postulated. The evidence of latency will play an important role in later chapters, in distinguishing elements for which it is or is not possible. We must therefore begin by separating this form of incompleteness, which is syntactic and of sentences, from four others which either do not concern us or will concern us in other ways.

The first is illustrated by the following example:

> There's football tonight. Will you be watching it?

where the *it* of the second sentence would refer, all else being equal, to the game of football, or the football programme on television, mentioned in the first. This sentence too is clear only in an appropriate context. I could not greet you out of the blue and say:

> Good morning! Will you be watching it?

'Watching what?', you might reasonably ask. Once more the context need not be verbal: the person addressed might be looking at a poster, announcing that a game of soccer, or whatever else is in question, will take place. In such sentences the pronoun *it* is a semantic variable, whose referent the hearer has in some way to identify. So are both *he* and *did it* in, for example, *He did it yesterday*. Suppose I greet you with this information:

> Good morning! He did it yesterday

Perhaps we had talked about it the previous evening. ('When IS Bloggs going to clear out his office?') Or perhaps there is some other indication. (Thus I see you nailing a reminder to Bloggs's door.) But in some way both the person and the action must be identifiable. Otherwise you will again be at a loss. ('Sorry, who did what?')

Ellipsis and variables have overlapping roles. Instead of *Will you be watching it?* one could also say *Will you be watching?*, with the object latent. The same remarks would apply – for example, if I said out of the blue:

> Good morning! Will you be watching?

There are also contexts in which *Did it* could be said in place of *He did it*:

> A. Has Bloggs cleared out his office?
> B. Did it yesterday

Instead of *He hasn't done it*, one could often use the elliptical *He hasn't*: *He hasn't* ⟨sc. *cleared out his office*⟩, *He hasn't* ⟨sc. *shaved*⟩, and so on. In some contexts one, in some the other form might be preferable. But from a syntactic viewpoint the phenomena are different. *Will you be watching it?* has an object *it*, just as *Will you be watching the football?* has an object *the football*. The incompleteness is lexical or semantic, and would be remedied not by adding an element, but by making the existing element more explicit. Likewise *He hasn't done it* has the same overall construction as *He hasn't shaved* or *He hasn't cleared out his room*: a main verb, with or without an object (*shaved, cleared out his room, done it*) is related to an auxiliary verb (*hasn't*) and a subject. But in *He hasn't* the auxiliary is left hanging; to remedy its incompleteness at least one other element (main verb, main verb plus object, and so on) must be supplied. Likewise the object must be supplied in *Will you be watching?*

Our second distinction is between an incomplete sentence and an incomplete utterance. Suppose that I would like you to open the window. Then I might gesture towards it and say:

> Please, would you mind opening . . . ?

But then I stop, or say 'Thank you', since I see you are already moving to do it. Or suppose that I forget someone's name: 'That girl over there is . . . Dammit, I was told only yesterday.' Such cases certainly involve incompleteness. But the reason I stop is not that I expect you to supply the words which are missing. In the second case you might indeed refresh my memory. ('Jane Bloggs, isn't she?') But I scarcely assume that you can do so. In the first case I was going to say 'the window', or 'that window', or 'that window over there'; it was only as I was speaking that I realised it was unnecessary. Perhaps you are still not quite sure what I want – for example, if you should open the window or a cupboard which is underneath. In that case you might simply pause, expecting or inviting me to continue. In these examples a sentence is attested only as a fragment: thus a fragment of what might have been the declarative sentence *That girl over there is Jane Bloggs*, or the request *Would you mind opening the window?* This fragment has no standing of its own.

For such cases the intonation is usually a sufficient guide. In the second example no word would carry nuclear stress; the pattern is one that should continue, with a nucleus in *Jane* BLOGGS, or whatever else might have been said. Otherwise there might indeed be ellipsis:

> That girl over THERE is ⟨*sc.* Jane Bloggs⟩

– which would not suit the context. Likewise an utterance of the incomplete *Will you be watching?*

> Will you be ˇWATCHing?

(high fall–rise with nucleus on *watch-*) is clearly distinguished from the fragment:

> Will you be watching … ?

which is an incomplete utterance of the complete *Will you be watching* FOOT*ball?*, *Will you be watching them ar*RIVE*?*, or the like. We will naturally find utterances in which both phenomena are attested. Thus:

> Are you listening ⟨*sc.* to the concert⟩ at home or … ?

– the hearer interrupting 'At home'.

Fragments are of no concern to syntax, except as a source of confusion in our data. But ellipsis is constrained by rules. The object can be latent with 'to watch', as above; also, for instance, with 'to play': *Do the children play* ⟨sc. *football*, sc. *bridge*, …⟩ *too?* But there are other verbs with which it has to be present. Suppose you asked me if I would like the window open or shut. I could not answer 'Would you mind opening?' or 'Could you please shut a little?'; with these verbs, or with the active sense of these verbs, the sentence must have the complete construction (*Would you mind opening it?* or *Could you please shut*

41

the window a little?). There may also be rules for the construction in general. We gave an example with ellipsis of the subject (*Did it yesterday*). But if the subject is latent there would also be ellipsis of a 'be' or 'have' auxiliary: *Bringing his wife, is he?* not *Is bringing his wife, is he?*, *Been drinking too much* not *Has been drinking too much*. Likewise for 'to be' as copula: *Stupid, weren't they?* not *Were stupid, weren't they?* It is easy to see why such a verb should tend not to be realised. But it is more than simply a tendency, and is therefore part of our field.

A third distinction may be drawn within syntax, between ellipsis recoverable from inside and from outside the sentence. In example *a*:

(*a*) Stolen another?

both words must be construed with latent elements: *stolen* with an auxiliary and subject, *another* with at least a head noun. So:

⟨*sc.* Had Bloggs⟩ stolen another ⟨*sc.* car⟩?
⟨*sc.* Have you⟩ stolen another ⟨*sc.* bicycle⟩?

and so on. The same two words can also appear in an example such as

(*b*) Bloggs has borrowed one car and stolen another

where we might again see at least two latent elements (. . . *and* ⟨sc. *has*⟩ *stolen another* ⟨sc. *car*⟩), subject to rules that are very similar. But as sentences these are not in the same category. Example *a* means different things in different contexts, and can naturally be misinterpreted. (For example, you arrive driving a car when I know your own has been smashed up. I greet you: 'Hullo! Stolen another?' But you have in fact stolen someone's umbrella, which is in your hand as I say it. Therefore you think it is the umbrella I am referring to.) But in example *b* the latent elements can be supplied uniquely. In such cases we will describe the sentence as **contracted**. Thus *b* can be understood as a complete sentence which may, however, be a contraction of one in which *has* and *car* are repeated.

There is again a parallel with semantic variables. In example *b*, *another* was taken to mean 'another car'; likewise in example *c*:

(*c*) Leave the books where they ARE

the pronoun *they* refers to the books. In:

(*d*) I'll fetch it if Bloggs HASn't

the ellipsis can be recovered either from inside or from outside the sentence ('if Bloggs hasn't fetched it' or, in context, 'if Bloggs hasn't got a car', 'if Bloggs hasn't time to go', and so on). Likewise in:

(*e*) Bloggs said he was coming

the pronoun *he* might refer either to Bloggs, or to someone quite different (A. 'What about Smith?' B. 'Bloggs said he [i.e. Smith] was coming'). In the first interpretation, *he* would be said to stand in a relation of **anaphora**; it relates back (Greek *aná* 'above', *phorá* 'a carrying') to the antecedent word or phrase *Bloggs*. Likewise *they* in example *c* is in an anaphoric relation to *the books*, and in an example which we gave earlier:

There's football tonight. Will you be watching it?

many scholars would see *it* as related anaphorically to an antecedent *football*. It will be obvious that a pronoun which can only be anaphoric (as in my reading of example *c*) is a special case of anaphora within the sentence (as in one interpretation of example *e*), which in turn is a special case in the interpretation of semantic variables, or of a certain type of semantic variable, in general. Likewise ellipsis that must or can be recovered from within the sentence (as in examples *b* or *d*) is a special case of a much more general phenomenon, illustrated by *Stolen another?*, *Will you be watching?*, and so on.

A fourth distinction is between an incomplete sentence and one that merely could have contained more elements. In *I was watching all the time* there is again ellipsis; this would not be said unless it was clear who or what was being watched. But in *I was reading all the time* there is simply no object. On occasion the person addressed might know what was being read, and the utterance might bring it to mind. ('Of course. You had that awful thesis, didn't you?') But it is not necessary. Suppose I have seen Bloggs sitting opposite you in a railway compartment; I might ask 'Did you talk to Bloggs on the train?' You could not reasonably reply 'No. I'm afraid I was watching all the time.' (Compare 'No. I was looking out of the window all the time.') But you could perfectly well reply 'No. I'm afraid I was reading all the time.' What you were reading is immaterial. Likewise if you reply: 'No. I was too busy eating.' With 'to watch' we establish a single construction, in which the object may however be latent. With 'to read' or 'to eat' we establish two distinct constructions, one with an object and the other without, each of which is equally complete.

This distinction is clear in principle, and clear in practice over many particular examples. But others are debatable, or raise complications. We said that 'to play' could also take a latent object – thus in the following interchange:

> A. I play chess a lot.
> B. Do the children play too?

where B means his hearer to understand *chess*. But we could also find examples like this:

> A. The children work a great deal.
> B. Do they play too?

where the verb is objectless, just like the verb in *Do they read too?* A natural solution is to say that the constructions are different:

Subject	*Predicator*	*Object*	*Adverb*
the children	do ... play	⟨ ⟩	too

Subject	*Predicator*	*Adverb*	
they	do ... play	too	

– the former elliptical, the latter not. We might also suggest that the verb has slightly changed its sense (from 'engage in a formalised game' to 'amuse oneself in general'). But this technique must not be abused. Suppose again that you were sitting opposite Bloggs; I ask you 'Did you talk to Bloggs?' Now perhaps this is pure curiosity: I would like to know how the two of you are getting on. But perhaps it is not: there is something specific you were meant to ask him. Should we then distinguish a separate construction, where *talk* construes with a latent adverbial? (Thus *Did you talk to Bloggs* ⟨sc. *about his car*⟩, ⟨sc. *about coming on Saturday*⟩, and so on.)

Surely not. For the test of ellipsis is that the person addressed can on occasion fail to supply it. I have it in mind that you play chess; perhaps I am pointing to a photograph of you doing so. I ask 'Do the children play TOO?', with the nucleus on *too*. Now perhaps you fail to make the connection; in that case you are at a loss, precisely because the object is unclear. ('Sorry. Play what?') But you would not simply take it as a non-elliptical sentence (compare *Do the children* PLAY TOO?). There could be no such difficulty with *Did you talk to Bloggs?* Perhaps I did have a specific point in mind; perhaps you have in fact forgotten it. You might even ask: 'Sorry. Was there some reason I should have ⟨sc. talked to him⟩?' (or 'Sorry. What about?'). But what you have failed to grasp is not my sentence – merely my reason for uttering it. We will not establish ellipsis unless it is clear that the latter explanation does not suffice.

GENERATIVE SYNTAX

The sentence is the domain of rules which specify that certain combinations of words are **grammatical**, and certain others are **ungrammatical**. For example, we have posited rules by which a grammatical arrangement *I am busy* is distinguished from the ungrammatical *I busy am*, with the wrong order; also from *I are busy*, with the wrong agreement; also from *I busy are*, with both. The set of rules established for a given language would together supply a definition of the total set of combinations which were in accordance with it. So, by the rules which we have posited, *I am busy* would be a member of this set, whereas *I busy am*, *I are busy* and *I busy are* would not be. Those members which are maximal, in that they are not part of larger combinations for which rules are also stated, would be defined as the **grammatical sentences** of the language. So, by the same rules, *I am busy* would be one such sentence. The more reliable the rules which a grammarian posits the more accurate, of course, will the definition be.

This is the basis for the notion of a **generative grammar**, as Chomsky first explained it in the 50s. As he pointed out, the set of grammatical sentences can be taken as infinite. For example, on the pattern of 'The House that Jack Built', we can establish a sentence *This is the house that Jack built*, then another sentence *This is the malt that lay in the house that Jack built*, then another sentence *This is the rat that ate the malt that lay in the house that Jack built*, and so on, in principle without limit. A grammar is said to **generate** such a set; just as in mathematics we can talk of a rule which generates an infinite set of numbers (*OED*, Supplement, s.v. 'generate', §2.d), so, for a given set of words or other minimal units, the rules of grammar can be seen as generating all the sequences of units which are established as grammatical sentences, and none of those established as ungrammatical. Chomsky's first, and in my view most impressive, achievement was to clarify this notion, and to show that such a system could be formalised.

There is nothing here that any language scholar need find disconcerting. If we accept that a construction is subject to rules, and define the sentence as the maximal unit of construction, then with respect to whatever rules we posit, there must be a set of sentences that follow them, which we are calling grammatical, and a set of combinations that break them, which we are calling ungrammatical. The notion is also of great heuristic value, since it is in trying to formulate a generative grammar, and seeing how far the sentences it generates are right, that the coherence and adequacy of a description are most rigorously tested. In that way Chomsky's insight has greatly deepened our understanding of what we are doing. But it has to be accompanied by three qualifications.

Firstly, there is no precise set of grammatical sentences, or set of sentences to be generated, which is given in advance of our analysis, or of the criteria by which the grammar is set up. There is much indeterminacy, and we must often draw a distinction for which the arguments are not conclusive. In such cases the generality of the rule may itself be a decisive factor (as in our discussion of tag questions). A grammar could in principle be limited to complete sentences. But that too is the grammarian's decision; by another criterion it would generate complete and incomplete alike. The choice is not dictated by our subject matter.

Secondly, just as there are aspects of language which are subject to rules, so are others which are not. For example, we posit no rules for collocations (Chapter 1), nor for word meanings in general. In Chomsky's earliest work these aspects were excluded from description, as in the Bloomfieldian theory of which his was an offshoot. But in the mid 60s the notion 'rule of grammar' was extended to all facets of the speaker's knowledge of, or competence in, his language – including collocational restrictions (the subject of 'selectional rules' in CHOMSKY, *Aspects*, p. 95), including the meaning of grammatical functions (thus the different meanings of objects which we discussed in Chapter 1), and so on. In my view both the earlier and later Chomsky were mistaken. Syntactic rules can furnish only one part of the description of a language. But it is only when they are limited to syntax, or to syntax plus some aspects of morphology, that generative treatments are sound.

Finally, it must be accepted that the formalisation of syntactic rules, which remained a dominant ideal until well into the 70s, is essentially a side issue. Our main problem is to distinguish different forms and types of construction, and to decide when they are instanced. If we can deal with that, we can ask what formalisation is appropriate. If we cannot, the pursuit of formalisation is not going to help us. The constructions themselves must therefore be the main topic of this book.

NOTES AND REFERENCES

Bloomfield's definition of the sentence is modelled on that of Meillet: see A. Meillet, *Introduction à l'étude comparative des langues indo-européennes*, 7th edn (Paris: Hachette, 1934), p. 355 (1st edn, 1903). Compare JESPERSEN, *Philosophy*, pp. 305ff. (definition, p. 307); see also Bloomfield's review of Ries, *Was ist ein Satz?* in *Lg*, 7 (1931), pp. 204–9 (reprinted in C. F. Hockett (ed.), *A Leonard Bloomfield Anthology* (Bloomington: Indiana University Press, 1970), pp. 231–6). Among earlier definitions those of Wundt and Paul were, in their day, important: see W. Wundt, *Die Sprache* (*Völkerpsychologie*, Vol. 2), 3rd edn (Leipzig: Wilhelm Engelmann, 1911–12), Part 2, p. 248 (discussion from p. 229 onwards); PAUL, pp. 121–3. But in Meillet's or Bloomfield's terms both were concerned with psychological and not with purely linguistic problems.

For a recent and important contribution see LYONS, *Semantics*, 1, pp. 29–31; 2, pp. 622–35. But I do not think that it is necessary to insist on all of Lyons's terminological distinctions, at least for our purposes. See too his earlier textbook (LYONS, *Introduction*, pp. 172ff.), which is more careful than others in the Bloomfieldian tradition; also D. J. Allerton, 'The sentence as a linguistic unit', *Lingua*, 22 (1969), pp. 27–46; HERINGER, pp. 139ff.

The 50s saw a determined attempt to reduce English intonation to discrete phonological and grammatical units: thus, in particular, G. L. Trager & H. L. Smith, *An Outline of English Structure* (Norman, Oklahoma: Battenburg Press, 1951); HILL, Ch. 2 and pp. 102–14; also HARRIS, *Methods*, especially pp. 45ff., 169f., 281f., and textbooks such as HOCKETT, Ch. 4 and pp. 168, 177. For early but definitive criticism see D. L. Bolinger, 'Intonation: levels vs. configurations', *Word*, 7 (1951), pp. 199–210 (reprinted in his *Forms of English: Accent, Morpheme, Order* (Tokyo: Hokuou Publishing Co., 1965), pp. 3–16). For the complexity of the phenomena, and a thorough survey of earlier analyses, see D. Crystal, *Prosodic Systems and Intonation in English* (Cambridge: Cambridge University Press, 1969), which remains a standard treatment. For the relation of intonation to grammar see Bolinger's essay 'Intonation and grammar', *Language Learning*, 8 (1958), pp. 31–8 (reprinted in *Forms of English*, pp. 95–100); Crystal, Ch. 6. On the status of intonation compare MARTINET, *Elements*, §§3.3f. *et passim*; but I cannot see it as, in toto, only 'faiblement linguistique' (section on the sentence, §4.33). For more careful views on what is or is not linguistic see Crystal, pp. 128ff. (on 'prosodic' and 'paralinguistic'); LYONS, *Semantics*, 1, Ch. 3. For a more recent study outside the English-speaking tradition (and stressing much that is familiar to scholars in it) see C. Hagège, 'Intonation, fonctions syntaxiques, chaine-système, et universaux des langues', *BSL*, 73 (1978), pp. 1–48.

The sentence has been defined as an intonational unit: thus, in particular, HILL, p. 336 ('a sequence of segmental material occurring under a single pitch superfix'). For a wider phonetic definition see DE GROOT, *Syntaxis*, Ch. 1 ('de klankeenheid voor het gebruik van woorden' – literally 'the sound unit for the use of words'); but de Groot stresses that the cues for sentencehood are not necessarily realised (note b, pp. 13f.). Compare, for example, the definition of H. Glinz, *Die innere Form des Deutschen: eine neue deutsche Grammatik*, 4th edn (Berne: Francke, 1965), p. 74, which refers to its physical production as a 'breath-unit'.

The transformational literature was at one time full of trivial discussion of tags. For two that are not so, see R. D. Huddleston, 'Two approaches to the analysis of tags', *JL*, 6 (1970), pp. 215–22; R. Cattell, 'Negative transportation and tag questions', *Lg*, 49 (1973), pp. 612–39. See JACKENDOFF, *Semantic Interpretation*, pp. 94–100 for similarities between sentential adverbs and one form of parenthesis.

There is no complete agreement as to when ellipsis should be recognised. For a standard definition see *OED*, s.v., §2 ('the omission of ... words ... which would be needed to complete the grammatical construction or fully to express the sense'); for earlier notions CHEVALIER, *passim* (see table of contents and index), especially on Sanctius (pp. 352–5). It is worth looking up the index references in JESPERSEN, *Philosophy* and *Syntax*, for uses current in the first part of this century. For present theories compare DUBOIS *et al.*, s.v.; LYONS, *Introduction*, pp. 174f. (and briefly in *Semantics*, 2, p. 589); HERINGER, pp. 101, 152f.; QUIRK *et al.*, pp. 707ff. (and more generally in Ch. 9, pp. 536ff.). Quirk *et al.* require that words should be 'uniquely recoverable' from the context (§9.2); this is too strong, even for their own examples (e.g. that of §9.14). For a wider and more traditional notion see R. B. Long, *The Sentence and its Parts: a Grammar of Contemporary English* (Chicago: University of Chicago Press, 1961), pp. 491f., on 'implied components': further illustrations *passim* on pp. 10ff., 76ff. These include cases where a standard transformational grammar posits obligatory deletions: compare, for example, HUDDLESTON, pp. 111–14 (on 'Equi NP deletion'), 187f., 201–3 (on deletion generally). But Huddleston is careful to distinguish ellipses in our sense (pp. 226ff.).

On ellipsis and pronouns see D. J. Allerton, 'Deletion and proform reduction', *JL*, 11 (1975), pp. 213–37. In earlier generative grammar anaphoric elements were introduced by transformations: see papers in REIBEL & SCHANE (ed.), Part 3, on 'pronominalisation'. But this treatment is now largely if not generally abandoned. For reasons see T. Wasow, *Anaphora in Generative Grammar* (Ghent: Story-Scientia, 1979), which includes latent elements as 'null anaphors' (p. 2 and Ch. 6). See too the helpful papers on ellipsis by T. Shopen, 'Ellipsis as grammatical indeterminacy', *FL*, 10

(1973), pp. 65–77; E. S. Williams, 'Discourse and logical form', *LIn*, 8 (1977), pp. 101–39. For a wider and very sound discussion of anaphora see LYONS, *Semantics*, 2, §15.3 (pp. 657ff.).

For elliptical and related types of sentence in English see Viola Waterhouse, 'Independent and dependent sentences', *IJAL*, 29 (1963), pp. 45–54 (reprinted in HOUSEHOLDER (ed.), pp. 66–81), which compares a group of Peruvian and Mexican languages; R. Gunter, 'Elliptical sentences in American English', *Lingua*, 12 (1963), pp. 137–50; also Elizabeth Bowman, *The Minor and Fragmentary Sentences of a Corpus of Spoken English* (Bloomington: Indiana University, 1966). Bowman's 'minor sentence' is from BLOOMFIELD, pp. 171f., 176f. For a suggestive study of their intonation see Gunter's 'Intonation and relevance', in BOLINGER (ed.), pp. 194–215; also his earlier 'On the placement of accent in dialogue: a feature of context grammar', *JL*, 2 (1966), pp. 159–79. Gunter's papers are reprinted, with an additional chapter, in his *Sentences in Dialog* (Columbia, S.C.: Hornbeam Press, 1974). On the general topic of connections between sentences see QUIRK *et al.*, Ch. 10 (with section on ellipsis cited already); also M. A. K. Halliday & Ruqaiya Hasan, *Cohesion in English* (London: Longman, 1976): textbook discussion in ALLERTON, Ch. 12. But a study of Halliday & Hasan should convince any reader that it is wrong to treat this as a grammatical problem.

Generative grammar originated in Bloomfieldian distributional analysis: compare HARRIS, *Methods*, pp. 372f., on the synthesis or prediction of utterances; CHOMSKY, *Structures*, pp. 13ff. (especially §2.2). In Chomsky's earliest writings 'utterance' and 'sentence' are used interchangeably: see 'A transformational approach to syntax', in HILL (ed.), pp. 124–58 (reprinted in FODOR & KATZ (ed.), pp. 211–45), where 'generate' collocates with both in the same clause (beginning of §3).

For Chomsky's mature theory see his *Aspects*, Ch. 1, especially pp. 4ff., *Topics*, p. 12; also *Language and Mind*, 2nd edn (New York: Harcourt Brace Jovanovich, 1972), especially pp. 26ff. (first published, 1968). Good secondary exposition by SMITH & WILSON, Chs. 1–2. For comments and criticism see my *Generative Grammar and Linguistic Competence*: senses of 'generative grammar' are discussed in §4.

3
Words

In the last chapter we treated the sentence as the maximal syntactic unit. We now turn to the minimal unit, which by tradition is the **word**. So, in a line from Ted Hughes which we cited earlier:

Takes his changed body into the holes of lakes

there are constructional links among *his* and *changed* and *body*, or among *the* and *holes* and *of* and *lakes*. But there is no syntactic relationship between the root *hole* and the plural suffix *-s*, or between *change* and the participial inflection *-d*, or between *in* and *to* in the compound preposition *into*. The structure of words belongs to another branch of grammar – **morphology** or the study of 'form' (Greek *morphḗ* 'form, shape').

This view has often been challenged, and for respectable reasons. We must therefore look carefully at the arguments that objectors have put forward, and the ways in which they can be met.

WORDS OR MORPHEMES?

In the sentence which we might transcribe [dʒilzdisəˈpiəd] all speakers will immediately identify three units: the proper name *Jill* [dʒil], a phonetically reduced form of *has* [z], and the participle *disappeared*. But

50

suppose we are asked to justify these divisions. Why should these units, and these alone, be set up?

A standard method is to make tests of replacement and insertion. For *Jill* we can substitute, for example, *John* or *my pencil* (*John's disappeared, My pencil's disappeared*). Between *'s* and *disappeared* we can insert, for example, *already* (*Jill's already disappeared*). *Disappeared* can be replaced with *vanished* or *finished her dinner*. These new forms fit together: one can also say *John's vanished* (combined substitution of *John* and *vanished*), *Jill's already vanished* (substitution of *vanished* combined with insertion of *already*), and so on. One might even try to make sense of *My pencil's eaten her dinner*. These changes of form are accompanied by regular changes of meaning. Thus *John's disappeared* differs in meaning from *John's vanished* as *Jill's disappeared* differs from *Jill's vanished*, the differences being attributable solely to the change of participle. Likewise *John's disappeared* differs in meaning from *John's already disappeared* as *Jill's vanished* differs from *Jill's already vanished*, and so on.

But why should the analysis stop at this point? In *disappeared* we can, for example, substitute *obey* for *appear* (*Jill's disobeyed*); we can also drop *dis-* (*Jill's appeared*), as again in *Jill's obeyed*. Although the change of meaning is less regular, *disobeyed* and *disappeared* are opposed to *obeyed* and *appeared* as broadly negative to positive. Alternatively, we might see *obeyed* as a form in which *obey* replaces the whole of *disappear*, leaving just the suffix (*-ed*) unchanged. In this way our example may be split not just into three successive words:

Jill + 's + disappeared

but into at least five partly smaller units:

Jill + 's + dis + appear + ed

with *'s*, or the full form *has*, perhaps divisible into two more.

Such results can lead to two forms of description. In the view adopted here the participle *disappeared* is one form in a **paradigm**. The paradigm as a whole is that of a verbal **lexeme** DISAPPEAR ('to disappear' in the traditional usage which we have followed in the first two chapters) which is distinct from other lexemes such as APPEAR, OBEY or DISOBEY. The place of *disappeared* in this paradigm can be characterised by the feature or **morphosyntactic property** Past

Participle; this in turn is distinct from other morphosyntactic properties such as Present Participle (the property which characterises the place of *disappearing*), Past Tense (the form here being homonymous with the past participle), and so on. In sum, the word or word form *disappeared*, as it appears in the example *Jill's disappeared*, is the past participle 'of' DISAPPEAR, or that **form of** DISAPPEAR which is so characterised. The lexeme and the morphosyntactic property, with their respective classificatory and other features, are all that is syntactically relevant. Of the smaller forms which we have isolated, *dis-* and *appear* are two parts of a complex root; but a root too is a purely morphological construct. The suffix *-ed* is an inflection serving as the exponent of past participle; but the exponent of a property in no way characterises the property itself.

The other view is that, since these smaller forms can be identified by the method which we have illustrated, it is they, and not the traditional words or word forms, which must represent the basic units of our field. In the usual formulation, APPEAR and past participle would be seen as **morphemes**, which precede and follow each other, in the construction of our example, just as the corresponding sequences of sounds, [əpiə] and [d], precede and follow each other in the form itself. Another morpheme – DIS-, let us call it – would be represented by the prefix. Likewise *'s*, as the reduced form of *has*, is the exponent of a verbal morpheme HAVE followed by a second, inflectional morpheme which is conventionally labelled '3rd singular'. In syntax, therefore, *'s disappeared* would be made up not of two units but of five:

HAVE + 3rd singular + DIS- + APPEAR + past participle

each of which enters into constructional relations.

There is no easy choice between these alternatives, largely because the status of the word, as a phonological, grammatical and lexical unit, varies greatly from one type of language to another. But whichever choice we make is absolute. If the morpheme is established as a syntactic unit we will soon find constructional relations that ignore word boundaries. Not only would the word be divisible, but for at least some purposes, or in at least one part of our grammatical description, we would be forced to set up complex units cutting across it. Conversely, if the boundaries between words are to be respected, the same constructional relations can only be stated over words as wholes. For the larger unit would be destroyed if smaller parts were seen as entering into them. Our syntax must be based either on the morpheme in defiance of the word, or on the word in defiance of the morpheme. We cannot treat both as fundamental.

The relationships in question can be revealed by further tests of substitution. Within the word *disappeared*, we can also make replacements for the suffix: thus, for example, *disappearing*. In terms of morphemes, we have replaced the exponent of past participle with a suffix representing present participle, itself another inflectional morpheme. But in the sentence *Jill's disappearing* the second word is also different, being the reduced form not of *has* but of *is*. In terms of morphemes, it no longer represents 3rd singular preceded by HAVE, but the same inflectional morpheme preceded by another verbal morpheme BE. We have thus discovered a co-variance between past participle and present participle on the one hand, and HAVE and BE on the other. This pattern holds independently of substitutions made in the remainder of the example. For instance, one can say *Jill has vanished* but not *Jill is vanished*, and conversely *Jill is vanishing* but not *Jill has vanishing*. Again, one can say *Jill had disappeared*, with the substitution of past tense, but not *Jill was disappeared*; conversely, *Jill was disappearing* but not *Jill had disappearing*. In short, we have evidence of a relation which is specifically between the verbal morpheme of one word and the inflectional morpheme of the word following.

In the same form, the rule of agreement can be stated not for the word *has*, but simply for the morpheme 3rd singular. In *The books are disappearing* and *The books were disappearing* we could also see a direct relation between *the books*, as subject, and an inflectional morpheme which would supply the final element in *are* and *were*. If we base our analysis on morphemes, the phrase *has disappeared* would therefore be divided into three parts, none of which coincides with a word. The verbal morpheme HAVE is directly related not to its own inflectional morpheme 3rd singular, but to past participle in *disappeared*; together these form one larger unit, representing the Perfect, which may be distinguished as a whole from forms of the Progressive or Continuous (present participle with BE). Both the verbal root in *disappeared* and the inflectional morpheme in *has* will likewise enter directly into their own constructions. Only the structure of *disappear* itself (APPEAR preceded by DIS-) would involve a relation that did not cross a word boundary.

At this point some scholars might already argue that the morphemic treatment was superior. For if a term which partly characterises word *x* must be related directly to another term which partly characterises word *y*, and these terms have isolable or at least partly isolable representations in the word forms (such as *-ed*, or the root *ha-* in the unreduced form *has*), it is an easy step to see these representations as the forms of successive units. But the constructions can be described as clearly in the traditional manner. In *Jill's disappeared* we have a subject, an auxiliary verb and a main verb. If the single auxiliary is a form of the lexeme HAVE (which form does not matter), then the main verb, whatever its lexeme, will have the morphosyntactic property past participle. If the subject is singular then the auxiliary (or, more generally, the first verb in the phrase) will typically have the property 3rd singular, unless some other property of the word excludes it. In short, we refer not to parts of words, but simply to the partial characterisations of words as wholes. The attraction of this form of statement is precisely that the word is not split up.

In arguing against the word it is not enough to show that morphemes, if established, must have a syntactic function. For any statement about such functions can be readily translated into the traditional form. But there is a stronger case when a word and a morpheme might be said to have functions which were the same. In the first of these examples:

> She is older than Jane
> She is more beautiful than Jane

older is one word, the Comparative form of the adjective OLD. In the traditional form of statement, it is related as a whole to the following word *than*, or to a larger unit *than Jane*. In the second sentence *more beautiful* is two words: the comparative form of an adverb followed by the only form of a different adjective BEAUTIFUL. But the change of meaning is attributable solely to the change of adjectives. One cannot say *She is beautifuller than Jane*; with this adjective one must use the form with *more*. Nor would one normally say *She is more old than Jane*. Even when both forms are natural (*She is prettier than Jane*, *She is more pretty than Jane*) their meanings do not differ, at least not in a regular way. On such evidence we are dealing not with two contrasting constructions, but with two variants of the same construction, each valid for a different range of adjectival lexemes.

The argument for morphemes will then run as follows. In *more beautiful than Jane* we can make substitutions for *beautiful* while holding *more . . . than Jane* constant: thus *She is more awkward than Jane, She is more delicate than Jane*, and so on. We can also drop *more . . . than Jane* as a whole (*She is beautiful*), but not any one word separately (*She is beautiful than Jane, She is more beautiful Jane, She is more beautiful than*). On such evidence *beautiful* is one syntactic unit and *more . . . than Jane* must be another, with its three words standing in close interdependence. In *older than Jane* we can make similar substitutions for *old* (*She is younger than Jane, She is taller than Jane*); all but this root can again be dropped (*She is old*); nor again can one say *She is old than Jane, She is older Jane*, or *She is older than*. On this evidence *-er than Jane* should also be taken as a unit, with the inflection *-er* precisely parallel to the word *more*. Accordingly *-er* must itself represent a syntactic unit: namely, the comparative morpheme.

Examples of this sort form the strongest case against a word-based syntax. But if the reasoning on one side is that the one-word *older* should be assimilated to the pattern of the two-word *more beautiful*, the traditional reply is that, on the contrary, the two-word *more beautiful* should be assimilated to the pattern of the one-word *older*. In *older than* we again relate *than* not to a comparative inflection, but to the whole word (the comparative of OLD) of which this is a morphosyntactic property. In *more beautiful than* we relate it to the comparative of BEAUTIFUL; the only difference is that, in the paradigm of this lexeme, the morphosyntactic property comparative has an adverb *more* and not the suffix *-er* as its exponent. When a form in a paradigm consists of two or more words it is **periphrastic**. So, in the paradigm of BEAUTIFUL the comparative form is the periphrastic *more beautiful*, whereas for OLD it is the simple or non-periphrastic *older*. For PRETTY it may be either (*more pretty, prettier*). The same would hold for the corresponding superlatives (*most beautiful* as compared with *oldest*). In *She is the oldest* there is a similar case for setting up a unit represented by *the . . . -est*, comparable to *the most* in *She is the most beautiful*. But alternatively we may argue that in the first the relation must be between *the* and the entire word represented by *oldest*. Accordingly, in the second it has to be between *the* and the whole unit which we call the superlative of BEAUTIFUL.

Neither form of statement can make the facts neater than they are. The description based on morphemes leaves us with two realisations of each construction; for although *-er* and *-est* would have functions which in some sense equal those of *more* and *most*, nevertheless the latter come before the adjective and the former after it, and they combine with it in respectively looser and closer ways, which at some point a description must acknowledge. Moreover, *more* and *most* are themselves morphemically complex, with comparative and superlative preceded by the same adverb. The traditional treatment gives a uniform account of the constructions (*older* or *more beautiful* related to *than Jane*; *the* related to *oldest* or *most beautiful*), but by putting the discrepancy somewhere else, in the description of paradigms. Moreover, it would tend to detach the structure of *more beautiful* and *most beautiful*, where there are non-periphrastic forms for other lexemes, from that of *less beautiful* and *least beautiful* (*She is less beautiful than Jane, She is the least beautiful*), where there are not. Either solution is bound to leave its own loose ends.

In these examples the periphrastic form has the same place in the paradigm (defined by the same morphosyntactic property, comparative or superlative) as the simple form with which we have compared it. But this is not a necessary condition. In *Jill's disappeared* we spoke of HAVE plus past participle, in a morphemic analysis, forming a syntactic unit to which we gave the semantic label 'perfect'. This may then be compared not only to the similar two-term unit which we called progressive (BE plus present participle in *is disappearing*), but also, for example, to the single morpheme past tense, in *Jill's disappeared*. In general, any verbal complex may display just one of these units, or two, or three, or none. In *Jill appears* there is none, the 3rd singular morpheme (*-s*) having a different role, as we have seen. In *had appeared* we would establish a sequence of morphemes

HAVE + past tense + APPEAR + past participle

with both past tense and the perfect (HAVE ... past participle). Likewise *was* or *were appearing* incorporates both past tense (*were* = BE + past tense, *was* = BE + past tense + 3rd singular) and the progressive, while in *has been appearing* or *have been appearing*:

HAVE + BE + past participle + APPEAR + present participle

we have both perfect and progressive. Finally, in *had been appearing* we have all three.

Alternatively, all eight combinations may be grouped into a paradigm, in which all forms except *appear(s)* are periphrastic. Just as past tense is a property of the word represented by *appeared*, so in *had appeared* or *was appearing* both it and the accompanying properties perfect or progressive would be ascribed to the complex as a whole. *Has been appearing*, for example, may be characterised as the perfect progressive 3rd singular non-past form of the lexeme APPEAR, opposed within this paradigm to the corresponding past tense *had been appearing*, to the corresponding non-perfect *is appearing*, and so on, and across paradigms to the entire periphrastic forms of other lexemes (*has been obeying* or *has been disappearing*). We are still dealing with three words: a 3rd singular form of HAVE, followed by the past participle of BE, followed by the present participle of APPEAR. As such they may be interrupted by words extraneous to the paradigm (the adverb *recently* in *has recently been appearing*, the subject *Jill* in the question *Has Jill been appearing?*); this naturally requires syntactic description. Nevertheless it is by treating the whole as periphrastic that the integrity of the individual words can best be respected. For in that way we can establish the categories of perfect and progressive, as elementary terms in the system of semantic oppositions, without resorting to morpheme-based units (HAVE ... past participle, BE ... present participle) by which all three are split up.

The integrity of the word can be respected only at a price. For if we speak just of morphemes, and the ordering of morphemes, and larger units made up of two or more morphemes, our conceptual apparatus is undoubtedly simpler. The issue must therefore be decided ad hoc, for the particular language and perhaps even for the particular problem that is being investigated. If there are no inflections the argument will not arise; the word may still be complex (thus a compound or a lexically derived formation), but no part of it will enter individually into wider relations. This defines a class of 'isolating' languages, of which the classic instance is Vietnamese. In other languages the decision will go in favour of the morpheme, especially if, within the word, we are faced with regular contrasts in the ordering of formatives. Such languages are called 'agglutinative'; in an ideal case the word would be no more than a phonological unit (for example, the domain of an accentual pattern). In a typical 'inflecting' language, such as Latin, the morpheme has no prima facie case. For the morphosyntactic properties which our description will particularly refer to (properties of number and person in the agreement of subject and verb, or of number and case and gender in the agreement of adjectives with nouns) cannot be identified by simple substitution and insertion of forms, in the way which we illustrated for English.

This does not mean that a morphemic description is impossible, but merely that a syntax based on words is more immediate and natural. In Latin the voice and aspect properties of the verb (passive versus active, perfect versus non-perfect) are shown by single words in three quarters of the paradigm, but periphrastically in the remainder. Thus for MONEO ('warn' or 'advise') we have forms such as *monet* '(he) is advising' (active non-perfect), *monetur* 'is being advised' (passive non-perfect) and *monuit* 'has advised' (active perfect), but the two-word *monitus est* (participle of MONEO combined with a 3rd singular form of SUM 'be') for the passive perfect, 'has been advised'. This too could be restated in a morphemic format, with a participial morpheme in *monitus* (represented by the suffix -*t*-) linked syntactically to the verbal morpheme in *est* (represented by the root *es*-) and forming a unit with it which can be opposed directly to a passive morpheme in *monetur* (represented by the final suffix -*ur*) or to a perfect morpheme in *monuit* (represented by -*u*-). The objection to such statements is not that they are infeasible or incoherent. For if the technique can be used for comparing exponents of the same property in different paradigms (as in the comparatives *more beautiful* and *older*), and for comparing exponents of different properties in the same paradigm (perfect *has appeared* and past tense *appeared*), surely it can also be used for exponents of the same properties in the same paradigm, when they are present in different combinations. But few Latinists would accept it, since it destroys a grammatical unit that is firmly established by all criteria.

In English there is more ground for argument, and descriptions in both styles can be found in the literature. On the one hand, the word is undoubtedly a unit, and the smallest that speakers themselves are consistently aware of. A sentence may be spelled out word by word (*Jill – is – appearing*), but only a grammarian might do it morph by morph, even where the sounds permit (*Jill – is – appear – ing*). Likewise each word may be stressed (JILL *is appearing*, *Jill* IS *appearing*, *Jill is ap*PEA*ring*), but in no ordinary utterance would one stress -*ing* (*Jill is appear*ING). On the other hand, no word has more than two inflections, and for the most part the exponents of morphosyntactic properties, or the exponents of putative morphemes, are separate and easily identifiable. Only in a few forms such as *was* and *were* (BE + past tense + 3rd singular, BE + past tense) have we referred to morphemes which substitution tests would not immediately reveal. For English in particular, as for languages in general, we must be prepared to think in either mode.

MARKERS AND DETERMINERS

Even apart from cases of periphrastic formation, we will often assign to a word a function which is in general like that of an inflection, or which can be compared to that of a specific inflection in some other language. In Latin, for example, two nouns may be linked by a genitive inflection: *Ciceronis orationes* 'the speeches (*orationes*) of Cicero (genitive *Ciceronis*)'. In English their equivalents may be linked either by the word *of* (*the speeches of Cicero*) or by an enclitic *'s* (*Cicero's speeches*); for other pairs only one may be usual (*John's house, the top of the hill*). In Italian all such linking will involve the word *di*: *la casa di Giovanni* (literally 'the house of John'), *la cima del monte* ('the top of-the mountain'), *le orazioni di Cicerone*. The range of these constructions is not identical; in Latin, for example, one would say *urbs Roma*, with the nominative *Roma* matching the nominative *urbs*, not *urbs Romae* (genitive *Romae*), for English *the city of Rome*. But it is clear that the roles of a morphosyntactic property in Latin, a word in Italian, and both a word and an enclitic in English, may be described in similar terms.

In the earliest Greek tradition such words are among those classed as *sýndesmoi*, literally 'things that bind together', or as *árthra* 'joints' or 'articulators'. (In later grammars these are the terms for the parts of speech called in English the conjunction and the article.) Among English grammarians *of* would often be called a **form word**, as opposed to a content word such as *speeches* or, we might say, a content lexeme such as SPEECH. Alternatively, it is a grammatical word (as opposed to a lexical word), or an empty word (as opposed to a full word). In a syntax based on morphemes, many writers would see both the *of* morpheme and the Latin genitive (represented by the suffix *-is* in our example *Ciceronis*) as grammatical morphemes, while the roots *Ciceron-* or *speech* would represent lexical morphemes. But the modern usage is not wholly satisfying. Firstly, it will be useful to have terms which are neutral between different minimal units. For similar

59

functions can be assigned to morphemes in one form of treatment, or to words and properties of words in the other. Secondly, it is not clear that all form words, or words with a quasi-inflectional role, are properly described as content-less. In *the speeches of Cicero* the article is classed as grammatical rather than lexical; nevertheless it does have a meaning – that of a definite article as opposed to an indefinite (compare the singulars *the speech* and *a speech*). We will accordingly distinguish two different types of function, each of which can be assigned to any term in a syntactic description, whether a word, a morphosyntactic property, or whatever. In the first type the item is, in a certain sense, content-less but in the second not.

A function is of the first type if, at that particular point in that particular construction, we establish no opposition of meaning. In *the plays of Shakespeare* we have another phrase with the same construction as *the speeches of Cicero*; likewise *the poems of Milton, the drawings of Michelangelo,* and so on. We will thus establish oppositions, at two points in this construction, among a set of nouns such as *speeches, plays, poems* or *drawings* and another set with members such as *Cicero, Shakespeare, Milton* or *Michelangelo*. But there is no other word with which *of*, as such, will be contrasted. In *the speeches and Cicero* we have put *and* in what is superficially the same place; but the construction is then of a different type. If we substitute *by* or *from* it changes only in part (*the speeches by Cicero, the speeches from Cicero*); but *by Cicero* and *from Cicero* have semantic functions also found in verbal constructions (*The speeches have been composed by Cicero, The speeches have arrived from Cicero*) into which a unit *of Cicero* cannot regularly enter. Whatever else we substitute, the construction alters in one way or another (*the speeches attacking Cicero, the speeches before Cicero,* and so on). In each case the change of meaning involves not just a contrast between *of* and a unit that replaces it (*of* as opposed to *by* or *attacking*, like *Cicero* as opposed to *Shakespeare* or *Milton*), but a change of relations in the phrase as a whole.

In such a case the form word has indeed no content, except as the source of one cue, or perceptual signal, by which the construction is identified. We will therefore describe its role as that of a **construction marker** (or simply a **marker**). In a Latin phrase with the construction of *Ciceronis orationes*, the genitive property is a similar marker (the suffix *-is* providing the direct cue) for the syntactic relationship between two nouns. On this basis grammarians will often talk of an English '*of*-construction' or a Latin 'genitive construction', referring to the relation itself, or the function of one noun within it ((*of*) *Cicero, Ciceronis*), by the marker which identifies it. Likewise, in *I want to go* or *She asked to leave*, the lexemes WANT or ASK are said to take an Infinitive construction, the relation between their forms and what follows being identified by the marker *to*, which supplies the formation traditionally called by that term. Alternatively, they might be said to take a *to*-construction as distinct, say, from the participial or -*ing* construction of *She wants washing*.

This definition does not cover, and is not meant to cover, the role of the articles. No grammarian (at least to my knowledge) would argue that *the* and *a* have a different constructional relationship to the noun. Nor would it cover, for example, the role of *has* (or of the morphemes HAVE and past participle) in *has appeared*. For by setting up a paradigm within which perfect *has appeared* is opposed to non-perfect *appears* (or an overall construction in which sequences of morphemes such as HAVE + 3rd singular + APPEAR + past participle are opposed to sequences such as APPEAR + 3rd singular) we are ascribing to the perfect property (or to a complex perfect unit) a semantic value beyond that of the construction itself. But by the same token this too is a quasi-inflectional item, having a role like that of the strictly inflectional past tense, with which it can be combined in the same structure. Forms such as *has*, or lexemes such as HAVE, are usually described as a restricted set of Auxiliary Verbs. The uses and meanings of both the auxiliaries and the articles fall within the field of the grammarian (we are still talking simply as the tradition sees it), whereas the individual meanings of lexical or full verbs, such as APPEAR or LEAVE, are left to dictionaries.

For this second type of form word a first condition is that it should enter into a **closed set**. In *the speeches of Cicero* we cannot say how many nouns might play the role of *Cicero*, any more than we can say how many nouns, or specifically how many proper names, there are. We are dealing with an **open set** of items, open in that new members can always be found. But for the article it is quite otherwise. In different settings a definite *the* can be contrasted with an indefinite *a* (*the speech* versus *a speech*) or with the reduced form of *some* (*the speeches* versus [səm] *speeches*); a grammar will also distinguish the case with no article (*the speeches* versus *speeches*). Perhaps the demonstratives might be assigned the same role: thus *these speeches* (with the plural form of

THIS) or *that speech* (with the singular form of THAT). But at some point the set has a definite bound. We can therefore establish a bounded **system** – we might more loosely say a paradigm – in which each item represents one term. So too does the case in which no article is present; just as in a morphological paradigm one term may be distinguished by the lack of an affix (singular *speech* as opposed to plural *speech-es*, non-past *appear* as opposed to past *appear-ed*), so the opposition between noun and *the* + noun, or noun and [səm] + noun, has its own semantic value.

There is the same distinction between the roles of *has* and *appeared* (or of HAVE ... past participle and APPEAR). For *appeared* it is impossible to say how many participles might fill the same role, again because we cannot determine how many verbal lexemes the language has. For example, is there or is there not a verb REDISAPPEAR (*He's just redisappeared*)? One would not expect to find it in a dictionary, and perhaps its use might be facetious; yet certainly the utterance can be understood. The set is also open to new borrowings, as STRAFE, for example, was adapted from German during the First World War. But for the auxiliaries we have already established a bounded paradigm, in which perfect is opposed to non-perfect (or perfect non-past non-progressive opposed specifically to non-perfect non-past non-progressive), and so on. As the partial exponents of these categories, the words which play the auxiliary role (such as *has*, or the 3rd singular non-past of HAVE) are themselves a limited set. Likewise, in a description based on morphemes, a semantic contrast would be assigned to sequences with or without the pair of morphemes HAVE and past participle, as also to sequences with or without the single inflectional morpheme past tense.

A distinction between open and closed sets is sometimes offered as the only basis for the distinction between lexical words and form words, including those we have treated as markers. But this will clearly not do. For in a detailed grammar there will be many constructions in which sets of lexical words (that is, what are usually called lexical words) cannot be extended. We referred, for example, to a construction in which WANT takes a present participle (*She wants washing*). But although verbs in general form a set that is open, there are only a few verbs (WANT, NEED, REQUIRE, MERIT, ...) which have that particular valency. One could not say, for instance, *She expects washing* (in the sense that she feels that someone has a duty to wash her) or *She desires washing,* even though EXPECT and DESIRE have meanings broadly similar to those of REQUIRE or WANT. Yet no grammarian would set up a grammatical system with these verbs as its terms. Here as in other constructions the differences between them are matters for the dictionary.

We therefore need a further condition, which is that implied, in the case of *has,* by the term 'auxiliary'. Of the two words in *has appeared,* the second plays an essential role in any larger construction. As a form of APPEAR it can take just a subject (*He has appeared*) but not both a subject and an object (*He has appeared the speech* or *He has appeared Cicero*). For other lexemes it can be the reverse: *He has distributed the speech* or *He has visited Cicero,* but not *He has distributed* or *He has visited.* A relation is thus established between *appeared,* or the morpheme APPEAR, and a subject element. But at that level the relation of *appeared* to *has,* or of the morpheme APPEAR to the discontinuous HAVE . . . past participle, is quite incidental. Occasionally it too is restricted by the lexical verb: for example, it is harder to see how one might use a progressive form of BELONG (*It is belonging to me now* or *They have always been belonging here*). But we will establish no direct co-variance between the auxiliary and a subject, or an object, and so on. The function of *has* can accordingly be said to **presuppose** that of *appeared*: there is no role for the auxiliary except in relation to the element that it is auxiliary to.

An article similarly presupposes the head element. On the one hand, there are clear restrictions on its relation to a noun. With the singular *meat* one can readily use *the* or the reduced form of *some* (*I must get the meat* or *I must get* [səm] *meat*); it may also appear with no article (*Meat is getting expensive*). But one would hardly use *a,* even with a relative clause following (*I must get a meat which they like*). With the singular *book* the range is different, *a book* being wholly natural (*I read a book*) but [səm] *book* – as distinct from [sʌm] *book* – being at best odd. On the other hand, there is a relation between the object noun and its verb. Thus in Chapter I we spoke of collocational restrictions which involved the lexemes MEAT and GRILL (*I grilled the meat*), BREAD and TOAST (*I toasted the bread*), and so on. Other restrictions apply to nouns in subject position: we cited ones which would relate *meat* and a subject complement *bad* (*The meat looks bad*), or *beer* and *flat* (*The beer tastes flat*). But there are none which establish a relation between, for example, a verb and the article in its object. If an article *t* can go with

63

a noun *n* (as *the* or [səm] go with *meat*) and the noun *n* can go with a verb *v* (as *meat* goes with *leave*, or *bread* with *toast*), the three together (*v* + *t* + *n*) will also fit.

In both cases the element without an independent function (*has* in *has appeared, the* in *the meat*) will be described as a **dependent** of the other. Similarly, in *He has been wandering* both the auxiliaries, *has* and *been*, will be seen as depending on *wandering*. Dependency is a notion of much wider application, which we will elaborate in the next and following chapters. For the moment, however, we are concerned with a case in which the dependent element has two special properties. The first is that it enters into a bounded system of oppositions, as discussed earlier. The second is that it can have no dependents of its own, or at most dependents which are themselves of a closed class. Thus there is no element that in turn presupposes either an article or an auxiliary. When both conditions are met (still for the particular point in the particular construction) the dependent will be described as a **determiner**, or said to have a **determining** function. So, in *the speeches*, the article is a determiner of *speeches*, or stands in a determining relation to it. Likewise, in *has appeared*, the auxiliary is a determiner of the participle *appeared*, and in *has been wandering* both *has* and *been* determine *wandering*. If we think in terms of morphemes, the root morpheme APPEAR, in a unit such as *had appeared*, would have as its determiners not only the complex HAVE ... past participle, but also the single morpheme past tense. Likewise, in *speeches*, a description based on morphemes would establish a plural morpheme (with the exponent -*es* [iz]) determining SPEECH.

In a detailed grammar, most of the words which have been thought of as form words will be classed, in specific uses, either as markers or as determiners. But there are three points which we must underline. Firstly, an item can be established as a form word (*sc.* as either a marker or a determiner) only with respect to a given function. *Has* is a determiner, we have argued, in its role as an auxiliary (*He has appeared*). But in *He has coffee* it must be either a full word or a marker, since it is not related to just the subject or just the object. In *He gave it to Bill* we will treat *to* as a marker; it supplies one cue for the indirect object, just as the dative case (in *Ciceron-i* 'to Cicero') supplies a cue in Latin. But in *He carried it to London* the same item will be put in contrast with other prepositions (thus *He carried it into London*). In this second construction *to* functions as a full word. A word is not in itself 'a form word', unless it is established as such in all its individual uses.

Secondly, both functions are established as part of a given description. In analysing a language we will make use of various sorts of **evidence**. Thus we will find that certain combinations of words are uttered or would not be uttered, that in certain contexts word *a* can be substituted for word *b*, that in other contexts word *c* can be dropped, with or without a relevant change of meaning, and so on. (For example, we will find that we cannot drop *'s* in *Cicero's speeches*, or that in *the speeches of Cicero* we can substitute *by* for *of*.) On that basis we will argue that a relation is of type *x* or type *y*, making appeal to various general principles or **criteria**, by which such decisions are guided. (So, for example, the arguments by which we sought to justify *has* or *the* as dependents, which made appeal to the criterion of co-variance.) In the course of our analysis, we will naturally say that certain bits of evidence are 'evidence for' one type of relation or another. (So, in *the speeches of Cicero*, the substitution of *by* for *of* is evidence against its role as a marker, except that we have claimed further evidence from which we may argue differently.) When we have balanced all our arguments, we will describe the constructions in terms of a certain abstract **model**, in which at least some types will be **primitive** or undefined terms. (In the model which we have assumed, dependency would be one such primitive.) It is only within this model that our remaining terms, such as 'marker' or 'determiner', would have their **definition**. Hence it is only in a particular application of this model, to the description of English or some other language, that the terms themselves will be applied to individual constructions.

Their application may therefore differ from one description to another, depending on the degree of detail we go into, or how precisely we argue from the evidence. In sentences such as

> Bill and Peter are coming
> Bill or Peter is coming

the roles of *and* and *or* are evidently similar. In both examples the construction is of a type that grammarians call Coordinative, linking two nouns with a common function. In both cases we can easily add more nouns (*John, Bill and Peter* or *Mary, Harry, Bill or Peter*), with the conjunctions regularly in next to last position. Just as *and* may be paired with *both* (*both Bill and Peter*) so *or* may be paired with *either* (*either Bill or Peter*), and so on. The main difference is that with *and* the agreement is normally plural (compare *Bill and Peter is coming*, with 3rd singular *is*), whereas with *or* it would be singular. But that could be ascribed to the meanings of these conjunctions, or to those of *Bill and Peter* versus *Bill or Peter* as wholes. Therefore we might argue that the constructions are the same; hence *or* and *and*, or the lexemes OR and AND, contrast as full words.

But this set of lexemes would be very restricted. Of the other conjunctions, BUT is similar in some respects (compare the possible *Bill but not Peter is coming*) and the pair NEITHER ... NOR in others (*Neither Bill nor Peter is coming*); but even their membership might be debated. Nor are there other constructions in which OR and AND do not belong to closed sets. (By contrast, WANT had limited contrasts in the construction of *She wants washing*, but belongs to an open set in that of *She wants the money*.) In that light the conjunctions must be seen as grammatical rather than lexical. Within a construction each form carries only a fixed amount of information: in one example AND will be differentiated just from OR and BUT, in others just from OR, and so on. (Whereas a form of WANT can carry an indeterminate amount of information, differentiating WANT from STEAL, from REIMBURSE, from an imaginable DISIMBURSE – *She disimbursed my money* – and so on.) By the same token *and* and *or* play an important role in differentiating constructions. Whereas an unknown verb can be recognised as such by its grammar (as when I first heard of someone being 'gazumphed'), not only are the conjunctions wholly known but they themselves will help to classify other items. For example, in *They were cheated or at best gazumphed* the conjunction shows that *gazumphed*, whatever it means, must have the same grammatical role as *cheated*.

Such properties cannot define an item as a form word (unless it also meets our second condition for determiners). But they provide an argument by which, all else being equal, we may decide to treat it in that way. To that end we will distinguish the constructions: so, in *Bill or Peter* there is one relationship between the nouns (we may call this a Disjunctive construction), while in *Bill and Peter* there is another (which we may describe as additive or Conjunctive). Likewise BUT will be assigned to one or more Adversative constructions. The difference of meaning between our two original examples, and the different verbal agreement resulting from it (*is coming, are coming*), are then explained not by the conjunctions themselves, but by a wider difference in syntax. Hence they are not full words, but markers. The problem here is typical of many that we will meet in later chapters, where the application of our model is bound up with the tests by which we divide and subdivide constructions, which in turn are bound up with the criteria for the types themselves.

Finally, just as constructions are not self-evident, neither are individual points or elements in constructions. In *Bill or Peter* we have tacitly assumed that, since there are three words, we must be dealing with just three syntactic functions. But that need not be so. In principle we could imagine a further solution, in which *or* and *and* have roles both as a marker of the coordinative relationship (thus of a link between the two terms *Bill* and *Peter*) and as determiners of this relationship (thus of a unit formed by *Bill* and *Peter* together). They would then be form words on both counts. In the second role they would contrast, *or* being the disjunctive determiner and *and* the conjunctive. But at that point in the construction they would also be dependents, insofar as we establish no direct relation between them and the verb *is coming* or *are coming*. In the first role they would not be dependents, since they relate equally to both nouns. But at that point in the construction they would not contrast, as the difference of meaning is assigned to their function as determiners.

This solution may seem somewhat ingenious. But there are other cases where a single element does fulfil both a marking and some other function. In *the man who came*, the word *who* is traditionally a pronoun; like the personal pronouns *I* or *he*, in *I came* or *He came*, it has a semantic role equivalent to that of a noun or noun phrase, such as *the man* in *The man came*. More specifically, it is a Relative Pronoun, defined as such by the relative clause, *who came*, which it serves to introduce. In the first capacity it is the subject of *came*, and in the second a marker for the clause as a whole; we may accordingly posit a construction like this:

$$\left\{ \begin{array}{l} Marker \\ Subject \end{array} \right\} \quad Predicator$$
$$\quad who \qquad\qquad came$$

in which two separate elements are **amalgamated** in a single word. Similarly, a conjunction such as *and* could, in principle, represent the amalgamation of a marking and a determining function. Although

67

the particular analysis may not appeal, there is no absolute objection to solutions of that sort.

NOTES AND REFERENCES

The first half of this chapter deals with topics also discussed in my *Morphology*: see especially Chs. 5 (for morphemes), 2 and 8 (for lexemes and morphosyntactic properties) and 9 (for the status of the word and morphology vs. syntax generally). For discontinuous units in the English perfect and progressive see CHOMSKY, *Structures*, pp. 38ff.; subsequent account in any transformational handbook (for example, HUDDLESTON, pp. 70ff.). See Chapter 12 below for corresponding rules for periphrastic formations. On the categories of perfect and progressive, and the paradigm of the English verb generally, see PALMER, Ch. 3. On the comparative see the textbook transformational account in B. Jacobsen, *Transformational-Generative Grammar: an Introductory Survey of its Genesis and Development*, 2nd edn (Amsterdam: North-Holland, 1978), pp. 327–31 (especially the tree diagram on p. 329). The periphrastic treatment is implied by, for example, DE GROOT, 'Classification', p. 150 ('compound adjectives', like 'compound verbs').

I remark that 'few Latinists' would accept the break-up of the word. See, however, the interesting paper by C. Touratier, 'Saggio d'analisi sintattica', in G. Proverbio (ed.), *La sfida linguistica: lingue classiche e modelli grammaticali* (Turin: Rosenberg & Sellier, 1979), pp. 91–150 (original French version, which I have not seen, in *Dossiers d'étude pour l'enseignement du latin*, 4 (1975–6), pp. 1–38). Note especially his analysis of prepositional government (*apud patres = patr- + apud ... -es*) and of agreement (*patres nostros = patr- + nostr- + -es ... -os*). For the former compare J. Kuryłowicz, 'Le problème du classement des cas', reprinted in his *Esquisses linguistiques*, 2nd edn (Munich: Fink, 1973), pp. 131–50, which is Touratier's source; also M. Bierwisch's early transformational monograph on German, *Grammatik des deutschen Verbs* (Berlin: Akademie-Verlag, 1965), e.g. for *in die Schule* (tree diagram, p. 87). For the latter compare HARRIS, *Methods*, p. 205; MARTINET, *Elements*, especially §4.21. (Both are sketched in my *Morphology*, p. 158.) In the periphrastic passive Touratier assigns the root of the verb 'to be' to a perfect and the suffix of the participle to a passive 'morpheme' (pp. 117ff.).

For 'form word' see SWEET, 1, p. 22 (words 'independent in form, [but] not independent in meaning'); *the* and *is* are also 'empty words' ('entirely devoid of meaning') as opposed to 'full words', which include 'full form-words' such as *become* (p. 23). Sweet remarks that 'it is not always easy – or even possible – to draw a definite line' (p. 24). Later and influential accounts in C. C. Fries, *The Structure of English: an Introduction to the Construction of English Sentences* (New York: Harcourt, Brace, 1952), Ch. 6, especially pp. 104ff. (on 'function words'); TESNIÈRE, pp. 53ff. ('mots vides' vs. 'mots pleins'), 80ff. (for the subtypes 'jonctif', 'translatif', 'indice'). On the indeterminacy between full and form words see H. A. Gleason, *Linguistics and English Grammar* (New York: Holt, Rinehart & Winston, 1965), pp. 186–9 (qualifying pp. 95ff.) and pp. 190ff. (on the issue of 'meaninglessness'); briefly in JESPERSEN, *Philosophy*, pp. 32f. See too my contribution 'Latin', to *Word Classes* (*Lingua*, 17 (1966), nos. 1–2), pp. 153–81 (relevant section pp. 169–73). For an acute conceptual account of the gradation see SAPIR, Ch. 5, especially pp. 100ff.; note the warning that 'these schemes must not be worshipped as fetiches' (p. 102).

For markers compare HOCKETT, pp. 153f. ('structural marker' or 'signal'); MARTINET, *Elements*, §4.12 ('monèmes fonctionnels'); also my contribution to *Word Classes*, *op. cit.*, pp. 159f. *et passim*, on 'syntactic constants'. For closed and open sets compare QUIRK *et al.*, pp. 46ff.; HALLIDAY, 'Categories', especially §2.1; also, for example, LYONS, *Semantics*, 2, pp. 383f., in defining 'lexical' and 'grammatical morphemes'; MARTINET, *Elements*, §4.19, for the corresponding division of monemes. The notion of a system is from Firth through Halliday through Quirk *et al.*; its special elaboration in the work of Halliday and his pupils need not concern us at this point (see, however, notes to Chapter 12). For the articles in English, including a widespread notion of a 'zero article', see QUIRK *et al.*, pp. 127ff. *et passim* (also for the usual English grammarian's sense of 'determiner', pp. 136ff.). On the auxiliaries see further argument (and references) in Chapter 7 below. For this type of form word generally compare MARTINET, *Elements*, §§4.19–20, on 'modalités'; in his terms these are 'déterminants' (criterion at end of §4.18) which are also grammatical monemes. On the amalgamated functions of relative pronouns (end of chapter) see, for example, HERINGER, p. 260; he describes them as having a 'kumulierende Bedeutung', as 'Translative' (in TESNIÈRE's sense) and as subjects, etc. Transformational grammars regularly treat '*wh*' as a separate item (for example, CULICOVER, Ch. 8, especially pp. 194ff., and earlier for interrogative pronouns). Compare Heringer's view of contrasting prepositions (HERINGER, pp. 198f.); also Hockett's, in which they are 'impure markers' (HOCKETT, p. 192, with acknowledgment to SAPIR, *loc. cit.*, on p. 197). On the status of conjunctions in coordinative constructions ('coordinators' in Chapter 9 below) see DIK, pp. 51f.

For *x* 'presupposing' *y* see, for example, DUBOIS *et al.*, s.v. 'présupposition', §1; the leading discussion is that of L. Hjelmslev, *Prolegomena to a Theory of Language*, tr. F. J. Whitfield (Baltimore: Indiana University, 1953), §§9 and 11, but is difficult. Note that the relation in the text is between elements, not individual items. In *I read a book*, neither *book* nor *a* can stand without the other (mutual presupposition between forms); in the construction of *a book*, determiner presupposes head but head does not presuppose determiner (unilateral presupposition between functions). Equivalent discussion of 'obligatoriness' in Chapters 6 and 7.

For dependency in general, and references, see Chapters 4 and 5.

At the beginning of the last section I refer to two of the ancient parts of speech. For the origins of this system see R. H. Robins, 'The development of the word class system of the European grammatical tradition', *FL*, 2 (1966), pp. 3–19 (reprinted in his *Diversions of Bloomsbury: Selected Writings in Linguistics* (Amsterdam: North-Holland, 1970), pp. 185–203). For the issues involved in word classification see again my contribution to *Word Classes*, *op. cit.*; recent discussion in LYONS, *Semantics*, 2, pp. 423ff. They are only partly syntactic and therefore I do not cover them here.

4
Constituency and dependency

Hierarchies of units; of relations. As basis for alternative models.
Constituency: Syntagms, constituents, immediate constituents; phrase structure grammars; generative interpretation.
Dependency: Dependents and controllers; dependency grammars. Weak equivalence of dependency and phrase structure systems.
Comparison and evaluation: Models not strongly equivalent: dependencies not derivable from constituency; constituents not always derivable from dependencies. Possibility of combined model. Inadequacies: for discontinuous constructions; for relations of non-minimal units; for specific functions; limitation to tree structures. Deep and surface structure; as distinguishing constructions and realisations.

Let us return to the sentence *Leave the meat in the kitchen,* which we discussed in Chapter 1. We established that it was constructionally ambiguous, with two alternative sets of constructional relations. But how should such relations be described?

Our arguments suggest two rather different answers. We showed that *it* could replace *the meat in the kitchen* (*Leave it*); alternatively, *it* could replace *the meat,* and *in the kitchen* could be replaced by *there* (*Leave it in the kitchen, Leave the meat there, Leave it there*). This suggests that *it* and *the meat in the kitchen,* or *it* and *the meat,* or *there* and *in the kitchen,* are comparable syntactic units. So, one construction might be represented as follows:

Predicator	*Object*
leave	the meat in the kitchen

with the whole of *the meat in the kitchen* standing in the object relationship to *leave.* The other might be shown like this:

Predicator	*Object*	*Adverbial*
leave	the meat	in the kitchen

with *the meat* as object and the whole of *in the kitchen* standing in the relation of an adverbial. Likewise *the meat in the kitchen,* as object in the first analysis, has a construction:

Determiner	Head	Modifier
the	meat	in the kitchen

where *in the kitchen* is in turn a unit in which *in* is related to *the kitchen*. In this way we establish a hierarchy of units. Each larger unit is divided into smaller units which are either minimal (*the* and *meat* in *the meat in the kitchen*, *leave* and *it* in *Leave it*) or themselves divided by some further construction.

We also pointed to the collocational relations between words. In the first analysis there are restrictions linking *leave* and *meat*, but none for the verb and preposition. We can therefore see the main construction as:

Predicator	Object
leave	meat

where the second element is not the phrase *the meat in the kitchen*, but its head noun. There are restrictions linking *meat* and the preposition, but none for *meat* and *kitchen*; hence a second relation which we might describe like this:

Head	Preposition
meat	in

whose second term forms its own construction with *kitchen*. In the other analysis *in* is linked to *leave* instead of to *meat*; therefore the main construction can be seen as:

Predicator	Object	Preposition
leave	meat	in

Finally, in both analyses, the articles are linked as determiners (Chapter 3) to their nouns. In this way we establish a hierarchy of relations, in which word *a* is linked to word *b*, which may in turn be linked to word *c*, which may in turn be linked to word *d*, and so on.

We can thus distinguish two notions of syntactic hierarchy, each of which has played some role in earlier chapters. By generalising the first we arrive at a **constituency** model of syntax, which in its crudest form permits the formulation of a **phrase structure** (or **constituent structure**) **grammar**. By generalising the second we arrive at a **dependency** model; in a crude form, this permits the formulation of a **dependency grammar**. Let us outline each in turn, and then compare them for the points which are important to us.

CONSTITUENCY

In the crudest form of constituency model, a unit *a* is related to a neighbouring unit *b* solely by their placement within a larger unit *c*. This larger unit we will call a **syntagm**: so, at the end of our example, a two-word syntagm *the kitchen* is established by the relationship of *kitchen* to the preceding *the*, and a three-word syntagm *in the kitchen* by that of *the kitchen*, as a whole, to the preceding *in*. This can be shown either by bracketing the units:

$$_b[\text{in }_a[\text{the kitchen}]_a]_b$$

with the smaller unit labelled *a* enclosed within the larger unit labelled *b*, or by the form of diagram in Figure 1 (in mathematical

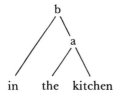

Figure 1

terms a 'tree graph' or tree diagram) in which words are joined together by successively higher nodes. Any unit which is enclosed within a syntagm may be described as a **constituent** of that syntagm. So, *the kitchen* is a constituent of *in the kitchen*; likewise each of the minimal units *in*, *the* and *kitchen*. Of these constituents, those whose relationship directly establishes the syntagm are its **immediate constituents**. So, the immediate constituents of *in the kitchen* are just *in* and *the kitchen*.

In the adverbial analysis of this sentence, another syntagm will be formed by *the* and *meat*:

$$_c[\text{the meat}]_c {}_b[\text{in }_a[\text{the kitchen}]_a]_b$$

the largest syntagm of all including both *the meat* and *in the kitchen* as the partners of *leave*:

$$_d[\text{leave }_c[\text{the meat}]_c {}_b[\text{in }_a[\text{the kitchen}]_a]_b]_d$$

The tree diagram is that of Figure 2 overleaf, with the highest node (the 'root' of the tree graph) eventually joining all the units together. In the other analysis, *the* and *meat* form a syntagm with *in the kitchen*

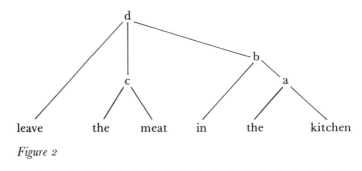

Figure 2

$_c$[the meat $_b$[in $_a$[the kitchen]$_a$]$_b$]$_c$

and *leave* is then related to this as a whole:

$_d$[leave $_c$[the meat $_b$[in $_a$[the kitchen]$_a$]$_b$]$_c$]$_d$

The equivalent tree diagram is that of Figure 3, with the node

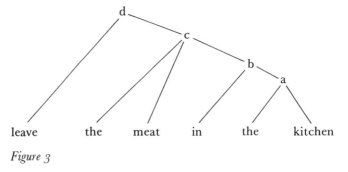

Figure 3

labelled *c* joining together all the last five words. Throughout this we are stating only one form of constructional relationship, between the immediate constituents of each successive syntagm. The constructional ambiguity resides in the different ways in which the units can be put together.

Since there are no other forms of relation, the construction of each syntagm can be characterised by the class of the whole, the class of each of its immediate constituents, and the order in which they appear. *The kitchen* is classed as a noun phrase (abbreviated NP); its constituents are classed as an article (Art) and a noun (N); the order of these is article first and noun second. We can therefore show its construction as follows:

$_{NP}$[$_{Art}$[the]$_{Art}$ $_N$[kitchen]$_N$]$_{NP}$

simply by labelling each unit for the category to which it is assigned. *In the kitchen* has a construction in which the noun phrase follows a preposition (P), the whole forming a Prepositional Phrase (PP):

$$_{PP}[\; _P[in]_P \; _{NP}[the \; kitchen]_{NP} \;]_{PP}$$

On the adverbial interpretation, the sentence as a whole (abbreviated S) has a construction in which the prepositional phrase follows a verb (V) and a noun phrase:

$$_S[\; _V[leave]_V \; _{NP}[the \; meat]_{NP} \; _{PP}[in \; the \; kitchen]_{PP} \;]_S$$

while in the other interpretation the prepositional phrase is itself part of a larger noun phrase:

$$_{NP}[\; _{Art}[the]_{Art} \; _N[meat]_N \; _{PP}[in \; the \; kitchen]_{PP} \;]_{NP}$$

the largest unit having a construction like this:

$$_S[\; _V[leave]_V \; _{NP}[the \; meat \; in \; the \; kitchen]_{NP} \;]_S$$

Just as class labels can be added to the brackets, so they can also be added to tree diagrams. In the adverbial analysis, the whole assemblage of constructions could be displayed as in Figure 4, the line

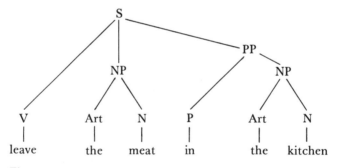

Figure 4

linking N to *kitchen* showing that *kitchen* is classed as a noun, those linking NP to *the* and *kitchen* showing that *the kitchen* is a syntagm classed as a noun phrase, and so on. In the other interpretation the structure of the sentence would be that of Figure 5 overleaf where, in particular, all the last five words are linked to the higher of the two nodes labelled 'NP'.

Tree graphs such as these are usually called **phrase structure trees**, the term 'phrase' (in this usage) being equivalent to our term

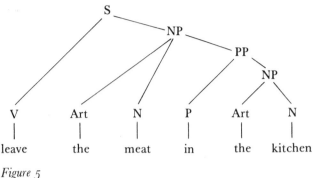

Figure 5

'syntagm'. The corresponding grammar will be a **phrase structure grammar**, consisting of a list of possible constructions, stated in terms of the constituents that a syntagm of a given class can have. At the highest point in our diagrams, a sentence can have as its constituents a verb followed by a noun phrase (V + NP), or a verb followed by a noun phrase and a prepositional phrase (V + NP + PP). This is stated as follows:

$$S \rightarrow V + NP$$
$$S \rightarrow V + NP + PP$$

where the arrow may be read as 'can be' or 'can consist of'. A noun phrase can in turn consist of an article followed by a noun:

$$NP \rightarrow Art + N$$

(*the* + *meat, the* + *kitchen*), or of an article followed by a noun and a prepositional phrase:

$$NP \rightarrow Art + N + PP$$

(*the* + *meat* + *in the kitchen*), and so on. Likewise a prepositional phrase can be a preposition plus a noun phrase:

$$PP \rightarrow P + NP$$

(*in* + *the kitchen*). These last two constructions allow for an infinity of possible structures. Thus a prepositional phrase could contain a noun phrase which in turn contains a prepositional phrase:

$$_{PP}[\text{on }_{NP}[\text{the table }_{PP}[\text{in }_{NP}[\text{the kitchen}]_{NP}]_{PP}]_{NP}]_{PP}$$

This too could be a constituent of a noun phrase which is in turn a constituent of a larger prepositional phrase:

$_{PP}[$in $_{NP}[$the meat $_{PP}[$on the table in the kitchen$]_{PP}$ $]_{NP}$ $]_{PP}$

and so on. In this sense, both NP and PP are **recursive categories**. A syntagm of each class can contain another syntagm of the same class (as *the table in the kitchen* included *the kitchen*, or *on the table in the kitchen* includes *in the kitchen*), with repetition at an indefinite number of levels.

By stating what constructions there can be we also state, by implication, what constructions there cannot be. For example, we would establish no construction in which a sentence consists of a preposition followed by a verb (*In leave, On dump*), or a noun phrase of a noun followed by an article (*meat the, kitchen a*) instead of the reverse. We can therefore interpret each of these expressions as a **phrase structure rule**, forming part of a generative grammar (end of Chapter 2) which defines, or aims to define, the set of grammatical sentences in the language. For example, there is one rule saying that a sentence can consist of a verb plus a noun phrase:

$$_S[_V[\quad]_V \; _{NP}[\qquad\qquad]_{NP} \;]_S$$

and another saying that the noun phrase can consist of an article plus a noun:

$$_S[_V[\quad]_V \; _{NP}[_{Art}[\quad]_{Art} \; _N[\quad]_N \;]_{NP} \;]_S$$

So, given that *leave* belongs to the class V, *the* to the class Art and *kitchen* to the class N, there is a grammatical sentence *Leave the kitchen*. Another rule says that the noun phrase could have a prepositional phrase as a third constituent:

$$_S[_V[\quad]_V \; _{NP}[_{Art}[\quad]_{Art} \; _N[\quad]_N \; _{PP}[\qquad\qquad]_{PP} \;]_{NP} \;]_S$$

another that the prepositional phrase can consist of a preposition plus a noun phrase:

$$_S[_V[\quad]_V \; _{NP}[_{Art}[\quad]_{Art} \; _N[\quad]_N \; _{PP}[_P[\quad]_P \; _{NP}[\qquad]_{NP} \;]_{PP} \;]_{NP} \;]_S$$

whereupon this further noun phrase could again be an article plus a noun:

$$_S[_V[\quad]_V \; _{NP}[_{Art}[\quad]_{Art} \; _N[\quad]_N \; _{PP}[_P[\quad]_P \; _{NP}[_{Art}[\quad]_{Art} \; _N[\quad]_N \;]_{NP} \;]_{PP} \;]_{NP} \;]_S$$

So, given a similar vocabulary, there are grammatical sentences *Leave the meat on the table, Leave the table in the kitchen,* and so on.

We need not go further into the formalisation of phrase structure grammars, which can easily be learned from other sources. But it can be seen that the generative interpretation, which was due to Chomsky in the mid to late 50s, follows naturally from the way in which the construction of a syntagm can be characterised. That in turn follows from the generalised relation of constituency, by which a syntagm is established solely by the smaller units of which it is composed. That in turn arose naturally from a procedure known as 'immediate constituent analysis', in which tests of substitution (of shorter sequences for longer, of longer sequences for shorter) were employed, as partly in our own discussion in Chapter 1, to determine what the syntactic units were. Some of the best work in this field was done by Chomsky's own teacher, Zellig Harris. In a more general way, the whole development springs naturally from Bloomfield's notion of 'linguistic forms' (Chapter 2 above) and from the categories of selection and order on which it is largely based. Not surprisingly, it is in Bloomfield's own work that immediate constituency is first formulated (BLOOMFIELD, p. 161).

DEPENDENCY

The constituency model is widespread in the literature, this notion of hierarchy being fundamental not only to the Bloomfieldian work of the 40s and 50s but also to the Chomskyan theory of transformational grammar, which was developed as an extension of it. But an equally simple model can be based on a generalised notion of dependency. In the traditional language of grammarians, many constructions are described in terms of a subordination of one element to another. A verb is said to 'govern' its object; so, in *Leave the meat in the kitchen*, the noun *meat*, which stands in a collocational relationship to *leave*, is seen as subordinate to (or 'governed by') it. A preposition is also said to govern the noun which follows. So, in the prepositional phrase *in the kitchen*, there is a relation between *in* and *kitchen* by which *kitchen* is the governed or subordinate element. The term 'modifies' implies the reverse; in this case it is the modifier that is subordinate to the head. So, in one interpretation of our sentence *in the kitchen* is subordinate to *meat*. But only *in* is directly linked to the head; we can thus describe a chain of subordination, first from *meat* to *in* by virtue of the modification, then from *in* to its own subordinate or governed element *kitchen*. In the other interpretation the adverbial modifies the verb, with which *in* is again collocationally linked. Accordingly both *meat* and *in* would be subordinate to *leave*, again with a subsidiary subordination of *kitchen* to *in*. In both interpretations the articles are subordinate to *meat* and *kitchen*, as 'determiners of' them.

In the recent literature the term 'dependency' covers all these forms of subordination. So, *in the kitchen* is a phrase in which *the* depends on *kitchen* (as already in the final section of Chapter 3) and *kitchen* in turn depends on *in*. We can display this as follows:

$$_a[in]_a \ _b[the]_b \ _c[kitchen]_c$$

where each arrow points towards the dependent term; alternatively in the tree diagram in Figure 6, where successive dependents are

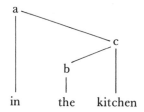

Figure 6

linked to successively lower nodes. When unit x depends on unit y we will describe y as the **controller**, or the **controlling term**, in the relationship. So, the word *in* (labelled a) controls *kitchen* (labelled c), which in turn controls *the* (labelled b).

In the adverbial analysis of this sentence, both *meat* and *in* are similarly dependent on *leave*. The whole assemblage of relations may accordingly be shown as follows:

$$_d[leave]_d \ _e[the]_e \ _f[meat]_f \ _a[in]_a \ _b[the]_b \ _c[kitchen]_c$$

with the first *the* again in a dependent relationship to *meat*. The equivalent tree is in Figure 7 overleaf with a single term, *leave*, standing at the head of the hierarchy of dependencies. In the other analysis, *meat* controls both *the* and *in*, leaving *meat* alone as the dependent (or, we might say, the direct dependent) of the verb:

$$_d[leave]_d \ _e[the]_e \ _f[meat]_f \ _a[in]_a \ _b[the]_b \ _c[kitchen]_c$$

The corresponding tree diagram is in Figure 8 – the constructional

79

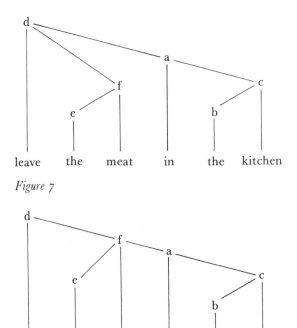

Figure 7

Figure 8

ambiguity residing in the different ways in which the chains of dependency are formed.

In the simplest form of dependency model, a group of units is constructionally related solely in that one is the controller of the others. For example, in the first of these analyses there is a group in which *leave* is the controller of *meat* and *in*. In that case, they can be separated only by units which the dependents in turn control, or the dependents of the dependents control, and so on. Thus the group of *leave*, *meat* and *in* is separated only by the first *the*, which depends on *meat*. The construction can then be characterised by the class of the controller, and the class and order of each of its dependents. In this example the controller is a verb (V); of the dependents which follow the first is a noun (N) and the second a preposition (P); the highest construction in the hierarchy can accordingly be shown like this:

again by a simple labelling of each unit. In the group controlled by *in* a single dependent follows and is classed as a noun; in those controlled by *kitchen* and *meat* a single dependent precedes and is classed as an article (Art); the whole assemblage of constructions can accordingly be shown like this:

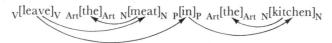

or by a **dependency tree** which is equivalently labelled (Figure 9).

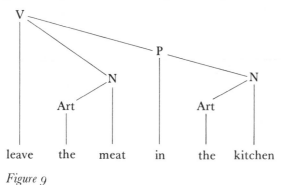

Figure 9

In the sense that a phrase structure grammar is a set of phrase structure rules, so a **dependency grammar** is a set of **dependency rules**, stating the controlling and dependent relations that each class of units can, and by implication cannot, enter into. For the analysis given, the first rule we must state is one by which verbs can appear with no controller – thus with V alone at the top of the hierarchy. In a notation introduced in the early 60s, this may be shown by the following expression:

$$* (V)$$

where V is paired with a controlling term, marked by the asterisk, which is left unspecified. The next rule states that a verb can control a following noun and preposition:

$$V (* , N , P)$$

– the initial controller, whose position is again marked by the asterisk, being specified by the V outside the brackets. Likewise we have a rule by which a preposition can control a following noun:

$$P (* , N)$$

and another by which a noun can control a preceding article:

N (Art , *)

– with the asterisk in the second position instead of the first. Finally, we must make explicit a rule by which articles can appear (and in the absence of other rules can only appear) with no dependents. Thus:

Art (*)

– where only a controlling term is specified.

The other analysis establishes the dependency tree in Figure 10,

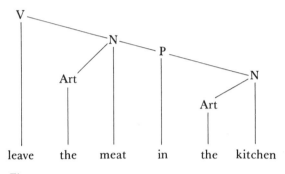

with the same class labels attached to our second hierarchy of nodes. For this we must state two further rules, by which a verb can have a following noun as its only dependent:

V (* , N)

and a noun can directly control both a preceding article and a following preposition:

N (Art , * , P)

– the asterisk thus being in the middle position. The total set of rules may again be interpreted generatively. For example, there are rules saying that a verb, with no controller, can itself control a noun which comes later:

Another says that the noun can control an article which comes earlier; since a controller and dependent cannot be separated by a higher controller, it follows that the article must come between the verb and the noun:

$$\text{v}[\;\;]_\text{V} \;_\text{Art}[\;\;]_\text{Art} \;_\text{N}[\;\;]_\text{N}$$

Another allows the article to have no dependents; so, given that *leave* is a verb, *the* an article and *kitchen* a noun, there is again a grammatical sentence *Leave the kitchen*. The rules would also allow an assemblage of constructions like this:

$$\text{v}[\;\;]_\text{V} \;_\text{Art}[\;\;]_\text{Art} \;_\text{N}[\;\;]_\text{N} \;_\text{P}[\;\;]_\text{P} \;_\text{Art}[\;\;]_\text{Art} \;_\text{N}[\;\;]_\text{N}$$

or again like this:

$$\text{v}[\;\;]_\text{V} \;_\text{Art}[\;\;]_\text{Art} \;_\text{N}[\;\;]_\text{N} \;_\text{P}[\;\;]_\text{P} \;_\text{Art}[\;\;]_\text{Art} \;_\text{N}[\;\;]_\text{N} \;_\text{P}[\;\;]_\text{P} \;_\text{Art}[\;\;]_\text{Art} \;_\text{N}[\;\;]_\text{N}$$

and so on. So, given the same vocabulary, there are grammatical sentences *Leave the meat on the table*, *Leave the meat on the table in the kitchen*, and so on.

It will be seen that just as NP and PP were recursive categories in our earlier set of phrase structure rules, so the dependency grammar has the recursive categories N and P. Thus a noun can control a preposition which in turn controls another noun, as in the structure just assigned to *Leave the meat on the table*; that noun can in turn control another preposition, which in turn controls another noun, as in the structure just assigned to *the meat on the table in the kitchen*; again this can be repeated an indefinite number of times. Therefore both grammars generate an infinite set of sentences, although the individual constructions are finite. Finally, both sets of rules generate the same set of sentences, assuming that the vocabulary is constant. In each case the set includes a further subset in which there is both an adverbial and a modifier of the object – in terms of syntagms like this:

[leave [the meat [on [the table]]] [in [the kitchen]]]

or in terms of dependencies like this:

leave the meat on the table in the kitchen

In each case it excludes, for example, sentences with a subject (*They leave the meat in the kitchen*), for which more rules would have to be added. In general, it can be shown that for any dependency grammar there is a phrase structure grammar which will generate an identical set of sentences; likewise, for any phrase structure grammar (or any phrase structure grammar limited to the form of rule which we have illustrated), the same set of sentences can be generated by a dependency grammar. In that sense the two are said to be **weakly equivalent**.

COMPARISON AND EVALUATION

If the models are weakly equivalent, how do they compare in other and more interesting senses? Is there anything we can say in a dependency grammar that we cannot also say, in substance, in a phrase structure grammar? Conversely, is there anything we can say in a phrase structure grammar that we cannot also say, in substance, in a dependency grammar? If both answers are no, the models are **strongly equivalent**. For any grammar of either type, there will be a grammar of the other type which not only generates an identical set of sentences, but also describes the construction of each sentence in a way that is effectively identical. If the first answer is no and the second yes then, regardless of weak equivalence, the phrase structure model is in that respect more powerful. If the first answer is yes and the second no, then the dependency model is in that respect more powerful. The fourth possibility is that both answers may be yes.

Let us imagine that the models are strongly equivalent. In that case there must be a procedure by which the constituents of a sentence can be derived from its dependency relations, and another procedure by which the dependencies can be derived from the constituency. In short, the accounts they give of the constructions will be intertranslatable. But we can see at once that the second of these procedures cannot exist. For given a bracketing

[x [y z]]

there is no way of determining whether the dependencies are like this:

or like this:

– or indeed like this:

x   y   z

or like this:

x   y   z

Therefore there cannot be strong equivalence, in the sense which we have defined. We must then ask if the account of dependencies adds something of value. So far we have justified it only in the case of determiners (Chapter 3). In other cases we have appealed to the practice of grammarians, in saying that x governs y or that x has y as a modifier. But later chapters will provide support for each of the dependencies which we have assumed: thus Chapter 5 especially, for the dependence of the object on the predicator, and Chapter 7.

An opposite procedure can be formulated quite simply. In any dependency diagram there will be at least one word on which no other word depends; for example, in

go into the kitchen

nothing depends on *the*. This word must form a syntagm with its controller; so, there must be a partial bracketing like this:

go into [the kitchen]

That controller can in turn depend on some higher controller; thus in this case *kitchen* depends on *into*. Therefore all three must form a larger syntagm:

go [into [the kitchen]]

including the first. In this way we proceed up the hierarchy of dependencies, until we reach a unit which has no controller. At that point the bracketing is complete:

[go [into [the kitchen]]]

having been derived from the dependencies by an entirely mechanical principle. In the same way, the constituency of

[leave [the meat [in [the kitchen]]]]

(the analysis which we assumed for the interpretation with *in the kitchen* as a modifier) can be mechanically derived from the dependency diagram:

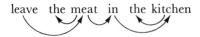

First the procedure brackets *the* and *kitchen*; then *in* and *the kitchen*. It then encounters a controller, *meat*, with two dependents, *the* and *in*. It therefore brackets all of *the* and *meat* and *in the kitchen*. Finally it brackets *leave* and all of *the meat in the kitchen*.

But there is a problem. In the noun phrase *the meat in the kitchen* we have assumed that *the* and *meat* and *in the kitchen* are all immediate constituents. Likewise in the adverbial interpretation:

[leave [the meat] [in [the kitchen]]]

we assumed that the verb, the noun phrase and the prepositional phrase were all immediate constituents of the sentence. But in any example where a controller has two or more dependents there might, in principle, be a hierarchy of syntagms which our procedure could not derive. In the noun phrase *the meat in the kitchen* we could in principle imagine two alternative analyses. In analysis *a*:

(*a*) [[the meat] [in the kitchen]]

the immediate constituents would be *the meat* and *in the kitchen*, with a subsidiary division between *the* and *meat*. In analysis *b*:

(*b*) [the [meat in the kitchen]]

they would be *the* and *meat in the kitchen*, with a subsidiary division between the noun and prepositional phrase. Neither could be derived from the dependency diagram given above.

Similarly, we could in principle imagine an analysis in which a verb and its object formed a unit distinct from a prepositional adverbial:

(*c*) [[leave [the meat]] [in the kitchen]]

or even one which grouped the object and adverbial:

(*d*) [leave [[the meat] [in the kitchen]]]

into a structure like that of *a*. Neither of these could be derived from the dependency diagram

since *meat* and *in* are equally controlled by *leave*. In principle, then, there is information that could be given in a constituency bracketing that would not be obtainable, by mechanical procedures, from the dependency diagram.

Of the two alternatives suggested in the last paragraph, *d* is unlikely to appeal to any student of the language. But textbook accounts of constituency often give analysis *c*, with the adverbial modifying not the verb, but a unit consisting of both the verb and the object. Of the two alternative treatments of the noun phrase, *b* would be unusual. But the textbooks often give analysis *a*, with the prepositional phrase modifying the article plus the noun, not the noun on its own. In phrases like *the sleek thrushes*, the same works make the opposite division:

[the [sleek thrushes]]

with the article determining the modifier plus the head. This again could not be derived from the dependency diagram

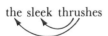

where our procedure would simply group all three together. So, although a procedure exists, it cannot derive from our account of dependencies everything that some accounts of constituency want to say.

In these examples, it is not clear that there is any real ground for bracketings more complex than those we originally gave. But there are other cases where dependents do stand in two separate constructions. In *up till Friday*, the first two words form a complex preposition (QUIRK *et al.*, pp. 301f.), in which *up* presupposes *till*; thus one can say *till Friday*, without *up*, but not *up Friday*. The noun is again a governed element, in the same way that *kitchen*, in *in the kitchen*, is governed by *in*. For a constituency analysis, this means that *up* and *till* form a syntagm distinct from *Friday*:

[[up till] Friday]

For a dependency analysis it means that both *up* and *Friday* depend on *till*:

up till Friday

But from the latter we have no way of telling that the constituents are not like this:

[up [till Friday]]

or simply like this:

[up till Friday]

with one construction overall. Another example is the constituency of auxiliaries and objects. In ⟨*Bill*⟩ *has brought the book*, the object *book* depends on *brought*. So too does the auxiliary *has*:

has brought the book

(the latter for reasons discussed in Chapter 3). But a verb phrase *has brought* must also be identified as a syntagm.

In short, there are things we can say in a constituency grammar which we cannot say in a dependency grammar, just as there are other things which we can say in a dependency grammar but not in a constituency grammar. At least some of these things are of descriptive value. As a first step we might therefore attempt to combine both forms of representation. For example, we could take the first of our phrase structure rules:

S → V + NP

and amend it to show a dependency instead of simply a sequence:

S → V NP

One rule for noun phrases could likewise be amended to

NP → Art N

on the understanding that the dependency relations holding in a larger construction (thus the dependency of NP on V) are operative for the controlling terms in any smaller constructions. On that understanding *Leave the meat* would have a structure like this:

$$_S[_V[leave]_V \; _{NP}[_{Art}[the]_{Art} \; _N[meat]_N]_{NP}]_S$$

which displays both the syntagms and the dependencies.

Let us then assume, for purposes of illustration, that *the meat in the kitchen* has the constituency given in the textbooks, with *the meat* as an immediate constituent. We might label this the 'head phrase' (abbreviated HP). The appropriate rules would then be written as

$$NP \rightarrow HP \; PP$$
$$HP \rightarrow Art \; N$$

with the rule

$$PP \rightarrow P \; NP$$

dealing with the internal structure of the modifier. On the same understanding as before, the dependency of PP on HP applies to the subsidiary controllers N and P, yielding a structure which is in relevant respects like this:

$$_{NP}[_{HP}[the \; meat]_{HP} \; _{PP}[in \; the \; kitchen]_{PP}]_{NP}$$

Another textbook analysis grouped together a noun and a modifying adjective (Adj) into a constituent that, for want of a label, we might call the 'head of the head phrase' (HHP). If we assumed this we would have to replace our rule for HP with

$$HP \rightarrow Art \; HHP$$

where one rule for HHP would be:

$$HHP \rightarrow Adj \; N$$

The sleek thrushes on the lawn would then have a structure which is in relevant respects

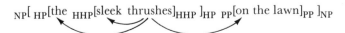

with *the*, *sleek* and *on* all depending on *thrushes*, but two successive constituency divisions, of NP into HP and PP and then of HP into the article and HHP.

We will return to this system in our discussion of coordination (Chapter 9). But in general it too is inadequate, if measured against the constructions that grammarians actually describe. A first point is that syntagms can be **discontinuous**. For example, in the interrogative *Has Bill disappeared?* the verb phrase *has disappeared*, which appears as a continuous unit in the declarative *Bill has disappeared*, is split in two by its subject. This cannot be shown by phrase structure rules, since our model was limited to relations between neighbouring units. Nor can it be shown by the system outlined in the preceding paragraph, which merely adds dependency relations to them. In a sentence such as *Eat it up!* there is a discontinuous Phrasal Verb (*eat ... up*), which then forms a syntagm with the intervening object. In *Has Bill eaten it up?* the total verb phrase might be assigned a bracketing like this:

[[has ... eaten] ... up]

where the smaller syntagm is split into two by its subject, and the larger into three, first by *Bill* and then by *it*.

Secondly, it is not clear that we will always want to see dependency as a relation between minimal units. In *Obviously he did it*, it is usual to class *obviously* as an adverb; it thus belongs to the same broad category as, for example, *badly* in *He did it badly* or *please* in *Please do it!*, whose non-paratactic use we discussed in Chapter 2. Nevertheless it is not related to the verb specifically; instead it is a Sentence Adverb or a Sentence-Modifying Adverb (thus already in SWEET, I, p. 125) whose relation is to the total syntagm formed by *he* and *did* and *it* together. The dependency relation is accordingly not like this:

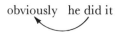

but rather like this:

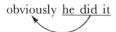

with the entire syntagm, *he did it*, as the controlling term. This cannot be shown by our original dependency rules: nor by our new system, since on the understanding which we stated the controller of *obviously* would have to be whatever is the controller in its co-constituent. Likewise in, say, *Please do not bring it* we would treat *please* as depending on the whole of *do not bring it.*

A third problem concerns the treatment of specific syntactic functions. In *Eat your dinner* the relation of *dinner* to *eat* is not merely that of a noun dependent on, or controlled by, a verb. Alternatively, *your dinner* is more than simply a noun phrase with which the verb forms a syntagm. For any grammarian, *(your) dinner* is specifically the object of *eat*, where 'being the object of' is an individual constructional relationship, just as 'being a noun' is an individual feature of class membership. To *Pass your sister the meat* the system we have outlined could assign a structure broadly like this:

where dependency, constituency and class membership are again the only primitive notions. But according to grammarians *(the) meat* and *(your) sister* have the specific roles of direct and indirect object: that is, the direct object OF, and the indirect object OF, the predicator *pass*. On the face of it, we need a system which can assign some form of structure such as the following:

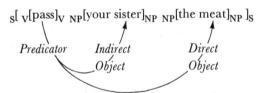

where the labelling of dependency relations represents another primitive.

Finally, it is not clear that every assemblage of relations can be correctly represented by a tree structure. In *It tastes nice*, the adjective has the specific role of subject complement: a complement which can be related to the subject, on collocational evidence which we discussed in Chapter 1. But it is also related to the verb, in that some verbal lexemes can take such a complement, whereas others (such as DRINK or BOIL) cannot. In addition, *tastes* can also be related to its subject *it*. In this way, each word is directly related to each of the others:

it tastes nice

with no single element that could be established as the controller.

Such considerations show that the combined model is unsatisfactory; they also provide further arguments against both the dependency and the constituency models in their pure form. But where we go from here is a matter on which theorists do not agree. Of the alternatives proposed, the theory of transformational grammar was developed on the assumption that, as part of its description, every sentence had to have either one or more structures that could be represented by a phrase structure tree. So, *Eat it up!*, which we gave as an example for discontinuity, would have to have a structure in which *eat*, *it* and *up* were equal constituents:

[eat] [it] [up]

But this is plainly inadequate, since *eat* and *up* should form a phrasal unit. Therefore we must posit another structure in which they are adjacent:

[eat up] [it]

with a relationship established between this second structure and the first. The construction of the sentence is then represented by both structures together. By the middle 60s the first of these trees had become known as the **surface structure**, and the second as the **deep structure**. The role of **transformational rules**, from which the theory takes its name, became that of deriving the surface structure from the deep structure, with as many intermediate stages as were necessary. So, in this case there would be a transformational rule which moves the second member of a phrasal verb (*up*) into a position after a following pronoun.

This has its attractions. For the basic defect of a phrase structure grammar is that it confuses information about constructions (for example, that *up* stands in a constructional relationship to *eat*) with information about the realisation of constructions (for example, that *up* can come after an object). In that sense it confuses what is 'deep' (the construction) with what is 'surface' (the realisation), to the inevitable detriment of the former. But it is not clear that the remedy lies in establishing two levels of phrase structure instead of one. In the surface structure of, say, *Eat up your meat!* a transformational grammar would give the information both that *up* immediately follows *eat* and, since there is no discontinuity, that *eat* and *up* are a constructional unit. This would precisely duplicate the information given in its deep structure. In the deep structure of both *Eat it up* and *Eat up your meat* a transformational grammar would give the information not only that *eat* and *up* form a constructional unit, but also that, in an allegedly 'deep' sense, *up* is ordered after *eat* and before *it* or *your meat*. In one case this duplicates what is in the surface structure. In the other it contradicts the surface structure; indeed it would contradict any likely surface structure for this combination, unless *it* is accompanied both by heavy stress and pointing (*Eat up* IT). If we multiply levels of phrase structure we multiply confusions between what is really 'deep' and what is really 'surface', instead of eliminating them.

No adequate alternative has been developed. Nor can this book try to solve the detailed problems of formalisation that would be involved. But in the chapters which follow we will assume that both the general relations of constituency and dependency, and the particular relations or types of relation between predicators and a direct object or indirect object, between a modifier and a head, and so on, should be studied independently of the order in which the relata are or can be realised, and of other purely realisational features. In the last two chapters we will return to the topic of realisation, and then (in Chapter 12) we will be able to take a fresh look at the 'deep' and 'surface' levels of description, as they might be conceived and also as the transformationalists themselves have seen them.

NOTES AND REFERENCES

My title recalls that of K. Baumgärtner, 'Konstituenz und Dependenz', in H. Steger (ed.), *Vorschläge für eine strukturelle Grammatik des Deutschen* (Darmstadt: Wissenschaftliche Buchgesellschaft, 1970), pp. 52–77; this is often cited, but I confess I do not find it entirely to the point. I know of no comparison which is quite of the sort that is given here.

For phrase structure grammar see CHOMSKY, *Structures*, Ch. 4; recursion and other technical details in his 'On the notion "rule of grammar"', in R. Jakobson (ed.), *Structure of Language and its Mathematical Aspects* (Providence: American Mathematical Society, 1961), pp. 6–24 (reprinted in FODOR & KATZ (ed.), pp. 119–36). Derivative accounts in sundry introductions to transformational grammar: those of BACH, Ch. 3 and HUDDLESTON, Ch. 3 are recommended. Note that my own discussion is limited to 'context free' (as opposed to 'context sensitive') systems. For immediate constituents see textbook accounts by HOCKETT, Ch. 17 and ROBINS, pp. 231ff.; but my term 'syntagm' is from the French (Saussurean) tradition (DE SAUSSURE, Ch. 5, §1; MARTINET, *Elements*, §4.13; overall survey in DUBOIS *et al.*, s.v. 'syntagme'). Primary accounts in R. S. Wells, 'Immediate constituents', *Lg*, 23 (1947), pp. 89–117 (reprinted in JOOS (ed.), pp. 186–207); Z. S. Harris, 'From morpheme to utterance', *Lg*, 22 (1946), pp. 161–83 (reprinted in JOOS (ed.), pp. 142–53; HARRIS, *Papers*, pp. 100–25); HARRIS, *Methods*, Ch. 16. Like other 'Bloomfieldian' studies these elaborate one aspect of Bloomfield's theory to the detriment of the remainder. But they are crucial for the development of Chomsky's. As he remarks in a passage referred to earlier, 'So far [*sc.* in outlining a phrase structure grammar] we have done nothing more than modify Harris' "Morpheme to Utterance" procedures ... showing how these ideas can provide us with a grammar which generates the sentences of a language in a uniform way, ...': p. 129 of 'A transformational approach to syntax', in HILL (ed.), pp. 124–58 (reprinted in FODOR & KATZ (ed.), pp. 211–45).

Two further points may be noted. (1) A syntagm need not have just two immediate constituents. Some scholars assumed that it should where possible (thus especially Wells, 'Immediate constituents', §53). Hence, in part, the textbook analyses of noun phrases with adjectival and prepositional modifiers. But binarism is not inherent in the model, as many Chomskyan rules (see already CHOMSKY, *Structures*, p. 29, n. 3) make clear. (2) Phrase structure rules are usually seen as 'rewrite' operations (hence the notation with the arrow); apart from Chomsky's own works see, for instance, WALL, Ch. 9 (for 'Type 2' (context free) grammars), or BACH's useful account of mathematical linguistics (Ch. 8). But other formulations are possible. For an attractive alternative see J. D. McCawley, 'Concerning the base component of a transformational grammar', *FL*, 4 (1968), pp. 243–69 (also in McCAWLEY, pp. 35–58) on 'node admissibility conditions'; further development, in a way that also affects the case for transformations, in a forthcoming paper by G. Gazdar, 'Phrase structure grammar', in P. I. Jacobson & G. K. Pullum (eds.), *The Nature of Syntactic Representation* (Dordrecht: Reidel). The account I have given is deliberately non-committal.

Dependency trees are introduced by TESNIÈRE ('hierarchie des connexions', pp. 13ff.), but in his account the constructional relation ('ordre structural') is abstracted from the linear sequence. For dependency rules see D. G. Hays, 'Dependency grammar: a formalism and some observations', *Lg*, 40 (1964), pp. 511–25 (reprinted in HOUSEHOLDER (ed.), pp. 223–40). I use 'control(ler)' for Hays's 'govern(or)' (Tesnière's 'régir', 'régissant'); although the latter is usual, its sense conflicts with those of ordinary grammarians (Chapter 11, notes to Chapter 6 below). Note that 'dependency grammar', in the strict technical sense, is only broadly related to the post-

Tesnièrean development of valency theory (notes to Chapters 5 and 6 below).

For weak and strong equivalence see Hays, 'Dependency grammar', §6 (but his 'equipotence' is not usual). Hays refers to proofs, by H. Gaifman, for the systems described. For similar theorems see Y. Bar-Hillel, *Language and Information: Selected Essays on their Theory and Application* (Reading, Mass.: Addison-Wesley; Jerusalem: Jerusalem Academic Press, 1964), especially pp. 185ff.; WALL, *passim*. For a linguist's view of strong equivalence compare LYONS, *Introduction*, pp. 226–31 (for phrase structure and 'categorial' systems). The combined system outlined in the text is not unlike that of HERINGER, Ch. 4, where rules for 'dependence' and 'interdependence' (see notes to Chapter 5 below) are added to a 'Konstitutionssystem' (HERINGER, Ch. 3) for unordered syntagms. Another proposal is that of HUDSON, but its formal character is less clear.

For a textbook analysis of phrases like *the sleek thrushes* and *the meat in the kitchen* see HOCKETT, p. 188; recently, and still with no explicit justification, in D. L. Bolinger, *Aspects of Language*, 2nd edn (New York: Harcourt Brace Jovanovich, 1975), p. 141. The constituency of the adjective is already in BLOOMFIELD (p. 195 for *this fresh milk*). ALLERTON, pp. 119f. discusses alternative analyses of *a new car*.

For defects of phrase structure (and, by implication, of dependency) grammars see CHOMSKY, *Structures*, Ch. 5 *et passim*; but 'deep' and 'surface' are later (CHOMSKY, *Topics*, p. 16; *Aspects*, p. 16). See also Postal's once influential polemic (POSTAL). A good textbook account is given, for the mid 60s, by N. Ruwet, *Introduction à la grammaire générative* (Paris: Plon, 1967), Ch. 3, §6 (English translation, *An Introduction to Generative Grammar*, by N. S. H. Smith (Amsterdam: North-Holland, 1973)); for the mid 70s, though now dated, by HUDDLESTON (Ch. 4 especially); see also LYONS, *Introduction*, pp. 247ff. For the discontinuity of the phrasal verb see Chomsky's 'On the notion "rule of grammar"', p. 23 (reprinted in FODOR & KATZ (ed.), p. 135). For a recent assessment of the arguments see my essay on 'Deep structure', in D. J. Allerton, E. Carney & D. Holdcroft (eds.), *Function and Context in Linguistic Analysis: a Festschrift for William Haas* (Cambridge: Cambridge University Press, 1979), pp. 148–58.

Deep structures are usually seen as an initial level of phrase structure. But dependency representations have been proposed: see Jane J. Robinson, 'Dependency structures and transformational rules', *Lg*, 46 (1970), pp. 259–85; J. M. Anderson, 'Dependency and grammatical functions', *FL*, 7 (1971), pp. 30–37 (also ANDERSON). Compare LYONS, *Introduction*, pp. 372ff., for the categorial system; also Chomsky's later model of 'X̄-syntax' (see notes to Chapter 7 below) which Robinson cites as a contemporary development.

5
Predication

General and universal categories.
Subject and predicate: Traditional analysis; types of predicate. Dependency
analysis: valency, predicators, complements. Semantic objection to traditional
analysis. Zero valency; subject and predicate vs. subject and object. Are
subjects universal? Justification for subject: cases, word order; active vs. passive; predicate as separate unit. An alternative system (Is there a subject in
Basque?); universality not establishable.
Copular constructions: Schema for dependency analysis. Copula no predicator; as
marking element. Prepositions as predicators.

Most of the terms which are used by grammarians refer to classes or
constructions peculiar to a particular language or to a particular
range of languages. For example, there is a category of phrasal verbs
in English (*ate ... up*, or the lexeme EAT UP, in *He ate it up*), but no
productive type to which the term could be applied in, say, Italian.
Both English and Italian have auxiliary verbs (*has* in *Mary has arrived*,
è in *Maria è arrivata*). That means: there are criteria for the application
of the term 'auxiliary verb' (defined, say, as a verb in a determining
relation to another verb) which, despite differences, both the English
and the Italian elements will meet. But there were no auxiliary verbs
– no elements satisfying such criteria – in, for example, Ancient
Greek. Both English and Italian have articles (*the* and *a* in *the book*, *a
book*; *il* and *un* in *il libro*, *un libro*); so did Ancient Greek (*ho* in *ho
ánthrōpos* 'the man'), though it did not have a comparable distinction
between the Definite article and an Indefinite (*the, il* versus *a, un*). But
there are no articles in Latin – no element to which this term could be
applied as distinct from, for example, 'demonstrative' (*hic* in *hic liber*
'this book'). Terms such as these are **general**, in that grammarians
do not transfer them arbitrarily from one system to another. But they
are not **universal**, since for any language we investigate we anticipate the possibility that they will not apply.

Other categories are such that every language can be expected to
display them. For example, we will always establish sentences, under

the theory developed in Chapter 2. It is only if we could imagine a language without syntax – without rules which constrained the possible combinations of words or morphemes – that the notion of a maximal syntactic unit would be inapplicable. We also expect that every language will have determiners, in the sense proposed at the end of Chapter 3. The particular types of determiner vary, as we have just remarked in the case of articles or auxiliaries. But in every grammar we establish certain oppositions between words or morphemes, which form a closed set and whose terms stand in a dependent relationship. A fortiori, we also anticipate that every language will exhibit relations of dependency; also constituency relations within syntagms, as explained in Chapter 4. Such categories form a system of **linguistic universals**, incorporated into a model (end of Chapter 3) that, to the best of our knowledge, every grammar can conform to.

What other types of element might be universally applicable? The question is nowhere more difficult than for the constructions which we will consider in this chapter, which concern the basic relationships within the clause, traditionally referred to under the heading of predication.

SUBJECT AND PREDICATE

Let us return to Orwell and discuss the analysis of the animals' seven commandments (*Animal Farm*, Ch. 2):

1. Whatever goes upon two legs is an enemy.
2. Whatever goes upon four legs, or has wings, is a friend.
3. No animal shall wear clothes.
4. No animal shall sleep in a bed.
5. No animal shall drink alcohol.
6. No animal shall kill any other animal.
7. All animals are equal.

According to tradition, each of these is divided into two parts. One part is the **subject**: in 1, *whatever goes upon two legs*; in 2, *whatever goes upon four legs, or has wings*; in 3–6, *no animal*; in 7, *all animals*. This is said to identify the topic which the sentence puts under focus: the original Greek term was *to hypokeímenon*, literally 'that which lies under'. Thus commandment 7 would be seen as making a statement about 'all animals', and commandment 1 a statement about 'whatever goes upon two legs'. The other part is a **predicate** (*is an enemy, is a friend, shall wear clothes,* and so on) which is said of, or **predicated of**, whatever the subject refers to. So, what is said of all animals is that they 'are equal', and what is said of a creature that goes upon two legs is that it 'is an enemy'. The division itself has been accepted by the majority of structural linguists, including the transformational grammarians. Thus in Chomsky's central work the first rule of English syntax deals with the construction of a noun phrase and a 'predicate phrase':

$$S \rightarrow NP + \text{Predicate phrase}$$

where the subject is defined as a noun phrase which is an immediate constituent of a syntagm labelled S (compare CHOMSKY, *Aspects*, pp. 71, 106).

The predicates are of three types, in each of which a **verb** (*is, shall wear,* and so on) is an essential element. In the first the verb has an **object**: thus in commandments 3, 5 and 6 the verbs *(shall) wear, (shall) drink* and *(shall) kill* have the direct objects *clothes, alcohol* and *any other animal*. In that case the construction is described as **transitive**: the act referred to by the verb (of wearing or drinking or killing) is said to pass across (Latin 'transire') from an actor to a goal. Likewise, in the imaginary commandment

No animal shall give aid to humans

the act of giving would be seen as passing across, first to a goal referred to by the direct object *aid* and then to a second or indirect goal, which is referred to by the indirect object *(to) humans*. The term is also applied to the verbal lexeme. Thus KILL is an inherently **transitive verb**, its sense implying a person or thing to whom the killing is done as well as a person or thing who is doing it.

In the second type of predicate the verb is a **copula** accompanied by a noun or an adjective: thus in commandments 1–2 the singular copula *is* is followed by the noun phrase *an enemy* or *a friend*, and in commandment 7 the plural copula *are* is followed by the adjective *equal*. In this case no action is referred to, and the verb is merely a linking element (the meaning of the Latin 'copula') between this second element and the subject. The noun or adjective is then described as **predicative**, or is said to stand in predicative position. Thus the predicative adjective in 7 is opposed to the Attributive adjective in, for example, *an equal amount*. The construction of a predicative noun or noun phrase is opposed, in particular, to that of an object, the predicate *is an enemy*, in 1, being fundamentally different from, for example, *saw an enemy* in *I saw an enemy*.

In the third type of predicate the verb may again refer to an action; but there is no goal to which it is directed. Thus in commandment 4 (*No animal shall sleep in a bed*) there is no goal for the process or activity of sleeping, and within the subject of commandments 1 and 2 (*whatever goes upon two legs*; *whatever goes upon four legs, or has wings*) the verb *goes* refers to an act that is not directed towards something 'being gone', or having going done to it. In this case the construction is described as **intransitive**, the verb being accompanied at most by adverbials. Thus in these examples (*shall*) *sleep* and *goes* are followed only by the adverbials *in a bed, upon two legs* and *upon four legs*; we could also imagine the preposterous commandment

> No animal shall sleep

whose predicate is the verb alone. The term may again be applied to the lexeme, SLEEP and GO being inherently **intransitive verbs**.

Given the basic division between subject and predicate, the rest of this analysis can be validated without difficulty. There is no doubt that the commandments with a copula differ syntactically from those with an object, for reasons which will be clear from Chapter 1, for the example *Terrifying are the . . . thrushes*. We can also justify the semantic notion of transitivity. For although there are many cases where no act is referred to (*I saw an animal* does not mean that I performed an act of seeing on it; *I smelled the carnations* may mean merely that their scent came to my attention), it is in general true, for English and for the classical languages for which this system was developed, that when such sentences do refer to the operation of one entity on another entity (as, for instance, in *No animal shall kill any other animal*), it is the operator or actor that is identified by the subject and the object that identifies its target. A construction cannot be justified on such evidence alone. But certain relations of meaning are typical of it, or more typical than others.

Nor is there any doubt that transitive constructions are distinct from intransitive. For here too there are specific lexical incompatibilities. A form of SLEEP cannot be construed with an object, unless it is a Cognate Object (*a good night's sleep* in *They slept a good night's sleep*; *the sleep of the just* in *He slept the sleep of the just*), where the noun is morphologically related, in this case by conversion or zero derivation, to the verb. With PREVARICATE or VANISH even that possibility is excluded: no object could be added to *No animal shall prevaricate* or *The man vanished*. The converse holds for many verbs which stand in the transitive construction. A form of WEAR cannot be construed with a subject only, except in examples such as *The carpet has worn badly*, where we have a different sense of WEAR, or perhaps a different lexeme altogether, from the transitive in *No animal shall wear clothes*. With PERUSE or SCRUTINISE the case is uncomplicated: even in ellipsis one would not normally say *He perused* or *They scrutinised*. In the literature on dependency grammar, such classes of verbs are described as having different **valencies**, or taking different sets of **valents**. Thus the valency of PREVARICATE includes a subject element only, while the valents of PERUSE are both a subject and a direct object. In our examples with WEAR we illustrate two senses with which different sets of valents are associated – or perhaps, again, homonymous lexemes which as such belong to different classes.

At this point it will be clear why objects are treated as depending on the verb (Chapter 4). For just as the function of a determiner presupposes the element it determines (Chapter 3), so an object function presupposes the element that it is object OF. Individual verbs exclude or require an object, independently of their relation to the subject, just as individual nouns restrict the range of articles (compare again *a book* and [səm] *book*, [səm] *meat* and *a meat*), independently of their own wider functions. But there cannot be an object without a verb; nor do individual nouns exclude the relationship. Thus it is the valency of the verb which determines how many other elements the construction may or must have (a subject alone, both a subject and a direct object, a subject with or without a direct object, and so on), not the valency of an object which determines that there must also be a subject and a verb or the valency of a subject which determines whether there may also be a verb and a direct object.

The dependency of objects is implicit in the usual statements of grammarians, as we remarked in Chapter 4. But in dependency grammars every valent, or every element that we have just referred to in our statements about valency, is treated in the same way. That includes the subject; so, in the intransitive *No animal shall sleep*, the relations are described like this:

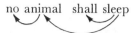

with *(no) animal* depending on *(shall) sleep* just as, in *Leave the meat*, the object *(the) meat* depends on *leave*. The transitive *No animal shall wear clothes* would then have a structure

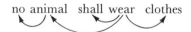

in which both the subject and the object depend directly on *(shall) wear*. In *No animal shall give aid to humans*, the verb *(shall) give* would have three dependents *(no) animal, aid* and *(to) humans*, since the valents of GIVE comprise all three elements subject, direct object and indirect object. In this form of analysis the main division is not between the subject and whatever is predicated of it, but between the element which we have already called the **predicator** *(shall sleep, shall wear, shall give)* and the various **complements**, as we will call them, which are required, according to the valency of the verb or the particular sense of the verb, if the construction is to be complete.

If we add the subject–predicate division we obtain a form of representation such as the following:

[no animal] [[shall wear] clothes]

where a construction which would be united by a single dependency rule:

V (N , * , N)

is split into two successive levels of phrase structure:

S → NP + Predicate
Predicate → VP + NP

the second of which relates a Verb Phrase (V plus its determiner) to the object alone. In principle, both could be right; we have already envisaged constructions where a constituent could not be predicted from the dependencies alone. But the traditional analysis can be questioned, especially if it is thought to represent a universal. According to some scholars, it is invalid even for languages such as English; an alternative view is that it is valid only for languages of certain types. But all languages have some form of construction in which predicators are related to different classes of complement. A division of subject and predicate would then be no more than a secondary feature.

Of the arguments against the division, the first and most obvious concern the semantic value attributed to it. Commandment 2 has the subject *whatever goes upon four legs, or has wings*; therefore it is a statement (it would be said) about all creatures having these characteristics. But in context it is also a statement about friends, defining who is a friend as opposed to an enemy. Let us suppose that animal A is catechising animal B: 'Right,' A asks, 'then who are our friends?' B could reply by uttering a sentence with *a friend* as subject: 'A friend is whatever goes on four legs, or has wings'. Alternatively, B could repeat the commandment:

> Whatever goes upon FOUR legs, or has WINGS, is a friend

with *four* and *wings* marked intonationally. In either case it is *a friend*, not *whatever . . . wings*, that refers to the topic of discourse. Similarly, it makes no difference if one says *I think John got it* (subject *John* and object *it*) or *I think it went to John* (subject *it* and *to John* adverbial), in answer, say, to *Who got the first prize?* Both are statements equally about John or about the prize, each of which may be said to underlie their utterance. The notions of subject and predicate originate in Aristotelian logic, where the study of language is subordinate to the aim of characterising valid arguments. It was only within that system (now superseded among logicians themselves) that they could be established on semantic grounds.

In the late nineteenth century a distinction was made between the **grammatical subject** of a sentence (*whatever . . . wings* in commandment 2, *John* in *John got it*, *it* in *It went to John*) and a **psychological subject**, which was said to represent its starting point in the mind of a particular speaker. In the context of the question asked by animal A, both of B's replies would have the psychological subject *a friend*, even though the second (*Whatever goes upon FOUR legs, or has WINGS, is a friend*) has it in a grammatically predicative position. The most we could claim is that the grammatical subject also tends to be the psychological subject (as would be said, for example, of *no animal* and *all animals* in commandments 3–7), or is so if no other factor disturbs the relationships. But that assumes that the category itself is valid. We must find other arguments by which it is shown to be so – arguments not just for a semantic or logical relation, but for a specific construction in which the grammatical predicate is established as a unit.

A second objection is that some predicates do not take subjects. Of what, for example, is *is raining* predicated in *It is raining*, or *pluit* in its Latin translation *Pluit*? In *Pluit* the verb is in the form of the 3rd singular, as also in, for example, *Cantat* 'He, she or it is singing'; but whereas *cantat* must be understood of some particular individual (*Cantat* ⟨sc. *imperator*⟩ '⟨The emperor⟩ is singing', *Cantat* ⟨sc. *puella*⟩ '⟨The girl⟩ is singing', and so on), there is no entity of which one would say that he, she or it 'rains'. Likewise for English *It is raining*: although this is superficially like, for example, *It is singing*, there is again no entity to which *it* refers or about which a statement is made. Nor could any other word or phrase be substituted (*He is raining*, *The cloud is raining*, and so on). In *It is singing* the pronoun is a semantic variable, as in examples discussed in Chapter 2. But in *It is raining* it is simply a marker, defined as an element with no semantic contrast (Chapter 3). In Latin *Cantat* the 3rd singular has variable reference; alternatively, there is ellipsis of a subject element (*puella, imperator, ...*) with which the termination agrees. But in *Pluit* there is again no choice of ending – no *Pluo* (with the same ending as *Canto* 'I am singing'), no *Pluis* (with that of *Cantas* 'You are singing'), and so on. Therefore it too has an empty role in the construction.

In dependency grammar, a verb which takes no complement is said to have a **zero valency**. Just as the valency of PERUSE comprises both a subject and an object, while that of VANISH comprises the subject only, so the normal valency of RAIN or PLUIT comprises no element whatever. It can now be seen why the subject stands in a dependent relationship. For a subject presupposes a predicator: it is only in cases of ellipsis that the construction can apparently consist of just a subject (*Bill* ⟨sc. *fetched Mary*⟩), or just a subject and an object (*And Bill* ⟨sc. *could fetch*⟩ *Mary*). But a predicator does not presuppose a subject: in the same way that a construction can be objectless, as in the intransitive *No animal shall sleep*, so, in *Pluit* or *It is raining*, it can also be subjectless. The predicator is the only essential element, and as such governs or controls a subject, precisely as it controls the direct object and other elements that enter into valencies.

According to tradition both the predicate and its subject are essential elements. A subjectless verb is therefore problematic, and requires some special explanation. Nevertheless the *it* of *It is raining* occupies what is otherwise the subject position, and the verb agrees with it by the normal rule (*is raining*, not *are raining*). Only under ellipsis is this position left vacant (⟨sc. *It*⟩ *won't rain tomorrow*, like ⟨sc. *Bloggs*⟩ *did it yesterday*). Even in Latin, *pluit* has to have a person suffix, which in other verbs would function as a determiner or in agreement with a subject noun phrase. In this respect a subject and object are still on an unequal footing. If a verb is objectless, no unit resembling an object enters into its construction; only in certain idioms might an empty *it* be established (as in the idiomatic sense of *They beat it out of the building*). Nor is its own form such that it could also mark an object relationship. But a subjectless construction is not simply reduced to a predicator. It also has a marker which is specifically subject-like in form.

This does not mean that it actually has a subject, in the sense intended by the Aristotelian tradition. The traditional subject represents an element in the semantic structure of the sentence, which the *it* of *It is raining* certainly is not. But it does suggest that the notion of 'subject' should be looked at in two different ways. On the one hand, there is a subject as opposed to an object. In that sense the animals' third commandment has the tripartite structure justified by arguments from valency:

Subject	Predicator	Object
no animal	shall wear	clothes

On the same level, *No animal shall sleep* has the two-term structure:

Subject	Predicator
no animal	shall sleep

and *It is raining* a one-term structure which we must simply show like this:

Predicator
is raining

with the marker left out of account. On the other hand, there is a subject as opposed to a predicate. In that sense the tripartite structure has a binary division imposed upon it:

Subject₁	Predicator	Object
no animal	shall wear	clothes

Subject₂	Predicate

(with the notions of 'subject' distinguished by subscripts). Likewise the intransitive has a structure like this:

Subject₁	*Predicator*
no animal	shall sleep
Subject₂	*Predicate*

in which *shall sleep* functions in relation both to subject$_1$ and to subject$_2$. In a language such as English the same pattern is imposed on cases of zero-valency:

	Predicator
it	is raining
Subject₂	*Predicate*

where the role of *it* is to supply a subject$_2$ which would otherwise be missing.

The remaining arguments concern the universality of these categories. For the subject in Latin or English, three main characteristics can be distinguished. The first is that the Agent noun in the transitive construction – the noun which tends to identify the actor as opposed to the goal of an action – is grammatically the same as the single noun in the intransitive. Thus in the following line from Virgil:

hostis habet muros; ruit alto a culmine Troia

(*Aeneid*, II.290),[1] the nominative *Troia* 'Troy' is the subject of the intransitive *ruit* 'is collapsing' precisely as the nominative *hostis* 'the enemy' is the subject of the transitive *habet* 'holds'. By contrast, the object of *habet* is accusative (*muros* 'the walls') and the adverbial accompanying *ruit* has a preposition (*a*) which governs the ablative case (*alto a culmine*, literally 'from the high summit'). The subject nouns are also singled out by agreement, the verbs *ruit* and *habet* being both 3rd singular. In English there is no case inflection; but both subjects occupy the same position in the sentence (*No animal shall sleep*, not *Shall sleep no animal*; *No animal shall wear clothes*, not *Shall wear clothes no animal*, *Shall wear no animal clothes*). The subject can again be marked by agreement, when the rule applies.

The second characteristic lies in the opposition between the active

---

[1] 'The foes already have possessed the wall;
Troy nods from high, and totters to her fall.' (Dryden)

and the passive construction. In a transitive clause the verb or verb phrase has the active form (*habet, shall wear*), matching the agent as subject. Once more there is identity with the intransitive (*ruit, shall sleep*). But in the passive construction it is the Patient noun – the noun which tends to identify a goal or 'undergoer' (Latin *patiens*) – that fills the subject function. Thus in place of the active sixth commandment

Agent	Predicate
no animal	shall kill any other animal

one could write an alternative version

Patient	Predicate
no animal	shall be killed by any other animal

where the predicate is stated of the potential undergoer of the killing. The verb phrase has the passive form, which in English is marked by BE with the past or passive participle: ⟨*shall*⟩ *be killed* versus ⟨*shall*⟩ *kill*. Likewise in the Latin sentence

> novae ab utrisque rationes reperiebantur
> 'New methods were found by both sides'

(compare Caesar, *Civil Wars*, III.50), the subject is the nominative *novae . . . rationes* 'new methods' and the verb the passive *reperiebantur* 'were being found', which is opposed to its active counterpart *reperiebant* 'were finding' by the addition of the suffix *-ur*. The agent is treated as an adverbial: Latin *ab utrisque*, with the same case and preposition as *a culmine* 'from the summit'; English *by any other animal*, with the same preposition as in, for example, *They killed him by stealth*.

It is the evidence of this construction, in particular, that establishes the subject as opposed to a predicate (subject$_2$ in our schemata) as a category distinct from that of the subject as opposed to an object (subject$_1$). For given a collocation of agent, verb and patient (*animal–kill–animal, utrique–reperire–rationes*), it allows either noun to be chosen for the subject$_2$ role. In English the choice is wider, in that the subject of a passive may also correspond to an indirect object. Thus for the collocation *I–give–money–children* there is a choice between an active with *I* as the subject (as in *I gave no money to the children*), a First Passive with subject *money* (*No money was given to the children by* ME) and a Second Passive with subject *children* (*The children weren't given any money by* ME). The 'subject$_2$' is thus independent of the agent or patient category. Yet the active is the basic term in the opposition. This is shown by the morphology of the verb (where the passive form is more complex than the active), by the lack of distinction (in English) between the verb of the first passive and the second, and also by the adverbial character which the passive imposes on the agent. This in turn is shown both by its morphology and by the readiness with which it can be dropped: thus *No animal shall be killed, The children weren't given any money, novae rationes reperiebantur* 'New methods were found', and so on. It is because the active is basic that we can identify the subject$_1$, or agent, with the subject of the intransitive.

The third characteristic is that the predicate can appear alone in various dependent positions. In *I saw him while visiting London* the predicator *visiting* has the object *London,* as in the finite clause *I visited London*; but while the main verb also has an explicit subject, *visiting* or *visiting him* does not. By contrast, there is no sentence like, for example, *I saw him while he visiting* (meaning 'while he was visiting me') or *I lost it while wearing* (meaning 'while I was wearing it'). Another case is when a main verb takes an infinitive: *Caesar tried to repair the bridges* (infinitive *to repair* forming a predicate with its object *the bridges*); Latin *conatus est Caesar reficere pontes* (infinitive *reficere* with object *pontes*). In other cases we can establish a contrast: *Buying that picture ⟨was a great mistake⟩, My husband buying that picture ⟨was a great mistake⟩.* But within the predicate the form of BUY retains its usual valency. As *visiting London* is a syntagm in . . . *while visiting London,* and *buying that picture* in *Buying that picture was a great mistake,* so, on this evidence, is *buying that picture* in *My husband buying that picture* .

[[my husband] [buying that picture]]

So, by extension, is *bought that picture* in the finite *My husband bought that picture*:

[[my husband] [bought that picture]]

These characteristics are decisive for the particular type of system in which all three are displayed. But there are many languages in which the first, in particular, is not. In Basque, for example, an intransitive sentence such as the following:

gizona   ethorri da
'the man'   'has come'[2]

---

[2] Cf. P. Lafitte, *Grammaire basque (navarro-labourdin littéraire)*, 2nd edn (Bayonne, 1962), §847; henceforth abbreviated LAFITTE.

has the noun *gizona* in the nominative or absolute case (root *gizon* with definite singular *-a*), while the auxiliary of the verb phrase (participle *ethorri* + auxiliary *da* 'is') is marked with a 3rd singular prefix *d-*. So far this is perfectly in line with other European languages. But in a transitive sentence such as

> aitak ogia jan du
> 'the father' 'the bread' 'has eaten'

(LAFITTE, §791) the noun which is in the nominative or absolute is not the agent *aitak*, but the apparent object *ogia*; it is with this noun, too, that the prefix of the auxiliary (*du* '(he) has') corresponds. *Aitak* itself is in a case which most scholars call the Ergative (LAFITTE's 'actif'), which is marked by a suffix *-k*; if the agent were anything but 3rd singular the auxiliary would then be marked with a suffix (*dut* 'I have ... (it)', *dugu* 'we have ... (it)', *dute* '(they) have ... (it)', and so on (LAFITTE, §§559–60)). In that way *aitak* is distinguished both from *ogia* and from *gizona* 'the man' in the first example.

Different scholars have proposed different analyses of these constructions. According to Martinet,[3] the sentence which we have called intransitive would consist simply of a verb and one dependent:

> [gizona [ethorri da]]

standing in a relation similar to that of a noun and a modifier. The sentence would in effect mean (1) that there had been an act of coming, and (2) that, more specifically, it was a coming of the man or in which the man was involved. In the sentence which we described as transitive the same relation would obtain between the verb and the patient:

> [ogia [jan du]]

– meaning (1) that there had been an act of eating, and (2) that, more specifically, it involved the bread. Since it is the same relation, the morphology of the noun and auxiliary (nominative/absolute with *d-*)

---

[3] Cf. A. Martinet, 'La construction ergative' (1958), reprinted in his *La linguistique synchronique* (Paris, 1965), pp. 212–28; also 'Le sujet comme fonction linguistique et l'analyse syntaxique du basque' (1962), reprinted in MARTINET, *Studies*, pp. 237–46. The latter replies to objections raised by Lafon: cf. R. Lafon, 'L'expression de l'auteur de l'action en basque', *BSL*, 55 (1960), 1, pp. 186–221.

is also identical. But in the transitive case the whole must form a syntagm with a second dependent:

[aitak [ogia [jan du]]]

– meaning (3) that, more specifically, the act of eating the bread was of the father. It is this higher constituent that is marked by the ergative.

If Martinet's analysis is right the language is without a subject category, either in relation to an object (subject₁) or to a predicate (subject₂). In that case all that is common between the Basque and the Latin or English constructions is the mere relationship of dependency (of Basque *aitak* and *ogia* on *jan du*, of Latin *hostis* and *muros* on *habet*), and the generalised semantic categories (*aitak* and *hostis* as agent, *ogia* and *muros* as patient) to which the dependents can be assigned. But if Martinet is wrong there are two ways, in principle, by which the notion of a subject might be reinstated. One is to ignore the morphology and treat the constructions precisely as we treat their Latin or English translations. So, while *ethorri da* 'has come' would be predicated of the nominative *gizona* 'the man':

Subject	Predicate
gizona	ethorri da

the ergative *aitak* 'the father' would be the subject of a transitive predicate *ogia jan du* 'has eaten the bread':

Subject	Predicate
aitak	ogia jan du

with the nominative *ogia* playing the syntactic role of the Latin accusative. This is the description presented by LAFITTE (Ch. 6 *et passim*), who writes very largely in Romance terms. The alternative is to see a subject role for the patient. So, just as *ethorri da* would be predicated of *gizona*, a syntagm formed by the verb and the ergative (*aitak ... jan du* 'the father ... eaten has') would be predicated of *ogia* 'the bread':

Subject	Predicate
ogia	aitak ... jan du

with both nominatives in the same role.

This last analysis is similar to that of a passive construction:

Subject	Predicate
the bread	has been eaten by the father

with the agent (*aitak, by the father*) marked in the predicate by *-k* or *by*. Some scholars have therefore classified it as such, even though there is no active to which it can be opposed. But without such an opposition it is hard to see how the description could be justified. For the essence of the passive lies in a choice between constructions, by which the subject as opposed to the predicate (subject₂) can be either the patient or the agent. In addition, it is the ergative or agent which is the obligatory element in the construction. According to Martinet, a sentence such as *Gizonak jaten du* (ergative *gizonak* 'the man', auxiliary *du* 'has' forming the present with a nominal infinitive *jaten* 'to eat') can mean simply 'The man is eating', with no patient referred to.[4] But with a patient alone the verb phrase would be different. Thus in a sentence such as the following:

Paulo	maitatua	da
'Paul'	'loved'	'is'

(LAFITTE, §644) the auxiliary, in particular, is *da* (compare the intransitive *ethorri da* 'has come') and not *du*. If we were dealing with a subject–predicate construction, we would expect the subject to be obligatory (thus in English there is no subjectless predicate *Has been eaten by the father*), with optionality of the agent (English *The bread has been eaten*).

The construction of this latest example (*Paulo maitatua da*) is the one which Lafitte himself describes as passive (*loc. cit.*). The relation between that and the construction which we described as transitive (*Aitak ogia jan du* 'The father has eaten the bread') might therefore be seen as parallel, morphology apart, to the relation between the agentless passive construction in Latin or English (*Novae rationes reperiebantur, No animal shall be killed*) and the basic active (*Hostis habet muros, No animal shall kill any other animal*). If this is right the transitive in Basque would itself be an active. Now that as such does not establish *aitak* as a subject, as Lafitte himself describes it. For there is still no evidence by which an ergative agent in the transitive, construed with

---

[4] MARTINET, *Studies*, p. 78. For the morphology of the periphrastic verb forms see LAFITTE, Ch. 29.

a verb which is in turn related to a nominative, can be classed together either with a nominative patient in the passive construction (such as *Paulo* in *Paulo maitatua da*) or with the single nominative in the intransitive (*gizona* in *Gizona ethorri da*). But could such evidence perhaps be found?

According to some recent contributions, it can be found in the interpretation of infinitive constructions. With the intransitive 'to talk' one could say, for example:

> mintzatzera   doa
> 'to talk'   'goes'

where an allative form of the nominal infinitive (the same case as, for example, *Parisera* 'to Paris') is understood of the same individual as the finite *doa*: 'He or she is going in order to – in order that the same he or she should – talk' (compare LAFITTE, §462). With the infinitive of a transitive verb, a similar example would be

> semearen   ikustera   noa
> 'the son'   'to see'   'I go'

(LAFITTE, §860), where the added noun is in the possessive genitive (*seme* 'son' plus definite -*a* plus -*(r)en*): so, literally, 'I go to the seeing of the son'. But this noun refers to the son who is to be seen; it is the individual who does the seeing, which in the finite transitive would be identified by a noun in the ergative, that one must understand from the main verb. So, a 'see-er' is understood with *ikustera* 'to see' in the same way that a repairer is understood with the English infinitive *to repair* (in *Caesar tried to repair the bridges*) or the Latin *reficere* (*conatus est Caesar reficere pontes*). Likewise, a talker was understood with *mintzatzera* 'to talk' just as a sleeper would be understood with English *to sleep* or the Latin *dormire* (in *Caesar tried to sleep, conatus est Caesar dormire*). Therefore (it is argued) the nouns which would refer to the 'see-er' and the talker in a Basque finite construction must be subjects like those of English or Latin, despite the difference in morphology.

I am not a specialist in Basque, and can make only hesitant comments. But, in the first place, it does not seem that the passive plays the same roles as in Latin or English. Lafitte remarks that its use is rare (§645, IV), and Lafon reports an experiment in translation, of a Latin passive into Basque, in which it was almost entirely avoided.[5]

---

[5] R. Lafon, 'Ergatif et passif en basque et géorgien', *BSL*, 66 (1971), 1, pp. 327–43.

According to Lafon himself, the only established passive has the role not of transposing an agent and a patient, but simply of converting a verb which is lexically transitive (such as IKUSI 'see') into the intransitive class. Hence, in particular, it is a passive without a grammatical agent (like the English *No animal shall be killed*); the construction with such an agent (as in the English *No animal shall be killed by any other animal*) is especially unusual. So far as the transitive is concerned, this would be compatible with any of the analyses which we have outlined. Thus in terms of Martinet's analysis, a verb whose ordinary valents are a nominative and an ergative, with the former an immediate and the latter a more remote constituent:

is converted to a construction with the close dependent alone:

[*Nominative   Verb*]

As for the infinitive constructions, it will be noted that the constituency bracketing which is imposed by Martinet's analysis, as shown above, is the same as that of the Latin subject and predicate:

[*Nominative* [*Accusative   Verb*]]
[*Nominative   Verb*]

except that the categories, and their case exponents, are changed. Now with each infinitive one noun, or whatever is referred to by that noun, is understood; in Latin or English it is naturally the subject, with the further possibility that, with a passive infinitive, it will be the patient instead of the agent (as in *Caesar tried to be seen*). In Basque the construction of the infinitive shows no contrast between active and passive, and in other respects resembles that of a noun; witness again the genitive of *semearen ikustera* 'to the seeing of the son'. In the light of the dependency analysis we may see this as a construction reduced, not from subject$_2$ and predicate to the simple predicate, or from subject$_1$, finite verb and object to the simple infinitive verb and object, but from a finite construction with both a closer and a more remote dependent:

[*Agent* [*Patient   Finite verb*]]

to one with the close dependent alone:

[*Patient   Infinitive verb*]

In that respect the agent may be said to fall together with the single noun, or the single non-oblique noun, in the intransitive. But it is not clear that we need a category of subject to explain why.

It emerges from this discussion that there is no element in Basque exhibiting all the characteristics of the Latin or English subject, as summarised earlier. The nominatives are subject-like in their morphology, with inflections on the verb (illustrated in our examples by the prefixes of *noa* 'I go', *doa* '(he, she or it) goes', *du* in *jan du* 'eaten has', and so on) to match. But if we assign them to that category it seems harder to explain the reduced construction with infinitives. The ergative is subject-like – that is, like a subject as we traditionally know it – both in its semantics in general (in that it is typical of the agent) and with respect to infinitives in particular. But if we treat it as such we are forced to seek some other basis for the noun and verb morphology. Explanations have been offered, but they become unnecessary if, on abandoning the hunt for subjects, we can find a common basis for all the features which have been outlined. Martinet's account has been rejected by at least one specialist (though not in favour of Lafitte's). But it explains more of the facts than any other that is at present available.

The argument has been limited to a single language, for which we have good and fairly detailed information. But the universality of subjects as opposed to objects (subject$_1$), let alone of subjects as opposed to predicates (subject$_2$), would not be supported by a wider study. In general, it is possible to establish a list of subject-like characteristics, involving case, agreement, agentivity, relations with non-finite verbs, and so on. Any language has elements that display some subset of them; in that sense it has subject-like elements. But a subject-like element is not by that token a subject, especially if there are others which are subject-like in other respects. If we look for a less vacuous universal, we will not find it.

COPULAR CONSTRUCTIONS

In a dependency analysis, transitive and intransitive are special cases of a general schema:

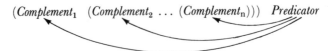

$$(Complement_1 \ (Complement_2 \ \ldots \ (Complement_n))) \quad Predicator$$

in which a single predicator is accompanied (the order is irrelevant) by zero or more dependent complements. When a lexeme allows no complement (like Latin PLUIT or English (TO) RAIN), it or its sense is zero-valent; if it allows just one it may be described as **monovalent** (English DISAPPEAR or Latin MORIOR 'die'), if two as **bivalent** (English KILL or Basque IKUSI 'see'), if three as **trivalent** (English GIVE in *No animal shall give aid to humans*), and so on. But so far we have not applied this schema to constructions with the copula. In the animals' first and last commandments:

> 1. Whatever goes upon two legs is an enemy.
> 7. All animals are equal.

the subject is once more a complement. But what exactly are the remaining elements?

One solution is to treat the form of BE as a predicator; the seventh commandment would thus be analysed as

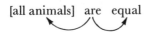

[all animals] are equal

where BE is a bivalent verb, but of a different class from KILL, WEAR, and so on. In the terminology of QUIRK *et al.* (pp. 820f.), it would be an Intensive verb, or a verb which takes intensive complementation, while the complementation of KILL and the like would be transitive or Monotransitive (*ibid.*, pp. 830f.). In this formulation, the term 'complementation' refers to the valency of verbs within their predicate: KILL is 'monotransitive' because its complementation comprises just a direct object; likewise GIVE is Ditransitive, in that its complementation comprises both a direct and an indirect object. In more traditional terms, the copula is seen as governing the predicative element (*equal, an enemy*), in the same sense that, in commandment 6, *shall kill* governs *any other animal*.

There are two arguments against such an analysis. In the first place, we have already remarked on the collocational link between a predicative adjective and a subject. This suggests a constructional relationship – between, for example, *equal* and *all animals* – which our diagram does not show. In the subject complement construction which we discussed in Chapter 1 (*It tastes nice, He sounded a fool*), there are restrictions relating the subject complement and the verb: for example, it would be unusual to say *His mother is turning old* or *The milk grew sour* (compared with *His mother is growing old* and *The milk turned sour*). But no such restrictions involve the copula BE. If a subject *s* can collocate with an adjective *a* – can collocate, that is, in any sentence with verbs such as TASTE, SOUND, TURN or GROW – then the collocation *s* + copula + *a* is also natural. Nor are there any special restrictions on the collocation of BE with a subject. So far as this form of evidence is concerned, we have no grounds, in *All animals are equal*, for establishing the dependency of either *equal* or *all animals* on *are*.

In the second place, an adjective can have semantic properties akin to valency. With OLD or SOUR the subject can be singular: *Boxer is old, This cream is sour*. But with EQUAL such a sentence would be very hard to interpret: *Any animal is equal* – but to who or to what? Only when the subject is at least notionally plural (*The cabinet are all equal*), or when two or more subjects are coordinated (*You and I are equal*), or with a *to*-phrase following (*A metre is roughly equal to a yard*), will the construction be complete. Likewise for SIMILAR or EQUIVALENT: *This book is similar* can be understood only under ellipsis ('similar to whatever we were talking about'). In this respect an adjective such as EQUAL is like a verb such as MEET. That too allows a plural or coordinate subject (*The pigs will meet, The politburo will meet, Squealer and Napoleon will meet*), or a singular subject with an object (*Squealer will meet Napoleon*); but for just one individual it does not make sense (*Squealer will meet*). An adjective such as OLD or LAZY can be compared to a strict intransitive such as VANISH. Just as the latter excludes an object, so there is no normal sentence *Squealer was lazy to us, Boxer was old at Napoleon*, or the like.

On this evidence it is the adjective and not the verb that serves as the controlling element in the construction. In terms of our schema, the predication is like this:

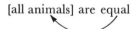

[all animals] are equal

with the predicative element in the role of predicator. A *to*-phrase would represent another complement (*A metre is equivalent to a yard*, with predicator *equivalent*). In commandments 1 and 2 the predicative element was a noun phrase: ⟨*Whatever goes upon two legs is*⟩ *an enemy*; ⟨*Whatever goes upon four legs, or has wings, is*⟩ *a friend*. We would accordingly treat the whole construction as dependent on the head nouns *enemy* and *friend*. In *Napoleon is our leader* the analogous relationship would be as follows:

Napoleon is [our leader]

– where, just as *No animal shall sleep* has as its predicator the verb or verb phrase *(shall) sleep*, so in this sentence the predicative role, or role of predicator, is played by the noun or noun phrase *(our) leader*.

The form of BE is then a marker. In scholastic and later grammars, up to at least the end of the eighteenth century, a verb is often treated as the combination of a participle and the copula: thus Latin *currit* represents *est currens*, English *runs* would represent *is (in a state of) running*. It is within this tradition, ultimately Aristotelian, that the term 'copula' has its origin. But instead of assimilating verbs to the pattern of an adjective or a noun, we may regard the copula as a means by which a predicator which is lexically non-verbal, and grammatically uninflected for tense and other verbal categories, is assimilated to a construction in which a verb is an essential element. In *It is raining*, the pronoun was seen as a marker by which a subject–predicate structure is imposed on a construction without complements. In *All animals are equal*, the copula BE is a marker by which an obligatory structure of verb plus complement:

Verb	*Complement*
are	equal

(QUIRK *et al.*'s 'intensive complementation') is imposed on a monovalent predicator:

Predicator
equal

which does not itself supply a verbal element.

This analysis might also be extended to sentences in which the verb 'to be' is construed with a Locative expression: *John was in the garden*, *Napoleon is outside*, and so on. At first sight there are restrictions linking the verb to the adverb or preposition. For example, one can say *John walked onto the lawn*, with a verb of motion WALK, but not *John is onto the lawn*, unless ONTO assumes a different sense (as in *John is onto the clue*). This would suggest that BE, like WALK, supplies a predicator which can take a locative complement. But there is another way of reading the evidence, by which, in *John was in the garden*, *in* would represent a further class of predicator to which ONTO, or ONTO in its ordinary sense, does not belong. The essence of the construction might be shown like this:

John [in [the garden]]

– where, since IN is non-verbal, the marker BE is again needed.

NOTES AND REFERENCES

For subject and predicate, and much else in this chapter, see LYONS, *Introduction*, Ch. 8; earlier discussion – and in spirit a good deal earlier – in M. Sandmann, *Subject and Predicate: a Contribution to the Theory of Syntax* (Edinburgh: Edinburgh University Press, 1954), especially Part 2, Chs. 1–2. It is instructive to compare a study by a modern philosopher: P. F. Strawson, *Subject and Predicate in Logic and Grammar* (London: Methuen, 1974).

For the 'psychological subject' see PAUL, pp. 124ff. and the brief critique by JESPERSEN, *Philosophy*, Ch. 11; textbook discussion (of 'psychological', 'grammatical' and 'logical' subjects) in HUDDLESTON, pp. 229ff. Recent work concerns the notion of 'theme' in functional sentence perspective. For representative studies see J. Firbas, 'On defining the theme in functional sentence analysis', *TLP*, 1 (1964), pp. 267–80; S. Kuno, 'Functional sentence perspective: a case study from Japanese and English', *LIn*, 3 (1972), pp. 269–320; also HALLIDAY, 'Transitivity and theme', Part 2, summarised in 'Options and functions in the English clause', *Brno Studies in English*, 8 (1969), pp. 81–8 (reprinted in HOUSEHOLDER (ed.), pp. 248–57); F. Daneš (ed.), *Papers on Functional Sentence Perspective* (Prague: Academia, 1974). For a good general discussion see LYONS, *Semantics*, 2, pp. 500ff. Note that this sense of 'theme' does not correspond to that of 'thematic relations' in, for example, CHOMSKY, *Essays*, pp. 6 *et passim*; the latter should be dropped.

For a standard traditional account of the subject see *OED*, s.v., §II.8; for 'indirect' vs. 'direct' object *ibid.*, s.v. 'indirect', §3.c, with Mason's definition (1881): 'the Indirect Object of a verb denotes that which is indirectly affected by an action, but is not the immediate object or product of it, as "Give *him* the book", "Make *me* a coat" '.

For valency see TESNIÈRE, pp. 238ff. (though a more general notion is already in DE GROOT, *Syntaxis*, pp. 114f., 154f., 242ff.). Later work is largely by Germanists, and is important both here and for Chapter 6. For early contributions see H.-J. Heringer, 'Wertigkeiten und nullwertige Verben im Deutschen', *Zeitschrift für deutsche Sprache*, 23 (1967), pp. 13–34; G. Helbig & W. Schenkel, *Wörterbuch zur Valenz und Distribution deutscher Verben*, 2nd edn

(Leipzig: VEB Verlag, 1973), pp. 11–92; also HELBIG (ed.), which has three papers by Soviet scholars. For a textbook account see BRINKER, pp. 91–118; valuable survey in KORHONEN. The model is extended to Latin by H. Happ: see 'Syntaxe latine et théorie de la valence: essai d'adaptation au latin des théories de Lucien Tesnière', in C. Touratier (ed.), *Linguistique et latin* (*Langages*, 50 (1978)), pp. 51–72, which I cite partly as a reference not in German; also his *Grundfragen einer Dependenz-Grammatik des Lateinischen* (Göttingen: Vandenhoeck & Ruprecht, 1976), though I find this very long for what it says. For a survey in English see T. Herbst, D. Heath & H.-M. Dederding, *Grimm's Grandchildren: Current Topics in German Linguistics* (London: Longman, 1980), Ch. 4; also H. Vater, 'Toward a generative dependency grammar', *Lingua*, 36 (1975), pp. 121–35 (discussion of relevant work in §3); S. R. Fink, *Aspects of a Pedagogical Grammar Based on Case Grammar and Valence Theory* (Tübingen: Niemeyer, 1977), pp. 6–25. Both Vater and Fink relate valency to Fillmore's concept of 'case frames' (FILLMORE and other references in notes to Chapter 1 above); see too Lyons's 'valency roles' and 'schemata' in semantics (LYONS, *Semantics*, 2, pp. 493–500). On a practical level, compare the grammatical classification of verbs in the *Oxford Advanced Learner's Dictionary of Current English*, 3rd edn by A. S. Hornby with the assistance of A. P. Cowie & J. Windsor Lewis (London: Oxford University Press, 1974) or the *Longman Dictionary of Contemporary English*, ed. P. Proctor *et al.* (London: Longman, 1978).

The dependency of the subject was proposed by Tesnière, contrary to most earlier grammarians: compare, for example, JESPERSEN, *Philosophy*, p. 97 (on successive 'subordination' in *The dog barks furiously*). For possible sources, for this as for Tesnière's diagramming technique, see E. Coseriu, 'Un précurseur méconnu de la syntaxe structurale: H. Tiktin', in *Recherches de linguistique: Hommages à Maurice Leroy* (Brussels: Éditions de l'Université de Bruxelles, 1980), pp. 49–62. Among recent proposals that of HERINGER, pp. 283ff. deserves comment (also in BRINKER, pp. 105f.). By Heringer's rules the predicator is in a relation of 'interdependence' to each of its complements; this is defined earlier (p. 107) as one of mutual presupposition between forms (see notes to Chapter 3 above). But it has a higher 'value index' ('Bewertungsindex', pp. 287ff.) in that (1) it enters into more such relations; (2) non-complements do stand in a relation of dependence (unilateral presupposition) to it. Hence it is central to the construction, and Tesnière's insight is said to have been put on a sound basis. But centrality must have been assumed; otherwise, why is the subject not interdependent with the objects, or non-complements dependent on each of the complements?

The term 'complement' is discussed in the notes to Chapter 6.

My 'zero-valent' has the sense of 'avalent' (TESNIÈRE, p. 279 and later literature). For the empty *it* (German *es*, French *il*, etc.) see JESPERSEN, *Syntax*, pp. 101f. (examples on p. 37 *et passim*); briefly in JESPERSEN, *Philosophy*, p. 25 (qualified p. 241f.); in the context of valency theory, Heringer, 'Wertigkeiten und nullwertige Verben im Deutschen', §2. Jespersen refers to earlier studies, especially that of K. Brugmann, *Ursprung des Scheinsubjekts 'es'* (Leipzig, 1914), which I have not seen. For previous discussion of subjectless sentences see PAUL, pp. 130–3.

The universality of the subject is assumed as often as it is challenged. For one recent view see E. L. Keenan, 'Towards a universal definition of "subject"', in C. N. Li (ed.), *Subject and Topic* (New York: Academic Press, 1976), pp. 303–33; criticised by D. E. Johnson, 'On Keenan's definition of "subject of"', *LIn*, 8 (1977), pp. 673–92. For so-called 'ergative languages' see R. M. W. Dixon, 'Ergativity', *Lg*, 55 (1979), pp. 59–138, which is now the best introduction to the topic. Dixon's 'pivot' (§6) is very like my 'subject as opposed to predicate' (subject₂); see, in particular, his discussion of the passive and 'anti-passive' (pp. 118ff.); also his critique of Keenan's definition (pp. 110–12). His 'subject' is universal, since it is defined by a notional criterion of 'potential agency' (pp. 108f.; syntactic consequences, pp. 112–18). For Basque ergatives as subjects see, in particular, S. R. Anderson, 'On the notion of subject in ergative languages', in Li (ed.), *Subject and Topic*, pp. 1–23 (Basque examples but, as throughout the paper, with no documentation, pp. 11–12). This case is accepted by Dixon (p. 129, n. 101); but note too his acute remark on p. 97 (top), on a semantic reason for identifying agent and intransitive subject in a purpose construction. On the term 'ergative', it is worth remarking that the *OED* definition (new supplement) is wrong; nor is it 'generally employed' of a relation between sentences such as English *The stone moved* and *John moved the stone* (LYONS, *Introduction*, p. 352).

For a quite different case in which the criteria are in dispute compare P. Schachter, 'The subject in Philippine languages: topic, actor, actor–topic, or none of the above?', in Li (ed.), *Subject and Topic*, pp. 491–518 and, for the opposite interpretation, M. Coyaud, 'Thème et sujet en tagalog. (Comparaisons avec le mandarin, le coréen et le japonais)', *BSL*, 74 (1979), pp. 113–39. Schachter's article may usefully be read with his review, in *Lg*, 53 (1977), pp. 707–11, of Teresita V. Ramos, *The Case System of Tagalog Verbs*.

The volume edited by Li is neatly summarised in an uncritical review by Pamela Munro, *Lg*, 55 (1979), pp. 372–80.

For the sense of QUIRK *et al.*'s 'intensive' see HALLIDAY, 'Transitivity and theme', Part 1, an intensive complement 'having, by definition, the same referent as another element in the clause' (p. 63); Halliday opposes 'intensive' and 'extensive', as subtypes both of complements and clauses (pp. 40ff.). Note that QUIRK *et al.* identify the copular construction with that of a lexical verb and subject complement (as in *It tastes nice*). For scholastic and later theories of the copula see G. A. Padley, *Grammatical Theory in Western Europe 1500–1700: the Latin Tradition* (Cambridge: Cambridge University Press, 1976), *passim* (see index); it is described by Scaliger (Padley, p. 205) as a 'nota coniunctionis' ('mark of linkage'). My treatment (here and in Chapter 12) follows that of LYONS, *Introduction*, pp. 322ff., at least in essentials. For parallels between predicative adjectives and verbs see G. Lakoff, *Irregularity in Syntax* (New York: Holt, Rinehart & Winston, 1970), pp. 115–33; Lakoff's conclusion – unwarranted in my view – is that the classes are identical. Predicative noun and prepositional phrases are discussed similarly by K. Allan, 'Complement noun phrases and prepositional phrases, adjectives and verbs', *FL*, 10 (1973), pp. 377–97. For predicative adjectives in valency theory see HERINGER, pp. 163–5; BRINKER, pp. 107f.; KORHONEN, pp. 170f.

In recent work Lyons distinguishes an 'equative' (*The chairman was Bill*) from an 'ascriptive' (*The chairman was foolish, … was an ass*) (LYONS, *Semantics*, 2, pp. 469ff.). But is this syntactic in English? The 'ambiguity' of *John is the author of this book*, which Lyons treats as grammatical (p. 472), can surely be explained by different sentence perspectives (in the sense of Firbas or Kuno, cited earlier).

6
Objects and adverbs

Distinction drawn by tradition; by various modern scholars. Complements vs. peripheral elements; predicative syntagms.

Complements and peripheral elements: Criteria: of participancy; from collocational restrictions; of obligatoriness; of latency; of exclusion. Indeterminacy of constructions and types (indirect object, directionals, locatives). Marginal codification.

Adjuncts: Conflicts of notional and other criteria (durationals, adverbs of manner). Adjuncts distinct from both peripheral elements and complements; indeterminacy of adjuncts vs. peripheral elements.

The traditional predicate consists of the predicator, in the sense of Chapter 5, with or without various other elements. Of these some are governed by the predicator: for example, in *I saw him yesterday* the verb *saw* governs the pronoun *him*. Such elements are typically nouns or noun phrases, or other units which are treated as their equivalent. For example, in *I said that I was coming* the verb governs a clause *that I was coming* which, for that reason, is often called a Noun Clause. Other elements are not governed, but modify either the verb or the whole. Thus in *I saw him yesterday* the verb and object are together modified by *yesterday*. Such elements are typically adverbs or adverbial units. For example, in *I saw him while I was in London* the place of *yesterday* is taken by the clause *while I was in London*, which for that reason is called an Adverbial Clause. The constituency structure could be shown as follows:

$$\begin{bmatrix} \text{saw} & \text{him} \\ \text{said [that I was coming]} \end{bmatrix} \begin{bmatrix} \text{yesterday} \\ \text{[while I was in London]} \end{bmatrix}$$

where *him* or the noun clause form a syntagm with *saw* or *said*, and *yesterday* or the *while*-clause are higher constituents.

A distinction of this sort is drawn by most scholars, but with striking differences in substance and in terminology. According to TESNIÈRE, the object *him* would be an 'actant', which refers to an 'acteur', or participating entity, in the process of seeing. It is the 'actants' that

121

make up the valency of a verb; so, in *I gave you the book yesterday*, the 'actants' are *I* as subject, *(the) book* as direct object, and *you* as indirect object, which are the dependents required by the trivalent GIVE. In Tesnière's account, the notion is limited to these three functions. An adverb or adverbial is not an 'actant' but a 'circonstant', referring to the setting or 'circonstances' in which a process or act takes place. So, in *I gave you the book yesterday*, the adverb is a 'circonstant' which indicates the temporal setting for the act of giving.

According to QUIRK *et al.*, whose usage was referred to briefly in the last chapter, both objects belong to the 'complementation' of the verb. An adverb like *yesterday* does not; instead it represents one type of 'adjunct', another being that of, for example, *clearly* in *I saw him clearly*. But the scope of complementation is wider than Tesnière's 'actants'. For example, *I put the meat on the table* would be said to have an adverbial complement *on the table*; the complementation of *put*, or the valency of the lexeme PUT, includes both an object and a locative. Similarly, *I went to London* would have a locative complement *to London*. These types are prominent in QUIRK *et al.*'s preliminary list (pp. 343f.), though a detailed survey of 'Types of Complementation' (pp. 819ff.) does not devote separate sections to them.

In a view once held by CHOMSKY (*Aspects*, Ch. 2), a distinction should be made between a 'predicate-phrase', which would include the whole of *saw him yesterday*, and a smaller constituent called the 'verb phrase', which would consist of *saw* and *him* alone. The category of *him* is again an element in valency restrictions; in Chomsky's terms, the relationship to such a constituent is part of the 'strict subcategorisation' of the verb (*ibid.*, pp. 95f.). But according to his rule (p. 102), the verb phrase also includes 'direction' elements (such as *to London* in *I went to London* or *I brought it to London*); also some 'place' elements (such as *in London* in *He remained in London*); also expressions of 'duration' and 'frequency' (*for three hours* in *It lasted for three hours*, *three times* in *He won three times*). All these belong to a category labelled 'prepositional-phrase'; this might also cover indirect objects, which Chomsky does not mention. The verb phrase also includes 'manner' adverbs, such as *clearly* in *I saw him clearly*.

Another formulation is that of Longacre, who distinguishes the 'nucleus' of a clause, such as *I saw him* in *I saw him yesterday*, from its 'periphery'; in *I saw him clearly yesterday*, the latter would include both *yesterday* and *clearly*. Another is basic to the theory of 'relational grammar', one of the more recent offshoots of transformationalism. In it a verb takes up to three 'terms': subject, direct object, indirect object. Other elements are non-terms, or are 'oblique'. In both these accounts the division echoes that of Tesnière. But in more recent work on valency or dependency theory the range of 'actants' or 'actant'-like elements is greatly extended, on a principle similar to that adopted by Chomsky.

It is hard to beat a clear path out of this tangle. Let us begin, however, with a broad distinction between the **complements** controlled by the predicator, in the sense already introduced in Chapter 5, and other elements which we will describe as **peripheral**. The predicator and its complements form a predication or **predicative syntagm**; so, in *I saw him yesterday* we have a predicative syntagm

[I saw him]

exemplifying a **predicative construction** in which the predicator is related to an object – forming perhaps a unit like the traditional predicate:

[I [saw him]]

– as well as a subject. A peripheral element depends on the predication as a whole:

I saw him yesterday

just as, in *Obviously he did it*, the sentence-modifying adverb *obviously* was related to the whole of *he did it* (last section of Chapter 4).

If we start from this model our main problem is to determine the limits of predicative constructions, especially with respect to locatives and other elements on which the authorities we have cited disagree. But we will find at the end that a simple binary typology, of complements and non-complements, will cover only part of the facts.

COMPLEMENTS AND PERIPHERAL ELEMENTS

Our authorities agree in placing a direct object, such as *him* in *I saw him yesterday*, in a different category from at least some temporal expressions, such as *yesterday*. There are five criteria by which this might be justified, all of which spring naturally from what we have already said, here or in previous chapters.

(1) The first is notional and arises from Tesnière's discussion of 'actants'. In Tesnière's account, the predicative syntagm (or 'noeud verbal') expresses a kind of performance ('tout un petit drame') which, like any other, may be characterised by its setting and the behaviour of the performers (TESNIÈRE, p. 102). The direct object readily refers to a performer: thus *Bill kissed his wife*, with performers Bill and his wife, or *David slew Goliath*. Therefore it is an 'actant' or, we will say in English, a **participant**. An adverbial of time does not refer to a performer; instead it sets a performance in context. Therefore it is a 'circonstant' or **circumstantial** element. The criterion, then, is that participants are complements and circumstantial elements are not.

This does not mean that direct objects always refer to performers. In *He loves music* or *He hates solitude* it would be fanciful to see a drama in which music or solitude engage in a performance with the relevant 'he'. But the syntactic role of *music* or *solitude* is the same as that of *Goliath* in *David slew Goliath* or *his wife* in *Bill kissed his wife*; there is no evidence, of the sort which we discussed in Chapter 1, which would warrant separating their constructions. Therefore they too are complements, by virtue not of their own semantic role but of the typical role, or simply a potential role, of the syntactic element. If taken in this way, a notional criterion is of considerable importance. For syntax has its basis in a codification of semantic relationships. We do not expect each category of meaning to be treated distinctly; therefore many elements, such as the direct object, are notionally heterogeneous. But when we do establish distinctions we expect them to make notional sense. For a major division between types of element, as between complements and non-complements, we expect it even more.

(2) The second criterion is based on collocational restrictions. With GIVE, for example, it is more usual to talk of 'giving protection' than of 'giving defence', or of 'giving help' than of 'giving' (as compared, say, to 'expecting') 'rescue'. These and other restrictions (such as those on TOAST and MEAT, GRILL and BREAD and so on, which we cited in Chapter 1) establish a direct constructional link between the object and the predicator. But no collocational restrictions affect adverbials of the class of *yesterday*. We can find absurdities of sense,

naturally: for example, it is difficult to think of contexts in which one might reasonably say *I will see him yesterday*. But they can be predicted from the general meaning of the lexemes and the morphosyntactic properties associated with them – thus, in this instance, from the past time reference of YESTERDAY and the future reference either of WILL or of the periphrastic *will see*. Restrictions such as that on GIVE or RESCUE, or on BAKE and CHESTNUT (Chapter 1), do not follow from the meanings which these lexemes have in other combinations.

(3) Thirdly, there are sentences in which a direct object cannot be dropped. Thus one can say *Bill got the prize* but not simply *Bill got*, *I am seeing him tomorrow* but not simply *I am seeing tomorrow*, and so on. So too for clauses in the object position: for example, one can say *I suggested that he should come*, but not simply *I suggested*. With these lexemes, or these senses of these lexemes, the object noun or noun clause realises an **obligatory** element. The criterion, then, is that a complement must be obligatory with at least some predicators.

QUIRK *et al.* cite similar examples as the only evidence for complementation (p. 344). But dropping can be a hard test to control. We must bear in mind the different senses of lexemes: thus SEE has different senses in *I can see you this afternoon* ('I can meet you' or 'I can give you an appointment') and in the intransitive *I can see*. We must also bear in mind the possibility of ellipsis. With WATCH the direct object can again be dropped: *Are you watching football tonight?* or *Are you watching tonight?* Nevertheless the element remains latent – compare again *I was watching* and *I was reading* (Chapter 2). We might therefore define two senses of 'obligatory'. In the stronger sense it means 'obligatory even in incomplete sentences'; in those terms the direct object is an obligatory element with GET (or with the sense of GET in *Bill got the prize*), but an **optional** element with WATCH. In the weaker sense it means 'obligatory only in complete sentences'; in these terms the direct object is obligatory with both GET and WATCH, but optional with the basic sense of READ. Just as the second use of 'obligatory' is weaker than the first, so the first use of 'optional' is weaker than the second. At least some types of time adverbial, such as that of *yesterday* or of the clause *while I was in London*, are optional with all predicators, weakly at least. Thus alongside *I can't see you this afternoon* there is also the sentence *I can't see you*, alongside *Did you watch it while you were in London?* there is the simple *Did you watch it?*, and so forth.

(4) The fourth point is that a direct object can indeed be latent.

Thus, to take some fresh examples, one may also say *I didn't finish* ($\langle$sc. *the job*$\rangle$, $\langle$sc. *the book I was reading*$\rangle$, . . .), *I didn't know* ($\langle$sc. *the solution*$\rangle$, $\langle$sc. *that they were coming*$\rangle$, . . .), *They noticed at once* ($\langle$sc. *that our car was new*$\rangle$, $\langle$sc. *where the door was*$\rangle$, . . .), and so on. Such sentences are incomplete; what we are calling a complement is the sort of element that will complete them.

The status of time adverbials is slightly problematic. In many cases they are optional in the strong sense; thus if we take a sentence such as

> Do your children play chess on Sundays?

and drop the adverbial *on Sundays*:

> Do your children play chess?

we obtain another sentence in which no element is lacking. If a speaker asks this out of the blue, the person he is addressing does not wonder what particular time is meant. Suppose, however, that he is greeted like this:

> Good morning! I'm afraid I was very drunk

The speaker means that he was drunk on some occasion known to his hearer, say at a party they were at the previous evening. If one did not grasp this one might well ask for an explanation ('Sorry, when?'). In Tesnièrean terms, the performance referred to cannot be identified unless the circumstantial element is understood. This form of incompleteness varies with the tense and aspect of the verb: compare *I bought some books*, in the past, with *I've bought some books*, in the present perfect. But by the tests assumed in Chapter 2, an adverbial such as *yesterday* or *last night*, in *I bought some books yesterday* or *I'm afraid I was very drunk last night*, would also meet our criterion.

But there are two vital qualifications. In the case of objects the effect varies with the lexeme of the predicator (GET, WATCH, READ, and so on). But it is constant for all types of clause – thus in a clause with *while* (*He fell asleep while he was watching*), in a relative clause (*I asked one man who didn't know*), and so forth. This confirms the syntactic link between a complement and its controlling element. In the case of time adverbials the effect is constant for all lexemes, but holds only for some types of clause. In a relative or temporal clause it disappears: compare *I asked a man who was very drunk*, or *He waited while I bought some books*. Thus no necessary link is demonstrated.

126

(5) Finally, instead of dropping elements, we can make tests of addition or insertion. Thus we can add a time adverbial to *I was watching*: *I was watching on Sunday*. Or we could add an object (*I was watching television*), which could also be inserted before *on Sunday*: *I was watching television on Sunday*. But objects cannot be added to every objectless sentence. Examples with VANISH were mentioned in the preceding chapter (*The men vanished* but not *The men vanished their clothes, The men vanished too much whisky*, and so on). Likewise one can say *The men were striking*, in the sense that they were on strike, but not *The men were striking the factory*, or *The men were striking their employers*, unless the verb changes its meaning. With VANISH and that sense of STRIKE the direct object is an **excluded** element, just as with GET, for example, it was obligatory. The criterion, then, is that a complement must be excluded by at least one class of predicators.

A time adverbial is never excluded. Thus we could add *on Sunday* to a sentence where the verb is zero-valent (*It rains on Sunday*), or trivalent (*No animal shall give aid to humans on Sunday*), or followed by a clause (*I shall know what has happened on Sunday, I shall know on Sunday what has happened*), and so on, free of any restriction but the need to make sense. This too classes the element as peripheral.

The results obtained by the last four criteria may be seen as confirmation of a distinction that is initially drawn on notional grounds, between the specific relationship of participants and the lack of it in non-participants. When all five coincide, there are no problems. The difficulties arise partly in cases where the notional category is intermediate, partly because the other criteria clash, and partly because a third type of relation (that of adverbs of manner and the like) must also be distinguished. But bound up with these there is the fundamental problem of identifying constructional elements. A direct object is not obligatory in every sentence (criterion 3); nor does it always refer to a performer (criterion 1); nor is every direct object subject to specific collocational restrictions (criterion 2); nor does every transitive verb allow it to be latent (criterion 4). In each case a subset of the forms which represent an element (those complements which do refer to a performer, those which do show collocational restrictions, ...) are criterial for the element in general. But this assumes that 'the element in general' can be identified. Are we always certain that form *a* has the same construction as form *b*? The answer is no, as we remarked for instrumental phrases (end of Chapter 1). This

127

also raises problems for the criterion of exclusion (criterion 5). On the one hand, we could argue that COME excludes an instrumental, as *He came with a stick* means something else. Therefore the instrumental is a distinct syntactic element (the issue of Chapter 1) and, by this criterion at least, a complement. On the other hand, we could argue that *with a stick* represents the same syntactic element in both *He came with a stick* and *He hit me with a stick*. A phrase of that class could always be added; therefore its role is peripheral.

In English grammar, problems of this sort arise with locatives especially. It will be recalled that these are just the elements on which our authorities most clearly differ. But the indirect object is already slightly less straightforward. Notionally it is a participant: in *They sold food to the enemy* or *They sold the enemy some food*, the enemy are performers entering into the transaction of selling. It is also excluded by some predicators: thus one would not say *They are seeing the candidates to us* or *They are seeing us the candidates*, *He wore a new suit to me* or *He wore me a new suit*. It can also be latent. *I gave away £10* means simply that I gave it away – to who or what is immaterial. But *I gave £10* means that I gave it to someone or to something understood: ⟨sc. *to the Red Cross*⟩, ⟨sc. *to the Staff Christmas Fund*⟩, and so on. Nor could a man say out of the blue:

Good morning! I have decided to bequeath my house

If he expects one to comment, he would have to explain what beneficiary he has in mind.

On the same evidence, an indirect object can be either optional (as with the phrasal GIVE AWAY) or obligatory in at least the weaker sense (as with BEQUEATH or the simple GIVE). But there are no verbs with which it is obligatory in the strong sense; at least if there are, I have failed to find them. It is equally hard to find collocational restrictions. For GIVE we cited restrictions on the direct object (of HELP or PROTECTION rather than DEFENCE or RESCUE); but are there similar restrictions on who, for example, one may talk of giving help to? Of course, there are collocations which might not immediately make sense: *I gave protection to anxiety* or *He bequeathed his house to Thursday*. But we need no specific lexical statement to explain why. In this and other respects the indirect object stands in a looser relationship. With a transitive verb X we often find a specialised sense, meaning 'to *x y*' in particular. Thus *He drinks too much* will typically mean that he drinks too much alcohol, *Thou shalt not kill* is taken to mean that one must not kill other human beings, *They are busy decorating* means that they are decorating the inside of their house, and so on. But I do not know of a basically ditransitive verb which can also be construed, without even a latent indirect object, in a specialised sense of 'to *x* . . . to *y*'. It is also common for direct objects to be incorporated in compound verbs (such as (TO) FOX-HUNT or (TO) FUND-RAISE). With indirect objects this is at best rare: a possible (TO) SELF-ADDRESS (compare the established adjective in *a self-addressed envelope*) is the nearest analogue that has been suggested to me.

This shows us no more, perhaps, than that an indirect object is 'indirect'. Notionally it remains an object, and this status is supported by criteria at least of latency (criterion 4) and of exclusion (criterion 5). But the element shows resemblances to others that are more circumstantial. The construction of *I gave it to Jill* or *I gave Jill a present* is usually distinguished from that of, say, *I made it for Jill* or *I made Jill a present*; where *(to) Jill* is an object, *(for) Jill* has a role that is called Benefactive. In traditional terms, the act of giving passes across to Jill as well as to 'it' or the present, while that of making passes across to the latter only. In Tesnière's metaphor, Jill would be an actor in one performance, but is in the wings for the other. Now on every account a benefactive is peripheral. It is never strongly obligatory; there is no scope for collocational restrictions; it would be hard to demonstrate a case of latency. Nor are there predicators which exclude this or similar phrases: compare *I would vanish completely for* JILL, *For Jill all animals are equal* (meaning 'For Jill's sake . . .'), and so on. But let us imagine that the constructions are not distinguished. By the criterion of latency both elements would be complements, on the strength of examples like *I gave £10*. But by the criterion of exclusion both would be peripheral.

Nor is the distinction quite so easily established. The indirect object has two realisations in English: with *to* in a position following a direct object (*They sold food to the enemy*), or without *to* in a position preceding it (*They sold the enemy food*). The second structure is often taken as a test for the element, as opposed to other *to*-phrases. Another test is based on the second passive: thus one may also say *The enemy were sold food* (with the same collocation of SELL, FOOD and ENEMY), *Jill was given a present*, and so on. But with benefactives the results are confused. With MOW or SWEEP a second passive would be wrong: *I mowed the lawn for my sister* but not *My sister was mown* (or *was mowed*) *the lawn, I have swept the carpet for you* but not *You have now been swept the carpet.* A structure without *for* would at best be awkward: *I have mowed you the lawn, I swept my sister the whole of her front garden.* With MAKE the latter is quite normal (*I am making her a footstool*); but *She is being made a footstool* would usually be understood differently. With SAVE one could readily say both *I saved Jill some petrol* and *Jill was saved some petrol.* In this respect, ⟨*I saved some petrol*⟩ *for Jill* is more like an indirect object than ⟨*I mowed the lawn*⟩ *for Jill*; also than the *to*-phrase in, say, *They donated £10 to the Red Cross*, since it would be less usual to say *They donated the Red Cross £10.*

It can also be difficult to find the boundary with Chomsky's 'direction' element. *I gave some books to Jill* is not unlike *I sent some books to Jill*; that too will meet both tests (*I sent Jill some books, Jill was sent some books*). In meaning SEND is similar to DESPATCH: thus *I despatched some books to my sister.* But is it so natural to say *My sister was despatched some books*, or *I despatched my sister some books?* In such cases it is often hard to trust one's judgment: for example, would one say *I carried Jill the shopping* (meaning that I took it over to her)? Perhaps so; but it seems less likely than, for instance, *I brought Jill the shopping.* Each of these verbs takes other phrases which refer to places: *I sent the books to New York* (where *I sent New York the books* could refer only to an office or institution in it); *I despatched them to his new address; I brought their mother to his house.* Does *I despatched some books to Jill* belong with these or with *I gave some books to Jill?* If the former then what of, say, *I presented some books to Jill?* For that too the tests are doubtful (*I presented Jill some books, Jill was presented some books*). This does not mean that the elements should not be distinguished. But the indirect object tends to merge with others that are not participants; as Tesnière observes, it shares something of the air of a 'circonstant' (TESNIÈRE, p. 127).

With locatives and directionals the problems are more serious. On the one hand, they are often purely circumstantial: in *I bought some books in London*, the locative *in London* merely supplies a setting for the transaction. The phrase could be added to any sentence where it makes sense: thus *All animals are equal in London, It is raining in London, I gave it to my sister in London* ('when she was in London'), and so on. By the same token neither the predicator and *in*, nor the predicator and *London*, would be subject to collocational restrictions. In such examples the locative is optional (*I bought some books*) – and strongly optional, at least in some types of clause (compare again *He waited while I bought some books*). All this suggests that the predicative syntagm should be limited to the first three elements:

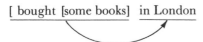

[bought [some books] in London

with *in London* peripheral.

On the other hand, there are directionals which are not circumstantial. In *I threw a stone at some pigeons* the action passes across to both the stone and the pigeons; they are being thrown at, just as it is being thrown. Other locatives are intermediate: in *He dumped his coat on the table*, the locative refers neither to an actor nor to the scenery in which the dumping is done. In Tesnière's metaphor, both coat and table are props for the dumper. Such phrases can also be obligatory: thus *I stuck it in the fridge* but not *I stuck it*, except with another sense of STICK. Likewise a directional with an intransitive: *I got to New York last Saturday*, but not simply *I got on Saturday* or *I got*. In the sense of 'arriving' GET requires an adverb or adverbial of place, just as, in another sense, it requires a direct object (*I got a present on Saturday*) or, in yet another, both (*I'll get it to New York quite easily*). In similar cases the adverbial can be latent. Thus one might send the message: *I'll be arriving on Saturday*. But the hearer must know where it is that I will be arriving; only with a special and unusual sense (I will 'arrive' or make my name in the world) would it be syntactically complete. A locative might perhaps be latent with PUT: *I told you to put the* BOOKS ⟨sc. *on the table, in the dustbin, . . .*⟩, *not my overcoat*.

We must also revise our findings with respect to collocational restrictions. With PLACE, for instance, it is easy to use IN or ON (⟨*I placed it*⟩ *in my study* or *on my desk*), but INTO or ONTO would be decidedly less usual (compare *I placed it carefully onto the exact spot* with *I lowered it carefully onto the exact spot*). With SET they would be even more so: ⟨*I set it*⟩ *on my desk*, not *onto my desk*. For verbs such as PUT or STICK the tendency is less strong: *Stick it in the fridge* is possibly more natural (also *Put it on the fire*), but *Stick it into the fridge* is not strikingly odd. With some, such as CHUCK or DUMP, there seems no preference either way: one can say ⟨*I chucked it*⟩ *in* or *into* ⟨*the fire*⟩ and similarly ⟨*I dumped it*⟩ *on* or *onto* ⟨*the table*⟩. But finally there are others, such as CART or SHOVEL, for which the tendency is clearly the opposite. One would say ⟨*He carted it*⟩ *onto* not *on* ⟨*the table*⟩, unless, of course, one means that the table was somehow used for carting (compare *He carted it on his bicycle*); likewise ⟨*They shovelled it*⟩ into not *in* ⟨*his sitting room*⟩, unless the phrase is once more purely circumstantial, with the room forming the surroundings rather than the receptacle.

Similar restrictions were invoked in Chapter 1, for the adverbial interpretation of *Leave the meat in the kitchen*. Together with the evidence of latency and obligatoriness, they suggest analyses such as the following:

I stuck it [in the fridge]

where the adverbial, like the object, is an element in the predicative construction. A similar pattern is suggested by restrictions on ARRIVE (*I arrived in London* not *I arrived into London*), on the corresponding use of GET (*He got to New York* not, in this sense, *He got at New York*), and so forth. If we took these on their own, the structure would again be like this:

I arrived [in London]

with the complements including both the subject and the adverbial. But this is the same phrase, *in London*, that, in *I bought some books in London*, was said to be peripheral. Which form of analysis is right? Or are they both right?

The basic question is whether we are dealing with a single construction, or with two or more distinct functions. If one, the element is peripheral by the criterion of exclusion (criterion 5), but a complement by those of obligatoriness and latency (criteria 3 and 4) and by virtue of collocational restrictions (criterion 2); for, again, we must merely show that there are cases where the evidence is positive, not that it is always so. But by distinguishing two elements the conflict can be made to vanish. Verbs such as THROW or ARRIVE would take a locative complement; this would sometimes be non-circumstantial (*I threw a stone at some pigeons*), and by the next three tests goes clearly with the participants. We would also limit it to certain predicators: to forms of STICK but not of BUY, of ARRIVE but not of DIE, and so on. With all other predicators the phrase would be peripheral: *It is raining in London, They painted off campus, We had dinner out of town*. It would then be peripheral by all criteria; for if any test were positive we would not assign it to that function.

If the distinction is accepted we can easily find both in the same sentence. An example such as

I keep it in the fridge in London

has one interpretation with *in London* modifying *fridge* ('the fridge which is in London'). But there is also an adverbial interpretation ('... in the fridge when I am in London') which would suggest a structure like this:

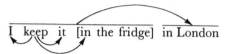

where the first locative is a complement but the second, as shown by the arc above the line, is peripheral. We might also adduce ambiguities. *He carried his umbrella home* could describe a journey with the purpose of transferring the umbrella; home, then, is the place to which he took it. For that interpretation we might argue that the structure should be

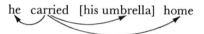

with *home* again part of the predication. (Compare *He brought his umbrella home* or *He led his daughter home*.) But the sentence could also mean that, on his way home, he carried an umbrella. So, we might argue for another structure in which the locative is peripheral:

– compare, for example, *He wore his overcoat home*.

But we would then have serious problems in deciding how particular cases should be analysed. In the fourth of the commandments which we discussed in Chapter 5:

No animal shall sleep in a bed

the locative can once more be dropped:

No animal shall sleep

– the shorter sentence being equally complete. Therefore the phrase might be peripheral: compare *I am never happy in a bed* or *I always get insomnia in a bed*. But let us consider the meaning of *shall sleep*. To 'sleep in a bed' could mean to get some sleep; the bed is merely the scenery in which this takes place. That is a natural interpretation if the verb is stressed:

No animal shall SLEEP in a bed

– or, with *his* in place of *a*:

No animal shall SLEEP in his bed

But it could also mean that the bed is used as a prop for spending the night in. If the nucleus is on *bed*:

No animal shall sleep in a BED

we might argue that SLEEP has a different sense, with which the locative is obligatory. Unlike the bare intransitive (*No animal shall sleep*), the commandment might still be broken, or there would be grounds for arguing whether it had or had not been broken, if the animal had never actually slept. Then perhaps there is a second structure with a locative complement: compare, for example, *He lives in a bed*? Or is that perhaps the only structure? It is hard to say how much weight this nuance should carry.

Similar uncertainties arise for phrases with a directional meaning. In *I got as far as Crewe* we would establish a complement, as in our earlier example *I got to New York*. In *I slept as far as Crewe* the same phrase would be peripheral: compare *They sang hymns as far as Crewe, I read the newspaper as far as Crewe, No animal shall drink alcohol as far as Crewe*, and so on. Then which construction have we in, for example, *I cycled as far as Crewe*? From one angle this is like the circumstantial interpretation of *He carried his umbrella home*: on the way to Crewe what I did was cycle. But from another angle its interpretation is goal-like: it was as far as Crewe that my cycling took me. The activity described is the same, and a mere change of focus tips our judgment one way or the other. Likewise for *I flew to New York*, compared with *I got to New York* and *I wore my overcoat to New York*. With FROM we would establish a complement in, for example, *He was expelled from Eton*: the bare *He was expelled* requires a 'somewhere' (*from Eton, from the Soviet Union*) to be understood. But the phrase can also be peripheral: *I am writing this letter from Eton, He will read it to you from Eton, The noise could be heard from Eton*, and so on. Then what of, say, *I posted the letter from Eton*? Does this mean that Eton formed the surroundings 'from which' it was posted, or was Eton one term in the letter's movement 'from' there 'to' somewhere else? With no supporting test we have no way of drawing the notional line.

This does not mean that the distinction should be repudiated. For it at least has the advantage of bringing our criteria into agreement. But the status of a locative or directional complement, both in its merging with the indirect object (*I threw it at the pigeons* versus *I gave it to the pigeons*) and in the further problems which we have just encountered, is an especially awkward case of marginal codification. In an example such as the following:

> (a) I told it to my brother

my brother refers to a person and not a place; for that and other reasons we assume that *to my brother* is a complement. We also assume that *a* has a different grammar from, for example, *b*:

> (b) I carted it to Manchester

in that *to Manchester* is locative. Nevertheless we found intermediate cases:

> (c) I despatched it to my brother

where the evidence is less decisive. If the locative in *b* is treated as a complement, then its grammar is in turn distinct from that of example *d*:

> (d) I wore it to Manchester

where it would be peripheral. But again there are intermediate cases – for example:

> (e) I pedalled it to Manchester

– where the constructions would merge. Now if *c* is intermediate between *a* and *b*:

$$a \rightarrow c \rightarrow b$$

and *e* intermediate between *b* and *d*:

$$b \rightarrow e \rightarrow d$$

is *b* itself, with the putative complement, more than one point on a

135

single gradation:

$$a \to c \to b \to e \to d$$

between a participant and an element that is purely peripheral?

It is not surprising that grammarians should vacillate. If we distinguish *b* from *d* we are distinguishing roles alone; the words and phrases which can fulfil them (*home, in bed, to Manchester, there,* and so on) are largely if not wholly the same. Since both can be realised in the same position (after the verb in *He lived in London* or *He disappeared in London,* after the direct object in *He put it on the table* or *He had a heart attack on the table,* and so on), we are left with a mass of boundary cases, subtle ambiguities, and gradience generally. If we do not make the distinction we are left with an element which our criteria classify both ways. In neither case can the problem of marginality be avoided.

ADJUNCTS

Of the adverbs or adverbials mentioned at the beginning of this chapter, two more raise problems of theoretical interest. One is the expression of duration in, for example, *It lasted for three hours,* and the other the adverb of manner in, for example, *I saw him clearly.*

In the former case the problem is merely that such expressions can be obligatory. Notionally they are circumstantial; at least it is clear that they are not participants. It would be hard to find collocational restrictions – for example, to find verbs whose forms go readily with *for* (*for three hours*) but not with *throughout* (⟨*He waited*⟩ *throughout the night*), or with *overnight* but not with *forever* (⟨*They will stay*⟩ *overnight,* ⟨*They might remain*⟩ *forever*). Nor are there obvious cases of exclusion: compare *It snowed for three hours, All animals are equal throughout August, They won every battle for a century, She fed them rice pudding the whole week,* and so on for whatever valency we choose. If particular combinations seem less likely to be uttered (*He will be murdered for three years* or *He passed away through the night*), a notional explanation will suffice. These expressions also fail to meet the test of latency, especially if we require (as for the non-durational *on Sundays, yesterday,* and so on) that it should hold for every type of clause.

Yet with LAST, in particular, they do not seem to be truly optional. If one can say *The race lasted,* it must mean that it lasted an unusually long time – compare:

It did LAST, didn't it?

with the verb emphasised. Just as DRINK can have the special sense of 'to drink alcohol' or 'to drink alcohol to excess', so we might see this as a special sense corresponding to what might otherwise be a verb plus an adverbial. In that one respect, an expression of duration has a 'completing' function. Nor can we assume that in *It continued for three hours* and *It continued yesterday*, or *It snowed for three hours yesterday* and *It snowed yesterday for three hours*, there is a syntactic as well as a semantic difference in the roles which the adverbials play. If the construction of each pair is the same, we must also qualify our statement earlier in this chapter, that an element such as *yesterday* or *on Sundays* is always weakly optional.

With an adverb of manner the problems are more fundamental. Notionally, it is neither a participant nor circumstantial. Thus in *I saw him clearly* or *He made it badly*, the word *clearly* or *badly* refers neither to an entity involved in the seeing or making (performer, prop or the like) nor to the scenery or framework, either of space or of time, in which it happens. To 'see clearly' is instead a degree or form of seeing, and to 'make badly' a form or quality of making. The semantic relation is similar to that of a noun and a modifying adjective: thus in *a clear view* or *a bad book*, the adjective *clear* refers to the nature or quality of the view, and *bad* to the quality or character of the book. We may also point to specific parallels between, for example, *He solved the problem correctly*, with the verb SOLVE and the adverb CORRECTLY, and *a correct solution to the problem*, with the derived noun SOLUTION and the simple adjective CORRECT, or *a beautiful lecture* and *She lectured beautifully*, with zero-derivation of the verb from the noun. In all these examples, the notional role can be described as one of **qualification**. Thus in *She lectured beautifully* the adverb adds a **qualifier**, as opposed to a participant or 'circonstant', to the simple *She lectured*.

In testing collocations one's judgment is often sorely tried. But it seems more natural to say, for example, *He wore his clothes neatly* than *He wore his clothes scrupulously*, *She dresses loudly* than *She makes up loudly*, *They build shoddily* than, say, *They cook shoddily*, or *I used to drink heavily* than *I used to fornicate heavily*. An adverb of this sort can also be obligatory. For example, one can say *This book reads well* but not simply *This book reads*; likewise *They treated him badly* but not *They treated him*, unless TREAT has a different sense (to treat him for an illness, or treat him to a drink or a meal). For BEHAVE there is a special sense of 'to behave properly': compare *The children behaved* with *The children behaved badly*. In these respects, an adverb of manner can share the characteristics of a direct object: for the example with READ compare the object in *Bill got the prize*, for the senses of TREAT compare those of SEE (*I can see you this afternoon* and *I can see*), and for BEHAVE compare once more the special sense of DRINK.

But, unlike the object, it is never a latent element. Suppose, for instance, that I remark how well this book is printed; you could not flatter me by saying 'And it READS too', or 'It is WRITTEN too', expecting me to understand *well* from my own utterance. Instead you would have to say 'It is well written too', or 'And it reads so too'. As for these, so for any other collocation in which such an adverb appears. There is no verb X, such that a sentence of the form I X-*ed*, *I* X-*ed it*, *It* X-*ed*, and so on, could be intelligible only if the ellipsis of an adverb of manner (*I* X-*ed* Y-*ly*, *I* X-*ed it* Z, and so on) could be supplied from the context of utterance. In terms which we used earlier, the element is always either strongly optional or strongly obligatory – not in between.

Nor is it certain that their syntactic element is ever excluded. According to CHOMSKY (*Aspects*, pp. 103f.), there is a set of verbs which do not take them 'freely'. This is a set of transitives which also excludes the passive (see Chapter 1 above): thus MARRY (in the sense of *She married him*), WEIGH (in the sense of *It weighed a hundredweight*), or FIT (in the sense of *The suit fits me*). Therefore he establishes a feature of valency – in his terms, of 'strict subcategorisation' – referring to a 'manner' element. Now with FIT we have a special sense, as with BEHAVE: an adverb is excluded only because the sense which a particular adverb might have (to 'fit well' or 'fit perfectly') is already covered by that of the verb. Otherwise one can say *This suit fits beautifully*, *It fits me very badly*, and so on. With MARRY there are collocational restrictions: thus *She married him well*, with MARRY transitive, is less likely than the intransitive *She married well* or, for example, *She married him quietly* or *She married him secretly*. But the element as such is not excluded – unless, in these last examples, the adverb is thought to have a different syntactic function. With the use of WEIGH in our example an expression of manner is semantically incongruous; it is hard to see how something could weigh a hundredweight in either a good way or a bad way, or by a competent or an incompetent method, and so on. But other qualifiers are possible. For example, one could say *It weighed a hundredweight easily* (or *It easily weighed a hundredweight*). One could also say of a weight-lifter that his grossness is not accidental: *He weighs that much deliberately*. Is the construction of *deliberately* and *weighs*, or even of *easily* and *weighs*, any different from that of *secretly* to *married*, *badly* to *fits*, *well* to *reads*, and so on?

Distinctions among adverbs are notoriously difficult to draw. *Deliberately* and *well* are in different semantic classes: one refers to the motives of the 'do-er', and the other to the character of his 'doing'. Likewise *willingly*, in *She married willingly*, is in an opposite class to *expensively*, in *She married expensively*. But what of *secretly* in *She married him secretly*? This refers to the character of her marriage, but also to her own secrecy (like her 'deliberateness' in *She married him deliberately*). Nor is *badly* so straightforward: in *He makes them badly* it is hard to distinguish the badness of his making from his own 'badness' at doing it. (Compare, for example, *He did it incompetently*.) In the example with WEIGH the meaning of *easily* may seem, at first sight, to belong with that of *almost*, *scarcely* or *precisely*: it qualifies the measurement itself ('easily a hundredweight', not 'barely a hundredweight', and so on). Or does it? Perhaps it refers instead to the uncertainty of the speaker's judgment: the thing was 'plainly over the hundredweight' (compare *It definitely weighed . . .* or *It seemingly weighed . . .*). But *easily* can also have a 'manner-like' use: thus *She cooked it quite easily*, meaning that it was an easy operation. For *She easily won* we might imagine three alternative analyses – one like *She nearly won*, another like *She obviously won*, and a third like *She won with difficulty*. That is scarcely a basis on which to draw constructional distinctions. But only if we did draw them would the criterion of exclusion give a positive result.

The discussion of these criteria will be resumed in the chapter which follows, where we will get similar results for adjectival qualifiers. But from the evidence of collocational restrictions (criterion 2) it seems clear that the adverb stands in a direct relation to the predicator; this is also attested by the cases in which it is obligatory (criterion 3). The structure of dependencies is therefore like, for example, this:

rather than like this:

– on the pattern of peripheral adverbials. But on the evidence of latency (criterion 4), it is not a 'completing' relationship; no sentence is syntactically incomplete, in the sense of Chapter 2, and could be made complete by adding an adverb of this type. In that respect the element is unlike the complements which we examined earlier: compare again such sentences as *Will you be watching?*, *I gave £10* or *He arrives tomorrow*. They also differ, in degree at least, by the criterion of exclusion (criterion 5). Finally, the element is neither a participant nor circumstantial (criterion 1). That too suggests that it is neither truly peripheral, which was also suggested by criteria 2 and 3, nor a true complement.

There is one explanation for these findings: namely, that we are dealing with a different type of element, standing in a different type of relation to the predicator. The typology will therefore have the form

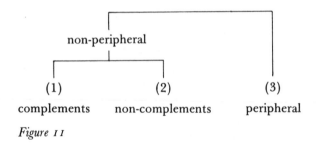

Figure 11

displayed in Figure 11, so that in, for example, *I saw him clearly yesterday*:

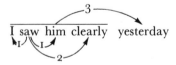

there is a major division between the peripheral element *yesterday* (labelled as type 3 in the dependency diagram) and all the elements controlled directly by *saw*. We then make a subsidiary distinction

140

between *clearly* (labelled as type 2) and both the complements (type 1). It is for an element standing in a relationship of type 2, with direct dependency within a predicative construction, that we may reserve the term **'adjunct'** which appears at the head of this section. Likewise, in *He weighs sixteen stone deliberately*, the subjective adverb *deliberately* is an adjunct, though arguably of a different syntactic class, controlled by *weighs*.

Now just as there were problems on the boundary between peripheral elements and complements, so we may expect some indeterminacy between peripheral elements and adjuncts. The status of a putative durational element, which would be obligatory in *The race lasted for three hours*, might be seen as corresponding, on the axis of type 3 versus type 2, to that of a locative or specifically directional complement, on the axis of type 3 versus type 1. We can show this by the form of diagram in Figure 12, where our three types represent the end-

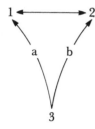

Figure 12

points in a triangular space, formed by the hierarchy shown in Figure 11. In terms of Figure 12, a durational adjunct would be schematically at point *b*, while a directional complement (as in *He went to New York*) would be at point *a*. An instrumental element, as mooted in *He walked with a stick*, would be one of the other adverbs and adverbials whose status might be seen as lying towards the centre of this space.

NOTES AND REFERENCES

'Govern' was introduced in Chapter 4, as one traditional term implying dependency. But it is used in stricter and in wider senses. In the narrowest, different lexemes govern an element in different forms: for example, some verbs govern a direct object in case *a* and others in case *b*. That is how we will use the term in Chapter 11. In a broader sense, element *x* has a form governed by element *y* in general: for example, all verbs govern objects in the

SAME case. Thus for SWEET, 1, §94, English verbs govern an object pronoun in the 'objective' (compare quotations in *OED*, s.v., §11; also BLOOMFIELD, p. 192; LYONS, *Semantics*, 2, p. 436). But the governed element is 'selected by' the governor; hence normal usage is restricted to complements, in a sense to be generalised in Chapter 7. Only in dependency theory (Chapter 4) are all dependents said to be 'governed'.

For 'nucleus' and 'periphery' see LONGACRE, p. 18 *et passim*; also PIKE, p. 468, for clause nucleus vs. 'margin' or 'satellite' elements. Compare LYONS, *Semantics*, 2, pp. 430ff. on nucleus and 'adjuncts'. It will be clear that I do not endorse Pike's wholesale generalisation of 'nucleus' to other syntactic and non-syntactic relations (especially in PIKE & PIKE, pp. 26ff.). For relational grammar see D. E. Johnson, 'On relational constraints on grammars', in COLE & SADOCK (ed.), pp. 151–78; brief and clear account by RADFORD, pp. 18ff. More substantial works have been promised – that of D. M. Perlmutter & P. M. Postal, *Relational Grammar*, since at least 1974. A specific proposal connected with it is that of E. L. Keenan & B. Comrie, 'Noun phrase accessibility and universal grammar', *LIn*, 8 (1977), pp. 63–99 (also 'Data on the noun phrase accessibility hierarchy', *Lg*, 55 (1979), pp. 333–51). For the range of complements in recent applications of valency theory see especially ENGEL, pp. 158–83 (list, p. 180).

Chomsky's distinction of predicate and verb phrase is abandoned in later work: hence it is not in BACH (rules 'adapted from' CHOMSKY, *Aspects* on p. 106) or other textbooks of the 70s. But see JACKENDOFF, $\bar{X}$ *Syntax*, pp. 57ff.

For the basic sense of 'complement' see SWEET, 1, §248: 'Transitive verbs … require a noun-word or noun-equivalent in the direct object relation to serve as complement to them, that is, complete their meaning'. But its use is variously confused:

(1) In French grammars (and Romance generally) a complement is ANY element that follows the predicator, even, and sometimes especially, those that are optional: thus, in *Hier, il y avait fête au village*, the expressions of time and place 'ne font que compléter [l'] énoncé [*Il y avait fête*], et c'est ce qu'on constate quand on dit, traditionellement, qu'ils sont des compléments' (MARTINET, *Elements*, §4.24). This passage is cited by the *OED* (new supplement), but is not representative of English usage. For a general definition of French 'complément' see DUBOIS *et al.*, s.v.; for its origin consult CHEVALIER, a valuable source for much in the history of our field.

(2) In English grammars it applies especially to 'subject(ive)' and 'object(ive)' complements (*happy* or *the treasurer* in *He became happy/the treasurer*, *They made him happy/the treasurer*). The logic is that of, for example, J. C. Nesfield, *English Grammar, Past and Present* (London: Macmillan, 1898), pp. 6–7, for whom the verbs are basically intransitive and transitive; however, they are 'of incomplete predication', in that they require the complement, or the complement as well as an object, for the sentence to stand. Nesfield and others limit the term to this sense: thus QUIRK *et al.*, for whom complement and object are different types of element in 'complementation' (pp. 342–4).

Some do not class objects as distinct: thus for HILL a complement is any 'noun or noun construction which is not the subject and which has its normal position immediately after the verb' (preliminary definition, p. 292; extended to adjectives, pp. 299ff.). Hill sees only a difference of meaning between 'object complements' (= objects) and 'non-object complements' (pp. 293–9). Others maintain a syntactic distinction, but as a subdivision of complements more generally: thus HALLIDAY, 'Categories' (for the elements S, P, C and A). But note that the subject is still separate, against my use in Chapter 5.

(3) In most transformational work the term refers to complements derived from an embedded sentence (notes to Chapter 8 below); a 'subject complement' is in subject position (originally the complement OF A NOUN in that position) and an 'object complement' in object position. For the leading analysis see P. S. Rosenbaum, *The Grammar of English Predicate Complement Constructions* (Cambridge, Mass.: MIT Press, 1967), presented briefly in 'Phrase structure principles of English complex sentence formation', *JL*, 3 (1967), pp. 103–18. Textbook accounts in CULICOVER, Chs. 9–10 (on 'verb complements'); HUDDLESTON, Ch. 8 especially (with the better term 'complement clause'). On this basis complementation is one type of embedding, and a complementiser (following Rosenbaum, Ch. 3) a marker by which a complement is introduced. But 'complementiser' has since been generalised in clauses of ALL types (the 'COMP' of, for example, CULICOVER, pp. 199f., 233f.; CHOMSKY, *Essays*, p. 7 *et passim*). And in a later 'notation' for phrase structure rules a 'complement' is any sequence that (in English) comes after the head of a phrase (the 'Comp' of LIGHTFOOT, p. 50 and earlier references in notes to Chapter 7 below). The history of such terms is a chastening lesson in semantic change and indeterminacy.

For 'participant' and 'circumstantial' see M. A. K. Halliday, 'Language structure and language function', in J. Lyons (ed.), *New Horizons in Linguistics* (Harmondsworth: Penguin Books, 1970), pp. 140–65 (and earlier in HALLIDAY, 'Transitivity and theme', Part 1); recent discussion in LYONS, *Semantics*, 2, pp. 497ff. Note that these are roles played by phrases, not by the individuals, etc. referred to; also that 'participant' is current in another sense, for the persons involved in an act of communication (LYONS, *Introduction*, pp. 275f., *Semantics*, 2, p. 570). Tesnière's reliance on these and other notional categories is criticised by R. H. Robins, 'Syntactic analysis', *ArchL*, 13 (1961), pp. 78–89 (reprinted in E. P. Hamp, F. W. Householder & R. Austerlitz (eds.), *Readings in Linguistics II* (Chicago: University of Chicago Press, 1966), pp. 386–95). The simile of a drama is also in JESPERSEN, *Philosophy*, p. 116 (for 'nexus' vs. 'junction'); compare LONGACRE, p. 35 (where a clause 'posits a situation in miniature').

Criteria for complements are discussed in the German literature on valency: see ENGEL, pp. 98–102; BRINKER, pp. 108–17; full survey in KORHONEN, pp. 129–61 (see too his concluding assessment, pp. 272–4). But tests are often for contingent differences. Thus certain locatives may move more easily to initial position (English *In* LON*don I* DO *drink*, rather than *To* LON*don I* DID *get*). They may also be followed by *nicht* 'not' (*Er erholt sich an der Ostsee nicht*, not *Er legt das Buch auf den Schrank nicht*). But while this might show a specific difference of construction, it is not, in itself, a criterion for peripherality. (For the insertion of *nicht* see G. Helbig, 'Theoretische und praktische Aspekte eines Valenzmodells', in HELBIG (ed.), pp. 31–49, examples 13–16.) Other tests are special instances of general principles. Thus Helbig notes that one can say *Er wohnte in Dresden* 'He resided in Dresden', but not *Er wohnte, als er in Dresden war* 'He resided when he was in Dresden' (*ibid.*, example 4). But as a formal criterion this is equivalent to dropping (compare *Er wohnte*). HERINGER remarks that the case or preposition of peripheral elements varies independently of their function (p. 244); we can see this as a special consequence of free insertability. It is essential to look beyond particular applications.

Standard references for obligatoriness are in the notes to Chapter 7. Note that for QUIRK *et al.* the READ of *He is reading* would be an intransitive derived by lexical conversion (reasons in note [a] on pp. 344f.); it is instructive to compare the practice of dictionaries, which commonly give separate transitive and intransitive uses. Transformationalists used to assume a syntactic process of object deletion (← *He is reading something*): first account in LEES, p. 33; see also LYONS, *Introduction*, pp. 360f. and balanced discussion by HUDDLESTON, pp. 226–9. But a lexical solution is put forward by BRESNAN, pp. 15–17, in terms identical to those of HERINGER, p. 153. Both Heringer and Huddleston distinguish this case from the one in which a complement is latent.

See D. J. Allerton, 'Generating indirect objects in English', *JL*, 14 (1978), pp. 21–33, for a careful study of that construction. On its realisation generally see Georgia M. Green, *Semantics and Syntactic Regularity* (Bloomington: Indiana University Press, 1974), Ch. 3. Most readers, or at least British readers, will find it instructive to compare her judgments with their own. I have not found a detailed study relevant to our problem with locatives.

'Adjunct' is originally a general term for a subordinate element (SWEET, 1, p. 16; compare *OED*, s.v., §B.5). For my usage compare QUIRK *et al.*, Ch. 8, where an adjunct is an adverbial element 'integrated in clause structure' (p. 421). But we differ as to the degree of integration. In their account an adjunct is distinguished from a 'disjunct' and a 'conjunct', which are described at one point as 'peripheral IN clause structure' (p. 421, my emphasis) and at another as 'not integrated within the clause' (p. 269). In fact they are typically sentence-modifying (see examples, pp. 508ff.); hence QUIRK *et al.*'s 'adjuncts' include many of the adverbials that in my analysis ARE 'peripheral in the clause' (for example, their 'time adjuncts', pp. 482ff.). My usage is likewise narrower than that of HALLIDAY ('Categories' and elsewhere) or of LYONS, *Introduction*, pp. 345f. (and briefly in *Semantics*, 2, pp. 435f.). Note that Jespersen's use (JESPERSEN, *MEG*, 2, p. 2, and later writings) has now been abandoned.

The adverbs in European languages can be divided into many semantic classes which (as I see it) are not clearly codified. The problem has bothered grammarians since antiquity: for recent contributions see QUIRK *et al.*, chapter cited (and their references, p. 532); JACKENDOFF, *Semantic Interpretation*, Ch. 3; also the logicised study by Renate Bartsch, *Adverbialsemantik* (Frankfurt: Athenäum, 1972), tr. F. Kiefer, *The Grammar of Adverbials* (Amsterdam: North-Holland, 1975). Some semantic distinctions I have not mentioned are discussed by R. H. Thomason & R. C. Stalnaker, 'A semantic theory of adverbs', *LIn*, 4 (1973), pp. 195–220. See also D. J. Allerton & A. Cruttenden, 'English sentence adverbials: their syntax and their intonation in British English', *Lingua*, 27 (1974), pp. 1–29, 'The intonation of medial and final sentence adverbials in British English', *ArchL*, n.s. 7 (1976), pp. 29–59, for the sentence-modifying types.

7
Phrases

Types of dependent; how are they distinguished?
Complementation and modification: Endocentricity. Objections: to classification (subjects in Italian vs. English); to incoherence of test. Determiners; complements of prepositions. Modifiers: can be obligatory; not subject to exclusion; as elements that cannot be latent. No positive test for modification. Apparent complementarities (status of English auxiliaries). Indeterminacy in direction and type of dependency (English noun-*of*-noun constructions).
Phrases as headed constructions: Noun phrase vs. noun clause. Definition of head; of phrasal construction; independent of type of dependency.

The last two chapters have dealt with dependencies within the unit that English-speaking grammarians call the clause. But we have also spoken of dependency within phrases. In the prepositional phrase *in the kitchen* we represented *kitchen* as dependent on *in*, a relation often described as one of government. Grammarians also talk of prepositions having objects (*OED*, s.v. 'object', §7), or having complements (QUIRK *et al.*, p. 299), again in the same way that they talk of verbal constructions. This implies a general relationship of **complementation**, which includes the dependency both of nouns on prepositions and of nouns and other complements (in the sense of Chapters 5 and 6) on predicators. Another such relationship is **modification**. Thus an attributive adjective is described as modifying a head noun (for example, *sleek* in *the sleek thrushes*); so too a prepositional phrase (for example, *on the lawn* in *the thrushes on the lawn*). Grammarians also talk of adjectives being modified by adverbs. So, in *some very sleek thrushes*:

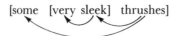

[some [very sleek] thrushes]

very modifies *sleek* within the syntagm *very sleek*, while *(very) sleek* in turn modifies *thrushes*. This too implies a general relationship, which includes both the relevant constructions.

But we cannot just appeal to the terminology of grammars. On

146

what grounds are these relations distinguished, and what is it that their individual instances have in common?

COMPLEMENTATION AND MODIFICATION

Many textbooks base their answer on a notion of 'endocentricity', which was introduced by BLOOMFIELD (pp. 194f.) in the 30s. To define this, they begin by asking if either term in a relation can be dropped. Thus in *very sleek* we can drop *very* (*some very sleek thrushes* or *some sleek thrushes*, *The thrushes are very sleek* or *The thrushes are sleek*) without changing the function of *sleek* in the larger construction. Another way of putting this is to say that *very sleek* can be replaced by *sleek*: the adjective without its modifier belongs to the same class (in the sense that it can appear in the same range of contexts) as its entire syntagm. But in *on the lawn* we cannot generally delete either *on* or *(the) lawn*: compare *the thrushes on the lawn* with *the thrushes on* and *the thrushes the lawn*, or *The thrushes are beautiful on the lawn* with *The thrushes are beautiful on* and *The thrushes are beautiful the lawn*. Another way of putting this is to say that neither the preposition nor the noun phrase belongs to the same class as the entire prepositional phrase. Similarly, neither *thrushes* nor *sang* belongs to the same class as *thrushes sang*: compare *Thrushes sang at sunset* with *thrushes at sunset* (which could only be a noun phrase) or *sang at sunset*. But the unmodified *(the) thrushes* does belong to the same class as the modified *(the) thrushes on the lawn* or *(the) sleek thrushes*.

In the textbook accounts, a construction is **endocentric** if at least one of its elements can be substituted for the whole. Alternatively, it is endocentric if this is possible in at least the majority of contexts; the part and the whole will then 'approach syntactic equivalence' (ROBINS, p. 234) or, in HOCKETT's terms, their 'ranges of privileges of occurrence largely overlap' (p. 184). An endocentric construction is then 'attributive' (or 'subordinative') if it has only one element that can be substituted. Thus we have seen that *sleek* can be substituted for *very sleek*. But we cannot also substitute *very* (*some very thrushes* or *The thrushes are very*); nor drop the head of *(the) thrushes on the lawn* (*The on the lawn* or *On the lawn ⟨are singing⟩*) as we can the modifier (*The thrushes* or *Thrushes ⟨are singing⟩*). In an attributive relation the element which can be dropped is an 'attribute' (or 'subordinate'). So, *very sleek* and *(the) thrushes on the lawn* have attributive constructions with the attributes *very* and *on the lawn*. The determiner in *some thrushes* or *the thrushes* is also classed as an attribute; thus one can say *The thrushes are singing* or *Thrushes are singing*, but not *The are singing*.

Any construction which is not endocentric is said to be **exocentric**. In *the thrushes on the lawn*, it is an exocentric construction that relates *on* and *(the) lawn*. Likewise, in a sentence such as *No animal shall wear clothes*, an exocentric construction relates the verb (*shall wear*) and its object. Both these are of a type that HOCKETT (pp. 191ff.) calls 'directive', in which one term is a 'director' (*on* or *shall wear*) and the other its 'axis' (*the lawn* or *clothes*). Another exocentric construction relates the subject and the traditional predicate: for example, *thrushes* and *sang at sunset* or *no animal* and *shall wear clothes*. This is of a type that Hockett calls 'predicative'. The basis for these subdivisions is not made clear. But in our terms all these constructions involve complementation.

Bloomfield's scheme has had such authority that there may still be scholars who are reluctant to give it up. But its inadequacy has long been apparent. Firstly, it is not clear that it draws the division in the right place. One purpose in having a typology is that it enables us to compare constructions in different languages (a point made by HOCKETT, p. 183). For example, French *les grives lisses* is like English *the sleek thrushes* in that both have attributive constructions, even though the attribute is realised in a different position (French *grives* 'thrushes' followed by *lisses* 'sleek'). But do we want to say that the subject–predicate construction in, for example, Italian is of a different type from its English counterpart? In *John is coming*, neither *John* nor *is coming* can be substituted for the whole; hence the construction is exocentric, of Hockett's predicative subtype. But the Italian case is different, as ROBINS (p. 235) points out. Beside the finite clause *Giovanni viene* 'John is coming' there is the simpler finite clause *Viene* 'He, she or it is coming.' In place of *Io vengo* 'I am coming' one can and normally would say *Vengo*; likewise for any other subject that we can think of. Therefore the Italian construction must be endocentric, and cannot be predicative by Hockett's criterion.

In the traditional view *Viene* is incomplete, with person and number agreement (3rd singular *viene*, not 1st singular *vengo* and so on) determined by a subject that is understood. Similarly, in a sentence such as *Sono nuove* 'They are new', the adjective *nuove*, which is in the feminine plural, is said to match a subject with identical properties: ⟨sc. *Queste scarpe* 'these shoes'⟩ *sono nuove*, ⟨sc. *Le case* 'the houses'⟩ *sono nuove*, and so on. This might be, and has been, disputed. But we do not have to accept it to establish that the construction is not like others in Bloomfield's endocentric class. In *Giovanni viene*, the subject is notionally a participant (Chapter 6 above), whereas an attribute in a noun phrase (*queste* 'these' in *queste scarpe* 'these shoes', *nuove* 'new' in *scarpe nuove* 'new shoes') is typically a qualifier. The subject is also an element in valencies: though compatible with the intransitive VENIRE 'to come', it is excluded, as in Latin, by verbs which are zero-valent (Latin *Pluit*, Italian *Piove* 'It is raining'). The Italian and English constructions are not identical. But they are not so dissimilar that they should be put in different major categories.

In such cases there is a logic in the way that Bloomfield's criterion is applied; we are questioning whether its results are sound. But for many other constructions it is not clear how coherent findings can be got. In *All animals are equal* we can substitute *animals* for *all animals* (thus *Animals are equal*). On that evidence the phrase is endocentric, with attributive *all*, like *the thrushes*, with attributive *the*. But one could not say *Animal shall sleep*, unless the noun is converted to a proper name (a person called 'Animal', a pop group called 'Animal', and so on). On that evidence *no animal* in *No animal shall sleep*, or *every animal* in *Every animal shall sleep*, must be exocentric. The result is not peculiar to these contexts. Over a range of functions plural nouns can regularly replace a plural with a determiner: as object in *I saw no elephants* and *I saw elephants*, after a preposition in *With some horses you must be careful* and *With horses you must be careful*, and so on. But singular nouns cannot regularly replace a singular with a determiner; by the textbook criterion, a word such as *animal* or *thrush* is far from syntactically equivalent to a phrase such as *no animal* or *each thrush*. Must the determiners therefore stand in two quite different constructions?

On all other evidence, *no animal* and *the thrush* have the same constructions as *all animals* and *the thrushes*; since the last two meet the criterion, it is tempting to argue that all four are endocentric, even though the first two fail it. But the relations called exocentric are no less problematic. We have already seen that direct objects can be dropped, as in *Bill left the room* and *Bill left*, *Bill was reading the newspaper* and *Bill was reading*, or *He was singing hymns* and *He was singing*. In the last chapter we argued that the object was a complement, for the reason, among others, that it is sometimes obligatory. But we could now argue that it is an attribute, like *no* in *no animal* or *the* in *the thrush*, for the reason that it is sometimes optional. For *inside the house* we can substitute *inside* (*the man inside the house* or *the man inside*, *They stayed inside the house* or *They stayed inside*); compare *It fell underneath the table* and *It fell underneath*, *He climbed up the tree* and *He climbed up*, and so on for several other prepositions. The textbooks would want to argue that the prepositional phrase is exocentric, again on the grounds that we cannot regularly drop nouns after *into* (*They walked into*, *the path into*) or, in our earlier example, *on*. Why is it right to argue like that, instead of saying that the case of *inside*, *up* or *underneath* makes it attributive?

To get out of this mess we have to refer to all the criteria discussed in earlier chapters, and not just that of obligatoriness. First we can deal separately with the case of determiners, on the lines already suggested in the final section of Chapter 3. In *no animal*, *no* belongs to a closed class of Quantifiers: although there are more of these than there are articles (*no*, *each*, *all*, *every*, *some*, *several*, and so on), we can again establish a bounded system of oppositions. In that respect the function is different from that of either a complement or a modifier, both of which involve open classes.

The remaining constructions may then be tested by the criteria introduced in the last chapter. In the prepositional construction, we have found that the object or complement is sometimes strongly obligatory: compare once more *the thrushes on the lawn* and *the thrushes on*, or *They walked into London* and *They walked into*. It can also be latent. Thus if I say *They live outside* I expect my hearer to understand outside what (*outside* ⟨sc. *London*⟩, and so on). Its sense may also be incorporated in that of the preposition: just as *They are drinking again* can mean that they are back on the booze, so, in *They were living opposite*, OPPOSITE could have a special sense of 'opposite where I or we were living'. Likewise *They stayed inside* could mean either that they stayed inside whatever is to be understood (*inside* ⟨sc. *the factory*⟩, *inside* ⟨sc. *the city boundary*⟩, and so on) or simply that they stayed indoors, with 'indoors' as a special sense of INSIDE. The complement can also be incorporated in a compound: compare adverbial compounds such as UPSTAIRS or DOWNHILL with compound intransitives such as FUND-RAISE.

Finally, it can be excluded. In *I walked away*, the last word is traditionally an adverb: whereas a lexeme such as INTO can be used only as a preposition (*I walked into London*), and OUTSIDE or OPPOSITE either as prepositions or as adverbs (*They lived opposite the church* or *They lived opposite*), AWAY, like DOWNHILL, belongs to a class that can be used only as adverbs (*I walked away* but not, for example, *I walked away the house*). In this respect a prepositional 'director' such as *into* is like a verbal predicator such as *perused* (*He perused the letter* but not *He perused*), while OUTSIDE or OPPOSITE are like WATCH or DRINK. Similarly AWAY is like, for example, VANISH. Both are inherently intransitive, in that, within the general structure of a predicate or a directional expression, both exclude the relevant 'object'.

Although its construction is not predicative, and its notional role not that of a participant, the complement of a preposition is similar to the direct object of a verb, with valencies determining when it is obligatory, optional and excluded. Therefore it is a dependent standing in a similar relationship of complementation. But in *sleek thrushes* or *very sleek* the relation is similar to that of an adjunct. Notionally the modifiers are qualifiers: compare, for example, the roles of COMPLETE and COMPLETELY in *a complete answer* or *a completely satisfactory answer* with that of the adjunct in *He answered us completely*. There are also collocational restrictions. For the adjectival modifier they are like those which affected subject complements and subjects (Chapter 1). For the adverb they are more tentative; but would one say, for example, *a very major artist* (compare *a pretty major artist* and *a very minor artist*), or *a slightly important painting* (compare *a fairly important painting* or *a slightly awkward painting*)? In this respect the modifiers are again like adjuncts, as distinct from peripheral elements.

Our other criteria were those of obligatoriness, exclusion and latency. In the last chapter we saw that adjuncts could be undroppable (for example, in *This book reads well* or *They treated him badly*). So can other qualifying elements. For instance, one can say *That is a separate matter*, with *matter* modified by *separate*, or *That is a matter of importance*, *That is a matter I must attend to*, and so on. But what could one mean by *That is a matter?* The unmodified noun will always have a different sense (as in *a theory of matter*), or may indeed be a different lexeme (in *What is the matter?*). Likewise one can say *She is a typical case*, with modifier *typical*, but not just *she is a case*. (Compare the special sense in, for example, *She really* IS *a* CASE!) In *a bizarrely constructed affair* the head *affair* is modified by the participle *constructed*, which is in turn modified by the adverb *bizarrely*. But in context it is hard to drop either: *Her hat was a constructed affair* or *Her hat was an affair*. Likewise

151

one could say *a badly made suit* (compare the adjunct in *His suit has been made badly*), but not *a made suit* (with a sense parallel to that of *His suit has been made*). The same holds for the participial adjective WROUGHT (*a finely wrought argument*, but hardly *a wrought argument*). In these cases the Bloomfieldian account would once more be defective. Thus *matter* cannot be substituted for *separate matter* or *wrought* for *finely wrought*, just as, in the case of determiners, *thrush* could not be substituted for *the thrush*.

Such examples are rare, and do not detract from the practical value of the test, as a first check on a category that will initially be set up by a notional analysis. But it is clearly not a sufficient criterion. For if a complement is a 'completing' element, and a completing element is simply one which can be an essential element in a syntagm, the modifier in *finely wrought* or *a separate matter* is as much a complement as the 'axes' in *on the lawn* or *No animal shall wear clothes*. There must be other grounds for seeing modification as a different type.

One of these is that qualifiers do not seem to be excluded by particular lexemes. Thus there is no noun in English, whose functions in a larger construction are like those of *thrushes* in *The sleek thrushes are coming* or *I saw some sleek thrushes*, to which no modifying adjective can be added. Likewise there is no adjective in English, with wider functions identical to those of *sleek* in *The thrushes are very sleek* and *some very sleek thrushes*, to which we can add no modifying adverb. Hence there is no need for special statements of valency. Whereas complements are often required and often excluded, and are therefore the basis for lexical classifications such as transitive, intransitive, and so on, a dictionary has no need to refer to modifiers, apart from the few exceptions, such as WROUGHT or MATTER, with which they can be obligatory.

But the application of this criterion is always open to dispute. Firstly, it is essential that the wider function should be controlled. In *the main factor* or *his principal achievement* we have a pair of adjectives, or what all grammarians call adjectives, whose class is nevertheless different from that of SLEEK, or IMPORTANT in *an important factor* or *his important achievement*. Neither MAIN nor PRINCIPAL can have predicative function: *This factor is main, His achievement is principal*. Nor do they take modifying adverbs: *a very main factor*, or *his equally principal achievement*. Their class also has a closed membership. We can therefore describe them as determiners, with a syntactic function distinguished from that of the adjectival modifiers and, in this respect, more like that of the quantifiers (*all*, *no*, and so on) which we mentioned earlier. But a grammarian might deny this, and equate their function with that of adjectives in general. In that case a dictionary would have to specify that they exclude adverbial modification, unlike the class of IMPORTANT (*a very important factor* or *an equally important achievement*).

A second problem concerns the possible distinctions between qualifying elements. In saying that there are no nouns which exclude adjectival modification I have assumed that, for example, *the lovely Miss Bloggs* has the same construction as *a large spoon*. But they could in principle be distinguished. In *a large spoon* the adjective is semantically Restrictive: thus in the command *Bring me a large spoon* it restricts the range of spoons from which the speaker wants one to be brought. But in *the lovely Miss Bloggs* the role of *lovely* is Non-Restrictive: in *I met the lovely Miss* BLOGGS (with the intonation nucleus on *Bloggs*) the speaker is not distinguishing her from another Miss Bloggs who is unlovely. This difference is often mentioned by grammarians, and some might wish to see it as constructional. If so, it might be argued that a proper name excludes restrictive modifiers. Any apparent counter-example (as in one interpretation of *the* LOVE*ly Miss Bloggs*) would have a noun converted to the common class.

Our best evidence, therefore, is that the qualifying elements are never latent. If a speaker uses a definite noun phrase, such as *the car* or *my sister*, it may of course be that the hearer knows it is a red car and not a blue car, or his elder sister and not his younger sister. But there is no noun x such that, in *the* x or *my* x, the hearer has got to supply some modifier from the context (*the* ⟨sc. y⟩ x, *my* ⟨sc. z⟩ x). Nor can a modifier be understood in an indefinite noun phrase. Thus if A asks *Did she wear a red coat?*, there is no x such that B could answer *No, but she did wear an* x, expecting A to understand *a* ⟨sc. *red*⟩ x. There is also no x such that, if the speaker says *an* x *car* or *the* x *man*, the hearer can or must understand an adverbial modifier (*a* ⟨sc. y-*ly*⟩ x *car*, *the* ⟨sc. z-*ly*⟩ x *man*). We get a similar result for adjuncts, which are initially set up as the qualifiers of verbs. By this criterion all three types of qualifier fall together, and are clearly distinguished from all types of 'object' element – direct, indirect, and of prepositions – and from locative and other marginal complements.

In short, the distinction between 'completing' and 'non-completing' elements is not, as the textbooks present it, between those that are strongly obligatory and those that are strongly optional, or even between those that are sometimes and those that are never obligatory, but between those which can and those which cannot complete an elliptical construction. The non-completing elements from open classes – adjuncts, modifying adjectives and others that are typically qualifiers – form the type of construction which most nearly corresponds to Bloomfield's 'attribution', and which is here called modification. But although this justifies the distinction, it is not as simple an answer as the one we have rejected, or as many linguists have apparently wanted. There are also various boundary problems, which we will illustrate in the rest of this section.

One basic point is that we have no positive test for modification. Suppose that *a* and *b* form a phrase, in which *a* alone can be dropped. Then *a* might be a modifier; but equally it could be a complement (like *London* in *outside London*) or a determiner (like *the* in *the thrush*). Suppose that, after checking all our examples, we have found no element like *a* that cannot be dropped. Then we can be pretty sure that *a* is a modifier, especially if it is notionally a qualifier. But we assume that the class is open; therefore there might be other examples, which we have not yet found, in which it is obligatory. Suppose that we find examples where an element like *a* is latent. Then we have positive evidence of complementation (as in *outside* ⟨sc. *London*⟩ or *underneath* ⟨sc. *the table*⟩). But suppose we have found none. Then *a* is provisionally an attribute, especially if it is again a qualifier. But our sample might in principle be skewed, so that we might find cases if we look at another. Suppose that we find clear examples where an element like *a* is excluded by a word like *b*. There too we have positive evidence of complementation (as in the ungrammatical *I went away the house*). But if we find none it may again be that we have not looked hard enough. In practice, these decisions have to be taken partly on notional and partly on statistical grounds.

A less obvious problem is that different relations often appear to be complementary. In *All animals are equal* it is possible to drop *all*: thus *Animals are equal*. This is part of the evidence by which we classed it as a determiner. But one could also say *All are equal*: this would be so precisely when the scope of *all* could be understood (*all* ⟨sc. *animals*⟩, *all* ⟨sc. *those who do what the pigs tell them*⟩, and so on). If we had no further evidence, we might be tempted to treat *animals* as a complement of *all*, reversing both the direction and the type of dependency.

One might also say *I'll take the blue*, meaning perhaps a blue counter in a game, or a blue shirt, and so forth. Instead of describing the adjective as a modifier of a latent head, we might at first be tempted to regard *blue* as a head with a latent complement, just as, in *Will you be watching?*, the predicator was seen as controlling a latent object.

A similar temptation can, and indeed does, arise in the analysis of the verb phrase. In Chapter 3 we argued that the auxiliaries depend on the lexical verb; they are forms which 'help to make up phrases' (QUIRK *et al.*, p. 65), but do not have a larger syntactic role. So, in *We must leave*, the modal *must* would be a determiner, in this instance droppable, of *leave*. But *leave* too can be dropped: thus *We must* (⟨sc. *leave*⟩, ⟨sc. *worship the Lord*⟩, or whatever else is intended). An alternative analysis might therefore be like this:

we must leave

with the lexical verb a complement of the auxiliary. In the commandment *No animal shall wear clothes*, we might propose a corresponding structure

[no animal] [shall [wear clothes]]

where the complement of *shall* is a syntagm formed by the remainder of the predicate. That too could be latent (*No animal shall* ⟨sc. *wear clothes*⟩, and so on). There is a respectable tradition, going back at least to the later nineteenth century, according to which the construction of a predicate like *shall wear clothes* is in one respect the same as that of, for example, *wants to wear clothes*, with both *shall* and *wants* governing an infinitive.

The objection is that *all*, *blue* or *shall* have no demonstrable relationship to elements outside the construction. In phrases like *all animals* the head noun enters into restrictions on the collocations of verbs and subjects, verbs and direct objects, and so on. But as with the article (Chapter 3), there is no direct relation between a quantifier and such wider elements. Thus if noun *n* goes with a predicative adjective *a*, and quantifier *q* in turn goes with noun *n*, all three go together in the construction *q n is a* or *q n are a*, without further restrictions on *q* and *a*. Likewise for a phrase such as *the blue bottle*: in *They decanted the blue*, it is the noun supplying the ellipsis (*the blue* ⟨sc. *bottle*⟩ or *the blue* ⟨sc. *liquid*⟩) that is limited by the collocability of DECANT. There is no direct relation between the verb and the adjective. In the case of the verb phrase there are a number of rules which differentiate between auxiliaries such as SHALL and main verbs such as WANT: for example, only the former can take negative *n't* as an affix (*They shan't leave* or *They mustn't leave*, but not *They wantn't to leave*). This establishes a construction within which there is again no evidence of a direct relationship between the auxiliary and the subject. By contrast, there is clear evidence relating the lexical verb and the subject.

We must leave will therefore have the structure

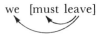

with the relation of *must* and *leave* conforming to a schema in which one element is 'non-completing' – either determiner or modifier:

– instead of one in which the other element is a complement:

But there are other cases where the choice between these schemata is not so clearly determined by our data. The phrase *a lot of people* is of type 1; LOT, in the expression *lots of* or *a lot of*, has no more than a general numerative function. But how many others have the same construction? A specific criterion is that of agreement: one says *A lot of people were there*, with plural *were* matching the head noun *people*, not *A lot of people was there*. But agreement in English is a notoriously variable matter. Would one say, for example, *A number of people was arriving*? I am reluctant even to write it, which would confirm that *a number (of)* is also a determiner or modifier. But my reluctance is not universally shared. For a noun such as PINT the evidence is balanced: *Three pints of beer was spilled* or *were spilled*, with plural *pints* and singular *beer*; *A pint of mussels were sold* or *was sold*, with singular *pint* and plural *mussels*. Then are *beer* and *mussels* the heads, with a construction of type 1, or are they not?

In other collocations the agreement is more clearly with the first noun. For instance, one would not usually say *Three glasses of milk was sold* or *A bowl of apples were brought in*. In all these phrases the second element can again be latent: thus *I drank three glasses* would normally mean that the speaker drank three glasses of something (*three glasses* ⟨sc. *of beer*⟩, ⟨sc. *of milk*⟩, and so on). Therefore the construction might appear to be of type 2, with *(of) milk* or *(of) apples* a complement of *glasses* or *bowl*. But the collocational evidence would again assign it to type 1. In *Three bottles of milk are sour* the restrictions link *sour* and *milk*, not *sour* and *bottles*. In the incomplete *Three bottles are sour*, the sourness is again that of the contents, not the bottles themselves; compare the complete *Three bottles are broken*. In that respect the example is just like *They decanted the blue*. The conflict is starker if we substitute nouns such as SORT or KIND. In *Three sorts of wine were served* the collocation is of *wine* and *served*, with *sorts* dependent. We might compare the reversed phrase *wine of three sorts*, where *wine* also dictates the agreement (*Wine of three sorts was served*). But one would not say *Three sorts of wine was served*. If agreement were our only evidence, we would say that in this order *wine* was the dependent.

Finally, there can be indeterminacy even when the direction of dependency is certain. In *the loss of Calais* the relation of *Calais* to *loss* resembles that of the finite ⟨*They*⟩ *lost Calais*; in meaning, *(of) Calais* is an objective genitive, like *(of) chocolates* in *the eating of chocolates* (Chapter 1). Moreover it is a complement. If dropped the element is at once latent: *The loss surprised us* would imply that the person spoken to knows what has been lost. Nor can such dependents be added freely in all combinations. Thus a phrase with LOSS can have both an inflected and a periphrastic genitive (*his loss of blood*, with subjective *his*). But a noun like DISAPPEARANCE can take only one: *his disappearance* or *the disappearance of the blood*, but nothing like, for example, *his disappearance of the blood*. Within the noun phrase LOSS and DISAPPEARANCE have different valencies, parallel to those of LOSE and DISAPPEAR in predicative constructions.

In these phrases the head noun is what JESPERSEN called a Nexus Substantive, 'nexus' being his term for what we have called the predicative construction (*Philosophy*, Ch. 10). But in other cases an *of*-phrase is more clearly a modifier. Thus *a model of solid silver* means the same as *a solid silver model*; with a bare noun the latter form would be more usual (*a silver cup* rather than *a cup of silver*), with longer phrases the former. Notionally, *of solid silver* can be classed with qualifiers such as *wooden* in *a wooden model, shiny* in *a shiny model,* and so on. Our other criteria do not disconfirm this. Testing for exclusion will again depend on how many *of*-constructions are distinguished; for although all nouns can take an *of*-phrase in some qualifying role (*an idea of great beauty, a loss of some importance*), their sense forbids that they should all take phrases telling what something is made of. Testing for latency will prove negative. Though *Bring me the* X could in context refer to 'the X made of Y', there is no X such that this could not reasonably be uttered unless *of* Y could be understood. We thus have evidence for both types of relation. Whereas *the loss of Calais* fits the schema which we represented as type 2, *a model of silver* illustrates a third schema:

(3)

differing only in the type of dependency.

But where is the boundary between types 2 and 3? For example, is *(of) Calais* in *a map of Calais* the complement or the modifier of *map*? One could say *I bought a map yesterday,* what it is a map of being irrelevant; although that might be known to the hearer on occasion, and the speaker might even be annoyed if he did not understand it, the sentence could also be uttered out of the blue. This might suggest that the relation is modifying. But it does not prove it, any more than the completeness of *I spent yesterday reading* proves that in *I spent yesterday reading a thesis* the object is a modifier of the predicator. The problem is again one of identifying constructions. Is *a map of Calais* like *the loss of Calais* – with MAP also a nexus substantive – or like, for example, *a map of painted silk,* with MAP a concrete noun that can be qualified in various ways?

The answer is that it is not entirely like either; we are in the middle of a chain of partial resemblances. As one can say *their loss of Calais* so one can say *his map of Calais,* meaning the map that he has made of it. But the latter phrase can also mean 'the map of Calais belonging to him', just as *his poster of Southend* could refer to a poster he owns or a poster he has designed, *his table* to a table he owns or one he is going to make, and so on. In that respect MAP and POSTER are like ordinary nouns, such as TABLE, and unlike a pure nexus substantive. Then does this concern the syntactic relationship of the genitive? The arguments against are, firstly, that many ordinary nouns are not compatible with the nexus-like sense: for instance, one could not readily say *his wall of Calais* (referring to a fresco of it in his sitting room) or *a flower bed of Southend*. Secondly, it is hard to dissociate *his map of Southend* from the construction of, for example, *his description of Southend*, where DESCRIPTION is the verbal noun from DESCRIBE. In *his postcard of Southend* we might say that *postcard* takes the syntactic relations of a derived noun, even though there is no verb 'to postcard'.

Then are there merely different degrees of nexus substantives, all of them (LOSS or DESCRIPTION, MAP or POSTCARD) having the same element in *of* as an obligatory or optional valent? *A model of the universe*, for example, would then have a different construction from *a model of solid silver* – again type 2 versus type 3. But this merely shifts the problem into another part of the spectrum. Although one is unlikely to say *a wall of Calais*, phrases such as *a screen of angels* are not unusual. But does this mean a screen 'representing angels' or 'consisting of angels'? Perhaps we might be tempted to think both: it could be a screen with angels painted on it, or one 'formed by angels' in a figurative sense. But would we then say that the first sense has *(of) angels* as a complement of *screen*? If so, it is not clear why *a screen of Calais* should be so much more awkward than, for example, *a picture of Calais*. Or is *(of) angels* a modifier in both senses? That seems to fit the case of SCREEN versus PICTURE: whereas a picture must by its nature be of something (*a picture of Calais* having *(of) Calais* as an overtly completing element), a screen is simply a screen. But is *a screen of angels* really quite like, for example, *a screen of bamboo*? Is there also modification in, say, *a facade of Corinthian pilasters* or, if so, in *a ceiling of the Last Judgment*, *a metope of Heracles and the Nemean Lion*, and so on?

Such indeterminacy should not surprise us, given the nature of our criteria and the variety and fluidity of the semantic connections. For although we might distinguish two constructions, one of one type and one of another, it is only in certain instances, where the direction of dependency is clear and there are definite cases in which the dependent is latent, that the type to which a particular form belongs could be recognised without appeal to notional criteria. In marginal instances all we can ask is whether form *a* is notionally more like form *b* or form *c*. That is, of course, precisely the problem which we encountered at a similar point in the last chapter, for forms like ⟨*No animal*⟩ *shall sleep in a bed*, or ⟨*This letter*⟩ *was posted from Eton*.

PHRASES AS HEADED CONSTRUCTIONS

The last section has dealt with relations in various sorts of phrase. But what exactly is 'a phrase', and what characterises particular classes, such as 'noun phrase', 'prepositional phrase', and so on?

Present usage is confused, and any definition would do violence to some grammarian's practice. But let us compare the complement phrase in *Leave the meat* with the complement clause in, for example, *Promise you will come*. Both have functions like those of a single noun: compare *money* or *satisfaction* in *Leave money, Promise satisfaction*. Therefore the first is called a 'noun' phrase and the latter is often called a 'noun' clause (as at the beginning of Chapter 6). But there is an important difference in their relationship to the predicator. In *Promise you will come* the clause has within it a controller *come*:

but there are no collocational restrictions which relate this directly to *promise*. Therefore *promise* controls the clause as a whole:

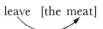

just as, in *Promise you will come tomorrow*:

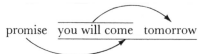

the whole predicative syntagm in turn controls the peripheral *tomorrow*. But in *Leave the meat* there is a direct relation between *leave* and the controlling element in the noun phrase:

leave [the meat]

Similarly, in *you will come* there is a direct relation between *you* and the controlling element in the verb phrase, and in *Go into the garden* the controller in the prepositional phrase is directly related to *go*.

For many linguists a noun clause is also a noun phrase, simply because it is a syntagm – the use of 'phrase' in, for example, 'phrase structure grammar' – which fills a noun-like role. But it is useful to restrict these terms, as many other writers do in practice, to a construction in which one element can, in at least some cases, stand in a

direct relation to some element in a larger unit. In the noun phrase
this is the head. The construction may accordingly be represented by
a schema like this:

$$[(Dependent_1 \quad (Dependent_2 \ldots (Dependent_n))) \quad Head] \quad (X)$$

(the order is immaterial) where a single head has zero or more
dependents (determiners like *the* in *the meat*, modifying phrases like *on
the lawn* in *thrushes on the lawn*, and so on) and may in turn be related, in
principle either as controller or dependent, to some further element
X. This last relation is not always instanced. A noun phrase can stand
alone, even without ellipsis: for example, in the title of a book. It can
also stand in apposition, as in *I met that other girl, the blonde*, where we
will establish no direct relation between *blonde*, as head of *the blonde*,
and the noun preceding. But the syntactic relation of *blonde* to *the* is
identical to that found in *I met the blonde*, where it is directly controlled
by *met*.

The same schema applies to a verb phrase like *will come* in *you will
come* or *must have been seeing* in *He must have been seeing her*, where the head
verb *seeing* is related both to *he* and *her*:

he [must have been seeing] her

Let us therefore generalise the term '**head**' to apply to any controlling
element which can fit this pattern. In *very sleek* we have a head *sleek*
which, in *the very sleek thrushes* or *The thrushes are very sleek*, is controlled
by or controls a noun. Likewise a Prepositional Phrase may be said to
have a head preposition. This does not always have a wider function:
for example, *in* may bear a direct relation to the predicator in *I put it in
the library*, but not as head of the peripheral element in *I worked all afternoon in the library*. The prepositions in a time expression like *on Friday* or
in the summer may never have a demonstrable relation of that kind. But
their relation to *Friday* and *summer* is syntactically identical to that of
on or *in* in locatives, which do.

A **phrasal construction** can then be defined as any construction
which has a head, and a **phrase** as any unit which exhibits such a
construction. An 'A phrase' (or 'A-(i)al' phrase) is specifically a
phrase the head of whose construction is an 'A'. *The meat* is accordingly a Noun Phrase, not simply because its functions can be filled by

single nouns, but because its head *meat* belongs to that class. In most grammarians' usage, these definitions would include the case in which the head is the only element. Thus *children* or *Mary* also satisfies our schema, with *n* (the number of dependents) as zero. Therefore they too are noun phrases, in *I can see children* or *Mary is coming* (or, appositionally, in *I met that other girl, Mary*).

Similarly, *will come* is a Verb Phrase by virtue of its head *come*. So too is *come* in, for example, *Deer come into their garden*, again in most grammarians' usage. *Very sleek* is an Adjective (or Adjectival) Phrase and *very carefully*, in *They did the job very carefully* or *a very carefully written letter*, an Adverb (or Adverbial) Phrase, defined as such by its head adverb *carefully*. *Very carefully written* is in turn a Participle (or Participial) Phrase, as (of a different sort) is *skidding badly* in *a car skidding badly*. In *Flying planes is dangerous*, the gerund *flying* is the head of a Gerundial Phrase *flying planes*, provided that we can argue a relationship between it and the predicative adjective. Finally, *in the library* is defined as a prepositional phrase by its head preposition *in*. Grammarians do not usually describe this as a head, but as a 'director' (as in HOCKETT's typology, cited earlier) or simply as governing the noun phrase. Hence it is not clear what a 'prepositional phrase' has in common with, for example, a noun phrase. But the relevant configuration of dependencies:

$$(X) \; [\text{in} \; [\text{the library}]]$$

conforms precisely (leaving aside the order) to the schema which we have given.

The notion of a head is therefore independent of the main types of dependency within the phrase. In prepositional phrases the dependent is a complement, as also in a noun phrase like *loss of blood* or an adjectival phrase like *similar to Mary*, in *Jill is similar to Mary* or *a girl similar to Mary*. In other phrases it is non-completing, as in a noun phrase like *sleek thrushes*. Others include dependents of both types, as in *heavy losses of blood* (modifier *heavy* and complement *(of) blood*) or *strikingly similar to Mary* (modifier *strikingly* and complement *(to) Mary*). The types of relation are themselves independent of headedness; in *Write the letter carefully*, a modifier *carefully* and a complement *(the) letter* depend on an element that, at least in our analysis, is not a head.

But it may be useful to have special terms for certain special cases. The term 'adjunct' was used for a modifier in a predicative syntagm (such as *carefully* in *Write the letter carefully*). Bloomfield's '**attribute**' might be retained for any other modifier. Thus *very* is an attribute in *very sleek, very similar to Mary* or *very carefully*. Likewise *sleek* is an attributive adjective (as it is always called) in *sleek thrushes*, and *on the lawn* again an attribute in *thrushes on the lawn*. '**Director**' might also be retained, for the special case in which a head can control only a complement. Thus *on* in *on the lawn* would be a director, but not *write* in *Write the letter carefully*. This type of head may not be exemplified in every language. But in many it is, and for some of them the more specific term 'preposition', which refers to the position of a director before its complement, would not be appropriate.

NOTES AND REFERENCES

For endocentric and exocentric see both the leading account by BLOOMFIELD (Ch. 12) and its elaboration by HOCKETT (Chs. 21–2). Other treatments are by ROBINS, pp. 234ff.; LYONS, *Introduction*, pp. 231ff., *Semantics*, 2, pp. 391ff.; most recently ALLERTON, pp. 126ff. Broadly speaking, the later the writer the more qualified his formulation.

Bloomfield treats coordination as another type of endocentricity (*loc. cit.*, p. 195). His hierarchy is thus as below, with the attributive *sleek thrushes* more like the coordinative *Jack and Jill* (see Chapter 9 below) than the exocentric *wore clothes*. (For the diagram see, for example, ROBINS, p. 236.)

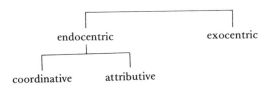

But this makes sense only in terms of Bloomfield's criterion. In general, coordination is easily distinguished from both attribution and exocentricity. The only indeterminacy is in distinguishing it from one case of apposition (Chapter 10 below). But the distinction between attributive and exocentric can be very difficult, as we have seen. Why so, if attributive vs. exocentric is a major division and attributive vs. coordinative only subsidiary?

I have assumed a different hierarchy, which first divides coordination from all types of dependency:

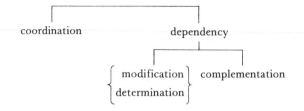

This has antecedents outside the Bloomfieldian tradition: see in particular
TESNIÈRE (for 'connexion' vs. 'jonction'); DE GROOT, *Syntaxis*, p. 59 ('Elke
woordgroep is òf nevenschikkend òf onderschikkend' – 'Every syntagm is
either coordinative or subordinative'). But de Groot's later classification
is more complex (and more traditional): see DE GROOT, 'Classification',
pp. 113–57; compare too MARTINET, *Elements*, §§4.31, 4.32, for coordination
and subordination as two types of 'expansion' of the predication. See the end
of Chapter 10 below for the eventual elaboration of my own scheme.

For the merging of prepositions and adverbs compare JESPERSEN, *Philosophy*,
pp. 88f.; Barbara M. H. Strang, *Modern English Structure*, 2nd edn (London:
Edward Arnold, 1968), p. 193 (especially for the parallel with transitive and
intransitive verbs); and JACKENDOFF, *X̄ Syntax*, p. 79 (with earlier trans-
formationalist references). Jespersen also discusses restrictive and non-
restrictive modifiers (pp. 110ff.); further references in notes to Chapter 10
below, for relative clauses. For adjectives which cannot be predicative, and
subclasses of adjectives generally, see QUIRK *et al.*, pp. 259ff.

For auxiliaries as governing verbs see *OED*, s.v. 'complement', §3.b (end
of quotation from Mason's *English Grammar*). But the term 'auxiliary' was
already established (*ibid.*, s.v., §B.3). For recent proposals see HUDDLESTON,
Ch. 14; also G. Pullum & Deirdre Wilson, 'Autonomous syntax and the
analysis of auxiliaries', *Lg*, 53 (1977), pp. 741–88 (with full references for
both sides of the argument). For special characteristics of the English auxiliaries see PALMER, pp. 18ff.; a useful debate is in Huddleston's review article,
'Some theoretical issues in the description of the English verb', *Lingua*, 40
(1976), pp. 331–83, and Palmer's reply, 'Why auxiliaries are not main
verbs', *Lingua*, 47 (1979), pp. 1–25. For a brief and (in my view) convincing
summary see Palmer's *Modality and the English Modals* (London: Longman,
1979), pp. 178ff. For discussion of another language compare KORHONEN,
pp. 235ff. on German.

Sweet has an interesting discussion of 'antilogical' constructions (SWEET,
1, pp. 45ff.), covering both the auxiliaries and *a number of...*, *a piece of...*,
and the like. In *shall have seen*, the participle is the logical 'nucleus' (p. 47); but
the grammatical prominence is 'shifted' to the finite *shall*. In *the majority of
Englishmen* the nucleus is *Englishmen*; but the 'logical relations of head-word
and adjunct-word' are 'reversed', so that, in *The majority of Englishmen are tall*,
the word which is 'least important logically' (relative to *Englishmen* and *tall*)

is 'put first and made the subject of the sentence' (p. 46). Compare *most Englishmen*, where logical and grammatical prominence coincide. But in the case of the auxiliaries, Sweet also says that 'even from a purely grammatical view' the complement function of the participle or infinitive is 'lost sight of' (p. 115). For a recent and interesting discussion of this type of *of*-construction compare A. Akmajian & Adrienne Lehrer, 'NP-like quantifiers and the problem of determining the head of an NP', *LAn*, 2 (1976), pp. 395–413. In their view phrases like *a bottle of wine*, or even *a herd of elephants*, are constructionally ambiguous.

For a fuller discussion of nexus substantives see JESPERSEN, *MEG*, 5, Ch. 7; also JESPERSEN, *Syntax*, Ch. 20 and pp. 159f. It is instructive to compare Chomsky's treatment (CHOMSKY, 'Nominalization').

My association of 'phrase' and 'head' is partly original. See, however, QUIRK *et al.*, pp. 43f., where verb phrases are one word or a 'head verb' plus auxiliaries, noun phrases a noun or pronoun or 'an indeterminately long structure having a noun as head', and adjectival or adverbial phrases are defined as 'having an adjective/adverb as their head'. A prepositional phrase is a structure 'consisting of a noun phrase dominated by a preposition'. But it is not clear how 'dominating' relates to being a head, and neither these nor 'phrase' have general definitions. Moreover 'noun phrase' is defined differently at the beginning of Ch. 4 (p. 127). See too P. L. Garvin, 'A study of inductive method in syntax', *Word*, 18 (1962), pp. 107–20 for a 'true phrase' as a unit with a head noun or verb (p. 292 in HOUSEHOLDER (ed.), pp. 68f. in GARVIN). But this refers to heads only in Bloomfield's sense (below).

'Head-word' is used by SWEET (1, p. 16) of any word to which another is subordinate: in *Bring the big book*, *bring* would be a head-word in relation to the 'adjunct-word' *book*, as *book* in relation to *big*. For Bloomfield the only subordination is in endocentric constructions; a head is therefore the obligatory element in an attributive relationship (BLOOMFIELD, p. 195). This is followed in the textbooks cited earlier (HOCKETT, pp. 184, 188; ROBINS, p. 236; LYONS, *Introduction*, p. 233; also LYONS, *Semantics*, 2, p. 391) and by at least one older generativist: R. P. Stockwell, *Foundations of Syntactic Theory* (Englewood Cliffs: Prentice-Hall, 1977), pp. 9, 74. For others the term seems merely a label: thus HALLIDAY, 'Categories', p. 257; LONGACRE, p. 24 *et passim* (but not indexed). Others introduce it only in special collocations: for example, 'head noun of a relative clause' in CULICOVER, p. 195. But in dependency grammar it can again be generalised: see, for example, Jane J. Robinson, 'Case, category, and configuration', *JL*, 6 (1970), pp. 57–80, especially for the representation of prepositional phrases. Likewise under the 'X-convention' (Robinson's paper and other references below).

A phrase is traditionally a combination of words that is not a clause: see *OED*, s.v., §2.c (citation from 1865); *Terminology*, p. 14. Compare HALLIDAY, 'Categories', p. 253 (where phrase or 'group' is one of a hierarchy of 'units'); likewise LONGACRE, pp. 17, 74; PIKE, pp. 439ff.; more developed model, with phrase as an expanded unit functionally similar to the word, in PIKE & PIKE, pp. 23f. See also LYONS's brief discussion of hierarchical models (*Introduction*, pp. 170f., 206ff.) and QUIRK *et al.* (as earlier). But for BLOOMFIELD a phrase is any unit consisting of two or more words ('a free form which consists entirely of two or more lesser free forms', p. 178); compare HOCKETT, p. 168 (with minor modification, pp. 178f.); also HILL, pp. 115, 124ff., for an attempted intonational definition. 'Phrase' is thus equivalent to my 'syntagm'. Hence clauses can also be phrases: compare BLOOMFIELD, p. 194 (on the 'actor–action' construction); also JESPERSEN, *Philosophy*, pp. 102ff. for subordinate clauses as word groups. Hence a noun clause can also be a noun phrase. This use of 'noun phrase' is general in transformational grammar from the later 60s: see, for example, HUDDLESTON, pp. 93f., for NP → S (alternative rule NP → (Det) N S, with deletion of all but S where appropriate, p. 108).

A minor question is whether a phrase can consist of a head, or what would otherwise be a head, alone. For QUIRK *et al.* it can (though the passage cited is not clear in the case of adjectival/adverbial phrases, p. 44). In this respect they follow HALLIDAY, 'Categories'; see again PIKE, p. 439 (with objections to Bloomfield on this issue, pp. 486f.). The opposite view was taken by DIK (tree diagrams e.g. on p. 209) and is doubtless nearer to that of earlier scholars; see criticism in my review, *Lingua*, 23 (1969), pp. 356f., 361f.

Standard phrase structure rules cannot show heads of phrases: partly because they do not show controlling relations (Chapter 4); also because NP or VP is a primitive category not, as such, related, to N or V. On the second point see LYONS, *Introduction*, p. 235. Nor can they show parallels between, for instance, prepositional and verbal constructions. P and V are again primitives, and their relation to NP merely that NP can or must follow.

Only in the 70s do we find an attempt to remedy these defects. For its earliest version see CHOMSKY, 'Nominalization', where the problem was to relate complements of verbs to those of nouns and adjectives. He proposes a 'uniform notation' (JACOBS & ROSENBAUM (ed.), p. 210) in which $\bar{\text{X}}$ and $\bar{\bar{\text{X}}}$ stand for successively larger phrases headed by an X. Thus a complete NP = $\bar{\bar{\text{N}}}$, VP = $\bar{\bar{\text{V}}}$ and adjective phrase = $\bar{\bar{\text{A}}}$, and we can write a single rule applying for all three values. Chomsky also suggested that N, V and A need not be primitive, but 'combination[s] of features of a deeper sort' (*ibid.*, p. 199); hence a rule could refer to features shared by any two. These proposals are soon combined: thus JACKENDOFF, *Semantic Interpretation*, p. 60. For their later elaboration see JACKENDOFF, $\bar{X}$ *Syntax*, especially Chs. 2 and 3; also, for the '$\bar{X}$-convention', LIGHTFOOT, pp. 50ff. All major categories, including P and PP, are now covered.

Detailed comment might be premature. But this plainly tries to represent, by an analysis of categories, what I see as similarities and differences of function. Jackendoff's 'head' is a controller: note that sentences or clauses are headed by V (JACKENDOFF, $\bar{X}$ *Syntax*, p. 36), as in dependency grammars. But he defines it not by its relations, but simply by its being an X within a larger X (p. 30). N and A share certain features: traditionally they are both 'nouns' ('substantive nouns' and 'adjective nouns'), as Jackendoff notes, unfortunately not quite correctly (p. 32). So do A and P, which 'are often thought of as "modifiers" '. But the relation of modification is not the same sort of concept as the part of speech 'noun'. V and P also share features; but this is precisely because they can both be related directly to an 'object' or, in my terms, complement (still p. 32).

Jackendoff's treatment of the clause is criticised by N. Hornstein, 'S and X′ convention', *LAn*, 3 (1977), pp. 137–76. If S is excluded from the convention a narrower sense of 'phrase' is again satisfactorily represented. But see notes to Chapter 8 below for the attractions of including it.

8
Clauses

Clauses distinguished by predications; functions of clauses; simple and complex units.

Clause and non-clause: Clauses as units which are transformationally related; as units which are not phrases; minor cases of incompleteness. Full and reduced clauses. Contraction: criterion of regularity (no contraction to locative phrases). Gradation between clauses and phrases (English participles and adjectives; gerunds; gradation between conjunction and preposition).

Fused constructions: Problems of constituency (catenatives and complex transitives); explainable by fused predications. Fusion as marginal subordination; fused constructions and marginal codification (English adjectives plus infinitive).

A sentence like *They rang me before I had finished breakfast* contains two predications. One is formed by *they*, *rang* and *me* and has the rest of the sentence as a peripheral dependent:

[[they rang me] [before I had finished breakfast]]

That element in turn consists of a second predication *I had finished breakfast*, controlled or introduced by a word traditionally classed as a conjunction:

[before [I had finished breakfast]]

In normal modern usage, the term '**clause**' is applied to both the units whose constituency has been displayed. So, in the sentence as a whole:

ₐ[they rang me ᵦ[before I had finished breakfast]ᵦ]ₐ

a smaller clause *b* is included within the larger clause *a*.

Clauses may stand in various types of relation. In

ₐ[I said ᵦ[it was a man ᵧ[I knew ᵨ[when I was in the army]ᵨ]ᵧ]ᵦ]ₐ

b, *c* and *d* are all **dependent clauses**. The last is peripheral to a partial predicative syntagm *I knew*:

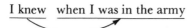

I knew   when I was in the army

It is thus a **peripheral clause**, as too is *before I had finished breakfast* in our first example. Clause *c* is a modifier in a noun phrase headed by *man*:

a   man   I knew when I was in the army

and is thus a **modifying clause** (or, more specifically, an **attributive clause**). Clause *b* is a second complement of the predicator *said*:

I   said   it was a man I knew when I was in the army

and is accordingly a **complement clause**. The relationship of complementation is established by the now familiar criteria of valency. With some verbs the element is strongly obligatory (*I mentioned they were coming* but not *I mentioned*). With others it can be latent: *They didn't say* (⟨sc. *my house was on fire*⟩, ⟨sc. *she was so beautiful*⟩ and so on), or *They didn't tell us*. With others it is excluded: thus *I read they were coming* but not *I perused they were coming*, *I gather they have arrived* but not *I pick they have arrived*. Other complement clauses function as subjects: for example, *b* in

$_a$[$_b$[why he did it]$_b$ still puzzles me]$_a$

as a valent of PUZZLE.

A clause may also stand in a relation other than dependency. In *Have you heard the news, that the Prime Minister is resigning?*, the noun clause *that the Prime Minister is resigning* is in apposition to the noun phrase *the news*; apposition is a further type of syntactic relation, which we will try to clarify in Chapter 10. In

$_a$[$_b$[he had asked them]$_b$ but $_c$[they wouldn't help]$_c$]$_a$

b and *c* are clauses linked by coordination (see discussion in Chapter 9); likewise in

he said $_a$[$_b$[he had asked them]$_b$ but $_c$[they wouldn't help]$_c$]$_a$

where an identical unit forms a complement of *said*. In principle, clauses can play any role other than those of markers or determiners, which are restricted to closed classes.

A sentence or clause can now be described as **complex** if it includes at least one smaller clause. Thus all the units labelled *a* are complex; so too, for example, is the attributive clause in *a man I knew when I was in the army*, since it includes the smaller clause *when I was in the army*. A sentence or clause which is not complex is **simple**: for example, *he had asked them* both as a sentence (*He had asked them*) and as a complement in *He said he had asked them*. Finally, a clause is a **main clause** if it forms a sentence or is one of two or more coordinated elements that together do so. Otherwise it is a **subordinate clause**. Thus in

$$_a[\text{I said } _b[\text{it was a man } _c[\text{I knew}]_c]_b]_a$$

a main clause *a* includes the successive subordinate clauses *b* and *c*. In such a structure, we will say that clause *c* is **subordinate to** (or **immediately subordinate to**) clause *b*, which is in turn subordinate to *a*. Conversely, *a* is **superordinate** (or **immediately superordinate**) to *b*, which is in turn superordinate to *c*. In *He said he had asked them but they wouldn't help* our analysis showed both clause *b* and clause *c* (*he had asked them* and *they wouldn't help*) as subordinate to the whole. With a different meaning the example could have another structure:

$$_a[\text{he said } _b[\text{he had asked them}]_b]_a \text{ but } _c[\text{they wouldn't help}]_c$$

where *a* and *c* are main clauses and *a* is superordinate to *b*.

These are conventional topics, which are treated with greater or less care in most grammar books. But although we have given examples of clauses, we have not yet said precisely what a clause is, or given criteria by which one is to be recognised. How then should the term be defined?

CLAUSE AND NON-CLAUSE

To answer this question, or rather to appreciate the difficulty of answering it, we must begin by looking more closely at the ways in which subordinate clauses resemble main clauses. In our original example

$$_a[\text{they rang me } _b[\text{before I had finished breakfast}]_b]_a$$

we remarked that *b*, like *a*, includes a predication. But it is clear that the predication does not have to be complete. In *It was a man I knew* the sense of KNOW is one that, in a main clause, would require a direct object: compare *I already know him.* But the subordinate clause *b*:

_a[it was a man _b[I knew]_b]_a

consists just of the predicator and its subject. Our main problem, therefore, is to determine what degrees or types of incompleteness, or, more generally, of differences between subordinate and main constructions, a definition should allow.

A first and limiting condition is that subordinate clauses should stand in a transformational relationship (Chapter 1) to main clauses. In

_a[he announced _b[that he had no money]_b]_a

or

_a[_b[that he had no money]_b certainly surprised us]_a

the construction of *b* is regularly opposed to that of the main clause *He had no money.* The only difference between them is that the former has a marking element *that,* which we will accordingly describe as a **subordinator**. Likewise in the German sentence

_a[sie   sagt   _b[dass   er   kein Geld   hat]_b]_a
  'she' 'says'   'that' 'he' 'no money' 'has'

b is transformationally related to the main clause

er   hat   kein Geld
'he' 'has' 'no money'

The difference between their constructions lies simply in the subordinator (*dass*) and in the ordering of elements (*kein Geld hat, hat kein Geld*).

But there are other constructions for which such a relation does not hold. For example, we found no regular opposition – no opposition meeting the minimal standard of regularity in Chapter 1 – between a main clause and such units as *the shooting of the hunters.* Therefore these are not clauses. To be precise, they do not have a predicative construction: although the relation of *hunters* to *shooting* may be in general one of complementation (Chapter 7), it is not differentiated, from a syntactic viewpoint, into the specific role of subject or object. If predication is essential to a clause, the basic definition is not met.

An alternative condition is that a clause should not be a phrase. In *The shooting of the hunters was criminal* or *Bill's shooting was erratic*, the subjects have the same construction as, for example, *the siege of Troy* or *Bill's arrival*, which in turn have the same construction, apart perhaps from the internal relation marked by *of* or *'s*, as *the back of the car* or *Bill's house*. *Shooting* is thus the head of a noun phrase. But there is no head in *that he had no money* or in German *dass er kein Geld hat*. For many grammarians clause and phrase are mutually exclusive categories. If a phrase is defined as a unit with a head, under the definition of 'head' suggested in the last chapter, a defining property of the clause might be its non-headedness.

These conditions can have different consequences, as we will see. But let us start by assuming that a subordinate clause should satisfy both. For each predication, it is the maximal unit which does so. For example, in

ₐ[he said ᵦ[he would be visiting London on Wednesday]ᵦ]ₐ

the subordinate clause is again the whole of the unit labelled *b*, not the predicative syntagm alone:

ₐ[he said [ᵦ[he would be visiting London]ᵦ on Wednesday]]ₐ

or, if we accept the traditional division of subject and predicate, just the latter:

ₐ[he said [he ᵦ[would be visiting London on Wednesday]ᵦ]]ₐ

since in each case there is a larger unit which is also in a transformational relation to the main clause *He would be visiting London on Wednesday*. A clause may also be defined to include the subordinator, if any. Thus the subordinate unit in *He announced that he had no money* is again *that he had no money*, not just *he had no money*.

Given a definition on these lines, the simplest case of incompleteness is that in which one of the elements corresponding to a main clause does not form a syntagm with the rest. For example, the relative clause in *the man who I think you saw* includes a complement clause with the predicator *saw*. But the object of *saw* is the relative pronoun *who*, which is also a marking element (by the analysis of Chapter 3) in the larger clause. Therefore the subordinate unit consists just of the predicator and its subject:

_a[who I think _b[you saw]_b]_a

Likewise, in ⟨*the place*⟩ *where I think it happened*:

where is peripheral to the predicative syntagm *it happened* (arc above the line). But it too is an element in the larger clause which it marks; therefore the complement clause is *it happened* alone (second arc below the line). These analyses are justified by the regularity of the relationship between relative and main clauses. Thus *who I think* [*you saw*] is to, for example, *I think* [*you saw him*] (with the complete clause *you saw him*) as *who you saw* is to *You saw him*; likewise *where* [*I think it happened*] is to *I think* [*it happened in London*] as the simple *where it happened* is to *It happened in London*, and so on for other elements.

Another straightforward case of incompleteness is that of the relative clause in *a man that I knew* or, in the form given earlier, *a man I knew*. *That* is traditionally a relative pronoun, like *who* in *who I knew* (or, for speakers who still use it) *whom* in *whom I knew*). Therefore *I knew* differs from *that I knew* merely in that the object pronoun, which could in principle complete the predicative construction, is omitted. Alternatively, *that* is merely a marker, identical to the equally omissible element in the complement clause *that he had no money*. But the argument then applies at another remove. In *a man (that) I knew* the construction is in every respect the same as that of *a man who(m) I knew*, except for the absence of *who(m)*, whose marking role *that* optionally fills. Similarly, the construction of ⟨*the man*⟩ *that came*, which on this view has no subject, is otherwise identical to that of ⟨*the man*⟩ *who came*, that of ⟨*the village*⟩ *(that) he lived in* to that of ⟨*the village*⟩ *which he lived in* or *in which he lived*, and so on.

In these examples, as in all the others given so far, a grammarian will describe the subordinate unit as a **full clause**. But our definition would allow for other, less venial forms of incompleteness. For example, in

_a[I hired a taxi _b[to get him to the airport]_b]_a

b is not a phrase and is transformationally related to *The taxi got him to the airport*, *I will get him to the airport*, and the like. But *(to) get* has no subject; nor could one be added, unless the construction is further changed (*for it to get him to the airport*, or *so that I could get him to the airport*). It is also non-finite, in that it lacks the inflections and determiners characteristic of the verb phrase in complete clauses (past tense *got*, perfect *have got*, and so on). Such units are described as **reduced clauses**. To be precise, we might suggest that this term should be used of any clause which is incomplete in either or both of these senses: in that at least one potential element of a main clause, or at least one of the potential categories of its predicator, is excluded. Thus in

_a[I hired a taxi _b[for him to get to the airport]_b]_a

b is again reduced, by virtue of the infinitive *(to) get*, even though the elements associated with it are identical in their predicative function to those of *He got to the airport*. If there were a dialect of English which had no relative pronouns, the construction of *I knew* in *a man I knew* might also be seen as reduced.

All this looks reasonably neat and perhaps, if formulated as a set of definitions, it might stand. But once a category of reduced clause is admitted, it becomes rather difficult to decide precisely when our basic conditions are met. Nor is it clear which of them is essential. Hence there is a gradation between clauses and other units which are not clauses but are still, to a limited degree, predicative.

For illustration, let us start from a type of clause that is usually described as elliptical or abbreviated. In

_a[I wear it _b[when cycling in the country]_b]_a

when has the same meaning as in *I wear it when I am cycling in the country*, where it introduces a full clause. It is therefore natural to postulate a contraction:

_a[I wear it _b[when ⟨*sc.* I am⟩ cycling in the country]_b]_a

in which the subject and a form of BE can be latent. Likewise in *I used to recite it [when on guard duty]* (*when* ⟨sc. *I was*⟩, ⟨sc. *I used to be*⟩ *on guard duty*), in *[Once taken out] it will melt quite quickly* (*once* ⟨sc. *it is*⟩, ⟨sc. *it has been*⟩ *taken out*), in *He wrote it [while sober]* (*while* ⟨sc. *he was*⟩ *sober*), and so on. *When, once* and *while* would then be items that can only introduce a full clause, either contracted or uncontracted.

But can contraction be limited to units where such items are present? In

> I got wet [walking across the park]

we might again see a contracted peripheral clause; in this case the conjunction would also be latent ($\langle$sc. *when I was*$\rangle$, $\langle$sc. *while I was*$\rangle$ *walking across the park*). In

> I opened a book [lying on the table]

we might see a contracted relative clause: $\langle$sc. *which was*$\rangle$ *lying on the table*. Similar analyses might be extended to locative expressions:

> you are quite safe [$\langle$*sc.* if you are$\rangle$ in a tank]
> I opened the book [$\langle$*sc.* which was$\rangle$ on the table]

Then are these also complex sentences?

Clearly, an important question is whether the contractions are regular. In the construction of *when on guard duty* or *when at church* the range of prepositional phrases is the same as in *when I was on guard duty, when I was at church,* and so on. For example, one cannot say *I wore it when to church* any more than *I wore it when I was to church.* Therefore the proposed contraction is feasible. But it is not so if *when* is removed. Thus one can say *I wore it to church;* similarly, *I wear it onto the stage* is not a contraction of *I wear it when I am onto the stage,* nor *I was travelling to London via Birmingham* of, say, *I was travelling to London while I was via Birmingham.* In other examples the meanings would not correspond. *I put on my overcoat through the customs* means that I put it on while I was going through; *I put on my overcoat when I was through the customs* means that I did so when I was already past them. Likewise *I was travelling to Anglesey along the coast* does not match *I was travelling to Anglesey when I was along the coast,* though the latter could be meaningful. In some of these examples it might seem tempting to posit alternative contractions: for example, *I put on my overcoat* $\langle$sc. *while I was going*$\rangle$ *through the customs.* But this merely confirms that there is no general rule.

It is the same for locative modifiers. Thus *the path to the kitchen* cannot be expanded to *the path which is to the kitchen* and *the road out of town* has an ordinary meaning ('the road leading out of it') which does not correspond to that of *the road which is out of town* ('the road situated outside it'). Therefore we will not speak of clauses consisting just of phrases of this kind. But in the case of participles this first criterion is not decisive. In *a book lying on the table,* the participle and locative

175

complement already form two elements of a predication, in that respect identical to those of the full clause. Likewise *the letter* is a direct object in *the man reading the letter*, as in *who was reading the letter*, *(to) Mary* an indirect object in *the man handing the letter to Mary*, as in *who was handing the letter to Mary*, and so on. Neither the valency nor the collocability of LIE, READ or HAND is altered. Nor is there a verb which cannot appear in participial constructions of this type, with either the attributive or the peripheral function.

There are perhaps a few instances where the analysis is less attractive. For example, BELONG is a verb that is not usually progressive: one would say *This book belongs to me*, rather than *This book is belonging to me*. Hence there would be a doubtful contraction in *a book ⟨sc. which is⟩ belonging to me*, where the participle is quite normal. But even if we reject ellipsis we can still establish a more general transformational relationship. In *to get him to the airport* the infinitive corresponds to the range of finite verbs in *I got him to the airport*, *It is getting him to the airport*, and so on. Similarly, the participle in *lying on the table*, if not specifically a contraction of the progressive *is lying* or *was lying*, is a non-finite form which is again relatable to the finite paradigm in general. In one way or the other, the first of our basic conditions is met.

However, these units can be assimilated to a phrasal pattern. Thus *the men lying on the floor* is like, for example, *the men asleep on the floor* except that the participle has been replaced with an adjective. But adjectives are heads of phrases. For example, in *the men older than me*:

the men [older [than me]]

older depends on *men* and has in turn a complement marked by *than*. In *the men lying on the floor* there is at least a collocational relationship between *men* and *lying*. That allows an equivalent analysis:

the men [lying [on the floor]]

in which *lying on the floor* is a phrase headed by the participle. In the same way the analysis of *the men sleeping*:

the men sleeping

would correspond to that of, say, *the men available*:

the men available

with an attributive phrase consisting solely of the head adjective. If these analyses are right, a participial unit meets our first condition only.

To avoid this conclusion, it might be suggested that we have the same contraction in the case of adjectives: *the men* ⟨sc. *who are*⟩ *asleep on the floor*, or ⟨sc. *who are*⟩ *available*. However, the syntax of post-modifiers, as in *the men available*, can hardly be detached from that of premodifiers, as in *the available men*. Where either is possible their meanings can be different. Compare, for example, *an inflatable dinghy* (one of a type that inflates) and *all dinghies inflatable* (those that actually can be blown up); similarly, *a ready helper* (always ready to do so) and *a helper ready, a working model* (as opposed to a solid model) and *the model working*, or *a drinking man* (of a type characterised as a drinker) and *a man drinking*. Hence one could say *all inflatable dinghies actually inflatable*, or *those working models still working*. But in other cases the position is dictated by the structure of the modifier. *A new book* has a simple adjective which, in normal style, can only precede. Thus *I bought a book new* has a construction with *a book* and *new* as separate constituents (compare *I bought it new*). But an adjective follows if it has a prepositional dependent: *a man new to this area*, not *a new to this area man*. A single comparative adjective may precede (*an older man*); but if it has its complement either both follow (*a man older than me*) or they are split (*an older man than me*). But note that we cannot always split other forms of adjectival phrase (*a dissatisfied customer with our service*, and so on). The position can also be dictated by the type of head (*someone larger*, not *(a) larger someone*), or by the shape of an element before the adjective: thus *a car a little older than ours*, not *an a little older car than ours* (compare *an even older car than ours*). Finally, a few adjectives can only come after: thus *a man asleep*, not *an asleep man* (though both *a man sleeping*, with the participle, and *a sleeping man*).

The rules affecting the position show that we are dealing with one construction, not two. Hence there is no syntactic difference between *the available men* and *the men available*, or *the sleeping child* and *the child sleeping*, despite any nuance of meaning we might be able to force. But premodifiers cannot be expanded into relative clauses (*the* ⟨sc. *who are*⟩ *available men, the* ⟨sc. *who is*⟩ *sleeping child*); so, if there were to be a general relation between modifiers and clauses it could not be one of simple contraction. Nor is there a regular transformation. For where premodifiers have a different meaning (as in *the inflatable dinghy* versus *the dinghy inflatable*), the copular construction does not always correspond. For example, *a ready helper* does not stand to *The helper is ready* as *a new car* stands to *The car is new*. There are also fragmentary correspondences with other constructions. *A ready helper* has perhaps a better parallel in the predicate *helps readily*; compare *a light sleeper* and *sleeps lightly* (not *The sleeper is light*). *His golfing brother* is paralleled only by *His brother plays golf* (though *his hunting brother* is matched by *His brother hunts* and *His brother plays tennis* has no correlate *his tennising brother*), and so on.

In short, the attributive relation forms a construction on its own, subject to restrictions only partly predictable from those in clauses which contain the same or similar words. In this light, participles are an intermediate category. On the one hand, they behave like adjectives: compare *a walking man, the men walking, the men walking into the house* with, say, *a willing man, the men willing, the men willing to do it* (all with the participial adjective WILLING) or *a sick man, the men sick, the men sick with malaria*. We remarked in Chapter 1 that there is no regular transformation for premodifying participles such as *flying* in *flying planes*. The parallel with adjectives is also valid in peripheral functions: compare, for example, *He wrote it lying on his back* with *He wrote it sober* or *He wrote it flat on his back*.

On the other hand a participle is, or at least can be, a predicator, taking objects, locative complements and so on under the same rules that apply to finite equivalents. In our example:

the men [lying [on the floor]]

the participial unit is thus clause-like in its internal structure (arc *b*), but phrase-like in its external dependency (arc *a*).

A similar uncertainty arises in the analysis of gerundial units. Traditionally, these too are not clauses, but contain forms of verbs used in a noun-like function. But we have distinguished the construction of, for example, *the shooting of the hunters* or *Bill's shooting*, which were excluded as clauses at the beginning of this section, from that of *shooting hunters* (in *Shooting hunters is forbidden*) or *Bill shooting* (in *Bill shooting is a very rare sight*). In the latter case the *ing*-form will be modified by adverbs rather than adjectives: compare, for instance, *the illegal trapping of red deer* with *trapping red deer illegally* (or *illegally trapping red deer*). We noted in Chapter 1 that there is also a regular transformation which would relate *shooting hunters* to *They shot hunters, I was shooting hunters*, and so on. This too has a status like that posited for the reduced infinitival clause in *I hired a taxi to get him to the airport.*

If such units are not clauses it is because, though distinct from phrases headed by nouns, they still have some continuity with them. In the simplest case our two constructions virtually fall together. For example, in *Typing is very boring work*, the single element *typing* might be grouped with that of either *typing this chapter* (in *Typing this chapter is very boring work*), which is a predicator taking a direct object, or *the typing of this chapter*, which again has a genitive complement. Perhaps the only crucial evidence is that one would not also say *typing of this chapter*, with a following genitive but no determiner. The regular gerund can also be preceded by a possessive noun or pronoun. Compare, for example, *Bill doing some work was a surprise* or *Them cooking dinner was a great help* and *Bill's doing some work was a surprise* or the more usual written form *Their cooking dinner was a great help*. These last forms are thus residually like an ordinary noun phrase, such as *Bill's dinner*. But it might be more revealing to see all four as neither truly clausal (like, for example, *that Bill should have done some work*), nor truly phrasal, like a unit whose head enters into wider selectional restrictions.

A final problem – or a final twist to this particular complex of problems – can be illustrated with the peripheral element in *He left before seeing me* or *He left after seeing me*. In *when seeing me* we would again be able to posit a contraction (*when ⟨sc. he was⟩ seeing me*). But with *before* or *after* we cannot, since one would not normally say *He left before/after he was seeing me*. Similarly, *He has done it since seeing me* ('since that time he saw me') does not correspond to *He has done it since he was seeing me* ('since the time when he used to come and see me' or 'because of seeing me'). Nor could one say, for example, *He did it before drunk* or *He did it after in the country*, with a contraction like that of *while ⟨sc. he was⟩ drunk* or *when ⟨sc. he was⟩ in the country*. So, we have a form of reduced clause:

$_a$[he left $_b$[before seeing me]$_b$]$_a$

whose construction differs from that of the participial *seeing me* (in, say, [*Seeing me*] *they ran away*) only in that it too is introduced by a conjunction.

Or have we? Unlike *when* or *while*, *before* and *after* can control noun phrases (*before Christmas, after the accident*). A form such as *before seeing me* is also syntactically like, for example, *on welcoming them to England* (*the speech he made on welcoming them to England*) or *in digging the garden* (*In digging the garden they found several old coins*), where *on* and *in* are words that cannot introduce full clauses. We might therefore suggest that the construction is not clausal, but one in which a preposition controls a gerund. *Before seeing me*, with gerundial *seeing me*, would thus correspond to *before Christmas*, with the noun phrase *Christmas*, as *on welcoming them to England* would stand to *on their wedding day*, *by cycling in the country* (in *I keep fit by cycling in the country*) to *by regular exercise*, *through being careless* to *through carelessness*, and so on.

In fact, this set of parallels is not exact. One can also say *through him cycling in the country*, with a subject *him*; likewise if we take the compound preposition IN SPITE OF (*in spite of him cooking dinner*) or BECAUSE OF (*because of them being so careless*). But one could not say *before him cooking dinner* or (with a purely temporal meaning) *after him cooking dinner*; similarly for *on me cycling in the country* or *in them digging the garden*. (Compare, for example, *before his shooting of the hunters* or *in their playing of Mozart*, where *shooting* and *playing* have a genuinely noun-like function.) The evidence for *on* and *in* would suggest that they too can introduce both a reduced clause and a prepositional phrase, while *through* and others are only prepositional.

But the broad picture is clearly one of gradation. If we distinguish just the constructions of

(*a*) before I had finished breakfast
(*b*) before finishing breakfast
(*c*) before breakfast

we find one class of items that can only introduce a full clause: (construction *a*): thus BECAUSE, AS (in *I gave up as I was so tired*) or the causal sense of SINCE (*Since he is such a fool I will have nothing to do with him*). This will also include WHEN, WHILE or ONCE, provided that forms like *while cycling in the country*, which at first sight have construction *b*, are again seen as contractions. We also find a class that can only introduce prepositional phrases (construction *c*): thus AT (*at breakfast* but not, for example, *at welcoming them to the country*) or DURING. This will also include THROUGH, provided that construction *b* is distinguished from that of *through finishing breakfast*, on the evidence in the last paragraph. But IN and ON satisfy both constructions *b* and *c*, while BEFORE and AFTER, with the temporal sense of SINCE, appear in all three. Moreover, there are no items that allow just the intermediate construction *b*.

Traditionally, words like BECAUSE, WHEN or WHILE are conjunctions, while those like ON, AT or THROUGH are just prepositions; BEFORE and AFTER are then both conjunctions and prepositions, and so assigned to two distinct functions. But some grammarians have argued that, for English at least, the distinction is unreal. Even if we do not entirely follow them, we must recognise that the clausal and phrasal units can be very hard to keep apart.

FUSED CONSTRUCTIONS

The preceding discussion has introduced many of the problems which surround the notion of 'reduced clause'. But in all our examples the constituency of the unit has been taken for granted. For example, in *I got wet walking across the park* we took as given that there is a syntagm *walking across the park*. An obvious reason is that a similar group can also appear in initial position (*Walking across the park I got really soaked*). In *Them cooking dinner was a great help* we assumed a unit in which *cooking* controls both *them* and *dinner*:

as opposed to the modifier in, say, *Men cooking dinner always make a mess*:

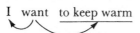

which includes just *cooking* and *dinner*. The crucial evidence is that one cannot say *Them cooking dinner were a great help*, despite the plurality of *them*. To the extent that these issues are clear, the problem becomes one of classification only.

But what, for instance, is the constituency of *I want to keep warm*? *To keep warm* would be a unit in *I shut the door to keep warm* (compare *to get him to the airport* in *I hired a taxi to get him to the airport*). Moreover, WANT can take an object in, say, *I want some firewood*. It is therefore natural to suggest that it can also take a clausal complement:

I want to keep warm

reduced in the same way. But this can easily be challenged. In *I want*

181

some firewood we can reorder the elements: *Some* FIRE*wood I* DO *want* (as opposed to other things which I do not). The construction can also be turned into the passive: THAT *firewood is* NOT *wanted*, or SOME *of the firewood is wanted by the* WO*man next door*. But neither test applies convincingly to the infinitive construction. The reordered form is unlikely: *To keep* WARM *I* DO *want*. One would surely use a more elaborate construction (*To keep warm is what I really want, To keep warm is something I* DO *want*), in which *want* and the infinitive are not directly related. A passive is scarcely better: *To keep warm is wanted by almost everybody, To get married is certainly wanted*. Again one would expect a more elaborate form (*To get married is a thing that is certainly wanted by* MOST *people*).

We are left with a broad analogy in which a putative infinitival object (*to keep warm* in *I want to keep warm*) would be compared to objects of other types (*the book* in *I finished the book* or *that he will come* in *I know that he will come*) in the same way that an infinitival subject (*To keep warm* in *To keep warm is advisable*) can be compared to subjects such as *the book* in *The book has arrived* or *that he will come* in *That he will come seems certain*. But in such an analogy 'object' is at best a generic term. There are verbs which take a noun phrase but cannot take an infinitive (*I have finished the book* but not, except with a purposive sense, *I have finished to keep warm*); others can take an infinitive but not a *that*-clause (*He started to read* but not *He started that he will come*), and so on. Each of these elements is a complement, by the criteria of valency elaborated in Chapter 6. But by the same criteria they are assigned to three distinct roles, only one of which (represented by *the book* in *I finished the book*) is that of an object, or direct object, in the strict sense.

Moreover, there is a gradience between the role of *want* in *I want to keep warm* and that of a Modal Auxiliary such as *must*, in *I must keep warm*, or *ought*, in *I ought to keep warm*. There are rules by which MUST and OUGHT are grouped together: for example, they can come before the subject in interrogatives (*Must I leave?, Ought I to leave?*) and can be followed by the reduced form of *not* (*I mustn't leave, I oughtn't to leave*). In that way both can be distinguished from WANT (*Want I to leave?, I wantn't to leave*), INTEND (*Intends he to leave?, They intendn't to leave*), and so on. But both OUGHT and WANT require *to* (*I ought to do it*, not *I ought do it*; *I want to do it*, not *I want do it*). In that respect OUGHT is distinguished from MUST (*I must do it*, not *I must to do it*). With DARE the pattern is further confused. In the present DARE largely goes with

MUST: *I daren't visit him* not *I daren't to visit him*, *Dare I visit him?* rather than *Dare I to visit him?* In the past it largely goes with WANT: thus neither *I daredn't visit him* nor *Dared I visit him?* However, one can say both *I didn't dare visit him* and *I didn't dare to visit him*; likewise, in the present, both *Do I dare visit him?* and *Do I dare to visit him?* Compare the discrepancy between the present and past tense of NEED: *Need I do it?* but not *Needed I do it?*, *I needn't do it* but not *I neededn't do it*.

According to the usual analysis, both *must visit* and *ought to visit* form a unitary verb phrase:

> I [must visit] him
> I [ought to visit] him

So would *daren't visit* and, in the past, the more literary *dared not visit*:

> I [daren't visit] him
> I [dared not visit] him

But for the latter the normal form is either *didn't dare visit* or *didn't dare to visit*. Are both these simple verb phrases:

> I [didn't dare visit] him
> I [didn't dare to visit] him

or the first alone, or neither?

It is perhaps between the last two examples that a line can plausibly be drawn. But the difference between them is not so considerable that, in addition to seeing a changed relation between *dare* and *visit*, we should also posit a change in the complexity of the sentence. Instead of a structure in which *dare* has a clausal complement:

> I didn't dare [to visit him]

we might establish a simple clause with four constituents:

> [I] [didn't dare] [to visit] [him]

in which there are direct links first between the subject and *dare*, then between *dare* and the infinitive, then between the infinitive and the object. A structure like this has been called Catenative (Latin *catena* 'a chain') and a verb like DARE a Catenative verb. We may then suggest the same analysis for WANT in *I wanted to visit him*:

> [I] [wanted] [to visit] [him]

183

This would at once explain why one cannot say *To* VI*sit him I* DO *want*, since *to visit* and *him* are two constituents and not one. Similarly INTEND would be a catenative verb in *I intended to visit him*, and so on.

A similar problem arises in the construction that QUIRK *et al.* (pp. 850ff.) describe as Complex Transitive. In *They painted it black*, the predicative construction has four terms:

Subject	Predicator	Object	Object Complement
they	painted	it	black

of which the fourth stands to the direct object in the same way that a subject complement, such as *nice* in *It tastes nice*, stands to a subject (Chapter 1, end of Chapter 4). Similarly, *They made him chairman* has a construction in which *chairman* is an object complement related to the object *him*. But what of, for example, *They made him do it*? This might seem to have the same construction:

Subject	Predicator	Object	Object Complement
they	made	him	[do it]

with a reduced clause:

Predicator	Object
do	it

in the fourth role. But there are no grounds for treating *do it* as a unit. It cannot be brought to the head of the sentence: DO *it they might make him* or *Eat* CHEESE *you can occasionally see him* (compare *You can occasionally see him eat cheese*). One cannot even say, for example, *Eat* CHEESE *is something they* DO *make him*. Here too the alternative is to establish *do* and *it* as separate elements:

[they] [made] [him] [do] [it]

with a catenative construction in which *do* relates to *made*, and *it* in turn relates to *do*.

The root of the problem is that in the construction with an object complement, as in that of *It tastes nice*, the relations between words do not reduce to a tree structure. In *They painted it black*, the object and adjective are linked by collocational restrictions analogous to those obtaining in the subject complement and copulative constructions: compare *It turned the milk sour* and *It turned the milk flat*, like *The milk went sour* and *The milk went flat* or *The milk was sour* and *The milk was flat*. On the strength of that we may propose a partial analysis

by which, all else being equal, *it* would depend on a predicator *black*. But the object complement is also a complement of the verb: compare the valencies of, for example, TURN and CHANGE (*That will turn it black* but not *That will change it black*) or, with a noun, of NOMINATE and SUGGEST (*They nominated him chairman* but not *They suggested him chairman*). If we add the roles of subject and object, we obtain a network

in which the complements which follow *painted* are themselves in a predicative relationship.

For Quirk *et al.*, the complex transitive is a fusion of the transitive and the copulative constructions (as in *They painted it* and *It is black*) into a single pattern of complementation. In this spirit, we may in general define a **fused construction** as any in which a single element is a complement of both a controlling and a dependent predicator. In *It tastes nice* we can now see *it* as a subject of both *tastes* and its predicative complement *nice*:

The construction is thus a fusion of the copulative (as in *It is nice*) with the intransitive (as, perhaps, in *It tastes*). In *They made him do it* we have a fused construction in which *him* is at once the object of *made* and the subject of *do*. The subject and object relationships are thus as follows:

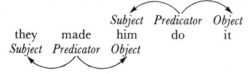

with fusion of the transitive and a second verbal predication. For *I want to do it* we may then suggest a construction in which *I* is the subject at once of *want* and of *do*:

185

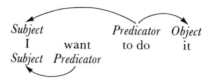

```
Subject              Predicator  Object
  I        want         to do      it
Subject   Predicator
```

The term 'catenative' would thus refer to the fusion of a dependent verbal construction with that of either the transitive or the intransitive.

Given this treatment of the subject and object relationships, it does not greatly matter whether, in the case of *They made him do it,* the first predicator is said to control the second plus its object:

they made him do it

– whereupon *do it* might again qualify as a reduced clause – or the second predicator alone:

they made him do it

For in neither case can a single tree structure be derived from the total set of dependency relations. In *I kept visiting him,* which apart from the participle has the same character as *I wanted to visit him,* we can see a fusion in which *kept* immaterially controls either *visiting him:*

I kept visiting him

or just *visiting.* Nor, if the latter, does it matter greatly whether the predicators are seen as a double-barrelled unit:

I [kept visiting] him

– to that extent like the verb phrase in, for example, *I was visiting him:*

I [was visiting] him

– or, again, as two constituents among four:

[I] [kept] [visiting] [him]

Any partial tree structure must, at some point, be inconsistent.

This treatment of such sentences is not usual, and perhaps goes somewhat beyond the hints and partial analyses that others have put forward. However, both the existence of fused constructions and the hierarchical indeterminacy that they give rise to might reasonably be expected from the way in which syntax can be assumed to be learned. At first, a child simply puts together collocations that make sense (*mummy–come, big–cake,* and so on). Such strings rapidly increase in length, partly by simple extension (*mummy–come + yesterday = mummy–come–yesterday*), partly by linking collocations with a common element (*mummy–want + want–cake = mummy–want–cake*) and partly, no doubt, by putting separate collocations together (*mummy–want + big–cake = mummy–want–big–cake, mummy–want + wear–hat = mummy–want–wear–hat, wear–hat + keep–warm = wear–hat–keep– warm,* and so on). This stage of learning may persist to an age at which most of the morphology, and a considerable amount of vocabulary, have apparently been mastered. For example, if a child of five says *Mummy wears a hat to keep warm,* we may have no compelling reason to assign this to a complex sentence construction (*Mummy wears a hat [to keep warm]*) rather than a simple collocational schema (*mummy– wears–a–hat–to–keep–warm*) in which, at successive points, an open or closed set of items can be substituted. To be precise, the question of what construction it has, or whether it is a simple sentence or a complex sentence, involve categories of 'construction', 'sentence' and so on which are not appropriate to the schemata with which learning begins.

According to our theory speakers do eventually conform to rules. Hence constructions are differentiated from collocations and, as one part of the process, those constructions which are indisputably simple, such as that of *I wear a hat,* are firmly distinguished from those which are indisputably complex, such as that of *I wear a hat so my head will be dry.* But this final stage of learning will again be carried only to the point at which a person's speech is fully acceptable in the community. So, just as it is natural that there should be cases of marginal codification, of the sort that we tried to explain at the end of Chapter 1, it is not surprising that there should also be cases of **marginal subordination**, in which it is undecidable whether a smaller clause is included. For example, there will be no effective difference among speakers if the recursion in *I kept wanting to try and see her* or *They forced him to make John do it* is learned as one involving successive layers of subordination, or as purely linear.

Finally, if this explanation is correct, it is not surprising that some of the trickiest cases of marginal codification should concern semantic relations for which a fused construction might be posited. In the adjectival sentence *She is eager to help*, the collocations are in other respects like those of the catenative *She wants to help*. We might therefore propose a structure

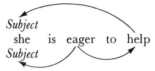

Subject
she   is eager to help
Subject

with *she* as subject of both *eager* and *help*. In transformational grammars, such sentences have been assigned a deep structure distinct from that of, for example, *She is easy to help*, where the relation of *she* to *help* would be that of an object. But there is also a difference between *She is easy to help* and, for example, *She is pretty to look at*. The former means that helping her is easy: the easiness is predicated of the action as a whole. But the latter does not mean that looking at her is pretty, any more than *She is eager to help* means that her helping is eager to come about. The prettiness is predicated not of the action, but of the individual who is looked at. Could this too be a difference of syntax? If so, one construction would be partly as follows:

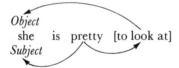

Object
she   is pretty [to look at]
Subject

with *she* at once the object of *look at* and the subject of *pretty*. The other might be seen as

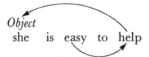

Object
she   is easy to help

where *easy* has the single complement *to help*.

A similar distinction could be drawn between, for example, *I tried to see her* and *I happened to see her*. In the first the trying is predicated of the speaker; we might therefore assign a structure like that of *I wanted to see her* or *I was eager to see her*. But the second describes his seeing her as something that happened – again a predication of the process, not of the individual. We might therefore see a structure

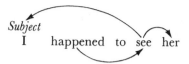

Subject
I happened to see her

in which *happened* takes the single complement *to see* or *to see her*. In *He promises to be a pianist* we might propose a constructional ambiguity. On the one hand, this can describe a promise he is making (compare *He is trying to be a pianist*). On the other hand, it can refer to something that promises to be so (compare *He happens to be a pianist*).

But there are many marginal examples. Which pattern have we in, for example, *They began to discuss it*? Was their discussion something which was begun by them (so like, for example, *They pretended to discuss it*), or merely something that began to happen (compare *They seemed to be discussing it*)? Does *It is dangerous to play with* mean that it is dangerous with respect to playing with it (compare, for example, *It is heavy to lift*), or rather that playing with it is a dangerous thing to do (like *It is difficult to play with*)? Such examples have been referred to as 'syntactic blends' – as forms which, like the locative in *No animal shall sleep in a bed* (Chapter 6), stand at the point of merger between two putative constructions. But is the term 'syntactic' appropriate? An alternative view is that the differences between *I tried to see her* and *I happened to see her*, or *She is pretty to look at* and *She is easy to help*, lie simply in the different meanings of TRY and HAPPEN or PRETTY and EASY. Likewise the ambiguity of *He promises to be a pianist* is just a reflection of two different senses of PROMISE.

We might also query the syntactic distinction between *She is eager to help* and *She is easy to help*. On one view, both might have a structure like this:

she is [*Adjective* to help]

where *easy to help* and *eager to help* are simply phrases with an infinitival complement. Their different interpretations we would explain, or seek to explain, by the meanings of EAGER, EASY and other individual lexemes. In the opposite view, the adjectives again have different valencies. The problem of hierarchical indeterminacy, which arose in a simpler form in the construction of *He wanted to do it*, is thus associated with a problem of marginality in codification, similar in principle to that originally illustrated, in a simpler form, by *He walked with a stick* versus *He went with a stick* (see again the end of Chapter 1).

In such circumstances, a grammarian should not be embarrassed if he cannot entirely resolve the argument.

NOTES AND REFERENCES

The sense of 'clause' has developed in this century, and the reader will encounter variations in its use.

(1) Earlier grammarians did not see one clause as including another. Thus for Sweet *If you are right, I am wrong* 'is made up of the two clauses *if you are right* and *I am wrong*' (SWEET, 1, p. 19); likewise, for instance, *Is it me you want?* has the first clause *Is it me?* (pp. 156f.). Compare the recommendation in *Terminology*, p. 14 (note 2). Criticism, in general effective, in JESPERSEN, *Philosophy*, pp. 105f. (expanding *MEG*, 2, pp. 14f.); but see end of Chapter 10 below for cases where the traditional view seems justified.

(2) The term has sometimes been restricted to subordinate elements: thus JESPERSEN, *Philosophy*, p. 103 (*MEG*, 2, p. 13), at the beginning of the sections referred to under (1).

(3) 'Sentence' is still normal for subordinate elements, as well as sentences in the Bloomfieldian sense. For older usage see again SWEET, 1, p. 19 *et passim*. In transformational grammar subordinate sentences (S) are 'embedded' in larger sentences: for example, in $_S[I\ said\ _S[it\ was\ a\ man\ _S[I\ knew]_S\ ]_S\ ]_S$, *I knew* is embedded in the structure of *it was a man I knew*, which is in turn the embedded complement of *said*. S is thus a recursive category (as NP and PP were recursive in the phrase structure rules of Chapter 4) of which our 'sentences' (Chapter 2) are maximal instances. For the standard formulation see CHOMSKY, *Aspects*, pp. 134f.; for textbook discussion HUDDLESTON, Ch. 7, which points out the reasons for not treating 'clause' as primitive (pp. 96f.).

(4) The term is traditionally restricted to units that contain, or under ellipsis can be said to contain, a complete predication. See *OED*, s.v., §1 ('containing a subject and predicate') and citation from Dalgleish (1865); also the range of examples given by JESPERSEN, *Philosophy* or *MEG*, *loc. cit.* (with the remark that 'as a rule it contains a finite verb', *Philosophy*, p. 103) and HUDDLESTON's definition, p. 97 ('essentially, ... a sentence having NP and VP as daughters'). For its wider extension see QUIRK *et al.*, Ch. 11; note, for instance, that they call *irresolute* a clause in *His gaze travelled round, irresolute* (p. 726). Their definition in an earlier chapter (p. 342) should be read in the light of its application to this and other 'verbless clauses' (p. 722).

For a brief summary of the traditional notion of the clause compare DUBOIS *et al.* for French, s.v. 'proposition', §1.

For 'full' and 'reduced clause' I have been helped, in part, by current work of Chomsky and his collaborators. In their theory, certain rules are subject to a 'propositional island condition' (earlier called 'tensed S condition'); this means that they cannot apply across the boundary of a clause which (in English) contains a finite verb. Nor can they apply unless the clause is, in ordinary terms, subjectless (one case of the 'specified subject condition'). In English, therefore, they are invalid unless a subordinate clause, or S, is reduced by both the criteria which I have stated. For these and related proposals see, in particular, N. Chomsky, 'Conditions on transformations', in S. R. Anderson & P. Kiparsky (eds.), *A Festschrift for Morris Halle* (New York: Holt, Rinehart & Winston, 1973), pp. 232–86 (reprinted, with other relevant papers and an index, in CHOMSKY, *Essays*, pp. 81–160); also Chomsky's 'On wh-movement', in CULICOVER *et al.* (ed.), pp. 71–132, and his *Rules and Representations* (Oxford: Blackwell, 1980), Ch. 4 (where these conditions are subsumed by the 'opacity principle'); summary of the version in 'On wh-movement' in LIGHTFOOT, pp. 62ff. This work has been criticised: for example, by E. Bach, 'Comments on the paper by Chomsky' ['On wh-movement'], in CULICOVER *et al.* (ed.), pp. 133–55. But despite continuing problems it does point to a narrower category – essentially that of clause or full clause in the traditional sense – to be distinguished from that of subordinate S, or surface derivate of subordinate S, in general.

For the category 'abbreviated clause' see QUIRK *et al.*, p. 725 and pp. 744ff. *passim*; this and other related or possible cases of ellipsis are discussed on pp. 540ff. For 'participle clauses' in postmodifying position *ibid.*, pp. 541, 876ff. Chomsky originally proposed a transformational account of adjectival modifiers (CHOMSKY, *Structures*, p. 72); standard formulation, integrated with a similar account of participial and prepositional modifiers, in, for example, HUDDLESTON, pp. 103f. This was persuasively criticised, especially by D. L. Bolinger, 'Adjectives in English: attribution and predication', *Lingua*, 18 (1967), pp. 1–34; earlier and less comprehensively by W. Winter, 'Transforms without kernels?', *Lg*, 41 (1965), pp. 484–9. For these or other reasons it is now increasingly abandoned: thus hesitantly by JACKENDOFF, *Semantic Interpretation*, pp. 59ff.; confidently in, for example, Culicover's textbook (CULICOVER, Chs. 2 and 8). I confess that I must also renounce an early suggestion of my own, regarding a clausal source for locative phrases (in my review article, 'Transformational grammar', *ArchL*, 13 (1961), pp. 196–209). On the status of gerundial units see P. Schachter, 'A nontransformational account of gerundive nominals in English', *LIn*, 7 (1976), pp. 205–41.

For a conflation of conjunction and preposition see JESPERSEN, *Philosophy*, p. 89, in a passage already referred to in Chapter 7 above for that of preposition and adverb; also references to Jackendoff and Vincent in the next paragraph. For HOCKETT, p. 192, both are subtypes of 'directive particle' and, in general, impure markers (notes to Chapter 3 above). For Heringer, conjunctions such as *weil* or *wenn* are 'Angabetranslative' ('adverbialisers'), again with both 'translative' and 'informative' meaning (HERINGER, p. 247; similar treatment of contrasting prepositions, pp. 198f., also referred to in Chapter 3 above). For relative *that* as a conjunction, which I mention briefly for *a man that I knew*, see JESPERSEN, *MEG*, 3, Ch. 8 (expanding JESPERSEN, *Philosophy*, p. 85); recent discussion, almost to the point of overkill, by H. F. W.

Stahlke, 'Which that', *Lg*, 52 (1976), pp. 584–610. See also LIGHTFOOT, in the section referred to below (pp. 313ff.), where *that* is treated like a role-filler (Chapter 12 below) for a 'COMP' or 'complementiser' position which is otherwise occupied both by relative pronouns and by other conjunctions.

A further question is whether the conjunction is rightly included in the clause. In Hockett's account the term 'clause' applies to just the 'axis' (complement) of the directive element (HOCKETT, p. 194): so, *They rang me when* $_{\text{Clause}}[I\ was\ in]_{\text{Clause}}$ or *I said that* $_{\text{Clause}}[it\ was\ Bill]_{\text{Clause}}$ not, as traditionally, $_{\text{Clause}}[when\ I\ was\ in]_{\text{Clause}}$ and $_{\text{Clause}}[that\ it\ was\ Bill]_{\text{Clause}}$. Nor is the conjunction an element in QUIRK *et al.*'s initial definition (p. 342), though included, in brackets, in the analysis of the example illustrating it. For one current resolution see, for instance, LIGHTFOOT, p. 316 (and earlier, p. 58), where, in such examples, S would dominate Hockett's clauses ($_{\text{S}}[I\ was\ in]_{\text{S}}$, $_{\text{S}}[it\ was\ Bill]_{\text{S}}$) and $\bar{\text{S}}$ – a higher level of S-hood under the $\bar{\text{X}}$-convention referred to in the notes to Chapter 7 above – those which are clauses in the traditional sense ($_{\text{S}}[when\ I\ was\ in]_{\text{S}}$, $_{\text{S}}[that\ it\ was\ Bill]_{\text{S}}$). But two tentative comments may perhaps be in order. (1) It is not obvious that conjunctions like *when* should be grouped with a pure subordinator such as *that*. Usually they are: see QUIRK *et al.*, p. 727; again HOCKETT, pp. 194f. (examples with *that* as directive particle). But note that one can say *What did you confess that you had done?*, with *what* as object of *had done*, while one would not say, for example, *What did you stop when you had done?* In Chomskyan terms this might be explained by the difference between an $\bar{\text{S}}$ ($_{\text{S}}[that . . .]_{\text{S}}$) and a phrase with an $\bar{\text{S}}$ as its complement (*when* $_{\text{S}}[. . .]_{\text{S}}$), the latter falling under his 'subjacency condition'. Compare again LIGHTFOOT, pp. 62ff. and other references given above, for the propositional island and specified subject conditions. (2) The treatment of conjunctions is quite unlike that of prepositions, which under the $\bar{\text{X}}$-convention are best seen as heads of $\bar{\text{P}}$, $\bar{\bar{\text{P}}}$ and so on (see again Chapter 7). Both objections are answered if conjunctions and prepositions are con-flated: compare JACKENDOFF, $\bar{X}$ *Syntax*, p. 79; full discussion in N. Vincent, 'Syntactic categories old and new: complementisers and conjunctions', to be published in *TPhS*.

On these matters I have deliberately stuck to traditional views, as I am not convinced that we should overstrain ourselves in searching for a mathematically elegant solution.

For *want to visit* as a 'catenative construction' see W. F. Twaddell, *The English Verb Auxiliaries*, 2nd edn (Providence: Brown University Press, 1965), p. 22. His first edition (1960) talks only of 'catenative verbs'; likewise PALMER, p. 16, Ch. 7. Palmer extends the term to verbs with an intervening noun phrase: thus WANT is also catenative in *wants them to go* (PALMER, p. 168). For arguments against catenatives taking objects see PALMER, pp. 176ff., and note his remark on gradience (p. 180). But he consistently avoids deciding issues of constituency, talking both of a subordinate clause and of a 'complex verb phrase'. For the former alternative compare JESPERSEN, *Syntax*, §§17.2 (catenative + infinitive), 15.1–2 (catenative + noun phrase + infinitive);

also 14.1 (for the non-verbal object complement). Full discussion of the last in JESPERSEN, *MEG*, 5, Chs. 2–5 (expanding *Philosophy*, pp. 122ff.). For the latter alternative it is worth recalling Chomsky's earliest account of object complements (CHOMSKY, *Structures*, pp. 76f.), which derived *considers John incompetent* from $_V$[*considers incompetent*]$_V$ *John*. See too HERINGER, p. 191 and earlier, for German *x findet y dumm* or *x lässt y schlafen*. In transformational terms a third alternative is to derive a complex verb phrase by an operation 'raising' the subordinate predicator. See RADFORD, §§1.7 and 3.5–6, on Italian; among his references especially Judith Aissen, 'Verb raising', *LIn*, 5 (1974), pp. 325–66 (on causatives in Turkish and Romance); L. Rizzi, 'Ristrutturazione', *Rivista di grammatica generativa*, 1 (1976), pp. 1–54. Application to English is less usual; compare, however, D. R. Dowty, 'Montague grammar and the lexical decomposition of causative verbs', in Barbara H. Partee (ed.), *Montague Grammar* (New York: Academic Press, 1976), pp. 201–45 (specifically §§5 and following, on the object complement construction).

Tree structures are so attractive that few linguists have considered the possibility that they might not be general. See, however, G. Sampson, 'The single mother condition', *JL*, 11 (1975), pp. 1–12, with diagram for *John wants to go* (p. 6); on the same construction P. M. Postal & G. Pullum, 'Traces and the description of English complementizer contraction', *LIn*, 9 (1978), pp. 1–29 (last section, especially p. 24). The latter is in terms of a then unpublished development of 'relational grammar' (notes to Chapter 6 above). Sampson's analyses are rejected by J. Anderson, 'Syntax and the single mother', *JL*, 15 (1979), pp. 267–87; see, however, pp. 269–71 for *the stories*, in *You expected the stories to terrify John*, as dependent on both *expected* and *terrify*. For an earlier and similarly limited proposal see S. C. Dik, 'Referential identity', *Lingua*, 21 (1968), pp. 70–97 (functional patterns on pp. 90f.); more recently HUDSON, pp. 167f. (on *He kept the wheel moving*). On the subject and object complements see my 'Complex intransitive constructions', in G. N. Leech *et al.* (eds.), *Studies in English Linguistics: for Randolph Quirk* (London: Longman, 1980), pp. 41–9. The relations in the latter construction are described precisely by SWEET, 1, p. 96.

For the syntactic blending of adjective constructions see D. L. Bolinger, 'Syntactic blends and other matters', *Lg*, 37 (1961), pp. 366–81; this is one of the most telling critiques of early transformational analyses, and widely unheeded. On the type of blend in general see F. R. Palmer, 'Noun phrase and sentence: a problem in semantics/syntax', *TPhS*, 1972, pp. 20–43; for verbal cases PALMER, pp. 183ff. See also my *Generative Grammar*, §§148–52. In standard generative accounts *I tried to see her* derives from a structure like *I tried* $_{NP}$[$_S$[*I see her*]$_S$]$_{NP}$ by deletion of the second *I*; *I happened to see her* from $_{NP}$[$_S$[*I see her*]$_S$]$_{NP}$ *happened* by the raising of *I* from subordinate position. Details in HUDDLESTON, Ch. 8 (summarised pp. 124f.); see also Ruwet's elegant discussion of French: N. Ruwet, 'La syntaxe du pronom "en" et la transformation de "montée du sujet"', reprinted in his *Théorie syntaxique et syntaxe du français* (Paris: Seuil, 1972), pp. 48–86. But such distinctions are now disputed. Against the former analysis see M. K. Brame, *Conjectures and Refutations in Syntax and Semantics* (New York: Elsevier/North-Holland, 1976), Ch. 5; consequences for the latter pp. 117f. and alternative account p. 137. Compare H. Lasnik & R. Fiengo, 'Complement object deletion', *LIn*, 5 (1974), pp. 535–71, against the standard account of examples like *She is easy to help*. In each case the movement is towards pre- or anti-transformational solutions. Another case of 'raising' is discussed at length by P. M. Postal, *On Raising: One Rule of English Grammar and its Theoretical Implications* (Cambridge, Mass.: MIT Press, 1974). For my notion of fusion it is worth looking back to HARRIS, 'Co-occurrence and transformation', on 'word-sharing' (§§3.6–7 and conclusion of §3 generally).

In the last section I have adopted what I conceive to be a commonsense view of the child's learning of syntax. An opposite view is that two year olds are already conforming to rules: see especially R. Brown, *A First Language: the Early Stages* (Cambridge, Mass.: Harvard University Press, 1973), following in this respect CHOMSKY, *Aspects*, Ch. 1. For reasons why I think it is wrong see my review of Brown, *JL*, 11 (1975), pp. 322–43: for specialist opinion in the same sense, Ruth Clark, 'Performing without competence', *Journal of Child Language*, 1 (1974), pp. 1–22; M. D. S. Braine, *Children's First Word Combinations* (Chicago: University of Chicago Press for the Society for Research in Child Development, 1976). On complex sentences compare D. Ingram, 'If and when transformations are acquired by children', in D. P. Dato (ed.), *Developmental Psycholinguistics: Theory and Applications* (Washington: Georgetown University Press, 1975), pp. 99–127. For up-to-date surveys of research in children's language see P. Fletcher & M. Garman (eds.), *Language Acquisition: Studies in First Language Development* (Cambridge: Cambridge University Press, 1979); but as a general introduction Jespersen's has not been surpassed: O. Jespersen, *Language: its Nature Development and Origin* (London: Allen & Unwin, 1922), Part 2.

9
Coordination

In Chapter 4 we discussed a form of recursion in which a syntagm of class *a* is a dependent within a larger syntagm also of class *a*. For example, in *the meat on the table in the kitchen*, a noun phrase *the kitchen* is the complement of *in*, forming a prepositional phrase *in the kitchen*; this in turn is an attribute of *table*, which is the head of a larger noun phrase *the table in the kitchen*; that in its turn is the complement of *on*, forming a larger prepositional phrase *on the table in the kitchen*, which is itself an attribute of *meat*. Clause types can be recursive in the same way. The pattern of 'The House that Jack Built' has already been mentioned (end of Chapter 2). In

$_a$[he said $_b$[that she had promised $_c$[she would come]$_c$]$_b$]$_a$

we have a similar structure in which clause *c* is a complement of *promised*, whose own clause (*b*) is in turn a complement of *said*; clause *a* could in its turn be a complement in

[I was told $_a$[he said that she had promised she would come]$_a$]

and so on. Alternatively, *b* could form part of an adverbial clause:

[before he had said [that she had promised she would come]]

which could be a peripheral element in a relative clause:

[who left [before he had said . . .]]

which might modify the object of a larger adverbial clause:

[when I followed the man [who left before . . .]]

which might itself be peripheral in, for example, a still larger relative clause. The example is becoming increasingly unwieldy. But there is no rule which restricts the number of layers.

A different form of recursion involves the relationship of **coordination**. In the first line of a poem by Christina Rossetti

I looked for that which is not, nor can be

('A Pause of Thought', line 1), the relative clause has two predicates, *is not* and *can be*, joined by the conjunction *nor*. We could, in principle, add a third (*which is not, nor can be, nor* SHOULD *be*), or a third and a fourth, and so on. In another line two verbs are joined by the conjunction *and*:

I watched and waited with a steadfast will

(line 4). We could easily add more (*I watched and waited and hoped, I watched and waited and hoped and prayed*), again with no fixed limit. Alternatively, *watched* might be a predicate joined by *and* to a second predicate *waited with a steadfast will*. Additional elements would also be predicates: *prayed endlessly* (in *I watched and waited with a steadfast will and prayed endlessly*), *stifled my anxiety*, and so on. Conjunctions apart, each sequence has a construction which conforms to the following schema:

$$X_1 \ldots X_n$$

where the *X*'s are syntactically similar and *n* has any value greater than 1. But no one *X* depends on any other. Thus in the first example *is not* is neither the controller nor a dependent of *can be*. Instead both predicates stand in an equal relation to the subject *which*.

A sequence of this sort can readily form a hierarchy. Thus in *She is seeing either Bill and Mary or Bill and Jane* the object is formed by four successive nouns: *Bill, Mary, Bill* and *Jane*. But there are two levels of coordination. At the lower level *Mary* is joined to the first *Bill* and *Jane* to the second *Bill*, both by *and*:

[Bill and Mary]   [Bill and Jane]

At the higher level *Bill and Mary* is joined to *Bill and Jane*, by the pair *either . . . or*:

[either [Bill and Mary] or [Bill and Jane]]

Again there is no dependency; all four nouns are related equally to *(is) seeing*. But in establishing the linear relation of coordination, by which the first *Bill* is coordinate with *Mary* or *Bill and Mary* with *Bill and Jane*, we also establish a syntagm formed by the **coordinates** and conjunctions which are involved. This type of syntagm we will call a **coordinative syntagm**. In the first example from Christina Rossetti, *is not* and *can be* are immediate constituents of the coordinative syntagm *is not, nor can be*:

which [[is not], nor [can be]]

In the example now before us, the coordinative syntagm *Bill and Mary* is a constituent of the larger coordinative syntagm *either Bill and Mary or Bill and Jane*.

A conjunction which joins the elements of a coordinative syntagm is a **coordinator**. In any grammar these will form a closed class: in English, *and* and *or*, the pairs *both ... and* and *either ... or*, the negatives *nor, neither* and *neither ... nor*, and so on. Alternatively, each grammar will establish a set of **coordinative constructions**, each with its own marker or set of markers (Chapter 3). In English, one construction might be represented by the schema

(either) $X_1 \ldots$ or X_n

with the possible combinations X_1 *or* X_2 (*Bill or Mary*), *either* X_1 *or* X_2 (*either Bill or Mary*), X_1 *or* $X_2 \ldots$ *or* X_n (*Bill or Mary or their daughter*), *either* X_1 *or* $X_2 \ldots$ *or* X_n (*either Bill or Mary or their daughter*), and $X_1 X_2 \ldots$ *or* X_n (*Bill, Mary or their daughter*). Another construction would be similar:

(both) $X_1 \ldots$ and X_n

but with further restrictions on *both*. In the schema which we might represent as

(neither) $X_1 \ldots$ nor X_n

neither and *nor* amalgamate the function of a coordinator, seen as the marker of a coordinative construction, with that of the negative particle.

So far there are no problems. But let us look more closely at the

197

sequences of elements that enter into coordinative relationships. We have remarked that there is a similarity between coordinates: for example, in *I saw Mary and her daughter*, both *Mary* and *her daughter* are noun phrases, and both stand in the direct object relationship to *saw*. But how close must the parallel be, and what form of rule restricts it?

COORDINATION BETWEEN WHAT?

We may begin by considering coordination within the framework of a phrase structure grammar. For a simple transitive sentence (*Bill saw her daughter*), the first rule could be of the form introduced in Chapter 5:

S → NP + Predicate

where the category of noun phrase is extended, as in Chapter 7, to cover single nouns as well as syntagms. The predicate would then be specified as follows:

Predicate → V + NP

where another rule for a noun phrase, here and in other positions, may be given as

NP → Possessive + N

('Possessive' = *my*, *Bill's* and so on). For the coordinative object in *Bill saw her daughter and her sister*, we could then envisage a rule

NP → NP + and + NP

by which the whole and its parts are assigned to the same category. This might be generalised as follows:

$NP \rightarrow NP_1 \ldots$ and $+ NP_n$

covering the case of three coordinates (NP → NP + NP + *and* + NP), of four (NP → NP + NP + NP + *and* + NP), and so on. The same formula allows for a coordinative subject (*Bill and my brother saw her sister*). Others of the same type would permit coordination in other categories: thus in verbs

$V \rightarrow V_1 \ldots$ and $+ V_n$

(*Bill saw and heard her daughter*) or in predicates

$$\text{Predicate} \rightarrow \text{Predicate}_1 \dots \text{and} + \text{Predicate}_n$$

(*Bill saw her daughter, swallowed his drink and left the room*).

We may also specify dependency relations. In terms of the combined system which we sketched in Chapter 4, the first two rules may be reformulated as follows:

$$S \rightarrow NP \qquad \text{Predicate}$$

$$\text{Predicate} \rightarrow V \qquad NP$$

where dependency is interpreted as obtaining between heads, in the sense since clarified in Chapter 7. Accordingly the subject, like the object, will depend on the verb, as head of the predicate:

$$_S[NP \ _{\text{Predicate}}[V \qquad NP]_{\text{Predicate}}]_S$$

For *her daughter and her sister* the rule could then be written as

$$NP \rightarrow NP \ \text{and} \ NP$$

where the double arrow indicates that both coordinates have a head-like character. In the predicate *saw her daughter and her sister*, the dependencies will therefore be interpreted as follows:

$$V \ _{NP}[NP \ \text{and} \ NP]_{NP}$$

with both coordinates standing in an equal relationship to the verb. The next rule will indicate the head of the noun phrase:

$$NP \rightarrow \text{Possessive} \ N$$

Therefore, more specifically, there is dependency between the verb and each of the following nouns:

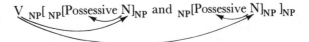

$$V \ _{NP}[\ _{NP}[\text{Possessive} \ N]_{NP} \ \text{and} \ _{NP}[\text{Possessive} \ N]_{NP} \ ]_{NP}$$

For the sentence *Bill saw her daughter and her sister*, the combined dependency and constituency structure will accordingly be

[Bill [saw [[her daughter] and [her sister]]]]

with only the coordinator, *and*, left out of the network of arcs.

For two or more noun phrases the rule of coordination may again be generalised:

$$NP \rightarrow NP_1 \ldots \text{and } NP_n$$

with similar formulae for verbs and predicates:

$$V \rightarrow V_1 \ldots \text{and } V_n$$

$$\text{Predicate} \rightarrow \text{Predicate}_1 \ldots \text{and Predicate}_n$$

and so on. In *Bill saw and heard her daughter*, we therefore see a structure:

[Bill [[saw and heard] [her daughter]]]

in which *saw* and *heard* are equal controllers of both *Bill* and *daughter*. *Bill* would have a similar role in our example with three predicates (*Bill saw her daughter, swallowed his drink and left the room*). The head of a predicate must again control its subject; but by the rule of coordination the predicate in this case has three equal predicates within it. Therefore the heads of all three must control equally:

[Bill [[saw [her daughter]] [swallowed [his drink]] and [left [the room]]]]

Finally, the dependency relations also carry through successive layers of coordination. Thus the grammar could include another formula

$$NP \rightarrow NP_1 \ldots \text{or } NP_n$$

for subjects and objects such as *Mary or her daughter*, or *Bill, Mary or her daughter*. But noun phrases joined by *or* may in turn consist of noun phrases joined by *and* (*Bill and Mary or Bill and Jane*). By the rule for *or* a head-like element is to be found within both *Bill and Mary* and *Bill and Jane*; by the rule for *and* there are then two head-like elements in each of these. A predicate *saw Bill and Mary or Bill and Jane* will accordingly have a structure like this:

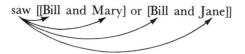

where *saw* has four dependents assigned to two layers of syntagms.

This formulation is appropriate for the examples which we have discussed so far, though it has the general defect, inherent in simple constituency and dependency models, that the relations of subject, direct object and so on are not labelled. But it makes explicit two related assumptions, neither of which we will be able to uphold. The first is that coordination is always between units of the same class. Thus in *I saw Bill and her brother*, both *Bill* and *her brother* belong to the class 'noun phrase'; in *I saw her brother and sister*, both *brother* and *sister* are nouns; in *Bill's and Peter's books*, both *Bill's* and *Peter's* are possessives, and so on. We might be tempted to advance an even bolder hypothesis, by which there is no class which cannot form coordinates. Our rules for *and* could then be covered by a single formula

$$X \rightarrow X_1 \ldots \text{and } X_n$$

where X is a variable ranging over the entire set of categories. Thus if there is a class 'possessive', as implied by our rule for noun phrases such as *Bill's books*, there is also a set of rules for syntagms of the form Possessive + *and* + Possessive, Possessive + Possessive + *and* + Possessive, and so on. Likewise for the categories 'N', 'NP', 'Predicate' and 'V', or any others that a grammar sets up.

The second assumption is implied by the first: namely, that coordination is always between units. *Bill saw her daughter* contains a syntagm *her daughter*, and *Bill saw her sister* a syntagm *her sister*; these same syntagms are joined as coordinates in *her daughter and her sister*. By the rule for NP + Predicate, *saw her sister* and *left the room* are syntagms in *Bill saw her daughter* and *Bill left the room*; so too in *Bill saw her daughter and left the room*. In general, such rules would allow no sequence of the form

$$A_1 \ldots A_n \text{ c } B_1 \ldots B_n$$

where c joins the coordinates $A_1 \ldots A_n$ and $B_1 \ldots B_n$, but neither of these could be a syntagm on its own. For the coordinates must themselves be of some class; in the rules envisaged, this is also the class of the

201

coordinative syntagm as a whole; therefore there must be at least one other rule which introduces it.

These assumptions can be defended, to some extent, by taking co-ordination as a criterion by which an analysis into constituents and classes is justified. In the Latin phrase

> per suum Meropisque caput
> 'by his own head and that of Merope'

(Ovid, *Metamorphoses*, I. 763), a coordinator -*que* unites a pair of words, *suum* 'his own' and *Meropis* 'of Merope', whose syntax is at first sight very different. *Suum* is a form of an adjective, inflected for number, case and gender in agreement with the noun *caput* 'head', while *Meropis* is a noun form, whose relationship to *caput* is marked by a genitive ending. If that were the end of their classification, our first assumption would be proved wrong. But rather than face this consequence we might argue that because *suum* and *Meropis* can be coordinated their classes must, at some level, be identical. Therefore we would establish a class 'Poss(essive)', as in the rule for English *her daughter* or *Bill's books*, by which the requisite pattern is achieved:

$$_{Poss}[_{Poss}[\text{suum}]_{Poss} \text{ -que } _{Poss}[\text{Meropis}]_{Poss}]_{Poss}$$

In this way the parallel would be presented in classificatory terms.

Similarly, in

> he asked [[her name] and [where she came from]]

the second coordinate is a clause, while the first is merely a phrase with a noun as its head. Unless the clause is itself a noun phrase, or both belong to some more embracing category, the parallel must lie solely in their role as complements of *asked*. In my view that is indeed where it does lie. But for many scholars the category of 'noun phrase' covers every unit, whatever its internal make-up, which plays a noun-like role. So, in *He asked where she came from*, the complement of *asked* would be a noun phrase *where she came from*. For a scholar who wished to defend the rules which we have outlined, the fact that it can be coordinated with phrases like *her name* or *three other questions* (*He asked where she came from and three other questions*) would seem important evidence for its classification.

In such examples only our first assumption is threatened. But the criterion has also been used to justify divisions between constituents.

In *her elder brother and younger sister*, the coordination separates the adjective and noun (*elder brother*, *younger sister*) from the possessive. Hence, in the non-coordinative *her elder brother* or *her younger sister*, we might suggest a corresponding division:

[her [elder brother]]   [her [younger sister]]

so that, it might be argued, the coordination can be explained. Similar analyses are common in Bloomfieldian handbooks, as we remarked in Chapter 4. In *He could have seen her and left the room*, the coordinative syntagm is as follows:

he could have [[seen her] and [left the room]]

and forms a larger syntagm with the auxiliaries *could* and *have*. But this cuts across the usual division between verb phrase and object, by which, in the non-coordinative *He could have seen her* or *He could have left the room*, the words *seen her* or *left the room* do not form a unit. Therefore we might question that analysis. An alternative treatment has been adopted by transformational grammarians, in which a constituent labelled 'Auxiliary' is divided from a second constituent which contains the verb and all the other elements of the predicate.

Such reasoning has an appeal for any grammarian whose model is wholly or primarily based on constituency relations. But it quickly leads to contradictions. If a phrase like *her elder brother* has one structure in which the adjective forms a unit with the noun, we can scarcely justify another:

[[her elder] brother]

in which it goes with the possessive. Yet these too can form a coordinate (*her elder and her younger brother*). Likewise one could say both *a blue coat and yellow scarf*:

a [[blue coat] and [yellow scarf]]

and *a blue and a yellow pullover*:

[[a blue] and [a yellow]] pullover

three common gulls and black-headed gulls or *three common and four black-headed gulls*, *some nail polish and furniture polish* or *some nail and some furniture polish*, and so on. In the last pair of examples, *nail* and *furniture* are usually seen as the first elements of compounds. In *He could have and might have seen her* the coordination would suggest that *have* forms a unit with a modal auxiliary: *[could have] seen her*, *[might have] seen her*. In *He could have seen her and have left the room* the same word is grouped with the remainder of the predicate: *could [have seen her]*, *could [have left the room]*. Neither analysis would be compatible with that suggested by *He could have seen and might have touched her*.

In other cases the coordinates do not stand in parallel constructions. In *I'll go to Leeds and visit Bill and then on to York to see Mary*, a smaller coordinative syntagm is formed by a pair of predicates less the auxiliary:

> [[go to Leeds] and [visit Bill]]

(compare *must have [[seen her] and [left the room]]*). This is in turn a coordinate in the larger syntagm

> [[go to Leeds and visit Bill] and [then on to York to see Mary]]

or alternatively, with *and then* as the coordinator:

> [[go to Leeds and visit Bill] and then [on to York to see Mary]]

But the second coordinate, *(then) on to York to see Mary*, cannot be construed with *will* (*I'll (then) on to York to see Mary*). To achieve a parallel we would have to establish the first coordinate as follows:

> I'll go [[to Leeds and visit Bill] and ...

beginning not with *go* but with the preposition. But then there is no parallel between *to Leeds* and *visit Bill*, since only the former can construe with *go*. The smaller coordinative syntagm fits our model only at the expense of the larger, and the larger only at the expense of the smaller.

So far, therefore, the defence is only partly successful. But for the last case, in particular, it is tempting to suggest that coordination is accompanied by contraction. In Chapter 2 we gave the example *Bloggs has borrowed one car and stolen another*, where the second coordinate, *stolen another*, consists of no more than a participle, parallel to *borrowed*, and a determiner or noun modifier, parallel to *one*. If there are just those elements, this too is not a unit. But for that reason most grammarians would posit at least two ellipses:

> Bloggs has borrowed one car and ⟨*sc.* has⟩ stolen another ⟨*sc.* car⟩

so that both the participle and the modifier are construed with latent elements:

Auxiliary	Head	Modifier	Head
⟨ ⟩	stolen	another	⟨ ⟩

Thus they would form a predicative construction on the same level as the first coordinate *has borrowed one car*. By this analysis both our assumptions can be saved. Similarly, the example in the last paragraph could be said to show ellipsis of at least a head verb:

> I'll go to Leeds and visit Bill and then ⟨*sc.* go⟩ on to York to see Mary

Of the two main coordinates, the first would again be formed by *go to Leeds* and *visit Bill*; in the second, the *go* understood construes with *I* and *will* just like the preceding *go* and *visit*. Alternatively, we could expand the second and third coordinates into complete predicates:

[will go to Leeds]   [⟨*sc.* will⟩ visit Bill]   [⟨*sc.* will go⟩ to York ...]

If we work through our other examples it will be clear that this defence could deal with all the problems raised so far. In *He could have seen her and have left the room* we would again posit a latent auxiliary: [*could have seen her*] *and* [⟨sc. *could*⟩ *have left the room*]. In *He could have seen her and left the room* we would posit two: [*could have seen her*] *and* [⟨sc. *could have*⟩ *left the room*]. Once such analyses are accepted, we have no need for constituency divisions such as

[could [have [seen her]]]   [could [have [left the room]]]

to save our hypotheses. Nor is there any contradiction between these and the straightforward coordination of verb phrases in *He could have seen and might have touched her*:

[[could have seen] and [might have touched]]

In *her elder brother and younger sister*, the construction of the second coordinate could be said to include a latent possessive:

Possessive	Modifier	Head
⟨ ⟩	younger	sister

(⟨sc. *her*⟩ *younger sister*). Accordingly, both coordinates have the syntax of full noun phrases. We then have no need for a syntagm which unites the noun and adjective ([*her* [*elder brother*]], [*her* [*younger sister*]]), at least not for present purposes. In *a blue coat and yellow scarf* the same contraction would affect the indefinite article ($\langle$sc. *a*$\rangle$ *yellow scarf*).

In the contrasting examples, the contraction would be **anticipatory** rather than **retrospective**. Like a pronoun (Chapter 2), an ellipse typically relies either on the context in which a sentence is uttered or, within the sentence, on some word or words preceding. Compare, for example, the pronoun in *He* (someone the hearer must identify) *is coming*, or *Bill says he* (Bill) *is coming*, with the ellipses in *Did it yesterday* (someone the hearer must identify did it), or, on one analysis discussed in the last chapter, *Bill collapsed while doing* (while Bill was doing) *it*. But within the sentence, the referent of a pronoun may also be identified from a phrase which follows: *when he visits us Bill always stays late* (when Bill visits us), or *Her illness frightened everyone but Jane herself* (Jane's illness). In the recent literature this is sometimes described as **cataphora** – a carrying forwards or downwards (Greek *katá* 'down') as opposed to anaphora (*ána* 'up'). Similarly, in examples like *He could have and might have seen her* or *a blue and a yellow pullover*, we could posit a contraction in which the first coordinate has a cataphoric relation to the second. In one case, a latent participle would suffice:

he [[could have $\langle$*sc.* seen$\rangle$] and [might have seen]] her

– whereupon the coordination is between full verb phrases. In the other we could posit an ellipsis of the head noun:

[[a blue $\langle$*sc.* pullover$\rangle$] and [a yellow pullover]]

paralleled in *her elder and her younger brother* (... *her elder* $\langle$sc. *brother*$\rangle$), and so on. Thereupon we are again dealing with full noun phrases.

Granted these possibilities, it is not surprising that some scholars have been tempted to reduce all coordination to that of full clauses. In *She wore a blue coat and scarf*, the relation is, on the face of it, between nouns:

$_N[\ _N[\text{coat}]_N \text{ and } _N[\text{scarf}]_N\ ]_N$

so that we would need a further rule

$$N \rightarrow N_1 \ldots \text{ and } N_n$$

in the constituency-cum-dependency format. But just as latent elements might be added to create a coordination of noun phrases:

[[a blue coat] and [⟨*sc.* a blue⟩ scarf]]

so we might also insert a latent subject and predicator:

[[she wore a blue coat] and [⟨*sc.* she wore a blue⟩ scarf]]

The apparent coordinative syntagm, *coat and scarf*, would be a structure resulting from the contraction of two distinct predications. In *Bloggs has borrowed one car and stolen another* we have already posited the ellipsis of an auxiliary and a noun. But we could also insert a latent subject: [[*Bloggs has borrowed one car*] and [⟨sc. *Bloggs has*⟩ *stolen another* ⟨sc. *car*⟩]]. In *She told Bill and Mary that she was coming*, we could posit a coordination not just of *Bill* and *Mary*, forming a coordinative noun phrase, but of a pair of complex clauses *she told Bill* ⟨sc. *that she was coming*⟩, with anticipatory ellipsis of a complement clause, and ⟨sc. *she told*⟩ *Mary that she was coming*, with retrospective ellipsis of subject and predicator. If all coordination were described in this manner, the set of formulae could be reduced to just one:

$$\text{Clause} \to \text{Clause}_1 \ldots \text{and } \text{Clause}_n$$

All the others we have given (for NP → NP$_1$ ... *and* + NP$_n$, Predicate → Predicate$_1$ ... *and* + Predicate$_n$, and so on) would be redundant.

This simplification had a natural appeal for transformational grammarians. In terms of their model, the ellipses form part of a series of transformational rules (in the sense mentioned at the end of Chapter 4) which relate deep structures of which one would be broadly like this:

[[the nail polish disappeared] and [the furniture polish disappeared]]

to surface structures showing varying degrees of contraction: [[*The nail polish*] and [*the furniture polish*]] *disappeared*; *The* [[*nail polish*] and [*furniture polish*]] *disappeared*; *The* [[*nail*] and [*furniture*]] *polish disappeared*. But the objection to such a treatment had been sketched by SWEET (1, pp. 141f.), more than half a century earlier. Firstly, there are many cases where the coordinates cannot be expanded. A verb like MEET will normally require reference to at least two individuals (*Bill and Mary met yesterday* or *Bill met Mary yesterday*, not *Bill met yesterday*). A similar restriction is associated with the preposition BETWEEN and with adjectives such as EQUAL and SIMILAR (Chapters 5 and 7). Since one cannot readily say *between Bill*, neither does one say, for example, *She is between Bill and she is between Mary*. One can say *Bill is similar and Mary is similar*, but only as an incomplete sentence (. . . *is similar* ⟨sc. *to John*⟩, ⟨sc. *to her mother*⟩, or the like). *Bill and Mary are similar* can be a complete sentence, meaning that they are similar to each other; for that sense no contraction can be postulated.

Coordinates with MEET, BETWEEN and so on must therefore be exceptions. In the terms used by the transformationalists, a grammar must contain at least one rule of Phrasal Coordination (NP → NP$_1$ . . . *and* + NP$_n$) in addition to the general schema for Sentential Coordination ('sentence' in the sense of our 'clause') posited when ellipsis is operable. But there is a second problem. For *Bill and Mary brought some roses*, we can easily propose contraction from *Bill brought some roses and Mary brought some roses*. But the semantic relations are not always as implied. Although the sentence could mean that they brought two lots of roses independently, another interpretation, and the natural one if Bill and Mary happen to be married, is that they brought one lot together. Similarly, *I wear cotton and wool shirts* could mean that the speaker wears both cotton shirts and wool shirts, or that he wears shirts in a cotton and wool mixture. In the first interpretation an ellipsis may not seem unreasonable: *I wear cotton* ⟨sc. *shirts*⟩ *and* ⟨sc. *I wear*⟩ *wool shirts*. But for the second it would evidently be wrong. In deep as in surface structure, the nouns *cotton* and *wool* must form a coordinative modifier of *shirts*, not separate modifiers, of two separate objects, of two separate predicators.

Some scholars have argued that, if such examples are ambiguous, they must therefore have alternative constructions. In one sense, *Bill and Mary brought some roses* would be elliptical, with *Bill* and *Mary* related to separate predicators (*Bill* ⟨sc. *brought*. . .⟩, *Mary brought*. . .). In the other, *Bill* and *Mary* would be phrasal coordinates, related to a single predicator on the pattern of MEET or EQUAL. *I wear cotton and wool shirts* would have one construction identical, at the deep level, to that of *I wear cotton shirts and wool shirts*; another would require a further rule of word coordination, by which *wool* and *cotton* form the attribute of a single head. Similarly, *I wear a yellow and a blue pullover* (referring to two pullovers) could be seen as a contraction of *I wear a yellow pullover and I wear a blue pullover*, whereas *I wear a yellow and blue pullover* (if referring to just one pullover) would show a straightforward coordination of adjectives.

But constructional distinctions cannot be founded on the evidence of ambiguity alone. Phrasal and sentential coordination are not distinguished by general rules of ordering or inflection. In particular, they make no difference to the grammatical rule of agreement: *Bill and Mary are meeting* (not *is meeting*) *tomorrow*, like *Bill and Mary are coming separately*. Even where the coordinates form a single notional unit there is no consistent preference for the singular: compare, for example, *Their steak and chips is/are very dear*. Nor do the categories enter into restrictions of valency. In *Bill and Mary are together* the coordination must be phrasal, since *Bill is together and Mary is together* does not readily make sense. But if TOGETHER has two sets of subjects, the second layer is sentential: [[*Both Bill and Mary*] *and* [*Peter and Jane*]] *are now together*. Similarly, MEET allows the sentential interpretation in, for example, *Bill and Peter have each met her*. In *Bill and Mary have got divorced* the natural understanding is that they are divorced from each other. But we can easily force a separate relationship (*Bill and Mary have both got divorced*). The distinction will also apply to simple plurals (compare *The Blogginses have got divorced*, *The Blogginses all get divorced after two or three years*). Such issues must be examined afresh in other languages. But in English, at least, the difference is purely semantic.

In the light of these arguments, we have to consider how the recourse to ellipsis is to be constrained. In *Bloggs has borrowed one car and stolen another* it was reasonable to posit an ellipsis of the head noun (*stolen another* ⟨sc. *car*⟩). But this is not to facilitate coordination. If the object had the single element *another*, it could form part either of a coordinated predicate (⟨sc. *has*⟩ *stolen another*) or of a predicate less its auxiliary (*stolen another*) without difficulty. The argument for ellipsis is that *another* is an element which requires a head: witness the incompleteness, in the sense originally discussed in Chapter 2, of simple sentences such as *Bloggs has stolen another*. Since no head follows, the hearer is taken to understand one, in the coordinative as in the simple case.

For the ellipsis of *has* the argument is quite different. In a finite verb phrase *stolen* will require a preceding auxiliary (compare the simple *Stolen yet another car?*). But in the coordinative example it can be related to the same auxiliary as *borrowed*:

Bloggs has [[borrowed one car] and [stolen another]]

just as, in our original analyses of *Bill saw her daughter and her sister* or *Bill and my brother saw her sister*, a single predicator is related to a pair of objects or subjects. Similarly, in *her elder and her younger brother*, a single head can be construed with both possessives and both adjectives; in *her elder brother and younger sister* both heads can be construed with a single possessive, and so on. The only problems lie in the classification of each pair of coordinates (*borrowed one car* and *stolen another, her elder* and *her younger, elder brother* and *younger sister*). Even in the most complex of our examples (*I'll go to Leeds and visit Bill and then on to York to see Mary*), *go* can be construed with both *to Leeds* and *to York* and both *go* and *visit* with both *I* and *will*. The problems lie not there but, in the first instance, in the imposition of a hierarchy of constituents.

So far as coordination is concerned, the most plausible contractions are those in which one coordinate could not stand for the whole. Thus in a written example:[1]

$_a$[$_b$[Hugford was among the earliest to forge]$_b$ and $_c$[Patch systematically to record]$_c$]$_a$ early Tuscan frescoes

coordinate *c* could not be substituted for the total coordinative syntagm *a* (*Patch systematically to record early Tuscan frescoes*). In Bloomfieldian terms, *a* is not endocentric (compare Chapter 7 above). Therefore it is attractive to postulate a contraction of a type often called Gapping:

and [Patch ⟨*sc.* was among the earliest⟩ systematically to record]

by which a gap is left within the unit. Again, in *I'll go to Leeds and visit Bill and then on to York to see Mary* the test for endocentricity would fail either at the higher level of coordination ([*go to Leeds* ...] *and* [*on to York* ...]) or at the lower ([*to Leeds*] *and* [*visit Bill*]), unless their boundaries are set in incompatible places. Hence the case for positing ellipsis of a second *go*.

But endocentricity is merely a property by which parts of forms – in this case, either of the coordinates – can replace the whole; it need not

---

[1] *The Burlington Magazine* (February 1980), p. 112.

imply, and in the textbook definitions does not usually imply, that they meet the stricter assumptions embodied in the forms of rule with which we began. If we were determined to preserve those assumptions the best we could do would be to require that contractions should never be carried beyond the point at which some schema of the form

$$X \rightarrow (\ldots) \; X_1 \; (\ldots) \; X_n \; (\ldots)$$

becomes applicable. For example, if COMMON GULL and BLACK-HEADED GULL are taken to be compound nouns, we could legitimately posit a contraction

twenty [[common ⟨*sc.* gulls⟩] and [black-headed gulls]]

so that the coordination meets the schema

$$N \rightarrow N_1 \; \ldots \; \text{and} \; N_n$$

(with $X = N$). But we could not posit a gratuitous contraction of noun phrases:

[[twenty common ⟨*sc.* gulls⟩] and [⟨*sc.* twenty⟩ black-headed gulls]]

or of other larger units. The constraint would apply regardless of whether twenty or forty gulls are referred to, since here too there is no syntactic distinction. Similarly, we could establish a coordination of noun phrases in *her elder and her younger sister* ([*her elder* ⟨sc. *sister*⟩] *and* [*her younger sister*]) only if, for other reasons, we reject the analysis by which an adjective forms a unit with the possessive.

The objection to this constraint is that, unlike the restriction of coordination to clauses, which is semantically interesting but unsustainable, it has no point apart from a strategy of expanding units. We must therefore ask if the strategy has any advantage. According to the proposal, any coordinate has either one or two sets of elements: a set of actual elements (or elements in surface structure), with or without a set of latent elements (or elements only in deep structure). For example, in *He could have seen her and run away*, the second coordinate would have an actual participle and adverb (*run away*) with two latent auxiliaries (⟨sc. *could have*⟩). Coordination is basically between full units (predicates, noun phrases, and so on), provided that they are syntactically equivalent. We must then specify the sequences of elements that can undergo ellipsis: thus there can be ellipsis of one or more auxiliaries (⟨sc. *could*⟩ *have run away*, ⟨sc. *could have*⟩ *run away*, ⟨sc. *could have been*⟩ *running away*), provided that they come at the beginning of the unit and match those in a coordinate preceding. Only under such rules can the actual elements form sequences that are not units.

But instead of giving rules for latent elements, and so specifying the sequences of actual elements that remain, why not describe the latter directly? On a simpler view, coordination is basically between sequences of elements, whether or not they could independently form a unit, which are equivalent in relation to other elements in the sentence. Thus *seen* and *run* are verb forms which can construe identically with, for example, a subject and a set of auxiliaries. Therefore there are sentences which consist of a single subject and a single set of auxiliaries, linked to coordinates composed of such a form plus whatever elements may or must follow it (*seen her and run away, seen your brother and run screaming from the room*, and so on). Naturally, we will find structures that in certain circumstances cannot form coordinates, just as, in the opposite account, we find structures that in certain circumstances cannot be latent. For example, a grammar must exclude a sentence such as

My elder [[brother was here] and [sister had gone to Leeds]]

where the coordinates consist of a predicate and the head of its subject, construed with a single determiner and modifier. Alternatively, a grammar must exclude the corresponding contraction:

my elder [[brother was here] and [⟨sc. my elder⟩ sister had gone to Leeds]]

In either account, this may be no more than an exception, or it may be explained by a general principle. In either account we would refer to sequences of elements within the coordinative syntagm and their relation to elements outside it. There is no obvious advantage in formulating rules for sequences that are said to be absent, instead of those that are present.

However ellipsis is constrained, there will be residual difficulties. Firstly, not every coordinative syntagm is, in the strictest sense, endocentric. In *Mary and Bill have brought some roses*, the coordinates *Mary* and *Bill* stand in identical relations to the predicator; nevertheless one would not say *Mary have brought some roses* or *Bill have brought some roses* unless, contrary to normal understanding, *Mary* and *Bill* were both to refer to groups of individuals. Therefore ellipsis cannot be invoked. In terms of the transformational proposal, by which the deep structure would consist of two coordinated clauses, its reduction to surface structure must involve not just the deletion of the first predicate:

$$_{\text{Clause}}[\text{Mary}]_{\text{Clause}} \text{ and } _{\text{Clause}}[\text{Bill has brought some roses}]_{\text{Clause}}$$

but the formation of a single clause with a single coordinative subject:

$$_{\text{Clause}}[_{\text{NP}}[\text{Mary and Bill}]_{\text{NP}} \text{ have brought some roses}]_{\text{Clause}}$$

with agreement accordingly.

The transformational proposal has already been rejected. But problems may arise in cases where contraction cannot be so confidently ruled out. In *I could sing and John play the piano*, only the first coordinate is syntactically equivalent to the whole. For example, one could say *He said that I could sing*, but not *He said that John play the piano*. It is therefore tempting to posit an ellipsis of *could* (*... and John* ⟨sc. *could*⟩ *play the piano*) so that endocentricity may be saved. But what if the speaker referred to John by a pronoun? I do not think I can say *I could sing and he play the piano*, with HE in the subjective form. We might restore *could* (*... and he could play ...*). But I can also use the objective form: *I could sing and him play the piano*. Now the relationship of *him* to *play* is, on the face of it, the same as that of *John* to *play* in the first example, which is, on the face of it, the same as that of *I* to *could sing*. But one cannot say, for example, *You said him could play the piano*. Therefore endocentricity cannot be preserved simply by positing a latent auxiliary (*... and him* ⟨sc. *could*⟩ *...*). If there is contraction, it also involves a consequential change in the morphosyntactic property of the pronoun.

Secondly, there may be problems with the notion of equivalent relationship. By this we do not refer to a mere semantic equivalence. In *The pavement and I felt cold, My patience and the lecture were at an end, He left in a Rolls Royce and a bad temper* or *A letter and her brother had told me*, we have a coordination traditionally referred to by the term **syllepsis** (Greek 'a taking together'), in which the semantic roles of the coordinates, as denoting actors, entities acted on, and so forth, do not match. Thus, in the first example, *I* refers to someone who experiences

213

a sensation of cold. But the pavement experiences nothing; the role of *the pavement* is semantically neutral, denoting neither an experiencer, nor an actor (compare *her brother* in the last example), nor a member of any other positive category. The oddity of such coordinations, or their facetious character when uttered, confirms the semantic analysis. But it could not establish a syntactic distinction. If *I felt cold* could be shown, on other grounds, to have a different construction from *The pavement felt cold*, the restriction would be explainable on that basis. Some might insist that it had; like *It happened to be cold* (compare *I happened to see her* at the end of Chapter 8), *The pavement felt cold* might be said to involve a predication of the state of coldness ('That the pavement was cold felt so', 'It felt that the pavement was cold'), while *I felt cold* would involve predication of an individual ('My coldness was what I, personally, felt'). Others would merely distinguish impersonal and personal senses of FEEL. On that view, the restriction on coordination would also be a matter of semantics only.

But there are other cases where the evidence from coordination is of greater interest. Instead of *You'll need the cakes on Wednesday*, one could say *The CAKES you'll need on WEDnesday*; for example, the speaker might be working down a list on which cakes are the next item, or might be correcting a suggestion that they would be needed on Tuesday, or (with another intonation) that some other commodity would be needed too. In the traditional account, both sentences have *the cakes* as direct object, with a stylistic difference in phrase order. Hence the tradition excludes coordinations such as

> the CAKES [[you'll need on WEDnesday] and [are better made FRESH]]

because, in the simple *The cakes are better made fresh*, the role of *the cakes* is that of subject to predicate. But is the exclusion justified? As an editor of the *Journal of Linguistics*, I once advised a contributor with too many footnotes: 'The others you do need but would be better in the text.' To the extent that such examples are found, we have to consider how the traditional account should be qualified.

According to a widely accepted analysis, *the others* is the Topic of both *The others you do need* and *The others would be better in the text*; the remainder of each sentence (*you do need, would be better in the text*) is sometimes called the Comment. It is in such terms, rather than in subject–predicator or object–predicator relations, that an equi-

valence might be sought. Just as *blue and yellow scarves* has a construction in which *blue* and *yellow* are two equal attributes of *scarves*:

Attribute		*Attribute*	*Head*
[blue]	and	[yellow]	scarves

so the example cited would exemplify a pattern in which
you do need and *would be better in the text* are comments in equal relation to
a single topic:

Topic	*Comment*		*Comment*
the others	[you do need]	and	[would be better in the text]

even though, in terms of the predicative construction, *the others* has
two different roles. It is because the predicative relations are at
variance that the coordination may seem awkward. It is because the
topic–comment relations are the same that it is possible.

But what sort of pattern, and what sort of equivalence, have we
shown? For many scholars, topic and comment are non-syntactic
categories, concerned with aspects of sentence organisation which,
like the semantic roles of actor, experiencer and so on, cut across the
patterns that are strictly subject to rule. Therefore coordination can
reflect an equivalence that is not syntactic, at least in marginal
instances. But we must consider the opposite argument: if such coordinations are possible, and coordination is a relation constrained by
syntactic equivalence, should it not follow that topic and comment
are themselves syntactic roles? *The* CAKES *you'll need on* WEDnesday
would then have a construction partly different from that of *You'll need
the cakes on Wednesday*, and partly similar to that of the passives *The
cakes will be needed on Wednesday* or *The cakes will be needed by* YOU *on
Wednesday*. We may reject this conclusion. But the case is worth
pondering.

NON-RECURSIVE COORDINATES

From the rules debated so far, the reader might conclude that all
coordinators can link an indefinite number of coordinates. But that is
not so. For example, one can say *I saw Bill, but not Mary* or *Bill came,
but didn't stay*. But it would be hard to add a third term: *I saw Bill, but
not Mary but Peter*; or *Bill came, but didn't see her, but still stayed*. If the

last example makes sense, it is as a structure with two layers of coordination:

Bill [[[came] but [didn't see her]] but [still stayed]]

both with *but* as the coordinator. Not every speaker will be happy to repeat *or* after *either* (*either John or Bill . . . or Mary*), or *and* after *both* (*both John and Bill . . . and Mary*), though in my own speech the former is normal. Multiple coordinates are a striking feature of particular coordinative constructions, as shown at the beginning of this chapter. But they do not define the type.

Its essence lies in the way in which coordinates are related. In dependency there is a connection between specific elements, each of which contracts its own connections, if any are possible, with elements elsewhere in the sentence. For example, in *He wore a bright red tie*, the relation of *red* and *tie* is that of the modifier and head of a noun phrase; this is different from that of an auxiliary and a head verb (in *was wearing*), or an adjunct and a predicator (in *wore it carelessly*), or a peripheral clause and a predicative syntagm (in *wore it when he came yesterday*), and so on. *Red* and *tie* are then linked independently, one to a modifier *bright* and the other to a determiner *a* and predicator *wore*. In coordination the case is the reverse. In *He was wearing a coat and tie*, the nouns stand in the same relation to other elements in the sentence; it is only within coordinates (for example, within the predicates in *I ate some mushrooms and felt ill*) that independent constructions are possible. But the specific parallel will vary. In the first example *coat* and *tie* are objects of *was wearing*, while in the second *ate* and *felt* are predicators related to *I*; yet the coordinative construction is the same.

In keeping with the symmetrical relation between coordinates, a coordinator does not construe with any one coordinate in particular. Sometimes it may appear that it does. For example, in the tag from Ovid which we cited earlier (*per suum Meropisque caput*), the coordinator *-que* is attached to the second of the two coordinates (*suum* 'his' and *Meropis* 'Merope's') to form a unit with a single accent (*Meropísque*). If we reverse the coordinates it will form a unit with *suum* (*Meropis suúmque*). But the reversal shows that the arrangement is fixed. We could not alter it to, for example, *Meropisque suum*, with reordering of *Meropis* plus the coordinator, instead of the coordinate alone. In English, the intonation often forms a similar unit: *I am happy, but exhausted* (perhaps with a pause at the comma), not *I am happy but, exhausted*. This might suggest an equivalent constituency: [[*happy*] [*but* *exhausted*]], instead of [[*happy*] *but* [*exhausted*]]. But here too we are dealing only with a pattern of realisation. Thus again one cannot say *I was but exhausted, happy.*

In certain cases this suggests a limiting criterion. At first sight, *but* and *though* are very similar: compare *I was happy, but exhausted* with *He is clever, though absent-minded, I met Bill, but not Mary* with *I met her brother, though not her sister, She might be helpful, but not him* with *Mary might help, though not Bill.* Both have a related use at the beginning of sentences (*But why is he wearing an overcoat?, Though how am I going to get there?*), as do *or* and *and* (*Or could you collect it tomorrow?,* AND *he brought his galoshes*). On such evidence, we might be tempted to treat *though* as a coordinator: *He is* [[*clever*] *though* [*absent-minded*]] or, with clauses, [[*he came*] *though* [*he didn't stay*]]. The objection is that one can also say *Though absent-minded, he is clever* or *Though he didn't stay, he* CAME, which establishes *though* and its sequel as a syntagm.

NOTES AND REFERENCES

The best general study of coordination is by DIK, in terms of a 'functional grammar' (notes to Chapter 1 above); this is also an exemplary survey of the earlier literature. But the transformational theory is important, both for its substance and for the problems it brought to light. For a good textbook account see HUDDLESTON, pp. 98–101 (and earlier pp. 93f.); a group of early studies – referred to separately below – is in REIBEL & SCHANE (ed.), Part 2 (pp. 71–142).

What I call a 'coordinate' generativists usually call a 'conjunct'; likewise coordination is 'conjunction' (as in the title of Part 2 of REIBEL & SCHANE), and the main rule which contracts coordinates is 'conjunction reduction'. For typical uses see, for example, A. Akmajian & F. Heny, *An Introduction to the Principles of Transformational Syntax* (Cambridge, Mass.: MIT Press, 1975), pp. 250ff. (indexed under 'conjunction', p. 408). This is potentially confusing, since in logic the terms are restricted to propositions joined by the *and*-operator (as opposed to 'disjunct' and 'disjunction', with the *or*-operator). It is also unnecessary, since terms derived from 'coordinate' are established from the later nineteenth century (SWEET, 1, p. 18 and earlier passages in *OED*, s.v. 'coordinative', §2.b). Nor can I see any point in trying to call a coordinate a 'conjoin' (QUIRK *et al.*, p. 560).

For Bloomfieldian treatments see BLOOMFIELD, p. 195, and other references in notes to Chapter 7 above; criticism, of at least the strongest form of this assumption, by DIK, Ch. 3. The transformationalists at first assumed that all coordination was sentential. There were two main reasons. (1) A phrase structure rule can only list a finite sequence of constituents: hence it could specify two or three coordinates (*John and Bill; John, Bill and Peter*), but not an indefinite number (*John, Bill, Peter, . . . and Jim*). See POSTAL, pp. 23f., 109f. (also LYONS, *Introduction*, p. 222). Therefore coordinates had to be introduced in separate derivations – $_S$[. . . *John* . . .]$_S$, $_S$[. . . *Bill* . . .]$_S$, and so on – with a so-called 'generalised' transformation (CHOMSKY, *Structures*, p. 113, rule 22) to put them together. (2) A phrase structure rule can deal with only one category: thus we could specify rules for the coordination of two NPs or two VPs (*John and Bill danced*; *John loves his wife and hates turnips*), but no single rule for coordinates of any class. Chomsky conjectured that such a generalisation could be made, and was stateable as a transformation which conflated any set of sentences (*John danced* and *Bill danced*; *John loves his wife* and *John hates turnips*) differing in just one phrase. See the leading argument of CHOMSKY, *Structures*, pp. 35–8. I confess that this reasoning convinced me as a junior lecturer. But its fallacies are now sufficiently obvious. As to (1), we CAN write an expression like those in the text ($NP \rightarrow NP_1$ . . . *and* $+ NP_n$) for a sequence of indefinite length. This is formalised as a 'rule schema' (see DIK, pp. 92ff.; HUDDLESTON, p. 94), and is already introduced in CHOMSKY, *Aspects* (p. 224, n. 7, p. 225, n. 11) in such a way that 'generalised transformations' could be eliminated. As to (2), we can also write a 'schema' like that in the text ($X \rightarrow X_1$ . . . *and* $+ X_n$), where X is a variable ranging over any category. An example is that proposed by Chomsky's pupil R. C. Dougherty: see 'A grammar of coordinate conjoined structures', Part 1, *Lg*, 46 (1970), pp. 850–98; Part 2, *Lg*, 47 (1971), pp. 298–339 (rule 133 in Part 1, p. 864 = rule 147 in Part 2, p. 315).

There remained a claim that, for example, *John and Bill danced* meant the same as *John danced and Bill danced*; so, by a common assumption, they should have the same deep structure (compare notes to Chapter 12). But what of verbs like MEET, or sentences like *John and Mary were dancing together*? On one view these required a rule of phrasal coordination: thus Carlota S. SMITH, 'Ambiguous sentences with *and*' (written by 1965; published in REIBEL & SCHANE (ed.), pp. 75–9). On another they too were sentential: see Lila R. Gleitman, 'Coordinating conjunctions in English', *Lg*, 41 (1965), pp. 260–93 (also in REIBEL & SCHANE (ed.), pp. 80–112). But Gleitman's proposals were persuasively criticised by G. Lakoff & S. Peters, 'Phrasal conjunction and symmetric predicates', in REIBEL & SCHANE (ed.), pp. 113–42 (originally in a report by various authors, *Mathematical Linguistics and Automatic Translation* (Cambridge, Mass.: Harvard Computation Laboratory, 1966)). By the end of the 60s it was questioned whether any coordinate phrases should be derived as Chomsky had proposed: see especially J. D. McCawley, 'The role of semantics in a grammar', in E. Bach & R. T. Harms (eds.), *Universals in Linguistic Theory* (New York: Holt, Rinehart & Winston, 1968), pp. 124–69 (reprinted in McCAWLEY, pp. 59–95; relevant discussion pp. 74–84, 89ff.); also Dougherty's papers mentioned earlier (indeed either of them, since they are repetitive).

A subsidiary problem concerned the rule or rules of contraction. For an attempt to unify their treatment see A. Koutsoudas, 'Gapping, conjunction reduction, and coordinate deletion', *FL*, 7 (1971), pp. 337–86 (which proposes just ellipsis); contra, R. A. Hudson, 'Conjunction reduction, gapping, and right-node raising', *Lg*, 52 (1976), pp. 535–62 (with various other mechanisms). For 'gapping' see R. S. Jackendoff, 'Gapping and related rules', *LIn*, 2 (1971), pp. 21–35 (with some examples that are still thought-provoking); earlier in J. R. Ross, 'Gapping and the ordering of constituents', in A. Graur *et al.* (eds.), *Actes du Xe congrès international des linguistes, Bucarest, 28 Aôut–2 Septembre 1967* (Bucharest: Academy, 1970), 2, pp. 841–52 (also in M. Bierwisch & K. E. Heidolph (eds.), *Progress in Linguistics: a Selection of Papers* (The Hague: Mouton, 1970), pp. 249–59). By the mid 70s it was clear that the restrictions could not be explained by syntax alone. For the special case of 'gapping' see S. Kuno, 'Gapping: a functional analysis', *LIn*, 7 (1976), pp. 300–18, with important emphasis on perceptual factors, and on into-nation and sentence perspective. For the pairing of coordinates in general see P. Schachter, 'Constraints on coordination', *Lg*, 53 (1977), pp. 86–103, which requires an identity both of category (as originally in CHOMSKY, *Structures*) and of 'semantic function'. I cannot see that either is strictly necessary.

The first transformational proposals are criticised by DIK, Chs. 5–7. But his own are also open to objection: see my review article in *Lingua*, 23 (1969), pp. 349–71 (especially pp. 362–7). For phrasal/sentential see also R. A. Hudson, 'On clauses containing conjoined and plural noun-phrases in English', *Lingua*, 24 (1970), pp. 205–53 (essentially for the factual discussion in §1). For a limited use of ellipsis compare QUIRK *et al.*, pp. 568ff. (for clauses), 598ff. and 608f. (for phrases). But their criteria are largely of economy and convenience (p. 569), and they too note cases where it cannot strictly be invoked (p. 597, §9.98; also p. 590, note [a] to §9.88). Compare, for example, HERINGER, pp. 275f. for German, specifically to save the assumption that coordination is of single constituents. But it is remarkable how often this assumption passes without qualification: thus the recent textbook account by ALLERTON, pp. 197–202, which is otherwise sound.

For the auxiliary constituent in transformational grammar see CHOMSKY, *Aspects*, especially pp. 106f. (significantly revising CHOMSKY, *Structures*, p. 39); further revision, with 'Aux' an immediate constituent of 'S' in, for example, CULICOVER, Ch. 3 *et passim*; yet more refinement in JACKENDOFF, *X̄ Syntax*, pp. 47ff. For 'topic' and 'comment' see HOCKETT, pp. 191, 201ff.; hence a transformation 'topicalising' objects and other elements (for example, in HUDDLESTON, pp. 229f.). See also references for 'theme' and sentence perspective in Chapter 5 above. I should add that Hudson (article cited, *Lg*, 52 (1976), p. 560) rejects out of hand the coordination of topics that I discuss.

For coordination vs. subordination compare QUIRK *et al.*, pp. 552ff.; also DIK, Ch. 4 (but see my review article, pp. 367–70). The constituency of the coordinator – [X] *and* [Y] or X [*and* Y]? – is an old issue: see DIK, pp. 53f.

10
Juxtaposition

The model so far. Juxtaposition neither coordination, nor dependency, nor parataxis.

Apposition: As intermediate between other relations. Apposition vs. coordination (criterion of coreference). 'Close apposition'. Apposition vs. attribution (non-restrictive relative clauses); vs. complementation (nouns with *that*-clauses); vs. parataxis and peripheral elements. Interest of apposition for syntactic theory.

Correlative constructions: A paradigm example (*qu*- and *t*- in Latin). As relation of clause not included in larger clause. Problem of correlation vs. peripherality.

In earlier chapters we distinguished two subtypes of dependency: modification (including, among others, the relationship of an adjunct to a predicator) and complementation. We also established a category of peripheral elements, whose relationship was neutral between those of adjuncts, or modifiers in general, and complements of the predicator. As relations of dependency, all three are distinguished from that of coordination; finally, both dependency and coordination differ from parataxis, where no syntactic relationship is posited. The typology so described may be displayed within a tetrahedral space (Figure 13), where the endpoints of the arrows represent extremes both of differentiation and of codification. Intermediate cases lie along the lines from one point to another. Thus the durational element in *The race lasted for three hours* was seen as intermediate between an adjunct, in the relation of modification, and a peripheral element (end of Chapter 6). The role of *please* in *Please do it* or *Could you please keep quiet?* might be described as intermediate between that of peripheral elements and parataxis (compare Chapter 2).

But does this typology cover all the constructions that may be recognised? From a tidy-minded viewpoint it is tempting to assume that it does: for any pair of units *A* and *B*, a syntactic relation must be either strictly symmetrical (*A* and *B* form all or part of a coordinative syntagm) or wholly asymmetrical (*A* and *B* form all or part of a **dependency syntagm**, of which one is the controller). But the more we look at texts, the more this assumption will be questioned. What,

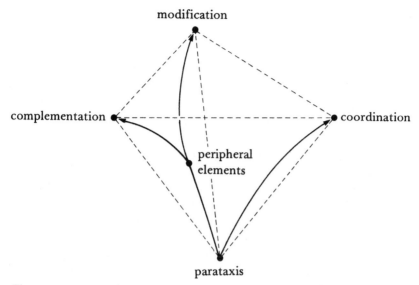

Figure 13

for example, is the structure of the sentence that I have just written? According to tradition, it contains two clauses ([*the more . . . at texts*], [*the more . . . will be questioned*]) which stand in a **correlative** construction. Should this be seen as a restricted form of coordination:

[the more [. . . at texts] the more [. . . will be questioned]]

(compare *Either we look at texts or the assumption will be questioned*)? Or should one clause be seen as subordinate within the whole? The term 'correlative' implies that neither alternative is correct. On the one hand it implies a symmetry, which is marked by the paired adverbials (*the more . . . the more . . .*). On the other hand it implies a positive relationship, which is more than a mere identity of function.

For a different illustration let us take a few lines from *The Ring and the Book*:

> I am just seventeen years and five months old,
> And, if I lived one day more, three full weeks;
> 'T is writ so in the church's register,
> Lorenzo in Lucina, all my names
> At length, so many names for one poor child,
> – Francesca Camilla Vittoria Angela
> Pompilia Comparini, – laughable!

(VII.1–7) which, like much of Browning's verse, so subtly mixes

221

literary and spoken styles. The first line fits our typology perfectly: *seventeen years* and *five months* are coordinates dependent on *old*, which in turn forms a predication with *I* and the copula. So does the second, *three full weeks* supplying a third coordinate, with a clausal dependent *if I lived one day more*. But what is the syntax from the third line onwards? The final *laughable!* can be established as a separate sentence, possibly paratactic. The unit beginning *all my names . . .* (line 4) might be seen as peripheral in the clause '*T is writ so . . .*; alternatively, it too might be paratactic (*All my names* ⟨sc. *were writ*⟩ *at length*), or intermediate between these types. But what, for instance, is the role of the preceding *Lorenzo in Lucina*? In meaning, at least, it is related to *church's* in line 3, telling the listener which church it is. Then is it a syntactic dependent – like, for example, *S. Lorenzo* in *the church of S. Lorenzo*? Or is it a second modifier of *register*, and so related to *church's* by coordination? If neither is justified, could this too be parataxis?

The traditional answer is that *Lorenzo in Lucina* stands to *church's* in a relation of **apposition**. Similarly, the list of names in lines 6–7 (*Francesca . . . Comparini*) is in apposition to the preceding phrase in line 5 (*so many names for one poor child*), which is in turn apposed to *all my names* in line 4. But this too is a term that implies an extension to our typology. For to say that *A* is apposed to *B* (Latin *appositus* 'set beside') is, on the one hand, to say that their relationship is not symmetrical: *Lorenzo in Lucina* stands in apposition to *church's*, not the other way round. Hence only *church's* is marked as a modifier of *register*:

and not both, in coordination:

On the other hand, it does not imply that *A* and *B* form a dependency syntagm: *Lorenzo in Lucina* is set beside *church's*, but as an independent phrase:

church's [Lorenzo in Lucina]

and not controlled by it:

[church's [Lorenzo in Lucina]]

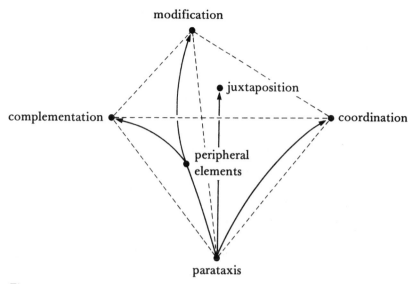

Figure 14

Yet, finally, the tradition recognises some constructional relation; otherwise grammarians would not need a term for it.

Both apposition and correlation may be characterised as relationships of **juxtaposition**. This is the most primitive constructional relation, being undifferentiated with respect to any of the specific types discussed in earlier chapters. It might therefore be represented by a point on the topmost plane of our tetrahedron (Figure 14) neutral between coordination and both subtypes of dependency. But only in special cases may the relation be seen as fully codified. In the second illustration, *Lorenzo in Lucina* comes as an afterthought to *church's* or to *the church's register*; though not readily analysed as paratactic, its role is at least more similar to parataxis than that of, say, the dependent in *the nave of Lorenzo in Lucina* or the coordinate in *St Peter's and Lorenzo in Lucina. So many names . . .* is in turn an afterthought in line 5. Their relation to *church's* and to *all my names* is indeterminate with respect both to codification (the vertical dimension of our figure) and to differentiation.

Of the cases of juxtaposition that we have mentioned, correlative constructions form a small class that is in general easy to identify. But the term 'apposition' has been used of a variety of constructions, which are not grouped together by any single criterion. We must look more closely at the resemblances between them, before returning to correlation in a final section.

APPOSITION

If apposition is an undifferentiated relation, we may expect boundary problems between it and every fully differentiated type. Thus in certain cases we can be sure that we are not dealing with dependency; but it is hard to determine whether it is apposition or coordination. In other cases we can be sure that it is not coordination; the problem is to distinguish between apposition and complementation. In other cases it is hard to decide between apposition and modification. These can be seen as problems of placement on the horizontal dimensions of our figure. But there are also distinctions in the degree of codification. In the tradition, apposition includes at least one fully codified construction. At the other extreme, it predictably shades into parataxis. Within our typology, the field of apposition is established by a set of five distinctions (Figure 15), numbered in the order in which we will

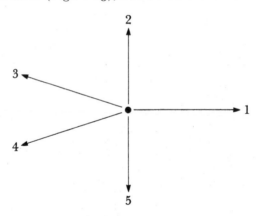

Figure 15

discuss them. The central point represents the paradigm case, at least as most grammarians see it. Case 1 is at the limit with coordination; cases 3 and 4 at the limits with attribution and complementation. Case 2 represents the maximal degree of codification; case 5 the minimal.

(1) The paradigm case of apposition is exemplified in *I met your brother, the poet*, where a noun phrase *the poet* is apposed to a preceding

noun phrase *your brother*, which is in turn the object of *met*. The relationship is realised by sequence alone, with no construction marker. But the term is also applied to phrases linked by words that may in other cases function as coordinators. A common example is where a species is referred to by both a scientific and a vernacular name: *Larus argentatus, or the herring gull; Rissa tridactyla, or the kittiwake*. Another is where two names are given for the same man: *Sir Winston, or Mr Churchill as he then was*. According to grammarians these are appositional, while in *a herring gull or a kittiwake*, or *Sir Winston or King George VI*, the relation is again coordinative. On what grounds is the distinction drawn?

One obvious test is that of **co-reference**. In the appositional *your brother, the poet* both phrases refer to the same individual, described in two different ways. But in the coordinative *your brother or the poet* their referents will normally be separate. In *Larus argentatus, the herring gull* the compound *herring gull* denotes the same species as *Larus argentatus*. That is also true of our example with *or* (*Larus argentatus, or the herring gull*); likewise, in *Sir Winston, or Mr Churchill ...*, *Mr Churchill* is co-referent with *Sir Winston*. Therefore these too would be seen as appositional, even though, in *Sir Winston, or possibly King George VI* or *a herring gull, or alternatively a kittiwake*, the same conjunction is classed as coordinative. The test can also be applied to phrases linked by *and*. In *He got a cheque and a medal* the cheque and medal are two different things; therefore the object is coordinative. In *He got a cheque, and a large one* the 'large one' is most probably the cheque already mentioned. If so, then by this test the object is *a cheque*, with *a large one* appositional. In general, two noun phrases would not stand in apposition unless their referents were to be understood as identical.

But if this were taken as a sufficient criterion, it would make the distinction in some odd, or at least untraditional, places. Consider the example *I met either his wife or his mistress*. This might suggest that he has both a wife and a mistress, but the speaker does not know which one he met; then the construction would be coordinative. But it could also mean that the speaker met some woman with whom he was living; however, it is not clear whether they are married. Would it then be appositional, since the same person is referred to by both phrases? Again, suppose that a man has his daughter Mary as his secretary. If one says *I met Mary, his daughter and his secretary* there is apposition between *Mary* and a phrase that follows. But is there further appo-

sition between *his daughter* and a co-referent *his secretary*? A grammarian would be unlikely to accept that there was. When singular
nouns are coordinated, the resulting phrase may still have singular
reference; hence the agreement in *His friend and colleague has finished it*
(compared with *His friend and colleague have finished it*). It is no different
when the coordination is of phrases themselves.

Nor is apposition necessarily between units that refer. In

it's $_a$[too expensive]$_a$, $_b$[much bigger than I need]$_b$

phrase *b* adds a gloss or explanation to phrase *a*, just as, in our original
example from Browning:

the $_a$[church's]$_a$ ... , $_b$[Lorenzo in Lucina]$_b$

Lorenzo in Lucina expands or explains *(the) church's* and, in a later
example, *the herring gull* supplies a gloss to *Larus argentatus*. In

he $_a$[acted terribly]$_a$, $_b$[kept forgetting his lines]$_b$

the predicates stand in a similar relation, the second stating at least
one respect in which his acting was bad. On such grounds there is
again apposition. But in the new examples only the pronouns *it* and *he*
have referents. There is no individual or mass that the predicates or
predicators refer to. Therefore it cannot be co-reference that distinguishes their role from that of the coordinates in *He acted terribly and
kept forgetting his lines* or *It's either too expensive or much bigger than I need*.

It seems clear that we are dealing with a broader resemblance,
some of whose features may not be exemplified in all languages. In
our paradigm example

$_a$[your brother]$_a$, $_b$[the poet]$_b$

a and *b* tend to be in different tone groups, with a potential pause at
the comma. In the examples in the last paragraph the tendency is
virtually compelling. In each case, the meaning of *b* elucidates that of
a; hence co-reference, when referents are involved. Similar features,
both semantic and intonational, are found in:

$_a$[a cheque]$_a$, and $_b$[a large one]$_b$

and other examples with apparent coordinators. We also find that *and*
and *or* can be dropped (*He got a cheque, a large one; Sir Winston – Mr
Churchill, as he then was – must have decided ...*), in conformity with the

paradigm case. So, by extension, these too are regarded as appositional, even though a particular feature, of co-reference or of divided intonation, can also be found in examples that we continue to class as coordinative.

But in arguing by extension it is often difficult to determine which resemblances should prevail. In *his wife or his mistress* the conjunction cannot be dropped, at least without further alteration. But what if we change it to *his wife, or maybe his mistress*? If the phrases are co-referent, this is like the case in which a name is amended (*Sir Winston, or Mr Churchill* ...); with that interpretation, the conjunction can easily be dropped (*I met his wife, maybe his mistress*). In the other interpretation it is like the construction with *and* (*His wife, and maybe his mistress, are coming*). Here too the conjunction can be deleted (*His wife – maybe his mistress – are coming*), but with plural agreement the referents of *his wife* and *his mistress* remain different. Is the example coordinative on both interpretations, or is it now constructionally ambiguous, coordinative in one sense but appositional in the other? When a relation is less clearly codified, questions concerning its type become increasingly academic.

We might also consider examples like *the mallard or wild duck*. Here there is a single tone group, though it is easily divided (*The mallard – or wild duck – is commoner*). Without the division the conjunction is undroppable (*The mallard wild duck is commoner*). Yet *mallard* and *wild duck* are alternative names, like the scientific *Larus argentatus* and *herring gull*. The treatment of such examples can only be a matter of grammarians' convention.

(2) A relation often cited is that between the components of a complex name: *King George VI, Mount Everest, Mr Churchill*, and so on. This is widely classed as appositional, though clearly differing from the paradigm case. Thus for Bloomfield these are examples of 'close apposition', close in that there is no 'pause pitch' (BLOOMFIELD, p. 186). But this comes near to a contradiction in terms. In Bloomfield's typology apposition is a special case of parataxis, 'parataxis' being defined, in the terms already cited in Chapter 2 above, as the relation of forms 'united by no other construction' than the same 'sentence pitch' (*ibid.*, p. 171). But is there no other construction here? The order is fixed: one does not say *Churchill Mr* or *Everest Mount*. (But in the paradigm case one can say either *your brother, the poet* or *the poet, your brother*.) Nor can the components be split: one can say *Your brother came,*

the poet but not *Mr spoke next, Churchill*. There are also restrictions on the first noun: *Mount Everest* but not *Mountain Everest*; *King George* rather than *Sovereign George*. Moreover, in these examples only the first element can be dropped: *Churchill spoke* but not *Mr spoke*; *They climbed Everest* not *They climbed Mount*. On this evidence not only do the names form a syntagm, but by Bloomfield's own test it is endocentric (Chapter 7 above) and attributive.

Our own tests seem scarcely more helpful. In *Mount Everest*, the components *Mount* and *Everest* are not phrases that refer separately; nor can Bloomfield's 'pause pitch' be introduced (*They climbed Mount, Everest*). With respect to codification, this is a clearly established pattern. Nevertheless there is a chain of resemblances connecting it to the paradigm case. In *President Truman* the relation is almost as tight; note that one would not say *President Mr Truman*, with a second title inserted. So too in *Captain Bloggs* (though one can also say, for example, *Captain Lord Bloggs*). But what of the journalistic *Prime Minister Churchill*? Here *Mr* can be inserted easily (*Prime Minister Mr Churchill*), and *Mrs* would be normal (*Prime Minister Mrs Gandhi*). In that way we can connect it with a general usage (*managing director Mr Joe Bloggs, ballet dancer Margot Fonteyn*) which is journalese for a form with an article (*the ballet dancer Margot Fonteyn* or, with a 'pause pitch', *the managing director, Mr Joe Bloggs*). These last are similar to paradigm examples like *Mr Bloggs, the man in the blue coat*. It would be hard to say exactly when we are dealing with a single phrase, or single referring expression, instead of two.

Such indeterminacy would not matter if, in the single phrases, we were sure what sort of relationship we had. But different grammarians have come to different conclusions. Sweet, for example, sees *King Alfred* as a case of modification (or, in his term, 'assumption'). Apposition then lies on a gradation between attribution and coordination: in *Alfred the king* or *Alfred, king of England* 'the subordination of [the] assumptive ... word to its head-word is so slight that the two are almost coordinate' (SWEET, 1, p. 33). Sweet's general view can be compared with that of Hockett: in apposition 'it is clear that [the] construction is endocentric, and reasonable to suppose that it is attributive, but difficult to tell which [term] is the head' (HOCKETT, p. 185). But for Hockett this also holds in Bloomfield's 'close' case (*Queen Mary, Lake Michigan*) and, despite these remarks, the whole type is presented as a variety of coordination. In my view such vacillation is entirely justified. The relations are appositional precisely in that they cannot be convincingly assigned to either of the fully differentiated types.

The case for dependency is at its strongest when one element cannot head its own phrase: thus in normal usage one does not say *A Mr spoke next*, like *A king spoke next* or *The President spoke next*. If all titles were like that we might be tempted to describe them as a special class of determiners. The case for coordination is at its strongest when either element can be dropped: thus in a form consisting of a Christian name and a surname (*Winston Churchill, Joe Bloggs*) or beginning with *the* (*the River Thames*). But still there is only one potentially referring expression, as in *Mr Bloggs* or *Mount Everest*, while the insertion of a coordinator at once creates two (*Joe or Bloggs*). In that respect 'close' apposition also differs from the apposition discussed in paragraph (1) above (*our river, the Thames*; *Joe, or Bloggs as I should call him*). But its type is similarly neutral or juxtapositional.

(3) Our next boundary is marked by the case of Non-restrictive Relative Clauses. In *I met the brother who used to live in London*, the relative clause *who used to live in London* is part of the specification of who the speaker met. Therefore it is said to have a Restrictive role, like that of, for example, the adjective in *a large house* or the prepositional phrase in *the house on the corner*. But one could also say *I met his brother, who used to live in London*. Here the relative clause does not help to specify the person referred to, but gives additional information. (For example, it might be explaining how the speaker happened to know him.) Therefore it is described as Non-restrictive. In that respect its role is like that of the adjective in *the lovely Miss Bloggs*, which we conflated with other modifiers in Chapter 7. (We might compare *I met Miss Bloggs, who is said to be so lovely.*) But its semantic role is also like that of the second phrase in *his brother, an old friend of mine* or *Miss Bloggs, a really lovely girl*. In the work of some scholars, a non-restrictive relative clause is called an 'appositive relative clause'.

There are partial cases both for modification and for apposition. On the one hand, only the relative clause can be dropped: *I met his brother*, but not *I met who used to live in London*. Nor can their order be reversed: *I met who used to live in London, his brother*. In both respects the pattern is like that of the attributive *the brother who lived in London*, but unlike that of the appositional *his brother, an old friend of mine*. (Compare *I met his brother*; *I met an old friend of mine*; *I met an old friend of mine, his brother*.) We might therefore establish an asymmetrical construction:

$$_c[_a[\text{his brother}]_a, _b[\text{who used to live in London}]_b]_c$$

where c is a noun phrase in which b is controlled by a. The difference between the restrictive and non-restrictive structures is that the latter would not show a direct relationship between the clause and the head noun. We remarked in Chapter 7 that there were nouns, or senses of nouns, with which dependents were obligatory (*That is a serious matter*, not *That is a matter*). But non-restrictive clauses do not satisfy the requirement (*That is a matter which I must attend to*, not *That is a matter, which I have already dealt with*).

On the other hand, there is evidence that c, in this structure, is not a single phrase. The clause can be separated from its alleged controller:

$$\text{I met }_a[\text{his brother}]_a \text{ yesterday, }_b[\text{who used to live in London}]_b$$

(Compare *I met his brother yesterday, an old friend of mine*.) Moreover, it is only the first element (a) that is, or need be regarded as, a referring expression. In the paradigm case of apposition a referring noun phrase is elucidated by a second noun phrase which is also of a referring or potentially referring nature. In the example now before us the referent is specified by the initial phrase *his brother*; though of a different category, the clause stands to it in the same form of semantic relationship. This suggests a juxtapositional analysis, in which a and b do not form a syntagm. The resemblance between restrictive and non-restrictive relative clauses would lie solely in their internal structure, not in the syntactic roles that they play.

The problem could, in principle, arise for other units that can play a modifying role. In *I met his brother, on a short visit to London*, it is reasonable to treat *on ... London* as peripheral, even when it is the brother, not the speaker, whose visit is to be inferred. But what of *I met her, up to her ears in work*? If *up to her ears ...* is not peripheral, then what is its connection to *her*? Is this another form of non-restrictive modifier? But personal pronouns do not readily take attributes (*I met her who you mentioned*; *Him over there I do want to speak to*). Or is it marginally appositional? But again only the apposed term could be dropped (*I met her*, not *I met up to her ears in work*). A choice between the three alternatives (peripheral, modifying, appositional) cannot be convincingly argued.

(4) The distinction between apposition and complementation is complicated by the construction with a noun and a noun clause: for example, *the fact that he did it*. In most grammars, this is assimilated to our paradigm pattern:

ₐ[the fact]ₐ ᵦ[that he did it]ᵦ

with the clause apposed to a preceding phrase. But according to other scholars the clause is a complement – in our terms a dependent of the head noun:

[the fact   that he did it]

There is again an argument for either alternative.

As with other types of complement, the case for the second analysis rests on evidence of valency. Although one can say *the fact that he did it* or *the circumstance that he was unfit*, one would not say, for example, *the happening that he did it* or *the matter that he was unfit*. Similarly, one can say *the signal that they should start* or *the danger that they might arrive*, but hardly *the shot that they should start* or *the peril that they might arrive*. Just as a *that-*clause is excluded by verbs such as PLAY or OCCUR (*They said that he had arrived* but not *They played that he had arrived*; *It seemed that he did it* but not *It occurred that he did it*), so it is excluded by PERIL, HAPPENING, and so on. In many cases the valencies of verbs and nouns are lexically related. For example, ANNOUNCEMENT and FEELING are derived from ANNOUNCE and FEEL; in keeping, one can say both *They announced that it was bust* and *the announcement that it was bust*, both *We felt that it would not happen* and *the feeling that it would not happen*. Just as there are verbal nouns which take an objective genitive (*the loss of blood, a description of Southend*), so these, at least, appear to govern an objective clause.

The case for apposition rests on examples with an intonational boundary. Without it, ENDING is another noun by which the clause is excluded (compare *with the ending that they got married* and *with the result that they got married*). But the restriction is cancelled if the clause forms a separate tone group: *Did you hear the ending, that they got married on Saturday?* Similarly for such nouns as POSTSCRIPT (*Have you read the postscript, that your mother is also coming?*), DISASTER (*the latest disaster, that his wife has had triplets*), RUBBISH (*some further rubbish, that Bill is leaving*), and so on. In these examples, the division is again between an initial noun phrase (*the ending* or *the latest disaster*) and a second unit which expands or explains what is meant. (Compare *the disaster, ⟨that is,⟩ that she had triplets* with *the church,* ⟨*that is,*⟩ *Lorenzo in Lucina.*) But now consider a noun such as NEWS. This can be used like ENDING or DISASTER: *Have you heard the latest news, that Bill is leaving?* But one can also say *the news that Bill is leaving*, with no intonational break. Similarly, one can say both *the general feeling, that it was not going to happen* and, as before, *the feeling that it would not happen*. In this light, the peculiarity of NEWS, FEELING and the like is not that they can take a complement, but merely that they allow close apposition (in Bloomfield's sense) as well as the looser form.

The case for complementation would be strengthened if there were nouns with which the clause was strongly obligatory. But in general it is not so: *The fact is indisputable, I saw the announcement, The feeling was to be expected*, and so on. Another criterion was that of latency: for example, the clause can be latent with a verb such as REALISE (*I have just realised* ⟨sc. *that she is coming*⟩, ⟨sc. *that what you said is true*⟩, and so on). But its application to nouns would involve an imaginary distinction of meaning. Take, for example, *The realisation surprised me*. Plainly there is something that the speaker had realised and, in speaking, he assumes that his hearer knows what it was. Therefore we might argue that the clause was latent:

Determiner	Head	Complement	
the	realisation	⟨	⟩

– the valency of the noun again reflecting that of the verb. But *the realisation* is a phrase with a definite article. If one says *I've cut down the rhododendron*, the hearer is expected to grasp what rhododendron is referred to (the rhododendron near the front gate, the rhododendron that is blocking the path to the compost heap, and so on). This does not show that *the rhododendron* has a latent modifier, but merely attests one meaning of *the*, or of phrases determined by it. In *I heard the announcement*, the phrase *the announcement* is likewise taken as sufficient to identify whatever announcement is meant. Similarly *the realisation* is enough, it might be argued, to identify a realisation. Therefore no latent element need be posited.

In *the fact that he did it*, the noun is simple and has no verbal nuance. But the same dilemma is posed. Is this a single referring expression, whose construction would be incomplete if *that he did it* were deleted? Then we must speak of complementation. Or is there a referring expression *the fact*, with *that he did it* a subsidiary aid to identification?

Then we are speaking of apposition. In such a case the distinction has little reality.

(5) The final indeterminacy is between apposition and parataxis. In

$$\text{I met } _a[\text{his father}]_a, \ _b[\text{a car salesman}]_b$$

b is again a phrase apposed to *a*. In

$$_b[\text{he is a car salesman}]_b, \ _c[\text{isn't he?}]_c$$

c is a tag syntactically related to *b* (compare Chapter 2); likewise in the incomplete sentence

$$_b[\text{a car salesman}]_b, \ _c[\text{isn't he?}]_c$$

(said as the speaker is pointing to the man in question, or in answer to the inquiry *What does that man do?*, and so on). But now let us put these elements together:

$$\text{I met } _a[\text{his father}]_a - _b[\text{a car salesman}]_b, \ _c[\text{isn't he?}]_c$$

Do *b* and *c* still form an incomplete sentence? If so, it must be paratactic to the whole of *I met his father*:

[I met his father] [a car salesman, isn't he?]

(compare *I met his father – isn't he a car salesman?*). But this relates *a car salesman* to a latent subject ($\langle$sc. *he is*$\rangle$, $\langle$sc. *his father is*$\rangle$, ... *a car salesman*), with no connection between it and the phrase preceding. Then is it just the tag that is paratactic:

[I met his father – a car salesman] [isn't he?]

with the phrases still in apposition? But this fails to make sense of the intonation, which will be broken at the dash, not at the subsequent comma. Then is there apposition between *his father* and the whole of what follows?

[I met [his father] – [a car salesman, isn't he?]]

The problem with that analysis concerns the construction of *a car salesman, isn't he?*, which is characteristic of a sentence and not of a subordinate unit.

All that seems certain is that, from *his father* onwards, the relations are of an undifferentiated form. Apposition is a type of juxtaposition, in the sense suggested in the preamble to this chapter. Tags stand in a juxtapositional relation to the preceding clause: this is a further case in which a choice between coordination and dependency could not be justified. Parataxis is another syntactically undifferentiated relation, since there is no construction at all. So, one analysis posits an undifferentiated relation of parataxis, whose second term exhibits an undifferentiated link between a subject complement and a tag. Another posits a different parataxis, with a first term which exhibits an undifferentiated relation of apposition. A third posits a different apposition, with a second term exhibiting subsidiary juxtaposition of a tag. There is little substantive difference between them.

Just as juxtaposition merges into parataxis so, in limiting cases, it can be indistinguishable from a peripheral form of dependency. In sentences such as

> They fought like tomcats, [hair and clothing flying everywhere]
> This train leaves at 10, [the next being due at 11]

the unit in brackets stands in what the tradition calls an 'absolute' construction; it is an element 'disengaged' or 'set loose' (Latin *absolutus*) from the remainder. Thus, according to the *OED*, an absolute element 'stands out of (the usual) grammatical relation or syntactic construction with other words' (s.v., §III.9). But what exactly would this mean? The definition allows for the possibility that there is no syntactic relation, usual or otherwise. Then there would be parataxis, as in

> [they fought like tomcats] [hair and clothing were flying every-where]

which could have the same intonation. But we could argue that the participle marks a subordinate clause:

> [they fought like tomcats [hair and clothing flying everywhere]]

In saying that it stands out of the usual relations, we mean that it neutralises the distinctions between all other peripheral elements. But we could also say that it neutralises the distinction between peripherality and coordination. (Compare the meanings of the second example and the coordinative *This train leaves at 10 and the next is due at 11*.) It stands out of the usual relations in that it is merely juxtapositional.

At this point the reader may feel that we are beginning to linger over problems of indeterminacy. But it is important to realise that a question which is perfectly sensible in certain contexts (for example, as to whether there is a syntactic relationship, or whether it does or does not involve dependency) may be perfectly silly in others. One error is to point to the silly cases and conclude that the distinction must be false, even in those for which decisive criteria can be offered. Since one of the questions concerns syntactic relationship as such, this leads to a denial of our field, with the description of sentence structure reduced to stylistics and the semantics of particular utterances. An opposite error is to deny that the indeterminacies are real: if we cannot answer our questions, it is because our arguments are deficient or the facts are not yet fully understood. This error is common and, of its nature, difficult to combat. For arguments are always open to objection and, naturally, new facts are always coming to our attention. We must therefore look at cases with some care, to show that no determinate solution is convincing.

It may also be asked why apposition should be considered at such length. Most introductions to linguistics either do not mention it or dispose of it very briefly. Nor is it certain that the type is universal. Earlier chapters have been illustrated largely or entirely from English, but with the knowledge that a wide range of languages, of divers families and in divers parts of the world, have been described in ways compatible with our model. But many descriptions do not mention apposition, or any construction to which the term seems applicable. It is conceivable that the topic is mainly of interest within the grammatical traditions of English and other European languages.

But its use by grammarians is instructive. As can be seen from our survey, there is no positive property that is common to all the constructions involved. In certain cases the first element is a complete referring expression (*your brother* in *your brother, the poet*). This is criterial for appositional relative clauses (*your brother, who was here yesterday*), if they are so described. But it is not so in *Mount Everest* or *Joe Bloggs*. In certain cases the elements are of the same class (noun phrase *your brother* plus noun phrase *the poet*). Most grammarians take this as criterial for the relation in *Joe Bloggs* (proper noun *Joe* plus proper noun *Bloggs*). But there is no internal parallel between a phrase and a following clause (*the announcement, that Bill is leaving*). In certain cases both elements can be substituted for the whole (*I met your brother, I met the poet*). This is criterial for elements that do not refer (*He acted terribly, kept forgetting his lines*). But relative clauses cannot; nor, in general, can *that*-clauses (*They tore up the announcement*, but not *They tore up that Bill is leaving*). There is a tradition in linguistics which requires that terms should be defined with respect to our data, with necessary and sufficient conditions for their use. Apposition is a striking instance of a category that cannot be elucidated in that way.

Instead we have a paradigm use, and other uses that are linked to it by various forms of resemblance. Where the resemblances end is naturally indeterminate.

CORRELATIVE CONSTRUCTIONS

Correlative constructions are especially clear in Latin. For illustration, let us take the last verse of a mediaeval poem:[1]

> Quot sunt apes   in Hyble vallibus
> quot vestitur   Dodona frondibus
> et quot natant   pisces equoribus
> tot abundat   amor doloribus

> 'As many as the bees that are in the valleys of Hybla,
> As many as the leaves with which Dodona is clothed,
> And as many as the fish that swim in the sea,
> So many are the pains with which love abounds.'

Lines 1–3 consist of three coordinate clauses (coordinator *et* 'and') which stand in a correlative relation to line 4. Each coordinate is marked by an initial *quot* which, apart from its marking function, also serves as a determiner of a noun. In line 1 this is the noun *apes* 'bees'; the constituency of the clause can thus be sketched as

> [quot   apes] sunt [in Hyble   vallibus]
> 'as many' 'bees' 'are' 'in' 'of Hybla' 'valleys'

with *quot apes* as subject. In line 2 *quot* construes with *frondibus*, which is in a case form translated by 'with';

> [quot   frondibus]   vestitur Dodona
> 'as many' 'with leaves' 'is clothed' 'Dodona'

[1] *Carmina Burana*, ed. A. Hilka & O. Schumann, Vol. 1: *Text*, Part 2: *Die Liebeslieder* (Heidelberg, 1941), no. 119.

('with as many leaves is Dodona clothed'). In line 3 it construes with *pisces* 'fishes':

> [quot   pisces]   natant equoribus
> 'as many' 'fishes'   'swim'   'in the waters'

Finally, line 4 has an initial *tot*, identical with *quot* except that it begins with *t-* instead of *qu-*. In its determining role *tot* construes with the noun *doloribus* 'with pains':

> [tot   doloribus]   abundat amor
> 'so many' 'with pains'   'abounds' 'love'

('with so many pains does love abound'). In its marking role it marks the second term in the correlative construction, just as *quot* marks the first.

The lexemes QUOT and TOT are one of a series of pairs that, in given constructions, serve as **correlators**, or markers of correlation. The initial *qu-* and *t-* recur in, for example, QUALIS and TALIS; these are used for parallels of type (*qualis X* 'an X of such a sort', *talis Y* 'a Y of the same sort'). From the simple QUOT and TOT we have the derived adverbs QUOTIENS and TOTIENS ('as many times', 'so many times'). Thus in the following quotation from Cicero (*Pro Balbo*, 20.47):

> si   tot   consulibus meruisset,   quotiens
> 'if' 'so many' 'consuls'   'he had served' 'as many times'
> ipse   consul   fuisset
> 'himself' 'consul' 'he had been'

('if he had served under as many consuls, as the times he himself had been consul'), a *tot* in the first clause, whose syntactic roles are identical to those of *tot* in the last line of the song, looks ahead to the adverb *quotiens* in the second. These words can mark other constructions: for example, the *qu-* words can begin interrogatives (*quot sunt pisces?* 'How many fishes are there?', *qualis est?* 'What sort is it?'). There are other correlative pairs whose morphology is not so transparent. But with *qu-* and *t-* together, the type is exhibited in a classic form.

The reason for distinguishing correlation from dependency has to do with the extension of clauses. When this term was first introduced into grammars, a clause was seen as excluding other clauses that might function within it. Thus the sentence *She will come when she is ready* would consist of two successive clauses *she will come* and *when she is ready*:

237

$_{\text{Clause}}$[she will come]$_{\text{Clause}}$ $_{\text{Clause}}$[when she is ready]$_{\text{Clause}}$

– not of a clause with another clause within it:

$_{\text{Clause}}$[she will come $_{\text{Clause}}$[when she is ready]$_{\text{Clause}}$]$_{\text{Clause}}$

as in the analysis that we have accepted. The argument against this is that *when she is ready* has the same syntactic function as, for example, the phrase *in two hours' time*; since one is an integral part of the main clause:

$_{\text{Clause}}$[she will come in two hours' time]$_{\text{Clause}}$

so is the other. Similarly, in *She said she was ready*, we describe *she was ready* not as a clause that follows a preceding clause *she said*, but as a complement within a clause of which *said* is the predicator. This is because it is a complement of *said*, and therefore part of the predicative syntagm by which the main clause is defined.

In correlative constructions such arguments are lacking. In an English example such as

$_a$[the less I do]$_a$ $_b$[the better I feel]$_b$

neither *a* nor *b* can readily be dropped. Nor can we substitute peripheral phrases (*Next week, the better I feel*; *The less I do, in my garage*) or clauses with peripheral roles. Similar restrictions hold for the Latin verses with which we began. For although a speaker could conceivably have uttered line 4 on its own, it would have been analysable as, for example, an incomplete correlative:

Tot abundat amor doloribus ⟨*sc.* quot ...⟩
'That (understood) is how many pains love abounds with'

or perhaps as having an exclamatory sense ('So many pains does love abound with'). A speaker might also have uttered a sentence identical to one of the coordinates in lines 1–3, but as a question:

Quot sunt apes in Hyble vallibus?
'How many bees are there in the valleys of Hybla?'

or again as an incomplete sentence ('As many as the bees in the valleys of Hybla') in answer, one might imagine, to a question about how many people were at the stadium. Yet the obligatory nature of the constituents is not due to the valency of either verb: in the English example any lexeme may be substituted, provided that it construes within its own unit. On that evidence neither clause is part of a larger predicative syntagm.

Under these circumstances the original conception of the clause seems fully justified. In the English example we have no evidence that *a* plays a role within a clause defined by the predicator *feel*:

[[the less I do] the better I feel]

or that *b* plays a role within the clause defined by *do*:

[the less I do [the better I feel]]

The only clauses we can justify are *a* and *b* themselves:

[the less I do] [the better I feel]

But the sentence role cannot be played by either clause independently; the evidence which shows that neither is peripheral to the other also confirms that their relation is not coordinative. It is in these conditions that a correlative construction is to be recognised.

The problem, of course, is to decide precisely when a clause is not an element within a larger clause. In *She will come if she is ready* the conditional *if she is ready* is to all appearances peripheral to *she will come*. (Compare *She will come when she is ready*, *She will come in two hours' time*, and so on.) There is the same construction if the order is reversed (*If she is ready she will come*). But let us add *then*: *If she is ready, then she will come*. On one view the *if*-clause is again peripheral:

$_{\text{Clause}}[_{\text{Clause}}[\text{if she is ready}]_{\text{Clause}} \text{ then she will come}]_{\text{Clause}}$

But the order can no longer be reversed: in *Then she will come if she is ready* we have a different construction, in which *then* is a potential sentence connector, syntactically peripheral to the whole of *she ... ready*. *Then* has the same syntactic role in the simple *Then she will come*; therefore, we might argue, the conditional cannot strictly be dropped. It is also relevant that one cannot say *Then if she is ready, then she will come*. Why not, if the internal *then* is merely an element in a single main clause? A possible hypothesis is that an *if*-clause and a *then*-clause form a correlative unit:

$[_{\text{Clause}}[\text{if she is ready}]_{\text{Clause}} \ _{\text{Clause}}[\text{then she will come}]_{\text{Clause}}]$

with which a clause-modifying adverb is unconstruable.

NOTES AND REFERENCES

My example from Browning can usefully be compared with conversational material. See specimens in D. Crystal & D. Davy, *Investigating English Style* (London: Longman, 1969), Ch. 4; for discussion, especially on the general topic of clause relationships, see D. Crystal, 'Neglected grammatical factors in conversational English', in G. N. Leech *et al.* (eds.), *Studies in English Linguistics: for Randolph Quirk* (London: Longman, 1980), pp. 153–66. Note especially Crystal's point regarding continuity with children's speech; as I have remarked before, the learning of rules for sentence-formation is neither a primary stage nor one that is ever complete.

Treatments of apposition are few while interesting treatments are fewer. For English examples, and an attempted taxonomy, see QUIRK *et al.*, pp. 620ff.; also JESPERSEN, *Syntax* (references in index), for one range of earlier uses. For apposition classed as modification see, for example, W. N. Francis, *The Structure of American English* (New York: Ronald Press Co., 1958), pp. 301f.; for its continued treatment as coordination compare ALLERTON, p. 127. Against the latter view it is worth stressing that the apposed term cannot always be substituted for the whole. Thus inflections may not necessarily agree: see ENGEL, p. 145 on modern German (example *meinem Bruder Philipp, ein wunderbarer Gesellschafter*); again the English type *the church's ... Lorenzo in Lucina* (adjacent in, for example, *It was the church's, Lorenzo in Lucina*). For apposition as a boundary case between coordination and dependency compare especially DE GROOT, *Syntaxis*, pp. 63–5.

The divergences among earlier scholars are reflected in the handful of studies under transformational influence. See Evelyne Delorme & R. C. Dougherty, 'Appositive NP constructions: *we, the men; we men; I, a man*, etc.', *FL*, 8 (1972), pp. 2–29 (with structure like that of coordination – $_{NP}[_{NP}[Bill]_{NP}, _{NP}[the\ boy]_{NP}]_{NP}$ – pp. 8ff.); R. D. Huddleston, *The Sentence in Written English: a Syntactic Study Based on an Analysis of Written Texts* (Cambridge: Cambridge University Press, 1971), pp. 251–5, especially for difficulties in deriving apposition from relative clauses; N. Burton-Roberts, 'Nominal apposition', *FL*, 13 (1975), pp. 391–419 (treating some paradigm cases as attributive). The last is the fullest recent study known to me.

For the criterion of co-reference see QUIRK *et al.* Note Burton-Roberts, *op. cit.*, against separate referring expressions in, for example, *the poet Burns* (p. 395). For 'close' apposition QUIRK *et al.* refer to four papers in *American Speech* between 1952 and 1955; note too JESPERSEN, *Syntax*, p. 19 (for *the Amazon River* as, in our terms, modifier + head), p. 21 (for *Dr Johnson*, etc. as a form of 'equipollent' construction). On non-restrictive vs. restrictive relative clauses see JESPERSEN, *MEG*, 3, Chs. 4–5 *passim*; QUIRK *et al.*, pp. 864ff. (with fuller references than usual, p. 934); also the neglected treatment by HILL, pp. 357ff. For an early transformational study see Carlota S. Smith, 'Determiners and relative clauses in a generative grammar of English', *Lg*, 40 (1964), pp. 37–52; for a current view JACKENDOFF, $\bar{X}$

Syntax, Ch. 7. Both Smith and Jackendoff use the term 'appositive relative clause' (similarly, for example, BACH, p. 267), and both raise the possibility, doubted or rejected in the studies already referred to, that these clauses are the source for apposition of the paradigm type (Smith briefly but confidently, p. 42; Jackendoff without commitment, p. 63). On the type *the news that . . .* see QUIRK *et al.*, both under 'weak apposition' (pp. 646f.) and in the sections on postmodification (pp. 874f.). It is treated as a paradigm case of complementation by HUDDLESTON, pp. 106f., BACH (very briefly, p. 107) and other transformational handbooks. For the traditional use of the term 'absolute' see, for instance, ERNOUT & THOMAS on Latin (references in index).

In Wittgensteinian terms, apposition is characterised not by a defining property but by a series of 'family resemblances': see L. Wittgenstein, *Philosophical Investigations* (Oxford: Blackwell, 1953), especially, §§66–7.

The term 'correlator' is my own, on the pattern of 'coordinator' and 'subordinator'. On the passage from correlation to subordination, with comparative arguments for the importance of correlative constructions in Indo-European, see J. Haudry, 'Parataxe, hypotaxe et corrélation dans la phrase latine', *BSL*, 68 (1973), pp. 147–86. References for the original sense of 'clause' are in the notes to Chapter 8 above.

11
Realisation

Realisation of syntactic relations. Forms of realisation: order; form words and inflection; intonation.

Agreement and government: Conventional distinction. Agreement not necessarily of inflections. Nor of identical properties. 'Agreement' determined by lexical class. Direction of agreement and government compared with that of dependency. When are agreement and government to be posited (preposition + noun in Latin)? Problems associated with historical change.

Free and fixed order: Complementarity of order and inflections; free and fixed word order. Distinction not absolute. Free word order vs. free phrase order (order of clausal elements in Italian). Balance of economy and redundancy. Marked and unmarked orders; freedom relative to syntax only.

Syntax covers both the constructional relations between units and the ways in which they are realised. In an example first discussed in Chapter 1

the construction relates *it* to *tastes*, and both (according to our analysis) to *nice*. The order and agreement are part of its realisation; the unit may also be marked intonationally, by a single tone group. Chapters 4–10 have dealt with the typology of constructions, which we took as our main topic. We must now look more closely at the devices by which they are shown.

A construction could often be determined from the lexemes alone, given the classes they belong to and their likely collocations. In our example, *it* is a pronoun; therefore it must be a subject or object or have some other role that such a pronoun can play. *Nice* is an adjective and, as such, might be either predicative or attributive. *Tastes* can be the form of either a noun or a verb. If nominal, it could collocate with *nice* (compare *He has nice tastes*), but that leaves no role for *it*. Therefore it must be verbal, whereupon *nice* and *it* must be its complements. That is why, in an experiment, one could understand a form such as *It taste nice*, without agreement, or *Nice tastes it*, with a

242

different order, and say how they should be corrected. Similarly, these lines by Matthew Arnold:

> For thee the Lityerses-song again
> Young Daphnis with his silver voice doth sing

('Thyrsis', stanza 19) are understood by virtue, in part, of the collocability of *Daphnis* and *song*, as subject and object rather than object and subject.

All this is obvious, and important to theories of the perception of language. But our concern is with cues specific to particular systems. These are of three types, already evident in our account of *It tastes nice*. The first involves the **order** of elements; it will be recalled that this is the first of Bloomfield's features of 'grammatical arrangement', referred to in our discussion of the sentence (Chapter 2 above; BLOOMFIELD, p. 163). The second involves the use of **form words** (Chapter 3) and **inflections**; this is in part wider and in part narrower than Bloomfield's category of 'selection'. The third involves **intonation** and is part, at least, of what Bloomfield called 'modulation'.

(1) A natural ordering feature is that of **adjacency**. Thus in English

> he brought [a [very large] suitcase]

very and *large* form a continuous stretch within a longer stretch *a very large suitcase*; this reflects constructions in which *large* controls *very* and *suitcase* controls *a* and *large*. These adjacencies are fixed by rule, in that one cannot say *He a brought very large suitcase*, *He brought very a large suitcase*, and so on. In *I saw them yesterday*, the adjacency of *saw* and *them* marks their relation in the predicative construction ([*I saw them*] *yesterday*); one cannot say *I saw yesterday them*, with the peripheral adverb coming between. In *I saw them there yesterday*, the added element is neither as clearly a complement nor as clearly peripheral (see Chapter 6), and is realised in the middle position. The examples in this paragraph suggest two general principles, which have some validity for English and other specific languages. The more general is that syntagms tend to be realised as a continuous stretch. A special principle is that, if a unit *a* has a clearer syntactic relation to a predicator than another unit *b*, *a* will tend to be nearer. Both have exceptions: for example, in *He has obviously not done it today*, the verb phrase *has … done* is interrupted by a sentence-modifying adverb *obviously*, whose semantic relation is to the whole of *he has … not done it today*, and by the particle *not*, which negates a unit including the positionally more remote adverb *today*. But even then there are usually alternative orders. Thus although the position of *not* is fixed, one can also say *Obviously he has not done it today*.

A further feature is **sequence**. In *a very large suitcase*, each modifier precedes its head. One cannot say *He brought a large very suitcase*; nor is one likely to say *He brought a suitcase very large*, even though, in another style or for another collocation, postmodification would be possible. In *I will see them tomorrow* the subject precedes the predicator, as also in, for example, the second line from Arnold (*Young Daphnis … doth sing*). The rule applies to this but not to every construction (compare the interrogative *Will I see them tomorrow?*, where *I* follows the auxiliary); thus the sequence realises both the particular relation of complementation and the clause type. In the same example the predicator is followed by its object. Here there is no rule, but a tendency: compare not only the poetic usage in the lines by Arnold (*the Lityerses-song … doth sing*) but also the pattern with the object as theme (*Them I* COULD *see* or THEM *I* COULD *see*) mentioned in Chapter 9. But the tendency is never gratuitously reversed.

(2) The role of inflections is illustrated by a Latin example discussed in Chapter 5

> hostis   habet muros
> 'the enemy' 'holds' 'the walls'

Here the subject and object are realised by case inflections: nominative *hostis*, accusative *muros*. Forms such as *hoste habet muros*, with ablative *hoste*, or *hostis habet muri*, with nominative *muri*, are unconstruable. For the role of form words compare English *of*, which was our original example of a construction marker (Chapter 3). In *a model of solid silver*, it is a partial realisation of the dependency of *(solid) silver* on *model*. In *the loss of Calais*, it realises what is arguably a different construction, with complementation in place of modification (see Chapter 7). But in both cases the construction would change if another word were substituted.

In these examples, *of* and the nominative are **independent** markers, in that they are determined by the construction as a whole, and not by any individual element. But in *It tastes nice*, the inflection of *tastes* is determined not just by its constructional relation to the subject, but also by the individual character of *it*, as singular rather than plural. In *hostis habet muros*, the number inflection of *habet*, as 3rd singular not 3rd plural, is selected by that of *hostis*; by the rule of agreement one could not say *hostis habent muros* (3rd plural *habent*) or *hostes habet muros* (plural *hostes*). In both examples the verb inflection is a **bound** marker, or the bound term in a rule of co-variance. The accusative of *muros* is another bound marker, in that, although most verbs take a direct object in the accusative, a few are traditionally described as exceptions. For instance, in *equis utuntur* 'They use horses', the noun *equis* 'horses' is in the ablative. If its syntactic relationship to *utuntur* 'they use' is the same as that of *muros* to *habet* – this could, in principle, be disputed – there is a pattern of co-variance in which the case of the direct object is a bound variable whose value is determined by the predicator: ablative with forms of UTOR 'to use', but accusative with those of HABEO 'to have' or 'to hold', and so on.

(3) Intonation has an obvious role in marking boundaries. In *It tastes nice*, a falling tone could mark the end of the sentence:

> It tastes ˋNICE

In

> It tastes ˊNICE, even if it ˎIS too sweet

a boundary between tone groups marks the beginning of the subordinate clause. In

> It tastes ˊNICE, a bit ˎSWEEter than usual

it marks a phrase in apposition. The intonation can also realise specific relations. Thus in an example from Chapter 10:

> I met his ˊBROther, who used to live in ˎLONdon

the boundary between tone groups marks both the beginning of the relative clause and that it is non-restrictive. The intonation could also distinguish, for example, *He did it naturally* (where *naturally* is an adjunct) and *He did it, naturally* (where, in writing, the comma marks it as sentence-modifying).

But we must stress that these intonations are not subject to rule. In part, this is for the reason already given in Chapter 2, that we cannot state rules for continuous differences. Thus in *He did it (,) naturally* we could easily find an intonation which will not distinguish the senses. But even gross features may not be obligatory. Thus sentences may stand in parataxis (Chapter 2), with no intonational boundary. Similarly, in

He vanished as soon as he ˏSAW me

with the subordinate clause *as soon as he saw me*, or in the appositional

I met his brother the ˋPOet

the intonation could be identical to that of *He vanished from over the* DOOR*way* or *I met his brother in* LON*don*. A limiting factor, therefore, is that no syntactic category can be justified by this form of evidence alone. In Italian, for example, a question such as *È possibile?* 'Is it possible?' is generally distinguished from a statement such as *È possibile* 'It is possible' – the former with a rising, the latter with a falling tone. But there is no distinction of order (compare English *Is it ...?* versus *It is ...*) or of markers. Therefore there is no difference of construction, unless Italian intonations, unlike English, can be shown to form a determinate system.

Intonation needs no further comment. But there are unclarities in existing accounts of bound markers (see paragraph (2) above). Let us try to deal with these, before returning to larger typological issues.

AGREEMENT AND GOVERNMENT

Agreement (or **concord**) is usually described as a relation between words that share a morphosyntactic feature. In Italian, for example, both a noun and a definite article are inflected for number; singular *ragazza* 'girl', plural *ragazze* 'girls'; feminine singular *la* 'the', feminine plural *le*. There is a rule by which one says *la ragazza* and *le ragazze* 'the girl' and 'the girls', not *le ragazza* or *la ragazze*. So, in this construction, there is agreement between the head and its determiner.

Agreement is then distinguished from **government**. In Latin *habet muros* 'holds the walls', *muros* is accusative. But there is no accusative inflection of *habet*; nor, in *equis utuntur* 'They use horses', any ablative inflection of *utuntur* 'they use'. The relation is not between words that share a morphosyntactic feature, but between a morphosyntactic feature and a word of a specific lexical class. The latter is said to **govern** the former. So, in this construction HABEO is a verb that governs the accusative, while UTOR 'to use' governs the ablative.

The distinction is fundamentally correct and useful. But a number of qualifications and warnings must be made. Firstly, it is not clear that all bound terms are inflections, or (to put it differently) that we have to treat them as inflections if a relation of agreement or government is to be posited. In Arabic, a noun may or may not have an article: Egyptian colloquial *bé:t* '(a) house', *(ʔ)il bé:t* 'the house'. But if the noun has one so must an attributive adjective: *bé:t kibí:r* 'a big house', but *(ʔ)il bé:t il kibí:r* 'the big house' (literally 'the house the big'). *ʔ il bé:t kibí:r* could only be predicative ('The house is big'). The Arabic article is usually described as a word rather than an inflectional prefix. But whichever it is, its repetition with a modifier has a realisational role like that of the repeated case and number inflections in, for example, the noun phrase in Latin. There is also no reason, in passing, why government should be determined only by lexical classes. Thus the same verb might govern different cases when it is in different tenses.

Secondly, it is well known that, as the term is used by grammarians, agreement is not, in every case, between words that share a relevant property. In the Italian sentence

le ragazze sono partite
'the' 'girls' 'are' 'gone away'

('The girls have left'), *sono* and *partite* are plurals – compare *Sono partite* 'They have left' – which agree with the plural subject *ragazze*. Likewise, in

la ragazza è partita
'the' 'girl' 'is' 'gone away'

singular *è* and *partita* agree with singular *ragazza*. But in

la ragazza e sua madre sono partite
'the' 'girl' 'and' 'her' 'mother' 'are' 'gone away'

sono and *partite* are plural, while both *ragazza* and *madre* are singular. Nevertheless the verbal elements are again said to agree with the subject. Similarly, in English *Bill and Mary were there*, plural *were* is described as agreeing with the coordinated singulars *Bill* and *Mary*.

The rule may be stated in two parts: (1) if there is a non-coordinative subject in the singular, the bound elements of the predicator are also singular; (2) in all other cases they are plural. Since generalisation 2 covers both a non-coordinative subject in the plural,

247

where the morphosyntactic features do match, and two or more coordinates, where they either may or may not, it is natural that the term 'agreement' should be extended beyond its basic definition. But the same examples also show what is described as an agreement in gender. In *Le ragazze sono partite*, both *le* and *partite* are feminine plurals, determined by *ragazze*; compare *I ragazzi sono partiti* 'The boys have left' (masculine plural *i* and *partiti*). Likewise for the singulars: *La ragazza è partita* (feminine singular *la* and *partita*), *Il ragazzo è partito* 'The boy has left' (masculine singular *il* and *partito*). But despite their endings *ragazze* and so on do not have morphosyntactic properties of gender. Instead they are forms of lexemes (RAGAZZA 'girl', RAGAZZO 'boy') which, like DONNA 'woman' and UOMO 'man', are of different lexical classes. Why is this agreement and not government?

Three answers may be deduced from the literature. One is that the term 'government' is traditional only when the bound term marks a complement of the word which selects it. Since an article is not the complement of a noun, nor a predicator a complement of its subject, the gender relations must be different. But this is not part of the definition given by handbooks. Nor have we prior reason to suppose that the typology of realisational rules corresponds to that of the syntactic elements realised.

By the traditional rule, the elements agree both in number and in gender. So, another motive is to preserve a generalisation, which would be destroyed if gender came under a different heading. But the parallel is only partly true. With coordinated subjects, the participle is plural, regardless of the number of each subject individually: thus our example *La ragazza e sua madre sono partite* 'The girl and her mother have left'. But by the gender rule the bound term is masculine unless ALL the selecting terms are feminine: in *La ragazza e il ragazzo sono partiti* 'The girl and the boy have left', with feminine *ragazza* but masculine *ragazzo*, the participle is masculine plural. Therefore the rules must, in part, be given separately. Moreover, grammarians would still speak of agreement even if no other category were involved. ROBINS (pp. 249f.) cites a Swahili sentence in which two other prefixes agree with that of a noun. That is also how grammars describe it, for this as for other Bantu languages.[1] But in this case the agreement is determined solely by the class of the noun lexeme.

---

[1] See, for example, E. O. Ashton, *Swahili Grammar*, 2nd edn (London, 1947), pp. 11f.

248

Another answer is that gender in nouns is the same category as gender in articles or participles, even though it is applied to units of a different sort. So, a masculine or feminine participle can be said to match a masculine or feminine noun, whereas, in the Latin example of government, accusative or ablative objects do not match accusative or ablative verbs. But is this more than a quirk of nomenclature? In Latin, VULPES is described as feminine simply because, in *vulpes rufa* 'a red fox' or *vulpes mortua est* 'The fox is dead', *rufa* and *mortua* have feminine inflections. Lexemes such as HABEO and UTOR are in different classes – call them A and B – simply because their objects are in different cases. Why not label A 'accusative' and B 'ablative', in the same way?

In fact, it would not be quite the same way, since the cases governed by verbs are only part of the total category. Thus no verb governs the nominative which, as we have seen, is a marker of the subject. For that reason, a 'lexical case' of verbs would not be identical to the inflectional case of nouns, whereas lexical and inflectional gender correspond precisely. But it is doubtful whether we have any stronger reason for treating the rules differently.

The remaining points are substantive. To begin, it is worth stressing that government and agreement are directional relations. In *habet muros*, the accusative is governed by the verb, not the verb by the accusative. In *le ragazze*, the article is in agreement with the noun, not the noun with the article. But the direction does not always match that of dependency. In these examples it does: *habet* controls its complement *muros*, and *ragazze* the determiner *le*. But in *Le ragazze sono partite* the remaining dependencies are like this:

while the determining of bound terms is like this:

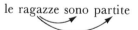

At the level of syntactic relations, the predicator controls both its subject and the auxiliary. At the level of realisation, the subject determines the agreement of both the auxiliary and the predicator.

Such discrepancies are real, and not a product of mistaken analysis. The reason for treating the agreement like this is that the inflections of the predicator can be predicted from those of the subject, but not vice versa. With *sono partiti*, the subject could be a masculine plural (*i ragazzi*), or two or more masculine singulars (*il ragazzo e suo padre* 'the boy and his father'), or a masculine and a feminine, and so on. But each of these uniquely selects the markers agreeing with it.

Older grammars describe the verb as subordinate to the subject, just as the object is in turn subordinate to – in our terms, dependent on – the verb. If that were correct the main discrepancy would vanish. But verbs can also agree with their objects. Thus, in another Italian sentence:

> le   ha   viste
> 'them' 'has' 'seen'

('He/she/it saw them/has seen them') the participle agrees not with a subject, but with the object pronoun *le*. Compare *Li ha visti* (same translation), with masculine plural *li* and *visti*. The agreement is also possible, though neither necessary nor usual, when the object is a noun: *ha viste le ragazze* 'has seen the girls', *ha visti i ragazzi* 'has seen the boys'. It appears that agreement follows the direction of dependency when the dependent is a modifier or a determiner (Latin *vulpes rufa* 'a red fox', with *rufa* modifying and agreeing with *vulpes*; Italian *le ragazze*, with *le* agreeing with and a determiner of *ragazze*), but is the opposite when it is a complement, or at least the complement of a predicator. Government, which is traditionally recognised only in complement constructions, follows the direction of dependency throughout. If these generalisations hold for all languages, and do not merely reflect the ways in which grammarians use terms, they attest the reality of the construction types and, perhaps, the unique character of predication.

We must also appreciate that an inflection which is bound in one sentence may be independent in another, even though the word has the same function. In our Latin example *hostis habet muros*, the 3rd singular of *habet* is selected, as we said, by *hostis*. But one could also say *habet muros* 'He/she/it holds the walls'; here there is no apparent subject, and the 3rd singular plays the role of a determiner. The corresponding construction in Italian was referred to briefly in Chapter 7, where we objected to a Bloomfieldian analysis with the subject said to stand in an endocentric construction. But we may also question the traditional account, by which, in a sentence such as *habet muros*, the verb agrees with a subject which is understood. The 3rd singular might instead be treated as semantically equivalent to a pronoun, whereupon no syntactic incompleteness need be posited.

But there are cases where it is more difficult to choose between analyses. In Latin

> veni   ad urbem
> 'I came' 'to' 'the city'

the preposition *ad* is followed by an accusative (*urbem*). In

> proficisci ab   urbe
> 'to set out' 'from' 'the city'

ab is followed, in the same construction, by an ablative (*urbe*). One could not say either *ad urbe* or *ab urbem*. But two considerations detract from the generality of this pattern. The first concerns a class of nouns (names of towns among them) which can function without a preposition. For example, one could say *Roma proficisci* 'to set out from Rome', where a simple ablative (*Roma*) has the same syntactic and semantic relationship to *proficisci* as *ab* plus the ablative (*ab urbe*). Likewise, in *domum veni* 'I came home', an accusative *domum* has the same relationship to *veni* as the phrase consisting of *ad* plus the accusative (*ad urbem*). In these examples, at least, the case is an independent feature.

The second point concerns a few prepositions which can be followed by either case. For example, one could say *in urbem veni* 'I came into the city' (*in* plus accusative *urbem*) or *in urbe remansi* 'I remained in the city' (*in* plus ablative *urbe*); *sub terram ire* 'to go beneath the earth' (*sub* plus accusative *terram*) or *sub terra habitare* 'to live beneath the earth' (*sub* plus ablative *terra*). Here the accusative is used with a directional meaning (motion into, motion into a position beneath) and the ablative with a static meaning (location in, location in a position beneath). Assuming that the clause construction is constant, and that the cases are not syntactically determined by the verbal lexemes (VENIO 'come' and REMANEO 'remain', EO 'go' and HABITO 'reside'), accusative and ablative must again be seen as independent determiners.

The usual account is that AD governs the accusative (*ad urbem*) and AB the ablative (*ab urbe*). Prepositions such as IN or SUB are said to govern, in a looser sense of having as their complement, either an accusative or an ablative. In *domum veni* or *Roma proficisci* the accusative or ablative is ungoverned. But an alternative at once presents itself. In *domum veni* 'I came home' the noun is a direct dependent – let us suppose – of *veni*:

domum   veni

For *in urbem veni* 'I came into the city', the traditional analysis would be like this:

[in urbem] veni

with no direct link between *veni* and *urbem*. But *urbem*, like *domum*, is a directional accusative (motion directed to the city, just like motion directed home). So, we might establish the alternative structure

[in urbem] veni

with *urbem*, not *in*, the head of the directional phrase. The dependent *in* would be one of a class of determiners – the prepositions are, in any case, a closed set – which are obligatory, in this construction, with most types of noun. In

[in urbe] remansi

('I remained in the city') the same determiner would depend on an ablative *urbe*, whose syntactic, though not semantic function could be identified with that of the ablative *Roma* in *Roma proficisci* 'to set out from Rome'. Nouns such as ROMA 'Rome' and DOMUS 'house, home' would form a semantic class with which the determiners were variously either optional or excluded.

Finally, in a phrase such as *ab urbe* (*ab urbe proficisci* 'to set out from the city'), we would have an obligatory determiner whose meaning is incompatible with directionals. That is the reason – we would argue – why one cannot say *ab urbem*: literally, 'away from ⟨the city⟩' construing with 'the city as the point to which motion is directed'. In the case of *ad urbem* (*ad urbem veni* 'I came to the city') we would argue that AD, which has a basic directional meaning, is semantically incompatible with an ablative. That is why one cannot say *ad urbe*. No syntactic rule, let alone a rule of government, would be invoked.

It is as well to realise that there are conditions under which such an account would be right. One is that there should be no evidence for a direct relation between the preposition, or putative determiner, and the verb. That means, in particular, that there should be no collocational restrictions, such as were found for at least some locative prepositions in English (Chapter 6 and earlier). Another condition is that the cases should have uniform semantic roles. Let us imagine a language, otherwise similar to Latin, in which a pair of features – call them case A and case B – are instanced only in this construction. Of these, case A is never used in phrases with a static or an 'away from' meaning (the meanings of Latin *in urbe* and *ab urbe*), while case B is never used in phrases with a directional meaning. Let us suppose that our first condition is also met. This system is not implausible; in it, A and B are clearly independent and not governed.

In Latin itself the facts are less obliging. It is possible that the verb and preposition were not related by collocational restrictions, though only a detailed study would allow us to assert this with confidence. But we have seen that the cases have at least one other role, as markers of a direct object. The construction of *habet muros* 'holds the walls' is different from that of *domum veni* 'I came home', since the former excludes a preposition whereas, in the latter, MURUS 'wall' requires one (*sub muros veni* 'I came into a position beneath the walls', and so on). The construction of *equis utuntur* 'They use horses' is similarly distinguished from that of *Roma proficisci*. This confirms that the hypothetical determiner is obligatory not just with a certain class of accusative or ablative nouns, but with nouns which, in addition, stand in one particular relationship. That in itself casts doubt on its status as a dependent.

Within this construction, we find that prepositions with an 'away from' meaning (AB or A 'from', E or EX 'out of', DE 'down from') regularly collocate with the ablative. But the opposition of static and directional rapidly dissolves. One would say, for example, *pro statua consedi* 'I sat down in front of the statue'; in the usual account, PRO 'in front of' must govern an ablative (*statua*). But for 'I sat down near the statue' we might say *propter statuam consedi* (compare Cicero, *Brutus*, III.25) or *iuxta statuam consedi*; both PROPTER and IUXTA are prepositions that collocate only with an accusative. In *ad urbem veni* the sense was clearly directional. But it is not so in, for example, *ad urbem habitare* 'to live close by the city'. Dictionaries treat these as separate senses of the preposition, since its translation tends to differ in modern European languages. But in reality AD is one of several prepositions that collocate indifferently with both static and motional verbs. Like AD, they generally govern an accusative. It is IN and SUB, with a distinction between accusative and ablative, that are the exceptions.

The arbitrariness of *propter statuam* as compared with *pro statua*, or of *ad urbem habitare* as compared with *in urbe habitare*, is the justification for recognising, in the first three, a relationship of government. But the pattern cannot be made entirely consistent. In *domum veni* the one-word *domum* cannot be reduced to the pattern of preposition plus complement. But neither can its relation to *veni* be reduced to that of a direct object. In *in urbe habitare* the construction of *in* with *urbe* is identical to that of the other prepositions. But it would be wrong to reduce the ablative of *urbe* to the rule of government. A preposition such as IN does not even restrict the range of cases that can follow since, in the construction of locative preposition plus noun in general, only the accusative and ablative are possible.

Problematic relations are often associated with historical shifts. The modern Romance languages have no cases and all prepositions control nouns in the same form. But at the prehistoric stage, the origin of prepositions lies in what appears to have been a class of adverbs, one of whose roles was as a modifier of locative and other case forms. Classical Latin shows a pattern which, on balance, is more like the modern. But it is a transitional system, in which the characteristics of earlier Indo-European are still partly in evidence. We might make a similar remark about the subject–verb agreement in modern English. For most subjects the choice of verbal root or verbal root plus -*(e)s* is determined by rule; therefore the form of the verb is regarded as bound. But the distinction is made only in the present, not in the past tense or for the modal auxiliaries. There is also a countervailing tendency towards what is described in the literature as notional or semantic agreement. *The committee*, for example, has a singular noun but would refer to a number of people; that is why one can say either *The committee has* or *The committee have reported*. Such instances give rise to the suspicion that there is no agreement, but only cases of semantic incompatibility (like the putative incompatibility of Latin *ad* with the ablative, or *ab* with the accusative) in which verb forms with or without -*(e)s* fail to collocate with subjects whose inflection and reference do not fit. Here too the conflict arises in a transitional state.

Although standard English retains a relic of the rule establishable in older or other Indo-European languages, it is nearer to the pattern of some dialects, where each tense has an invariant form.

FREE AND FIXED ORDER

It is a commonplace of linguistic typology that the more relations are realised by inflections, the more the order is, or can be, syntactically free. In Latin, it was possible to write a line of poetry such as

> ultima Cumaei venit iam carminis aetas
> 'The final age of the Cumaean song has now arrived'

(Virgil, *Eclogues*, IV.4) where none of the noun phrases is continuous. The first word, *ultima* 'final', modifies the last, *aetas* 'age'. The second, *Cumaei* 'of Cumaean', modifies the second to last, *carminis* 'of song'. The four together form a larger noun phrase, still divided by *venit iam* 'has come already'. Such ordering would be unusual in other styles; in prose one is more likely to write *Cumaei carminis aetas ultima iam venit* (continuity of all phrases), *Cumaei carminis iam venit aetas ultima* (continuity at least of modifiers and heads), and so on. But no rule excludes it. Of the seven words that make up Virgil's line, no pair need be adjacent, and none need follow or precede any other.

Instead all the relations are realised by inflections. The nominative singular feminine *ultima* 'final' agrees with the nominative singular of the feminine AETAS 'age', thus marking the dependency shown by arc *a*:

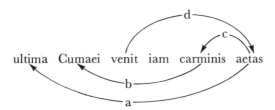

The genitive singular non-feminine *Cumaei* 'of Cumaean' agrees with the genitive singular of the neuter CARMEN 'song'; that marks the dependency shown by arc *b*. The genitive of *carminis* 'of song' is an independent marker of its dependency on *aetas* 'age' (arc *c*). Finally, the nominative of *aetas* is an independent marker of its role as subject (arc *d*); this is also marked by the bound 3rd singular of *venit*. Given

255

the inflections, and the part of speech to which each word belongs, there is no other way in which the line can be construed.

In the light of such examples Latin is described as a language with **free word order**. By contrast, English is described as having **fixed word order**. In the translation of Virgil's line:

> The final age of the Cumaean song has now arrived

the dependency of *song* on *age* is shown by the sequence as well as by *of*. In *the Cumaean song of the final age* it would be *age* that depended on *song*. In the smaller phrases (*the final age*, *the Cumaean song*) the relations are realised by sequence and adjacency alone. There is also a fixed sequence of subject plus predicator. For these words, in these syntactic relations, the order could vary only in the position of the peripheral *now*: with appropriate intonation, one could also say ... *has arRIVED now* or ... *has arrived NOW*. But even there not every sequence is possible. In particular, one would not say ... *now has arrived*, with *now* preceding the auxiliary.

There is thus a complementary relationship between a type of system with free order and rich inflections – in particular, with an extensive pattern of agreement – and one with few inflections and fixed order. But again some qualification and clarification is needed.

To begin with, the distinction is clearly a matter of degree. It is doubtful whether any language has completely free order. In Latin, prepositions must generally precede their complements: although one can say *ad urbem veni* or *veni ad urbem* 'I came to the city', one cannot say *urbem ad veni*, *veni urbem ad* or *ad veni urbem*. It is significant that, of the traditional parts of speech, only the prepositions are named after a realisational feature (Latin *prae* 'in advance, in front of' plus *positio* 'placing'), rather than a constructional role (thus the conjunction as a word that 'joins together') or notional type (the noun or *nomen* as, in what was seen as the typical or 'proper' case, a word that names some entity). Nor is the order in English entirely fixed. We have remarked that adverbs can appear at more than one point, though, of the many restrictions on adverbs that have been investigated, some are absolute constraints. One could also say either *He took off his hat* or *He took his hat off*, with a so-called 'adverbial particle' preceding or following the object. It is doubtful if there is any language where the order is wholly subject to rule.

But apart from differences of degree, it would be well to recognise a qualitative distinction between free word order, as exemplified in

Latin, and **free phrase order**. In Italian, as in English, the order within phrases is largely fixed. For example, one can say *le ragazze* 'the girls', but not *ragazze le*; *tutta la famiglia Pirelli* 'the whole Pirelli family', but not *la tutta famiglia Pirelli, tutta la Pirelli famiglia,* and so on; *la casa di Giovanni* 'John's house', but not *la di Giovanni casa.* As for noun phrases so for verb phrases. For example, one says *Sono arrivate* 'have arrived', not *Arrivate sono*; *Le ha viste* 'has seen them', not *Ha le viste.* In this last example, the object pronoun *le* is a clitic attached to the verbal unit.

But between phrases the order is largely free. For 'The girls have arrived' one could say either *Le ragazze sono arrivate* or *Sono arrivate le ragazze.* The choice is not empty, but the only absolute restrictions are those of sequence and adjacency within the subject and predicator blocks. For further examples let us cast an eye through the second chapter of di Lampedusa's novel *Il Gattopardo* 'The Leopard'.[2] In a sentence such as

> Tutta la famiglia Salina discese dalle carrozze
> 'The whole Salina household got down from the carriages'

a subject constituent (S), predicator (P) and adverbial (A) follow each other in the same order as the English translation: $_S$[*tutta la famiglia Salina*]$_S$ $_P$[*discese*]$_P$ $_A$[*dalle carrozze*]$_A$. In

> Al basso della scalinata le autorità si congedarono
> 'At the foot of the stairway the authorities took leave'

the sequence is A S P: $_A$[*al basso della scalinata*]$_A$ $_S$[*le autorità*]$_S$ $_P$[*si congedarono*]$_P$. In

> Nella prima stavano il Principe ... e Concetta
> 'In the first stood the prince ... and Concetta'

it is A P S: $_A$[*nella prima*]$_A$ $_P$[*stavano*]$_P$ $_S$[*il Principe ... e Concetta*]$_S$. Here too the order can be preserved in translation, but the English pattern is more restricted. For example, one would not translate *Vicino al pozzo incominciò la colazione* by 'Near the well began lunch.'

For other orders phrase by phrase translation becomes impossible. In

> Seguiva il Principe a braccio della Principessa
> 'The prince followed arm in arm with the princess'

[2] Giuseppe Tomasi di Lampedusa, *Il Gattopardo* (Milan, 1958); examples from pp. 68, 70, 78, 79, 106, 108.

the sequence is P S A: p[*seguiva*]p s[*il Principe*]s a[*a braccio della Principessa*]a. In

> Entrò nel parlatorio afoso la frescura del chiostro
> 'Into the stifling reception room came the coolness of the cloister'

it is P A S: p[*entrò*]p a[*nel parlatorio afoso*]a s[*la frescura del chiostro*]s. To replicate these in English, one could at best add *there* in the usual position of a subject: 'There followed the prince . . .', 'There came into the reception room . . .'. Finally, in

> Lui in quell'ammirazione rumorosa ci nuotava come un pesce nell'acqua
> 'He swam in this noisy admiration like a fish in water'

we have the sixth combination S A P: s[*lui*]s a[*in quell'ammirazione rumorosa*]a p[*ci nuotava*]p . . . In this example, the locative adverbial is picked up by a locative clitic (*ci*) attached to the verb. But the clitic can, and in written style would usually, be dropped.

Much the same freedom is allowed for other clause constructions, including those with a subject and object. But unlike the free word order in Latin, the free phrase order in Italian is only partly facilitated by inflections. Some roles are distinguished by the presence or absence of prepositions: thus in the first example from 'The Leopard', *dalle carrozze* (preposition *da* + article *le* + noun *carrozze*) cannot be a subject or object. Others may be distinguished by agreement: for example, in

> i ragazzi   il vino   l'hanno bevuto
> 'the boys' 'the wine' 'him/it have drunk'

the plural *hanno* matches a subject *i ragazzi*, and the singular clitic *l'*, backed by the masculine singular participle *bevuto*, matches the object *il vino*. But Italian has no case inflections; so, in an example like

> Giovanni il vino   l'ha bevuto
> 'John'   'the wine' 'him/it has drunk'

(alternatively *Il vino Giovanni l'ha bevuto*) there is nothing, apart from the sense, context and intonation, to show which element is which. Similarly, in *Tutta la famiglia Salina discese dalle carrozze*, no realisational feature confirms that the first phrase is subject ('The whole Salina household got down . . .') and not object ('He/she/it descended the whole Salina household . . .').

As elsewhere in language, there is a variable balance between economy and redundancy. In these respects the English system is less economical than the Italian, since a relatively fixed phrase order will often show relationships that would be evident from the context, collocations and so on. But the agreement is more rudimentary, as we have seen. There is also much homonymy between noun and verb forms: for example, *fishes* is a noun in *He caught three fishes* but a verb in *He fishes every Saturday*. To that extent the restrictions on order are less redundant. In another respect the Italian system is less economical than the English. For within the noun phrase the relations are often marked redundantly, by both order and agreement: English *a red tie*, with uninflected *a* and *red*; Italian *una cravatta rossa*, with feminine singular *una* 'one, a' and feminine singular *rossa* 'red', in agreement with the head noun.

But the variation falls within limits. A highly economical system would be one which combined a relatively free word order, as in Latin, with a relative poverty of inflectional markers, as in English. But that would lead to excessive ambiguity: for example, in an imaginary sentence

> John Paul will visit said Mary

there might be no way, even in context and with appropriate intonation, to determine which nouns stand in which relationships to which verb. This does not mean that such ambiguities are impossible. In the following line of Latin verse:

> aio te, Aeacida, Romanos vincere posse
> 'I say' 'you' 'descendant of Aeacus' 'the Romans' 'beat' 'can'

Ennius (*Annals*, VI. 179) records a somewhat unhelpful prophecy which can mean either '... that you can beat the Romans' or '... that the Romans can beat you'. This is because the complement clause is in a construction called the Accusative and Infinitive, with an infinitive verb, *posse*, that does not show agreement, and a subject, either *te* or *Romanos*, which is in the same case as the direct object. But although ambiguity is possible, communication would suffer if it could not generally be avoided.

A highly redundant system would be one that had both a relatively fixed word order and a relative richness of inflectional markers. At first sight, German tends towards this pole. Like Latin, it is described

259

as having case inflections, with finite verbs agreeing in person and number with the subject, and agreement within noun phrases in respect of case, number and, in the singular, gender. Yet the order in phrases is largely fixed, and the order within clauses is not as free as in Italian. But there is an important qualification, in that German has a very high degree of morphological homonymy. In a phrase like *den alten Baum* 'the old tree' the article, *den*, is in a form that could be either dative plural, or accusative singular masculine. The adjective, *alten*, is in a form that, with a definite article preceding, could be anything but nominative singular, or accusative singular feminine or neuter. The noun, *Baum*, is masculine, but in a form that could be either nominative singular, accusative singular or dative singular. It is only the phrase as a whole that is shown, by elimination, to be accusative singular. In the plural *die alten Bäume*, the article could in principle be either nominative or accusative plural, or nominative singular or accusative singular feminine; the adjective is as before; the noun could be nominative plural, accusative plural or genitive plural. Therefore the phrase as a whole could be either nominative or accusative, as could a feminine singular like *die alte Frau* 'the old woman' or a neuter singular like *das kleine Haus* 'the small house'. The notion that German is an 'inflected language', in a sense which has significant bearing on its potential for 'free word order', is in fact quite wrong.

Finally, in saying that a construction can be realised by two or more alternative orders, we do not, of course, imply that every order is equally likely or that there are no differences of meaning between them. In many cases one or more alternatives are **marked**, in that they tend to be used only in certain circumstances, or in certain styles. We have seen that a declarative sentence in English can begin with an object: THESE *he will* LIKE. But this is not usual except in a conversation, or in a latinised literary style (as, for instance, in the lines by Matthew Arnold cited at the beginning of this chapter). Nor is it usual, in conversational style, unless there is some reason to make this phrase the centre of attention: THOSE (pointing to them) *he surely* WOULD*n't want*; *An encyclo*PAE*dia* (the suggestion you have just put forward) *he might* WELL *find useful*; PAR*snips* (of the various vegetables I might consider serving) *I believe they* WON'T *eat*. The position after the predicator is **unmarked**, in that it is usual in all styles and can also be used, with appropriate intonation, in just the same contexts. Compare *He will like* THESE or *He will* LIKE THESE, *He surely wouldn't want* THOSE, and so on.

When there is no general tendency there may well be specific lexical differences. We remarked that in Italian it is possible to say either *Le ragazze sono arrivate* 'The girls have arrived' or *Sono arrivate le ragazze*; likewise either *Le ragazze sono partite* 'The girls have left' or *Sono partite le ragazze*. But Lepschy and Lepschy remark that the second order (predicator + subject) is unmarked for ARRIVARE, whereas the first (subject + predicator) is unmarked for PARTIRE.[3] This is only partly explained by the contexts in which these verbs are most likely to be used ('Someone has arrived – it is the girls'; 'The girls have done something – they have left').

We remarked that in English one can say either *He took off his hat* or *He took his hat off*. But this does not mean that the orders cannot carry a semantic difference. *He must pull his finger out* can be literal or idiomatic ('He must proceed faster'). But *He must pull out his finger* is likely to be taken only in the literal sense. The tendency is less clear in, for example, *He must pull his socks up* and *He must pull up his socks*, though we might find a difference of frequency. With other collocations it is reversed. *I'd like to take up your offer* will usually have the idiomatic sense of TAKE UP ('accept', 'agree to'). *I'd like to take your offer up* will generally be taken literally (compare *I'd like to take your suitcase up*), unless it is *up* rather than *offer* that carries the stress. Contrast *I'd like to take your* OFFer *up* and *I'd like to take your offer* UP. *He coughed up £10* can be either literal or idiomatic, but *He coughed £10 up* tends, in my usage, to be literal only. However, this tendency is in turn less clear in, for example, *I'll dig up some books for you* ('find you some' or literally 'dig up') and *I'll dig some books up*.

It is always foolish for a linguist to assume that, because we cannot immediately find a difference of meaning or of statistical tendency, a difference of form can play no communicative role. But the opposite error is also foolish, of supposing that, because a difference of form does carry a difference of meaning, it must necessarily realise a difference of construction. In this light, the complementarity of languages like Latin and English reflects a difference in the roles that ordering can play. In Latin order may not have been free in an absolute sense. A speaker might often have had little choice in a

---

[3] Anna L. & G. C. Lepschy, *The Italian Language Today* (London: Hutchinson, 1977), p. 154.

particular context of utterance. But it was syntactically free, or largely so, in that its role is not primarily to realise constructional relations. In English it has that role to a strikingly greater degree. To that extent it is syntactically fixed, and its role in Latin must often be supplied by differences between constructions or by intonation. We will not make sense of either type unless we understand how and why our field is limited.

NOTES AND REFERENCES

For earlier typologies of realisational devices see PAUL, pp. 123f.; SWEET, 1, pp. 30ff.: fuller discussion in DE GROOT, *Syntaxis*, Ch. 8, especially pp. 246ff. See also W. Porzig, *Das Wunder der Sprache: Probleme, Methoden und Ergebnisse der modernen Sprachwissenschaft*, 2nd edn (Berne: Francke, 1957), pp. 142ff.; again, BLOOMFIELD, pp. 163f.

On the continuity of syntagms see de Groot, who speculates that the primary tendency might be towards intonational unity; his remarks remain suggestive (DE GROOT, *Syntaxis*, pp. 251, 256). On the relation of elements to the predicator compare, for example, HUDSON, pp. 92ff.; for detailed discussion and illustration see D. L. Smith, 'Mirror images in Japanese and English', *Lg*, 54 (1978), pp. 78–122, especially pp. 99ff. (on a supposedly universal 'proximity principle'). The last reference forms part of a growing literature on tendencies in the ordering of elements, whose value is as yet unclear. For the leading study see J. H. Greenberg, 'Some universals of grammar with particular reference to the order of meaningful elements', in J. H. Greenberg (ed.), *Universals of Language* (Cambridge, Mass.: MIT Press, 1963), pp. 73–113; a recent theoretical essay is that of P. Garde, 'Ordre linéaire et dépendance syntaxique: contribution à une typologie', *BSL*, 72 (1977), pp. 1–26, which seeks to base Greenberg's conjectures in the theory of dependency relations. But note that only tendencies are postulated: see, for example, D. C. Derbyshire, 'Word order universals and the existence of OVS languages', *LIn*, 8 (1977), pp. 590–9, against one restriction that had seemed temptingly absolute. These studies assume a notional universality of categories such as subject and object, and they usually have little regard for the different roles that order plays in particular languages.

The study of means of realisation might be advanced if we knew more about the way sentences are understood. In fact we seem to know surprisingly little: see W. J. M. Levelt, 'A survey of studies in sentence perception: 1970–1976', in W. J. M. Levelt & G. B. Flores d'Arcais (eds.), *Studies in the Perception of Language* (Chichester: Wiley, 1978), pp. 1–74, and other papers in that volume, for a recent and depressing survey.

Agreement and government are treated in most general introductions: for example, in LYONS, *Introduction*, pp. 239ff. But see especially HOCKETT,

Ch. 25, for their association with modification and complementation ('endo-' and 'exocentricity'). Hockett has an intermediate category of 'governmental concord' which would cover the gender agreement illustrated from Italian: for its classification as government see F. R. Palmer, *Grammar* (Harmondsworth: Penguin Books, 1971), pp. 102f.; earlier in DE GROOT, *Syntaxis*, p. 244. For transformational treatments compare POSTAL, pp. 43ff., with rules which begin by introducing gender morphemes in the head noun; BACH, pp. 249f., which treats both gender and number, etc. as 'syntactic features' (in the spirit of CHOMSKY, *Aspects*, pp. 170f.). For an early critique of the traditional notion of government, including the division made between it and agreement, see L. Hjelmslev, 'La notion de rection', *Acta Linguistica*, 1 (1939), pp. 10–23 (reprinted in his *Essais linguistiques* (Copenhagen: Nordisk Sprog- og Kulturforlag, 1959), pp. 139–51); this must be read in the context of his glossematic theory, which was then developing. For wider senses of the term see notes to Chapter 6 above; see also notes to Chapter 3 above, for government and agreement in models ignoring word boundaries.

On preposition and case in the history of Latin see ERNOUT & THOMAS, pp. 9ff.; A. Meillet, *Esquisse d'une histoire de la langue latine* (Paris: Klincksieck, 1928), pp. 158ff.; on their wider development, J. Kuryłowicz, *The Inflectional Categories of Indo-European* (Heidelberg: Winter, 1964), pp. 176ff. For the use of cases with particular prepositions see J. B. Hofmann, *Lateinische Syntax und Stilistik*, new edn by A. Szantyr (Munich: Beck, 1965), pp. 219–82. For agreement of verbs in English see QUIRK *et al.*, pp. 360ff.; also my *Generative Grammar*, pp. 89ff.

The complementarity of inflections and order is regularly noted: thus, with qualification, by ROBINS, p. 256. It should be obvious that there can also be systems in which neither is syntactically redundant; for a reminder see T. F. Mitchell, 'Aspects of concord revisited, with special reference to Sindhi and Cairene Arabic', *ArchL*, n.s. 4 (1973), pp. 27–50 (modified version, without discussion of Sindhi, in his *Principles of Firthian Linguistics* (London: Longman, 1975), Ch. 5). On the systems of realisation in different types of language see Sapir's brilliant and as yet unsurpassed survey (SAPIR, especially pp. 109ff., 136ff.).

The freedom of order in Latin has in the past been such a commonplace that most handbooks neglect to illustrate it. But it is correctly emphasised by HILL, pp. 475–82. For some tendencies that did exist see ERNOUT & THOMAS, pp. 161–3, and the studies by Marouzeau that they refer to; note that in my terms they are not 'LINGUISTICALLY without significance' (HILL, p. 476; my emphasis). For the type in general compare K. J. Dover, *Greek Word Order* (Cambridge: Cambridge University Press, 1960); this is short and parts may be read with profit even by those who cannot understand the examples. On the quite different case of, for instance, German see ENGEL, pp. 190–226 (on the rules of order in simple main clauses). This difference is often suppressed by writers on theoretical topics: thus, for example, H. U. Boas, *Syntactic Generalizations and Linear Order in Generative Transformational Grammar* (Tübingen: Gunter Narr, 1975), which limits discussion of Latin to the order of subject and object (pp. 47ff.); JACKENDOFF, *Semantic Interpretation*, p. 67 (following a review by S. J. Keyser, *Lg*, 44 (1968), p. 372), for the 'hopeful' extension to it of a principle that self-evidently will not do. See also CHOMSKY, *Aspects*, p. 126 ('In every known language the restrictions on order are quite severe').

For detailed discussion of Italian see Tatiana Alisova, *Strutture semantiche e sintattiche della proposizione semplice in italiano* (Florence: Sansoni, 1972), pp. 130–53, and the collective work by the Gruppo di Padova, 'L'ordine dei sintagmi nella frase', in *Fenomeni morfologici e sintattici nell'italiano contemporaneo* (Rome: Bulzoni, 1974), pp. 147–61; for the intransitive verb and subject compare Lidia Lonzi, 'L'articolazione presupposizione–asserzione e l'ordine V–S in italiano', *ibid.*, pp. 197–215. For a formulation of one form of restriction see F. Antinucci & G. Cinque, 'Sull' ordine delle parole in italiano: l'emarginazione', *Studi di grammatica italiana*, 6 (1977), pp. 121–46. On the type of system compare H. Contreras's fuller and more developed account of Spanish, *A Theory of Word Order with Special Reference to Spanish* (Amsterdam: North-Holland, 1976) – physically unpleasant to read but worth the eye-strain. For German compared with English see H. W. Kirkwood, 'Aspects of word order and its communicative function in English and German', *JL*, 5 (1969), pp. 85–107. For the most recent account of German phrase inflection see O. Werner, 'Kongruenz wird zu Diskontinuität im Deutschen', in B. Brogyanyi (ed.), *Festschrift for Oswald Szemerényi on the Occasion of his 65th Birthday* (Amsterdam: Benjamins, 1979), pp. 959–88 (stimulating on this and on agreement generally).

On the roles of order in general see F. Daneš, 'Order of elements and sentence intonation', reprinted in BOLINGER (ed.), pp. 216–32 (originally in *To Honour Roman Jakobson: Essays on the Occasion of his Seventieth Birthday* (The Hague: Mouton, 1967)); the theoretical framework is explained in his 'A three-level approach to syntax', *TLP*, 1 (1964), pp. 225–40. See too notes to Chapter 5 above, for general references on 'theme' and functional sentence perspective. The principle that no difference can be assumed to be meaningless is argued to the brink of excess by D. L. Bolinger, *Meaning and Form* (London: Longman, 1977); this has much that also bears on our discussion in the next chapter. Among his earlier papers see especially 'Linear modification', *Publications of the Modern Language Association of America*, 67 (1952), pp. 1117–44 (reprinted in HOUSEHOLDER (ed.), pp. 31–50).

12
Syntactic paradigms

Paradigms of clauses: basis in transformational relations.
Kernels and transforms: Direction of derivation. Kernels, transforms, kernel
sentences. Intermediate stages. Transformations.
Abstract representations: Abstraction from agreement; from morphology; from
periphrastic formations. Base rules, transformational rules, realisational rules.
Role-fillers (English DO, *it,* copula). Redundant vs. minimal representations
(subject and objects in English). Free order.
Transformational grammar: Bloomfieldian origins. Treatment of functions;
obligatory and optional transformations; implications of changes in mid 60s.
Integration of syntax and semantics: in generative semantics; in revised
extended standard theory. Persistence of phrase structure representation.

Of the following sentences:

    1. The police have impounded his car
    2. His car has been impounded by the police
    3. Have the police impounded his car?
    4. Has his car been impounded by the police?

the first is declarative and active; the second declarative and passive;
the third and fourth respectively interrogative and active, and interrogative and passive. This may be represented as a paradigm:

	Active	*Passive*
Declarative	1	2
Interrogative	3	4

whose vectors refer to properties of clauses or, more generally, of the
clause constructions which these examples illustrate. The paradigm
can be extended. In

    5. The police having impounded his car, ⟨he had to walk⟩
    6. His car having been impounded by the police, ⟨he had to
       walk⟩

the initial clauses are participial, not finite. These fit in like this:

		Active	*Passive*
Finite	{ *Declarative*	1	2
	{ *Interrogative*	3	4
Participial		5	6

with declarative and interrogative a subdivision of finite. In

> 7. Having impounded his car, ⟨they charged him with obstruction⟩
> 8. Having been impounded by the police, ⟨it cost £50 to collect⟩

the participial units are without a subject, and so on.

A paradigm of this sort is established by an analysis of transformational relations. Example 1 is transformationally related to example 2; likewise to examples 3, 4, 5 and 6. In short, each of the first six clauses is transformationally related to each of the others. We can show this by the diagram in Figure 16, with double-headed arrows

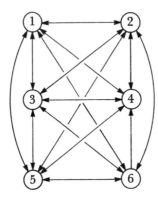

Figure 16

connecting each node. On the same principles, each of these is transformationally related to the participial units in examples 7 and 8.

But within such networks there are further correlations of form and of syntactic or semantic function. The clauses in 5–8 function only as subordinate clauses, while those in 1–4 may or must function as main clauses; this corresponds to a difference of form between the participle *having* and the finite *have*. That divides the network into two main blocks. Within the finite block, 1 is to 3 as 2 is to 4; this is an opposition of meaning, corresponding to a formal difference in the place of *have* or *has* (*The police have ...*, *Have the police ...*; *His car has ...*, *Has his car ...*), with a tendency towards different intonations. Likewise 1 is to 2 as 3 is to 4. We can accordingly simplify this part of the network (Figure 17), with the arrows reduced to those representing direct oppositions.

Within the participial block, 5 is to 7 as 6 is to 8, the presence or

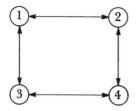

Figure 17

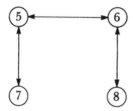

Figure 18

absence of a subject allowing a different range of subordinate roles. The arrows may accordingly be reduced as in Figure 18, where, in addition, 5 stands to 6 in the same active to passive relationship as 1 to 2 or 3 to 4.

Let us call this a **syntactic paradigm**, to distinguish it from a paradigm in morphology. But there is a limited analogy between them. In treating inflectional morphology, a grammar gives rules relating morphosyntactic properties to their exponents. For example, in the paradigm of the Italian adjective NUOVO 'new':

	Singular	*Plural*
Masculine	nuovo	nuovi
Feminine	nuova	nuove

it will state that -*o* is an exponent of masculine and singular, -*i* of masculine and plural, and so on. For our partial syntactic paradigm, it must make clear a similar relationship between, for example, the form of the verb phrase (*have/having impounded, has/having been impounded*) and the clausal properties of active and passive. This should be done by general statements, each of which applies to as many paradigms as possible. In

> The police impound his car
> His car is impounded by the police

267

the opposition is realised by a partly different pair of forms, *impound* and *is impounded*. But, on further analysis, the same statement covers both.

These are matters on which few scholars would, in substance, disagree. But how best can such a description be formulated?

KERNELS AND TRANSFORMS

The earliest answer, and one whose possibilities are still worth exploring, is to begin by characterising one term in the network of oppositions, and derive the others from it. The starting point is determined by various criteria.

Firstly, the relevant construction must allow the maximum number of valents. In the reduced *having impounded his car, having been impounded by the police*, each verb has one complement; elsewhere in the paradigm they have two. Therefore the same clause will appear in many different paradigms: for example, the active *having impounded his car* stands in the same opposition to *the chief constable having impounded his car, the students' rag committee having impounded his car*, and so on. Our starting point will be a construction in which the paradigms are maximally differentiated.

It will also be one which can be generalised over paradigms with different terms. An intransitive verb allows oppositions between declarative and interrogative:

> His engine has stopped
> Has his engine stopped?

between both and a participial

> his engine having stopped

and so on, but none between active and passive. In that respect the paradigm has different vectors. But apart from the difference in valency, the realisation of these clauses is the same as that of the actives. We therefore characterise that pattern once, and then derive the passive pattern from the actives, instead of deriving the active from the passive, and then characterising the intransitives separately.

We will also start from a construction which allows the predicator to be maximally determined. In finite clauses the verb carries a distinction of tense (present or past). But this does not apply to participles. Hence *the police having impounded his car* is a reduced clause (by the definition suggested in Chapter 8) opposed to both *The police have impounded his car* (present perfect with *have*) and *The police had impounded his car* (past perfect with *had*). Nor are there participles of modal auxiliaries. So, there is no participial counterpart of, for example, *The police could have impounded his car*.

Otherwise, we start from the construction to which the others, in general, bear the most resemblance. By earlier criteria it must be active rather than passive, finite rather than participial. Of the two constructions which remain, the declarative is more like the complete participial: subject before the first auxiliary, not after, as in the interrogative. In a subset of paradigms it is also closer to the subject-less participial. Thus a declarative *The police impounded his car* (past tense with no auxiliary) corresponds to an interrogative *Did the police impound his car?* (auxiliary supplied by the past tense of DO). But the participial units are again without an auxiliary: *(the police) impounding his car*, not *doing impound his car*. Our starting point must be the declarative.

A clause construction which is not derived from another is a **kernel construction**, and a clause which has such a construction a **kernel clause**. All other terms in the network are described as their **transforms**. Thus there is a transformational relationship between *Has his engine stopped?* and *His engine has stopped*; the latter has the kernel construction; therefore the construction of the interrogative is a transform of it, and the specific clause *Has his engine stopped?* is a transform of the specific declarative. A kernel clause which is both a sentence and a simple sentence, like *His engine has stopped* or *The police have impounded his car*, is a **kernel sentence**. Within this model the construction of any other sentence, or any other sentence that consists of clauses, will be reduced to that of kernel sentences wherever possible. Thus the following:

> The police have impounded the car which he left outside the stadium

is a kernel clause, with transforms *Have the police impounded the car which he left outside the stadium?*, and so on. It is not a kernel sentence, as it is not simple. But the relative clause, *which he left outside the stadium*, is a transform of the kernel sentences *He left a car outside the stadium*, *He left the car outside the stadium*, *He left a bicycle outside the stadium*, and so on.

269

When this modifying clause is set aside, the remainder of the main clause, *The police have impounded the car*, is itself a kernel sentence.

If we return to our fragmentary paradigm, we will find that there are arguments not just for the starting point, but also for intermediate stages in the derivation. The clauses numbered 5 and 7:

    5. the police having impounded his car
    7. having impounded his car

both have a participle. So, to achieve a generalisation, we will derive first one, and then the other from it. Likewise for the passives 6 and 8:

    6. his car having been impounded by the police
    8. having been impounded by the police

But in that case the subjectless units must be derived from those with subjects, on the principle, once more, that we make better generalisations if we proceed from points of greater differentiation. So, starting from the declaratives

    1. The police have impounded his car
    2. His car has been impounded by the police

the first stage of derivation is from 1 to 5 and 2 to 6; this involves an operation changing the first verb to a present participle. The second stage is from 5 to 7 and 6 to 8, involving an operation which deletes the subject element.

Within the finite block

    1. The police have impounded his car
    2. His car has been impounded by the police
    3. Have the police impounded his car?
    4. Has his car been impounded by the police?

we have a choice of deriving the active interrogative from the active declarative (3 from 1), and then deriving the passives (2 from 1, 4 from 3), or deriving the declarative passive from the declarative active (2 from 1), and then deriving the interrogatives (3 from 1, 4 from 2). But consider again the case in which the kernel clause has no auxiliary. To derive *Did Bill cook dinner?* from *Bill cooked dinner* we must introduce DO; this requires a special statement, additional to the general process deriving *Have the police . . . ?* from *The police have . . .* If we derive the passive interrogative from the active interrogative, we must then remove DO: *Was dinner cooked by Bill?*, not *Did dinner be cooked by Bill?* This would require another special statement, additional to the general process by which *Dinner was cooked by Bill* is derived from *Bill cooked dinner, His car has been impounded by the police* from *The police have impounded his car*, and so on. If we derive the passive interrogative from the passive declarative, only the first of these special statements is needed. *Was dinner cooked by Bill?* derives from *Dinner was cooked by Bill* in just the way that *Has his car been impounded by the police?* derives from *His car has been impounded by the police.*

In conclusion, the order of derivation can be shown by the directed graph in Figure 19. The graph is rooted in the node labelled 1,

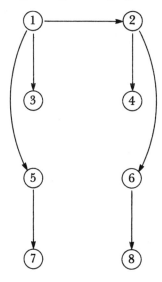

Figure 19

representing the construction of the active declarative. It shows a path from node 1, through node 2 (passive declarative), to node 4 (passive interrogative), for the reasons just given; likewise paths from 1 and 2, through 5 and 6 (participial clauses with subjects), to 7 and 8 (subjectless participials), following the paragraph before.

Within this model, a **transformation** describes the operations by which a new vector is added to the paradigm. One states the operations by which a passive construction is opposed to the active: mapping of the active onto the passive verb phrase, of the subject and object of the active onto the agent and subject of the passive. Together these form the Passive Transformation. Another is the Interrogative

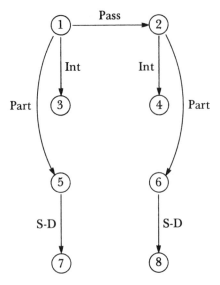

Figure 20

Transformation, by which interrogatives are opposed to declaratives. A third can be called the Participial Transformation, describing just the operation by which a finite verb is mapped onto a participle. A fourth is the Transformation of Subject-Deletion. This will also apply outside our fragmentary paradigm: for example, to the opposition of the subjectless infinitival *to have impounded his car* and fuller infinitivals such as *for the police to have impounded his car*.

The structure of the paradigm may now be represented by a directed graph in which the arcs are labelled for the transformations which apply. For our illustration this is as in Figure 20, where Pass = Passive, Int = Interrogative, Part = Participial and S-D = Subject-Deletion.

ABSTRACT REPRESENTATIONS

The success of our criteria, in determining both the kernel constructions and at least some of the subsequent stages of the derivation, is a notable confirmation of the model. This is brought out by the comparison with inflections. In morphology, a traditional technique is to derive a paradigm from a leading form: for example, the paradigm of Latin nouns from the nominative singular. But the choice of leading form is hard to justify, and intermediate stages are often unhelpful. In syntax we do not find corresponding difficulties, especially in establishing the kernel. The fact that kernel sentences are determined uniquely, without unresolvable clashes of criteria, is good reason for believing that the category is genuine.

There is a problem, however, as to how the opposed constructions are to be characterised. A particular paradigm shows contrasts among individual clauses: for example, between *She cooks dinner* and *Does she cook dinner?* Each pair have a common description in respect of certain lexemes and certain word forms (*cooks* and *cook* are both forms of COOK, *she* is a word distinct from *her*), in respect of certain features of order (*cooks* and *cook* precede *dinner*), in respect of certain functions (*she* is subject and *dinner* object), and so on. In certain respects they have different descriptions (*cooks* differs from *does . . . cook*). But how many of the similarities and differences are relevant to the general characterisation of their opposition? It will be obvious in a moment that some are irrelevant; to that extent constructions have an **abstract representation**, which does not show all the features by which individual clauses are realised. But the more abstract the representation becomes, the less the role of transformations will be, and the more the difference between kernels and transforms will be reduced.

Let us begin with the agreement. In our original paradigm, the actives had a plural verb (*The police have . . .*), the passives a singular (*His car has . . .*). But this is merely a consequence of the change in subject: in *A policeman has removed his wheels*, *His wheels have been removed by a policeman*, the effect is the reverse. It has nothing to do with·the opposition between constructions. We will therefore adopt an abstract representation in which the verbs are not inflected for this category. It is in that form that the kernel construction will be specified, and for that form that the passive transformation will be stated. The agreement is irrelevant at this level.

The next obvious candidate is the morphology. A representation of syntax is already abstract in that it ignores variation between inflectional paradigms. For example, it is irrelevant to syntax that *removed* has a regular past participle in *-(e)d*, while *taken* has the irregular *-(e)n*. But let us look more closely at the passive verb phrase. If we stated it word by word, the change of active to passive would involve two operations: one turning the head verb into the past participle (*cook(s)* → *cooked*, *took* → *taken*), another inserting the corresponding form of BE (present *cook(s)* → present *am/are/is* + *cooked*, past *took* → past *was/were* + *taken*, *have/has* + past participle *removed* → *have/has* + past participle *been* + *removed*, and so on). But this pattern is similar to that of the perfect and progressive (Chapter 3). For *cooks* and *has cooked* the difference is between a simple present and a past participle preceded by the present of HAVE. For *took* and *was taking* it is between a simple past and the past of BE followed by a present participle. In passives, as in these, there is a link between an auxiliary lexeme and a property of the verb which follows it. Only the particular relata (BE and past participle, not HAVE and past participle or BE and present participle) are unique to the transformation.

One solution is to treat the forms as periphrastic. *Cook(s)* is the simple present (non-perfect, non-progressive, non-passive) of COOK. Its place in the morphological paradigm may be represented by V_{Pres}, with an abbreviation for the morphosyntactic property subscripted to the symbol for 'verb'. *Have/has cooked* is a periphrastic perfect and may be represented, in the same style, by $V_{Pres, Perf}$; likewise the periphrastic progressive, *am/are/is cooking*, may be represented by $V_{Pres, Progr}$. To these representations the passive transformation merely adds another property: $V_{Pres, Pass}$ = *am/are/is cooked*, $V_{Pres, Perf, Pass}$ = *have/has been cooked*, $V_{Pres, Progr, Pass}$ = *am/are/is being cooked*. That the passive is formed by BE and a following past participle; that this auxiliary immediately precedes the head verb (*has been cooked*, not *is had cooked*); that the perfect and progressive are similarly formed by HAVE with a past and BE with a present participle; that these auxiliaries appear before a passive auxiliary – all this is a matter for separate morphological statement.

If we pause for a moment we can now see that a generative account of syntax (Chapter 2) would need rules of three sorts. The first specify the abstract representations of the kernel. For example, they state that the clause includes a predicator and its complements; that one possible set of complements comprises a subject and a direct object; that the predicator may be present or past, perfective or non-perfective, may take one of a set of modal auxiliaries, and so on. We will refer to these collectively as **base rules**.

The second derive the abstract representation of the transforms. These are the **transformational rules**, or transformations, in the sense already referred to. Thus the passive transformation states, among other things, that in a passive clause the predicator has passive as a further morphosyntactic property.

The third relate the abstract representations to a sequential representation of words or morphemes. These will deal with, among other things, agreement; also with periphrastic formations. For example, a rule will state that $V_{X, Pass}$ (where X is any set of one or more properties) is realised by $BE_X + V_{PaP}$ (PaP = past participle). Another will state that $V_{X, Perf}$ is realised by $HAVE_X + V_{PaP}$. Successively these relate $V_{Pres, Perf, Pass}$, the abstract representation of forms such as *have been cooked*, to a word by word representation $HAVE_{Pres} + BE_{PaP} + V_{PaP}$. Let us refer to these collectively as **realisational rules.**

The problem we face is to decide how much belongs to the realisational rules, and not to the abstract representations. They already deal with certain markers, such as the bound '3rd singular' (-*s*) of *She cooks*. Others relate directly to a clausal property: thus the passive morphology of the verb phrase *is cooked* marks the passive syntax of clauses such as *Dinner is cooked by Bill*. But there are many which, at first sight, might be handled at either level. Since all markers are realisational devices, is there any reason why, wherever possible, they should not be handled by realisational rules? It is the same with order. Some features of order relate to clausal properties: thus the position of the auxiliary in *Has Bill cooked dinner?* is a direct mark of the interrogative construction. But the rest are either irrelevant to syntax (in cases of free order), or mark particular relations within the construction. Again we may ask if there is any reason why the abstract representations should include them.

Of the various types of form word, the most interesting are those that can be described as **role-fillers**. One such is the DO of *Does Bill cook dinner?* The form of an interrogative is, in general:

Aux + Subject ...

with an auxiliary (Aux) preceding the subject. In *Can Bill cook dinner?* the preposed element is supplied by the modal (CAN). In *Has Bill cooked dinner?* or *Is Bill cooking dinner?* it is supplied by the auxiliary of the perfect or the progressive; in *Is dinner cooked by Bill?* by that of the passive. If no such word is available the role is filled by DO. So, the kernels *Bill cooks dinner* and *Bill cooked dinner* (present and past tense with no auxiliary) have transforms *Does Bill ...?* and *Did Bill ...?*, with the corresponding tenses of DO occupying a place that would otherwise be empty.

We therefore need another rule of periphrastic formation, by which a residual Aux V_X – residual in that none of the other rules is applicable – is realised by DO_X V. But the reason for separating this from the transformation is not just that it fits in neatly with the other realisational structures. In simple negation, *doesn't cook* is to *cooks* as *can't cook* is to *can cook, hasn't been cooked* to *has been cooked*, and so on. In each pair *n't* is attached to an initial auxiliary (Aux + *n't*); here too this is DO if nothing else is available. Similarly, *Bill* DOES *cook* (affirmation or confirmation that he does so) is to *Bill* COOKS or BILL *cooks* as *Bill* CAN *cook* is to *Bill can* COOK or BILL *can cook, Bill* IS *cooking* to *Bill is* COOK*ing* or BILL *is cooking*, and so on. In this pattern an auxiliary carries the nucleus of a tone group (Aux); again it is DO if the role would otherwise be unfillable. The rule for DO is thus more general than the particular transformation with which we began.

Another role-filler is the *it* of, for example, *It is raining* (Chapter 5). The verb RAIN is zero-valent; so, in that respect, the abstract representation might be simply RAIN$_{Pres, Progr}$. But a full clause has, in general, a subject (S) and a predicate. With a transitive or intransitive the subject is supplied by a complement: $_S[it]_S$ *is coming*, $_S[she]_S$ *hit me*. When nothing else is available, the role is filled by *it*: $_S[it]_S$ *is raining*.

This too is characteristic of more than one construction. In *It is quite clear that she is not coming* we have what is called Extraposition. The predicator *clear* takes a single complement, the clause *that she is not coming*. This could, in principle, supply the subject: *That she is not coming is quite clear*. But the more usual pattern is with the clause removed outside the subject–predicate relation (Latin *extra* 'outside'); this leaves no subject and *it* is supplied. The same pattern is found in passives such as *It is reported that she is not coming*. In *It was Bill who cooked it* we have a Cleft construction. The elements of the predication *Bill cooked it* are split between two structures, of which the second relates *cooked it* to the pronoun for an unspecified complement (compare *Who cooked it?* and *the man who cooked it*) while the first has *Bill* as a predicative noun. Only *it* can supply a subject for *was Bill*. A single generalisation covers the role of *it* in cleft and extraposed and zero-valent clauses. But the condition for stating it is that this too should be eliminated from the individual abstract representations.

There is also a case for eliminating the copula. In predications of the form *It is dear, He is a fool, She is in the garden, It is for slicing beans*, we have described BE as a marker. As such it appears in no other construction, and we would lose no generalisation if we introduced it in the base rules. But the copula is like an auxiliary with respect to interrogation (*Is she in the garden?*, like *Is she coming?*), negation (*She isn't in the garden*, like *She isn't coming*) or the affirmative/confirmative pattern (*She IS in the garden*, like *She IS coming*). Moreover, it is hard to detach it from the BE of the passive and progressive formations (*is impounded*, *is coming*). In the passive the linked element is a past participle (V_{PaP}), in the progressive a present participle (V_{PrP}); these are the inflections by which, in other constructions, a verb assumes an adjective- or noun-like role. The copula precedes a non-verbal predicator (adjective, noun, prepositional phrase). Could this be the basis for a partial generalisation?

It is easy to see how it might be formulated. In *It is dear* we describe *dear* as the predicator; on that analysis BE is a verb which carries distinctions of tense and so forth, regularly associated with a verbal predicator (*It breaks*, *It broke*, *It is breaking*) but not compatible with non-verbal predicators such as adjectives. If the kernel *It breaks* has the construction

Subject	Predicator
it	BREAK_{Pres}

that of *It is dear* may be shown equivalently as

Subject	Predicator
it	DEAR_{Pres}

The place which BE will occupy may then be introduced by a realisational rule

$$\text{Non-verbal predicator}_X \rightarrow {}_V[{-}_X]_V \text{ Non-verbal predicator}$$

where '—' marks the slot for an as yet unspecified verb (V), with whatever morphosyntactic properties (X) the abstract representation gives. This rule is presented as an operation by which, for example, *They* $\text{CHEAP}_{Pres, Perf}$ (the abstract representation of *They have been cheap*) is changed to *They* $-_{Pres, Perf}$ *cheap*. Rules for the passive and progressive may be given similarly:

$$V_{X, Pass} \rightarrow {}_V[{-}_X]_V\, V_{PaP}$$
$$V_{X, Progr} \rightarrow {}_V[{-}_X]_V\, V_{PrP}$$

Thus an abstract *It* $\text{COOK}_{Pres, Progr, Pass}$ *by Bill* (for *It is being cooked by Bill*) would undergo successive changes first to *It* —$_{\text{Pres, Progr}}$ COOK$_{\text{PaP}}$ *by Bill*, and then to *It* —$_{\text{Pres}}$ —$_{\text{PrP}}$ COOK$_{\text{PaP}}$ *by Bill*.

The rule for the perfect may be written as

$$V_{X, \text{Perf}} \rightarrow {}_V[\text{HAVE}_X]_V \ V_{\text{PaP}}$$

changing, for example, *They* —$_{\text{Pres, Perf}}$ *cheap* (our intermediate representation of *They have been cheap*) to *They* HAVE$_{\text{Pres}}$ —$_{\text{PaP}}$ *cheap*. This covers the exceptional case, in which a participle is linked with an auxiliary other than BE. The general case may then be covered by the rule

$${}_V[\text{---}_X]_V \ \text{Non-verbal} \rightarrow {}_V[\text{BE}_X]_V \ \text{Non-verbal}$$

(Non-verbal = a participle or non-verbal predicator), changing *They* HAVE$_{\text{Pres}}$ —$_{\text{PaP}}$ *cheap* to *They* HAVE$_{\text{Pres}}$ BE$_{\text{PaP}}$ *cheap*; likewise *It* —$_{\text{Pres}}$ —$_{\text{PrP}}$ COOK$_{\text{PaP}}$ *by Bill* (our intermediate representation of *It is being cooked by Bill*) to *It* BE$_{\text{Pres}}$ BE$_{\text{PrP}}$ COOK$_{\text{PaP}}$ *by Bill*. That rule might in turn be seen as an exception to a final

$${}_V[\text{---}_X]_V \rightarrow {}_V[\text{DO}_X]_V$$

by which all other blank verbs as in —$_{\text{Pres}}$ *Bill cook dinner?* (for *Does Bill cook dinner?*) are supplied by DO.

At this point we can reasonably pause again, and ask not what might with profit be removed from the abstract representations, but what they, and in particular those of the kernel constructions, must contain. Clearly they must give the form of a predicative construction: for example, *Bill told Mary a story* has a construction which we would display like this:

(direct object *a story*, indirect *Mary*) according to the schema of Chapter 5. They must also specify the roles of adjuncts and peripheral elements: for example, the construction of *Bill told a story to Mary in the hospital* has the same elements plus a peripheral locative. Other base rules must describe the morphosyntactic categories of a predicator: in English, those of past versus present, perfect versus non-perfect and progressive versus non-progressive. But given that *Bill* is the subject it cannot but precede *told*, and given that *Mary* is an indirect object it can either follow a direct object and be marked by *to* (*told a story to*

Mary) or precede it without *to* (*told Mary a story*). To specify such features would be redundant at this level.

That does not mean that they cannot, in fact, be specified. In principle, the base rules could provide a **partly redundant representation**. For the subject this would show a kernel order:

> *Subject* + *Predicator*
> Bill $TELL_{Past}$

(with the plus-sign symbolising a sequential relation). The passive or first passive transformation maps the direct object of the kernel construction onto a subject which retains this feature:

> *Subject* + *Predicator*
> a story $TELL_{Past, Pass}$

Similarly for the second passive and the indirect object of the kernel: $Mary + TELL_{Past, Pass}$. The interrogative transformation reorders the subjects with respect to a first auxiliary: $Aux + Bill + TELL_{Past}$, and so on. The realisational rules would be no more than those already stated or implied.

Alternatively, the base rules could provide a **minimal representation**. For the subject this would show no order:

> *Subject,*   *Predicator*
> Bill $TELL_{Past}$

(with the comma symbolising an unspecified sequence). The passives have the same structure: *a story*, $TELL_{Past, Pass}$; *Mary*, $TELL_{Past, Pass}$. The interrogatives supply just the order of the subject and a first auxiliary: $Aux + Bill$, $TELL_{Past}$. Finally, we would need a realisational rule which might simply take the form

> Subject, V → Subject + V

– V being any verb whose order is not already fixed.

The first treatment is attractive in that the order can be stated as the element itself is introduced. No further rule would then be needed. The second is attractive in that, by dealing with the order separately, we can state a generalisation ranging over all constructions, not just the kernel. But the order of objects is a more interesting problem. In one analysis, *Bill told a story to Mary* has the same construction as *Bill told Mary a story*, where it is merely realised differently. The indirect object could also precede the subject (*To* MA*ry Bill told a* STO*ry* or MA*ry Bill told a* STO*ry to*), like the direct object (*The* OTH*er story Bill told to* MA*ry*). A minimal representation would be neutral:

Subject,	Direct Object,	Indirect Object,	Predicator
Bill	a story	Mary	told

with realisational statements to the effect that an indirect object may take *to*; that otherwise it cannot follow the direct object (*told Mary a story*, not *told a story Mary*); that normally both objects follow the predicator; that in special circumstances one element may be preposed (indirect object + subject ..., direct object + subject ...); that a preposition may or may not accompany such an element; that a preposition not accompanying it cannot precede the direct object (MA*ry Bill told a* STO*ry to*, not *Mary Bill told to a story*). Parts of this are or may be generalised to other constructions: thus for other prepositions (*In the* OTH*er box I keep* BUT*tons*, or *The* OTH*er box I keep* BUT*tons in*), or for an indirect object and agent (*The story was told by Bill to Mary*, or *The story was told to Mary by Bill*).

In another analysis, *Bill told a story to Mary* and *Bill told Mary a story* have two different constructions, occupying different places in their paradigm. Let the former be the kernel construction. It would then be simpler to begin with a redundant representation:

Subject +	Predicator +	Direct Object +	Indirect Object
Bill	told	a story	to Mary

From this we would transformationally derive:

Subject +	Predicator +	Indirect Object +	Direct Object
Bill	told	Mary	a story

Another pair of transformations would derive distinct constructions with preposing: *To + Mary + Bill ...*; *Mary + Bill ... to*. Yet another would derive that of, for example, *Bill told to Mary a story about the people we met last summer*, with both *to* and a position before the direct object. Again, the realisational rules would be no more than those already envisaged for agreement, periphrastic formations, and so on.

But the alleged relationships are not regular. One can say *They explained the circumstances to Mary* (proposed kernel), but not, or not usually, *They explained Mary the circumstances*. Likewise *They presented a painting to the managing director*, but not *They presented the managing director a painting*; here one would have to say . . . *with a painting*. This use of *with* is like that in, for example, *This lands us with a problem*; but, conversely, one cannot say *This lands a problem to us*. One can say *They fined the chairman £10* (proposed transform), but not *They fined £10 to the chairman*. Likewise *They refused Mary a council flat*, but not, or at least not usually, *They refused a council flat to Mary*; compare *They refused the loan to Mary*, understood with the single object $_{NP}[\textit{the loan to Mary}]_{NP}$. The choice of kernel or transform would even vary for the same verb. Thus we find *He charged Mary £20 for doing it*, rather than *He charged £20 to Mary for doing it*; but, with a different sense, *You can charge the bill to my insurance company*, in preference to *You can charge my insurance company the bill*. We met part of this problem earlier, in considering the distinction of indirect objects and directionals (Chapter 6). Here as there, there are many cases where one's judgment is not certain.

We must also consider the weight of the object phrases. We gave an example with a *to*-phrase before the direct object (*Bill told to Mary a story about the people we met last summer*). But the length of the direct object is important: one would not usually say *Bill told to Mary a story*. There are further complications with pronouns. One would say *They told it to Mary* (pronominal direct object) in preference to *They told Mary it*; conversely *They told her a* DIF*ferent story* (pronominal indirect object) in preference to *They told a* DIF*ferent story to her*. This is due to a stylistic tendency to put new or contrasted information (that it was Mary to whom it, already known, was told; that she, already known, was told a different story) later in the sentence. Hence the last example is better if *her* is also tonic: *They told a* DIF*ferent story to* HER. These tendencies may affect one's judgment for particular lexemes. Thus with REFUSE it seems more likely that one might say, for example, *They can't refuse one to* MA*ry*.

In short, there is every indication that our first analysis is right: that in, for example, *They handed it to Mary, They handed her a sheaf of papers, They handed to Mary a sheaf of papers about drainage in Greater Manchester*, we are dealing not with a series of distinct but related constructions (like active and passive, declarative and interrogative, and so on), but with a single construction whose realisation varies in a way bound up, in part at least, with stylistic and lexical factors. The base rules should be restricted to what is in common between them.

English is not, by and large, a language with free order. But the argument here is not dissimilar to those that would apply more

281

generally to Latin or Italian (Chapter 11). There are again two alternatives. We could specify minimal representations without order. We would then add realisational rules for the minority of cases where the order is fixed: thus in Latin the preposition must precede its complement in the construction of *ad urbem* 'to the city', *per agros* 'through the fields', and so on. Thus, a sentence like *ad urbem veni* 'I came to the city' would have an order partly specified as follows: *ad* + *urbem, veni*. But the remaining choice, between *ad urbem veni* and *veni ad urbem*, is left for, perhaps, stylistic comment. Similarly, an Italian sentence like *La famiglia Salina discese dalle carrozze* 'The Salina family got down from the carriages' has a construction with the minimal representation

Subject,	*Predicator,*	*Adverbial*
la famiglia Salina	discese	dalle carrozze

(commas again meaning that no sequence is specified). Such phrases can appear in variable order; hence no further syntactic statement is required.

Alternatively, we could specify one order by the base rules, and derive the others from it. But the different patterns are not different constructions: for example, *La famiglia Salina discese dalle carrozze* is syntactically no different from *Dalle carrozze discese la famiglia Salina*, or *Discese dalle carrozze la famiglia Salina*, and so on. Accordingly the derivations cannot be transformational, in the sense in which we are using this term. It is also misleading to give specific realisational rules. Let us suppose that, in the Italian case, the base rules give the order subject + predicator + adverbial (S P A). Then one way to proceed would be to posit rules saying: 'starting from this the adverbial may be moved to the beginning' (S P A → A S P); 'in either of these structures the predicator and adverbial may be interchanged' (S P A → S A P, A S P → P S A); 'in any of these the subject may be moved to the end' (S P A or P S A → P A S, S A P or A S P → A P S). But the true generalisation is not that the elements must be either in this order or in that order, but simply that any order is possible. That is, there are no general rules for order at all.

The choice is ultimately very simple. Either we give minimal representations, and add realisational rules for specific cases where the order is fixed; or we give a single base order, with a realisational statement saying that, except for specific cases where the order is fixed, every other permutation is also allowed. This is a choice between saying 'there is no rule' and saying 'there is a rule but, after all, it is in point of fact not a rule'.

The scope for argument varies from one language to another. But perhaps we could turn the question round and ask not whether, in given cases, there are positive grounds for favouring a minimal representation – to which the answer is that sometimes there are and sometimes there are not – but whether it would ever lead to positive disadvantages. Does a partly redundant representation, such as *Bill + told* ... instead of *Bill,* ... *told,* ever offer more than a particular sort of expositional simplicity or clarity? It is not obvious that it does.

TRANSFORMATIONAL GRAMMAR

The preceding sections sketch the course that transformational grammar should have taken, in my view, after its brilliant beginning in the late 50s. But it makes only limited contact with what actually ensued. What, if the question is not too impertinent, went wrong?

The answers are to be found partly in preconceptions taken over from the generativists' Bloomfieldian predecessors, and partly in notions of their own, which became prominent in the middle 60s. The Bloomfieldians had been especially concerned with distributional analysis, which had led in syntax to an elaboration of Bloomfield's notion of immediate constituents. *Eat it,* for example, is segmentable into the immediate constituents *eat* and *it.* The longer *Finish your rice pudding* can be segmented into distributionally similar constituents *finish* and *your rice pudding:* compare *Finish it, Eat your rice pudding, Leave it* and *Leave your rice pudding, It is too sweet* and *Your rice pudding is too sweet,* and so on. This led to descriptive statements which are the precursors of phrase structure grammar (Chapter 4). For example, *it, pudding, rice pudding, your rice pudding,* and so on are all classed as 'noun' constituents.

The distributional criterion is valuable, and formed part of our own analysis of the example *Leave the meat in the kitchen* (Chapter 1). But the resulting statements leave out two crucial things. Firstly, they do not say that in, for example, *Tell the story to Mary* and *Tell Mary the story* the elements have identical functions: predicator, direct object, indirect object. The question could not arise. One sentence has a verb followed by two noun constituents (V + N + N); the other a verb followed by one noun constituent, then by *to*, then by another noun constituent (V + N + *to* + N). To talk of functions, other criteria are needed.

Secondly, they do not say that, for example, *You have eaten your rice pudding* is opposed, as a whole, to the distributionally dissimilar *Have you eaten your rice pudding?* A traditional paradigm was already alien to contemporary accounts of morphology. For Bloomfield's successors, a form such as *took* could be characterised as past tense only if a morpheme 'past tense', identical to that represented by the *-ed* of *walked* or *waited* or *wailed*, could be discovered or posited within it; that *took* and *walked* simply stand in the same opposition to *takes* and *walks*, *taking* and *walking* or *taken* and *walked*, was not seen as a sufficient form of statement. In syntax, any paradigm was strictly inconceivable. In an account of immediate constituents, *You have eaten* ... has a pattern beginning with a noun constituent followed by an auxiliary (N + Aux ...), *Have you eaten* ...? one beginning with an auxiliary followed by a noun constituent (Aux + N ...). There is nothing else that such an account could, in principle, say.

Chomsky's first achievement was to formalise phrase structure grammar and to demonstrate, in part with reference to relations already explored by Harris, that it was inadequate. But having done so he declined to reject it. Instead he added a second syntactic level, defined by rules which mapped one phrase structure representation (the type of structure shown as a tree diagram in Chapter 4) onto another. For a sentence like *You have eaten your rice pudding*, a transformation mapped a phrase structure representation in which the past participle morpheme forms a unit with *have* (compare again Chapter 3) onto another in which it forms a suffix of *eat*. Another transformation related the first of these representations to an equivalent representation of interrogatives like *Have you eaten your rice pudding?* For *Did you eat your rice pudding?*, a transformation related a representation with no DO to one in which DO was inserted. In general, wherever there was anything that phrase structure rules could not appropriately handle, the remedy was to add a transformation to them.

Chomsky's first book ignored functions such as subject and direct object. But in the middle 60s he tried to define these two, at least, on the basis of phrase structure. Thus, given a representation which in essentials is like this:

$$_S[\ _{NP}[Bill]_{NP}\ _{VP}[ate\ _{NP}[the\ pudding]_{NP}\ ]_{VP}\ ]_S$$

the subject was defined as a noun phrase (NP) which is an immediate constituent of a sentence (S), and the direct object, or simply 'object', as a noun phrase which is an immediate constituent of the 'verb phrase' (VP). How we define the indirect object was not made clear. The essential, however, is that instead of saying that the direct object and indirect object are distinct elements in a construction, which some verbs could and others could not take as valents, and then detailing the structures by which they can be realised, a transformational grammarian had to begin by detailing one particular phrase structure representation – say

$$_S[\ _{NP}[Bill]_{NP} \ _{VP}[told \ _{NP}[the \ story]_{NP} \ _{PP}[to \ _{NP}[Mary]_{NP} \ ]_{PP} \ ]_{VP} \ ]_S$$

(PP = prepositional phrase) – then define the functions over that (say, the indirect object as one sort of PP that is an immediate constituent of a VP), and finally, if there is any correspondence with phrases in other structures – say

$$_S[\ _{NP}[Bill]_{NP} \ _{VP}[told \ _{NP}[Mary]_{NP} \ _{NP}[the \ story]_{NP} \ ]_{VP} \ ]_S$$

– state a transformation. The possibility that these might simply have the same construction was excluded by the representational technique.

In such cases the distinction between transformation and realisation (as these terms are used in the previous section) was already confused. But in others Chomsky's model did at the outset make a useful division between 'optional' and 'obligatory' transformations. The forms to be generated include both declaratives and interrogatives; so, the transformational rule deriving the phrase structure representation of *Has Bill eaten the pudding?* had to apply optionally in order not to eliminate that of *Bill has eaten the pudding*. So too did the transformation deriving the representation of passives such as *The rice pudding has been eaten by Bill*. But a grammar must exclude sentences identical to these except that the verbal suffixes are in the wrong place, or identical to *Did Bill eat the rice pudding?* except that there is no form of DO. Therefore the transformations dealing with these matters (in our terms, the realisational rules) were obligatory. This division was reflected in the standard definition of a kernel sentence, as a simple sentence to which either no, or only obligatory transformations applied. In that the rules had names, there was also the possibility that those of the optional transformations (the 'passive transformation', the 'interrogative transformation , and so on) could be interpreted, as in the previous section, as referring to vectors in a paradigm.

But in the mid 60s the application of the model was changed in ways which excluded any interpretation of that kind. From being optional operations on an abstract representation which was also that of declaratives or actives, transformations such as the interrogative or passive became obligatory rules applying only to sentences whose abstract representations, simultaneously christened 'deep structures', were already marked as requiring them. In the first accounts of this type, an interrogative was assigned a deep structure that began with an element Q (for 'question'); the requisite transformation applied only to structures containing Q, and mapped them onto corresponding structures with Q deleted and other elements appropriately reordered. The deep structure of a passive was said to contain *by* plus an element *'passive'*, which Chomsky treated as together forming an adverb of manner; the passive transformation applied only to structures which included this adverb and, among other things, replaced *'passive'* with the agent noun phrase.

This had three effects. Firstly, the distinction between obligatory and optional transformations, insofar as it did distinguish realisational rules from transformational rules in our sense, was collapsed at the expense of the latter. The only separate category were the optional transformations dealing, in our terms, with optional or alternative realisations: for example, one deriving a structure for *Bill told Mary a story* from a deep structure which is also that of *Bill told a story to Mary*.

Secondly, the notion of kernel sentences was lost. For if *Bill has eaten the pudding* was derived with only obligatory transformations, so too, in this treatment, were *Has Bill eaten the pudding?*, *The pudding has been eaten by Bill* and *Has the pudding been eaten by Bill?* That might not have mattered had interrogative or passive been described as paradigmatic categories: for example, by assigning sentences as wholes to oppositions of '+ interrogative' or '+ passive' (marked interrogative or passive) and '− interrogative' or '− passive' (unmarked declarative or active). But this could not be done by phrase structure rules, and indeed no wish to do it was discernible. Instead they were described as if they were morphemes, each with its place in the constituency structure, before or after other constituents. So, the deep structure of

Bill has eaten the pudding was distinguished from that of *Has Bill eaten the pudding* merely in that it did not have a *Q* as an initial constituent. In Chomsky's account, the deep structure difference between *Bill has eaten the pudding* and *The pudding has been eaten by Bill* was that the latter had *by + passive* as an adverbial constituent of the verb phrase. The earlier distinction between kernel and transform was replaced by one of just the same sort as that between, for example, the deep structures of *Bill has eaten the pudding* and *Bill has eaten the pudding surreptitiously*.

Thirdly, the way was opened to a new sort of abstractness. In the previous section, we tried to decide what part of the total characterisation of a clause (order of words and phrases, markers and determiners, dependency and constituency relations, and so on) was relevant to the abstract representation of its construction. But that does not allow us to add elements that are not there. For example, we decided that the DO of *Does Bill cook dinner?* was irrelevant to the interrogative transformation. Therefore it was eliminated from the abstract representations, and introduced by a realisational rule. But if our aim were merely to regularise the transformation we could have achieved it equally well by adding DO to the kernel. *Bill cooks dinner* might have an abstract representation like, let us say, *Bill* DO$_{Pres}$ COOK *dinner*; the interrogative transformation would move DO just as it moves other auxiliaries; a rule would then delete DO whenever its position or some other factor does not require it.

But from the mid 60s the only constraint on deep structure is that a structure with the eventual sequence of morphemes, christened 'surface structure', can be derived from it. This allowed *Q* to be added to the interrogative; for, if transformations are merely rules relating deep to surface structure, and can among other things delete parts of a constituency representation, there is no problem in removing it at some point. Nor was there difficulty in reanalysing role-fillers. We treated *it* as a role-filler in, for example, *It is clear that she is not coming*. But most transformationalists have not dealt with it in that way. Instead both this sentence and *That she is coming is not clear* are assigned an initial *it* in deep structure; it is then deleted in the latter. Some transformationalists have proposed a similar account of DO; to achieve further regularity, they have been tempted to assign it the deep structure of a main verb, so that, at that level, the construction of *Bill cooks dinner* would be the same as that of, for example, *Bill tries to cook dinner*. For one or two, this has raised the possibility that the tense might also be treated as a main verb; so, the deep structure of *Bill cooked dinner* would have a main clause with the verb 'past tense', taking as a complement a subordinate clause with DO, which in turn takes a subordinate clause with COOK. Such proposals were naturally disputed. But once transformational grammarians began to introduce disposable elements such as Q, or to treat the passive as if it had the structure of an active with an adverb of manner, these and other fantasies were hard to check.

I began by describing these developments as changes in the application of the syntactic model. As such they were enough to turn transformational grammar into a path different from that sketched earlier in this chapter. But they also formed part of a major theoretical reorientation, in which syntax was mistakenly integrated, or integrated in a mistaken way, with semantics. In Chomsky's terms a grammar, or total account of a particular language, was now seen as having three components: a set of syntactic rules, consisting of base rules, a lexicon and transformational rules; a set of semantic rules, relating the syntactic descriptions of individual sentences to appropriate 'semantic representations'; and a set of phonological rules, relating syntactic descriptions to 'phonetic representations'. The syntactic descriptions had two parts, a deep structure and a surface structure, of which only the second was relevant to the rules of phonology; in the same spirit the deep structure was defined as the part relevant to semantics. So, for every sentence or sense of a sentence, rules of various types related a semantic representation to a phonetic representation, via a deep structure and a surface structure.

But if syntax and semantics are integrated, how is it decided what belongs to which? The line we have taken is that syntax deals with patterns subject to rule. Thus we have talked of transformations (such as that deriving passives from actives, or interrogatives from declaratives) only where we could establish regular oppositions. But in Chomsky's theory 'rule' became no more than a term for 'unitary statement made as part of the description of a language'. The syntactic component consisted of 'rules', some of them transformations (in the new sense) which relate deep structures to surface structures. The semantic component also consisted of 'rules', which relate deep structures to semantic representations. What real division was there between them?

Later years have seen apparently conflicting movements, one to assimilate deep structure to semantic representation and the other tending to limit syntax to surface structure. The first emerged very quickly. Thus it was soon proposed that sentences like *The door opened* and *I opened the door*, in which *the door* bore (it was said) the same semantic relationship to *opened*, should be related transformationally to structures in which both this relationship, and that of *I* in the second, were directly represented. It was also suggested that a sentence like *I cut the cheese with a bread-knife* should have the same deep structure as its paraphrase (it was said) *I used a bread-knife to cut the cheese*, dealing directly with the similarity of meaning between USE and the instrumental. Such proposals both fed and fed upon the new sort of abstractness. Thus, in the second pair, we had to disregard the 'surface' difference between a one-verb and a two-verb construction.

This led to the theory known as 'generative semantics', in which Chomsky's syntactic and semantic components were reduced to a set of semantic base rules, detailing the semantic representations of sentences, and an undifferentiated set of transformations, relating them to surface structures. Our erstwhile realisational rules – the obligatory transformations of earlier generative grammar – became the tail-end of a component which also covered the meanings of *with*, a similarity between the roles of an adverbial *with a bread-knife* in *I cut the cheese with a bread-knife* and, for example, the subject *a bread-knife* in *A bread-knife won't cut it*, and so on.

The opposite movement has emerged since 1970. It began in the field of derivational morphology, where transformationalists had earlier assumed that, for example, *Bill's arrival* was related syntactically to *Bill arrived*. But Chomsky now rejected this, arguing (rightly) that the relation was not regular. There is merely a lexical relation between ARRIVAL (noun) and ARRIVE (verb) which, in Chomsky's model, would also determine a similarity in semantic representation.

In later work he has revised the model itself, arguing at first that the semantic rules should refer not to deep structure alone (the so-called 'standard theory') but to both deep and surface structure (the 'extended standard theory'), and subsequently that they should refer just to surface structure (the 'revised extended standard theory'). So, for a pair like *Bill cooked dinner* and *Dinner was cooked by Bill*, we must envisage syntactic rules which assign to each sentence an appropriate morpheme by morpheme classification of constituents. We must then envisage semantic rules which, on the basis of the individual surface structures, assign semantic representations that are at least partly identical. But if the semantic rules themselves explain the semantic similarity, what do we gain by retaining a syntactic similarity in deep structure? At the time of writing the argument has not run its full course. But the natural conclusion is substantively the same as that reached earlier by proponents of generative semantics. Where their theory had base rules for semantic representations, plus mapping rules – called 'transformations' – pairing them with surface structures, the ultimate 'revised extended standard theory' seems likely to have base rules for surface structures, plus mapping rules – called 'rules of semantics' – pairing them with semantic representations. In either case the integration is superficially impressive. But the real distinctions, between constructions and meanings and constructions and the realisation of constructions, have been lost.

Finally, none of these developments touched the basic reliance on phrase structure representation. By the mid 6os this had been accepted as a kind of standard notation for syntactic argument, which few wished to challenge and none challenged effectively. For it was not a matter of notation alone. To meet Chomskyan aims, a critic would have had to provide a new formalisation, which restricted the possible form of a grammar, and thus the possible character of a language, in the way that they were believed to be restricted (wrongly, as it happens) by the formalisation that had been implied (or, it was widely believed, given) by Chomsky himself. Some attempts were made, notably on the basis of dependency relations. But even these had few supporters.

The results are ironic. From the late 6os the literature is full of the most abstract deep or semantic structures of sentences, some inane but many fundamentally insightful, all couched in a notational system which was derived not even from the main linguistic tradition, but from a specifically Bloomfieldian segmentation and classification of parts of utterances. Some proposed an order different from that of the surface: for example, a deep order (in English) of verb + subject + object. Yet they could not propose no order, since order was a basic relation in immediate constituent analysis, and hence in phrase structure rules. In recent years, Chomsky has proposed a series of conditions on the operation of syntactic rules, which he posits as universal. These involve, for example, clauses and subjects of clauses. But they too are stated in terms of phrase structure trees, with an

English-like sequence of an NP and a VP constituent or of verb and complement S. It is hard to see how generalisations can be usefully proposed and assessed unless the categories are set up independently of the details of constituency and order in particular languages.

It will be clear from this book where, in my view, we might begin to look for alternatives, though the problems of formalisation, if indeed they are important for our purposes, are not solved. But a sufficient negative lesson is that a standard way of talking grounded solely in phrase structure grammar, and thus essentially in the Bloomfieldian analytic procedures of the 40s and 50s, ought to be thrown out.

NOTES AND REFERENCES

The first half of this chapter draws on several sources, but does not follow any in detail.

(1) The notion of transformational relations is closest to that of HARRIS, 'Co-occurrence and transformation'. But his criterion does not control the opposition of meaning (§1.3; subsequent 'practical evaluation' of meaning, §5.7). Instead he insists on strict recurrence of collocations: thus a transformation could relate *the barking of dogs* to *The dogs are barking* (said to be related, §4.303) only if *the* xing *of* ys and *The* ys *are* xing were equally acceptable, as Harris must have supposed, for every x and y. The test is later refined: see Z. S. Harris, 'Transformational theory', *Lg*, 41 (1965), pp. 363–401 (reprinted in HARRIS, *Papers*, pp. 533–77). But this admits many transformations which its predecessor would apparently have excluded: compare §§3 and 5 (especially §3.2) with HARRIS, 'Co-occurrence and transformation', §4 (especially the section on 'quasi-transformations', §4.5). The reasons are clearer in the light of recent work: Z. S. Harris, 'Grammar on mathematical principles', *JL*, 14 (1978), pp. 1–20; more fully in French, *Notes du cours de syntaxe*, tr. M. Gross (Paris: Seuil, 1976).

(2) For syntactic paradigms compare K. L. Pike, 'A syntactic paradigm', *Lg*, 39 (1963), pp. 216–30 (reprinted in HOUSEHOLDER (ed.), pp. 195–214); also his 'Dimensions of grammatical constructions', *Lg*, 38 (1962), pp. 221–44 and, for recent discussion, PIKE & PIKE, pp. 139–44. But these include oppositions which are not transformational (such as transitive vs. intransitive). Another parallel is with the later development of 'systemic grammar' (earlier model compared with Pike's in notes to Chapter 1 above). In its terms *The police have impounded his car* and *Have the police impounded his car?* realise distinctions within a 'system network' of mood, those of *The police have impounded his car* and *His car has stopped* an intersecting network of transitivity, and so on. The system networks will thus describe the structure of paradigms of a particularly complex form. For the earliest statement see M. A. K. Halliday, 'Some notes on "deep" grammar', *JL*, 2 (1966), pp. 57–69; more

specifically in HALLIDAY, 'Transitivity and theme', especially (for the model) Part 1, pp. 38ff.; also R. A. Hudson, *English Complex Sentences: an Introduction to Systemic Grammar* (Amsterdam: North-Holland, 1971); M. C. McCord, 'On the form of a systemic grammar', *JL*, 11 (1975), pp. 195–212. For a brief account of 'system network' see Halliday's *Language as Social Semiotic: the Social Interpretation of Language and Meaning* (London: Edward Arnold, 1978), pp. 40f. (originally in H. Parret (ed.), *Discussing Language* (The Hague: Mouton, 1974)).

(3) For kernel constructions and sentences see HARRIS, 'Co-occurrence and transformation', §5.4; CHOMSKY, *Structures*, pp. 45ff., Ch. 7 *passim*; also Harris, 'Transformational theory', §4; LYONS, *Semantics*, 2, pp. 467ff. But these accounts are only broadly related. Thus for Lyons kernel sentences do not include 'optional, or omissible, expressions' (p. 468); hence a special relevance to valency, which he discusses later in the same chapter (Ch. 12). Likewise Harris, 'Transformational theory', has transformations adding optional elements (§3.2 on, for example, 'adverbial inserts'). But that was not his earlier treatment (HARRIS, 'Co-occurrence and transformation'), nor Chomsky's. For kernels within a paradigm see Pike, 'Dimensions of grammatical constructions', pp. 226ff.; for the factorisation of transformations compare HARRIS, 'Co-occurrence and transformation', §§5.1–2, on 'elementary transformations'. On derivations and leading forms in classical treatments of inflection see my *Morphology*, pp. 69ff.

(4) An unordered level of representation was posited in the 60s within 'stratificational' grammar: S. M. Lamb, 'The sememic approach to structural semantics', *American Anthropologist*, 66 (1964), pp. 57–78 (see p. 70); H. A. Gleason, 'The organisation of language: a stratificational view', in STUART (ed.), pp. 75–95 (p. 81, for a 'network' model). This is acknowledged by Halliday ('Some notes on "deep" grammar'), who was then close to Lamb's school. For a more explicit proposal see W. L. Chafe, *Meaning and the Structure of Language* (Chicago: University of Chicago Press, 1970): note his rules of 'literalisation' and 'linearisation' (for English verbal auxiliaries, pp. 246ff.). Compare too the 'set system' – phrase structure with order abstracted – of, among others, J. F. Staal, *Word Order in Sanskrit and Universal Grammar* (Dordrecht: Reidel, 1967). The case against this is presented, within standard generativist assumptions, by E. Bach, 'Order in base structures', in C. N. Li (ed.), *Word Order and Word Order Change* (Austin: University of Texas Press, 1975), pp. 308–43 (earlier CHOMSKY, *Aspects*, pp. 124–7). But I see no reason why we should investigate this matter holding constant every other part of Chomsky's theoretical package.

See notes to Chapters 1 and 11 for other references on order generally.

For DO as a role-filler compare PALMER, p. 25 ('a special type of auxiliary, . . . used *only* under those conditions where an auxiliary is obligatory'); JACKENDOFF, $\bar{X}$ *Syntax*, p. 50 (where it fills an empty 'M' position); earlier, for interrogatives, in JESPERSEN, *Philosophy*, p. 26 (immediately after discussion of empty *it*). For its introduction in deep structure, cited later for abstractness, see S. J. Keyser & P. M. Postal, *Beginning English Grammar* (New York: Harper & Row, 1976). Ch. 27; CULICOVER, Ch. 4 (both with earlier references). Keyser and Postal treat it and other auxiliaries as deep main verbs; hence all sentences are basically complex (derivation of *Mary sang*, p. 346). For tense as a deep verb see J. D. McCawley, 'Tense and time reference in English', in C. J. Fillmore & D. T. Langendoen (eds.), *Studies in Linguistic Semantics* (New York: Holt, Rinehart & Winston, 1971), pp. 97–113 (reprinted in McCAWLEY, pp. 257–72).

For empty *it* see notes to Chapter 5 above; for cleft constructions and extraposition, QUIRK *et al.*, pp. 951ff., 963ff. For the *it* of extraposition as already present in deep structure see, for example, HUDDLESTON, p. 108, Ch. 8 *passim*; opposite solution in FILLMORE, pp. 41ff. For copular BE see again Chapter 5 and notes. In the later 60s Bach suggested that BE and HAVE should not appear at all in underlying structures; see E. Bach, '*Have* and *be* in English syntax', *Lg*, 43 (1967), pp. 462–85 (with reduction of auxiliaries to the non-auxiliary pattern, pp. 473ff.). His paper is a good illustration of the way in which transformationalists have tended to argue such issues.

On the realisation of the English indirect object see references to Allerton and Georgia Green in notes to Chapter 6; also QUIRK *et al.*, pp. 845ff. The usual transformational treatment is that of, for example, CULICOVER, pp. 153ff. (also in HUDDLESTON, pp. 231f.).

For distributional analyses see notes to Chapters 1 and 4 above, and for their link with Chomsky's theory. This continuity has been obscured by propaganda: see already R. B. Lees, review of CHOMSKY, *Structures*, *Lg*, 33 (1957), pp. 357–408, which substantially misrepresents the earlier school. But it is emphasised by D. Hymes & J. Fought, 'American structuralism', in T. A. Sebeok (ed.), *Current Trends in Linguistics*, 13: *Historiography of Linguistics* (The Hague: Mouton, 1975), pp. 903–1176. On Bloomfieldian treatments of inflection see my *Morphology*, especially pp. 116ff. Bloch's remarks on process models are revealing: see B. Bloch, 'English verb inflection', *Lg*, 23 (1947), pp. 399–418 (reprinted in JOOS (ed.), pp. 243–54), §1.

The history of transformational grammar has yet to be written, and I will therefore give general bibliographical indications, as well as references for points in the text.

(1) For the early period CHOMSKY, *Structures* is essential: note again the definition of 'kernel sentence' (p. 45). Most enthusiasts also read, or tried to read, his unpublished *The Logical Structure of Linguistic Theory* (eventual published version, New York: Plenum Press, 1975). For characteristic studies see LEES; R. B. Lees, 'Grammatical analysis of the English comparative construction', *Word*, 17 (1961), pp. 171–85; R. B. Lees & E. S. Klima, 'Rules for English pronominalisation', *Lg*, 39 (1963), pp. 17–28 (the last two reprinted in REIBEL & SCHANE (ed.), pp. 303–15; 145–59). These are not directly relevant to my argument, but introduce issues that have obsessed generative grammarians ever since. For the earliest textbook see E. Bach, *An Introduction to Transformational Grammars* (New York: Holt, Rinehart &

Winston, 1964); comparison with his revised version (BACH) should be instructive.

Throughout this period there was much polemic against other schools: see POSTAL especially. But the theory was already developing under its own momentum, without response to work outside the group.

(2) For the so-called 'standard' theory see CHOMSKY, *Aspects*: for its sources, J. J. Katz & J. A. Fodor, 'The structure of a semantic theory', *Lg*, 39 (1963), pp. 170–210 (reprinted in FODOR & KATZ (ed.), pp. 479–518), which added a semantic level; J. J. Katz & P. M. Postal, *An Integrated Theory of Linguistic Descriptions* (Cambridge, Mass.: MIT Press, 1964), which reduced transformations to those which were said not to affect meaning; also E. S. Klima, 'Negation in English', in FODOR & KATZ (ed.), pp. 246–323. For the definition of 'deep' and 'surface' see CHOMSKY, *Topics*, p. 16 (also in *Aspects*, p. 16); note that this is all the justification Chomsky ever gave for these terms. For that of subject and object see CHOMSKY, *Aspects*, pp. 70ff.; good account in SMITH & WILSON, pp. 100–4. Compare too C. Touratier, 'Comment définir les fonctions syntaxiques?', *BSL*, 72 (1977), pp. 27–54. For *Q* see Katz & Postal, *An Integrated theory*, pp. 79ff.: compare their treatment of imperatives (pp. 74ff.); also J. P. Thorne, 'English imperative sentences', *JL*, 2 (1966), pp. 69–78, whose style is typical of its time. For *by* + 'passive' see CHOMSKY, *Aspects*, pp. 103f. The last major reference to kernel sentences is in *Aspects*, pp. 17f.

For criticism see my review of CHOMSKY, *Aspects*, *JL*, 3 (1967), pp. 119–52, which I could cite in detail for several points. A wider assessment is by E. M. Uhlenbeck, 'Some further remarks on transformational grammar', *Lingua*, 17 (1967), pp. 263–316, the second of five papers in his *Critical Comments on Transformational-Generative Grammar 1962–1972* (The Hague: Smits, [1973]). Among later critiques see especially E. Coseriu, *Leistung und Grenzen der transformationellen Grammatik* (Tübingen: Gunter Narr, 1975).

(3) The argument for generative semantics was, in retrospect, very simple. Assume that deep structures 'determine' the meaning of sentences (CHOMSKY, *Topics* or *Aspects*, *loc. cit.*); then (*a*) any ambiguity must involve a difference at that level. (So, for instance, HUDDLESTON, p. 88, commenting on Katz & Postal, *An Integrated Theory*.) Assume, as a heuristic principle, that paraphrases have the same deep structure (Katz & Postal, p. 157); then (*b*) any similarity of meaning will involve an identity at that level. Hence deep structures and meanings will be in one: one correspondence, and the former can be eliminated.

But the actual discussion was more complex and perhaps more reputable. For *a* and *b* see G. Lakoff, 'Instrumental adverbs and the concept of deep structure', *FL*, 4 (1968), pp. 4–29. See too FILLMORE, which combined a 'deeper' deep structure with a search for universals which was then very popular. For comments on this last aspect I hope I may refer to my 'Chomskyan grammar – a more skeptical view', *Aristotelian Society Supplementary Volume* 44 (1970), pp. 175–90 (§2); see too E. Coseriu, 'Les universaux linguistiques (et les autres)', in L. Heilmann (ed.), *Proceedings of the*

Eleventh International Congress of Linguists, Bologna: Florence, Aug. 28-Sept. 2, 1972 (Bologna: Il Mulino, 1974), 1, pp. 47–73 (also in English in A. Makkai *et al.* (eds.), *Linguistics at the Crossroads* (Padua: Liviana; Chicago: Jupiter Press, 1977), pp. 317–46). In the late 60s the tendency to abstractness is clearly illustrated by the work of J. R. Ross: see especially 'On declarative sentences', in JACOBS & ROSENBAUM (ed.), pp. 222–72. For the argument that abstract structures would equal semantic representations see R. B. Lees, 'On very deep grammatical structure', in JACOBS & ROSENBAUM (ed.), pp. 134–42; classic statement in P. M. Postal, 'On the surface verb "remind"', *LIn*, 1 (1970), pp. 37–120 (passage on pp. 101–3). For an independent argument see J. D. McCawley, 'The role of semantics in a grammar', in E. Bach & R. T. Harms (eds.), *Universals in Linguistic Theory* (New York: Holt, Rinehart & Winston, 1968), pp. 124–69 (postscript, on *respective*); reprinted in McCAWLEY, pp. 59–98.

For comments on a representative collection see my review of JACOBS & ROSENBAUM (ed.), *JL*, 8 (1972), pp. 125–36. For remarks on later generative semantics see my *Generative Grammar, passim*; but this is not mainly of concern to syntax. For the order verb + subject + object (end of chapter) see J. D. McCawley, 'English as a VSO language', *Lg*, 46 (1970), pp. 286–99 (reprinted in McCAWLEY, pp. 211–28); later in Keyser & Postal, *Beginning English Grammar*. McCawley's paper is also in P. A. M. Seuren (ed.), *Semantic Syntax* (London: Oxford University Press, 1974); this selection gives a good picture of how generative semantics saw itself at the outset of what now seems its final phase.

(4) The so-called 'extended standard theory' has two major sources. One is the attempt to limit the operation of transformational rules: see already N. Chomsky, *Language and Mind* (New York: Harcourt, Brace, 1968), Ch. 2, especially on the 'A-over-A' principle; also J. R. Ross's unpublished but influential thesis, *Constraints on Variables in Syntax* (Massachusetts Institute of Technology, 1967). This was stimulated by the realisation that transformational grammars had excessive power: see P. S. Peters & R. W. Ritchie, 'A note on the universal base hypothesis', *JL*, 5 (1969), pp. 150–2; WALL, Ch. 11. Also by the opposite development of generative semantics: compare especially G. Lakoff, 'Global rules', *Lg*, 46 (1970), pp. 627–39. The other source is in an improved account of the lexicon: see CHOMSKY, 'Nominalization', using techniques already implicit in CHOMSKY, *Aspects* (Ch. 2, especially pp. 164ff.). For the model of semantic interpretation see JACKENDOFF, *Semantic Interpretation*; earlier N. Chomsky, 'Deep structure, surface structure and semantic interpretation', in CHOMSKY, *Studies*, pp. 62–119 (originally in R. Jacobson & S. Kawamoto (eds.), *Studies in General Linguistics Presented to Shigo Hattori on the Occasion of his Sixtieth Birthday* (Tokyo: TEC Co., 1970)). For the 'revised extended standard theory' see R. Fiengo, 'On trace theory', *LIn*, 8 (1977), pp. 35–61; for Chomsky's later contributions, CHOMSKY, *Essays*; also his and other papers in CULICOVER *et al.* (ed.), and LIGHTFOOT. Alas, no introductory treatment to date.

The latest tendency is towards a wholesale abandonment of transformations. See already F. Heny, review of Chomsky, *The Logical Structure of Linguistic Theory*, *Synthese*, 40 (1979), pp. 317–52; BRESNAN (in notes to Chapter I above for the passive). Note too the enthusiastic review by P. Schachter, *Lg*, 54 (1978), pp. 348–76, of an anti-transformational monograph (HUDSON).

INDEX OF NAMES

Bis or *ter* are used where an author is cited in more than one paragraph of a page of notes and references.

SUBJECT INDEX

Page numbers in italics refer to the notes and references.